Blackstone's Guide to the

PENSIONS ACT 1995

Blackstone's Guide to the
PENSIONS ACT 1995

Meryl Thomas BA, LLM

&

Brian Dowrick LLB

BLACKSTONE
PRESS LIMITED

First published in Great Britain 1995 by Blackstone Press Limited,
9-15 Aldine Street, London W12 8AW. Telephone 0181-740 1173

ISBN: 1 85431 485 8

Brtish Library Cataloguing in Publication Data
A CIP catalogue record for this book is available from the British Library

Typeset by Style Photosetting Ltd, Mayfield, East Sussex
Printed by Livesey Limited, Shrewsbury Shropshire

Contents

Preface

A significant amount of time and taxpayer's money were chanelled into the formulative stages of the Pensions Act 1995. Yet, whilst not the flagship in the government's legislative programme, it found itself to the fore due to the lacuna occasioned in the programme when other, more contentious issues did not bear fruit. Nevertheless, it is a statutory measure that attempts to address some fundamental issues troubling pensions law. However, it is suggested in some quarters that an opportunity to tackle these and other related issues fully was missed.

It is hoped that most of the significant aspects of the Act will be brought into force by April 1997, though some measures were effective on Royal Assent, for example, the provisions relating to war widows pensions (s. 168) and those relating to official pensions and equal treatment provisions relating to official pensions (ss. 170 and 171).

In tackling this guide, we have attempted to make the text accessible and wherever possible straightforward — not always an easy task with this or any new Act. Further, we have addressed our minds, and we hope the reader will agree, to what we believe are the areas of the Act that have the greatest impact. This is not to undermine other areas of the Act that may have an important effect on the lives of some people, for example, those provisions relating to war widows pensions. As a result, any errors lie, of course, with the authors.

We would like to extend our thanks and gratitude to the staff at Blackstone Press for their enthusiasm for the project, their energy, efforts, professionalism and (of course) their patience throughout a long hot summer. Brian would like also to extend his thanks to his Head of School for his support and assistance.

Meryl Thomas
Brian Dowrick
October 1995

Abbreviations

APP	appropriate personal pension
AVC	additional voluntary contribution
COMPS	contracted-out money purchase scheme
COSRS	contracted-out salary related scheme
DSS	Department of Social Security
EAT	Employment Appeal Tribunal
ECJ	European Court of Justice
EPA 1970	Equal Pay Act 1970
FSA 1986	Financial Services Act 1986
FSAVC	free-standing additional voluntary contribution
GMP	guaranteed minimum pension
Goode Report	Pension Law Review Committee, *Report*, vol. 1 (Cm 2342-I) (London: HMSO, 1993)
HRP	home responsibilities protection
IMRO	Investment Management Regulatory Organisation
LEL	lower earnings limit
LPI	limited price indexation
MFR	minimum funding requirement
MSR	minimum solvency requirement
OPB	Occupational Pensions Board
OPRA	Occupational Pensions Regulatory Authority
OPS	occupational pension scheme
PA 1995	Pensions Act 1995
PSA 1993	Pension Schemes Act 1993
PSO	Pension Schemes Office
RPI	retail price index
SERPS	State earnings related pension scheme
SIB	Securities and Investments Board
UEL	upper earnings limit
White Paper	Department of Social Security, *Security, Equality, Choice: the Future of Pensions* (Cm 2594-I and II) (London: HMSO, 1994).

Chapter 1
Introduction

1.1 PURPOSES OF THE ACT

In introducing the Pensions Bill to the House of Lords during second reading, Lord Mackay of Ardbrecknish, Minister of State for Social Security, described the subject area touched by the Bill as one of the topics of which it could be said 'truly that it affects every man and woman in our country' (Hansard, HL, 24 January 1995). For most people, beside the home they own (if at all), and especially given the numbers of people facing a negative equity in their property, their pension is likely to be the most significant asset they own.

The provisions of the Pensions Act 1995 (PA 1995), which received Royal Assent on 19 July 1995, are a response to a mixture of stimuli but it is probably true to say that in terms of generating a momentum for the Act's genesis, the late Robert Maxwell's well-documented conduct in relation to particular pension funds was the catalyst for this significant legislative measure. This is mirrored in the view of the Social Security Select Committee who stated:

> The single good deed Robert Maxwell has done for pensioners generally is to ensure that . . . the ownership and control of pension schemes is now high up on the political agenda (*2nd Report, The Operation of Pension Funds* (House of Commons Papers Session 1991–2, 61-II), para. 13).

Mr Maxwell's misappropriation of some £400 million of pension fund assets caused the Social Security Select Committee to expand its investigations into the ownership and control of pension fund assets and led to its call, in its March 1992 report, for further investigation into the detailed structure of a Pensions Act (ibid., para. 10). This call was answered in June of that year by the goverment which established the Pension Law Reform Committee to:

> review the framework of law and regulation within which occupational pension schemes operate, taking into account the rights and interests of scheme members, pensioners and employers; to consider in particular the status and ownership of occupational pension funds and the accountability and roles of trustees, fund managers, auditors and pension scheme advisers; and to make recommendations.

The Committee's report (Cm 2342–I, the Goode Report) made over 200 recommendations. Principal among these was a call for a Pensions Act to 'lay out a properly structured framework of rights and duties, and a Pensions Regulator ... with overall responsibility for the regulation of occupational pension schemes' (para. 4.1.3). The government embraced these recommendations in its White Paper (*Security, Equality, Choice: the Future of Pensions*, CM 2594–I). This stated that it would provide for greater pensions security by measures designed to achieve the 'the greatest practicable security' and that the new legislation would provide a clear framework of statutory obligation on employers, trustees, managers, professionals and members. Perhaps to some extent with the benefit of '20/20 hindsight', this is no more than can be expected in the light of the prominent role that pensions law (unwillingly) found itself in.

The significance of the Act should not be underestimated:

(a) It is the first measure to provide for a public regulator of schemes charged with specific statutory duties and powers for enforcing the terms of the Act.

(b) It provides in statutory form an attempt to crystallise duties and responsibilities of scheme trustees.

(c) It signifies the prominence of the trustee in scheme security and operation.

(d) It obliges professionals involved with schemes to be part of the policing of them.

(e) It provides for a quota of trustees to be made up of those nominated by members.

(f) It provides for a compensation scheme to be established.

(g) It requires that men and women be provided with equal benefits and the equalisation of the State pensions scheme.

The net result is a large (181 sections and 7 schedules) and unwieldy statute. It also authorises the making of regulations to provide much of the detail to the Act to be provided at later dates. This is both fortunate, in that much of the minutiae can be provided after proper consultation and consideration, and unfortunate, in that much of the purpose and direction of the provisions can only be assessed at this stage by consideration of the formulation of the Act.

1.2 NATURE OF THE PENSION AGREEMENT

The PA 1995 is principally concerned with occupational pension schemes (OPSs) and to a lesser degree with State, public sector and personal pension schemes. The history and development of the OPS is compendiously dealt with in L. Hannah, *Inventing Retirement: the Development of Occupational Pensions in Britain* (1986), but for these purposes it is worth noting that a significant aspect was the more uniform approach to pension provision for employees by the utilisation of the trust concept. The taxation benefits provided to schemes formed under 'irrevocable trusts' (see now Income and Corporation Taxes Act 1988, s. 592(1)(a)) established a suitably attractive climate for a more systematic provision of pension benefit. The financial attractiveness of tax reliefs was buttressed by the linking of State and private pension schemes in terms of the ability to 'contract out' of the State earnings related pension scheme (SERPS). This demands benefits payable that replace SERPS and there is a concomitant reduction in national insurance contributions paid by the employer. It is right to say that, today, some form of pension provision is a common feature of most employment contracts, albeit not necessarily directly, to the point that the pension benefits are part of the remuneration package (see R. Nobles, *Pensions, Employment and the Law* (1993)).

The use of the trust concept as the basis of the OPS has distinct tax advantages. In a trust the trustee holds property for the benefit of another on terms and obligations that require the trustee to act in that other's interest - in a fiduciary relationship. These obligations arise not only from the trust deed but also largely from the general law of trusts (for a more detailed examination, see for example Petit, *The Law of Trusts* (1994)) and require the trustee, for example, to act in the beneficiary's interests and not to act in a capricious or unreasonable manner. However, the trust is an uneasy, if relatively long-lived, import into the pensions field, as far from being concerned with its conventional family trust setting, it has to be adapted to the requirements and needs of a commercial operation, though it must be pointed out that adaptation in this and other areas has not been detrimental to its use. Beneficiaries under a pension scheme, unlike those in the family trust, are not mere donees: they earn their benefits from their employment duties and the contributions they make to the scheme. Also, though there are some conceptual difficulties, in a pension setting there is a contractual backdrop wherein an employer may offer as part of the employment a pension to the employee or alternatively where the courts imply a term into the contract of employment requiring the employer to procure those benefits for the employee to which he or she is entitled under the scheme (see *Mihlenstedt* v *Barclays Bank International Ltd* [1989] IRLR 522). To this end it is possible for the contract of employment to be a source of rights and duties between the parties and to delineate the terms of the relationship between them as they affect those that arise under the scheme. In the final analysis, the trust deed and rules are to a great extent a manifestation of the employer's desires, and this ability to form and shape the scheme in the employer's best interests (for example, in terms of the variations permissible) causes serious concern in some quarters over the degree of control and influence exercised over the scheme by the employer and to some extent the potential for a conflict of interests where trustees also place the financial survival of the employer to the fore. This has led to a questioning of the desirability of the trust as a basis for the provision and protection of the pension promise. However, as was pointed out by the Goode Committee, 'Trust law cannot in itself prevent breaches of trust any more than criminal law can prevent the commission of crimes' (Goode Report, para. 4.1.12). In any event, the Goode Committee expressed its faith in trust law as a continuing basis for OPSs (see Goode Report, para. 4.1.14) and it is within the trust framework that the Act's provisions relating to OPS must be read.

Chapter 2
Public Regulation

2.1 REGULATORY SYSTEM

Before the PA 1995, there was a plethora of regulatory provisions pertaining to all stages of 'pension scheme life', from genesis of a scheme — through the maintenance and enforcement of tax and social security provisions; during maintenance, administration and financial management — through the Occupational Pensions Board (OPB), the Financial Services Act 1986 (FSA 1986), the Securities and Investments Board (SIB) which has devolved powers to the Investment Management Regulatory Organisation (IMRO); and sometimes the 'death' of a scheme — through social security provisions and the OPB. The PA 1995 does nothing to diminish this — on the contrary, it provides for a significantly enhanced regime.

Whilst it is undesirable to rehearse the Maxwell affair, which, though not the only pension fund disaster is surely, the most notorious to date, it demonstrates that something was lacking in the ability of the previous regulatory regime to police effectively the operation and management of schemes. There was a lack of powers to ensure the safety and good management of pension scheme assets, and the OPB, even given its limited remit, was passive in the discharge of its functions (see also the Social Security Select Committee's report, *The Operation of Pension Funds,* (House of Commons Papers Session 1991–92, 61-II)). The PA 1995 introduces a significantly enhanced regulatory framework to implement the principal recommendations of the Goode Committee (Cmnd 2342-1). Central to the Committee's recommendations was that a pensions regulator should be established and PA 1995 has implemented this by creating the Occupational Pensions Regulatory Authority (OPRA). Sections 1 to 15 and 96 to 108 and sch. 1 establish OPRA and lay out OPRA's functions and powers. Unfortunately the Act does nothing to resolve the obvious difficulties caused by the addition of a new piece in the regulatory jigsaw and the multitude of jurisdictions concerned with pension regulation.

OPRA will have to coexist and cooperate with the regulation of pension schemes by the Inland Revenue and the Department of Social Security (DSS). Pension schemes are controlled by the Inland Revenue through the Pension Schemes Office (PSO) and by the DSS through the OPB. OPRA will have to work alongside these authorities which are, however, concerned with different areas of the design and operation of schemes. The regulatory framework can be said to be broadly concerned with four areas:

(a) fiscal regulation,
(b) contracting-out regulation,
(c) investment regulation,
(d) administrative regulation.

2.1.1 Fiscal regulation

Approval of a scheme by the Inland Revenue, though not mandatory, brings with it income and capital gains tax advantages on investment activities, and the employer can set its contributions to the scheme against income or corporation tax liability. The Inland Revenue through the PSO administers the tax reliefs relating to pension schemes. As a result, the Inland Revenue is primarily concerned with what may be termed 'fiscal regulation', that is, ensuring that the scheme meets the conditions for approval and that the contributions to and benefits provided by the scheme fall within the limits provided by taxation provisions and Revenue discretions.

2.1.2 Contracting-out regulation

Regulation by various social security provisions is broadly geared toward what may be termed 'contracting-out regulation'. The OPB has exercised powers conferred by the Social Security Acts concerning, amongst other things, administration of the contracting out of SERPS provisions contained in, for example, the Pension Schemes Act 1993 (PSA 1993). Schemes were required to satisfy the OPB that, for example, the guaranteed minimum pension (GMP) and protected rights were secure. This function will remain within the purview of the DSS under the Contributions Agency. Further roles for the OPB include being involved in the design of pensions policy, the provision of information for members and acting as Registrar of the Occupational and Personal Pensions Schemes Register. The Pensions Register enables persons who have preserved benefits in schemes with which they have lost contact to trace the schemes. Any scheme with, or proposing to have, Revenue approval is required to register. Section 6 of the PSA 1993 currently requires the establishment and maintenance of the Register. The OPB was appointed Registrar by regulations (SI 1990/2278). This role may be undertaken by OPRA.

2.1.3 Investment regulation

This form of regulation arises from the trustees' duty to invest the funds of the scheme to produce income and/or to arrange for capital growth of the funds invested. Different questions arise in relation to the type of investment and manner of business that is conducted, but the 'investment regulation' framework broadly concerns whether the trustees of a scheme are authorised by IMRO as an 'OPS member' (that is, subject to the regime in the FSA 1986 relating to the management and investment of OPS funds) — in which case the trustees can manage the investment of scheme funds themselves — or, as is normally the case, the trustees will authorise an external fund manager, who is authorised by IMRO, to conduct the management of the investment. Alternatively, pension scheme funds may be managed and invested by an insurance company under an investment contract, which, again, is subject to the provisions of the FSA 1986.

It was the 'investment regulation' framework that came under the most stringent and stinging criticism of the Social Security Select Committee (House of Commons Paper Session 1991–92, 61-II) in its examination of the operation of pension funds. Since that time the rules relating to the regulation of IMRO authorised members have been reinforced. These include, in the context of an OPS, many of the facets of regulation relating to 'ordinary' members of IMRO. Accordingly, this rationalisation has enhanced the regulatory protection afforded to OPS members in the investment of scheme funds.

Both the Inland Revenue and the DSS exercise powers in the context of 'investment regulation'. As part of its approval of schemes, the Revenue imposes restrictions on the ability of small self-administered schemes to 'self-invest', that is, to invest the scheme assets in investments that are directly or indirectly related to the employer (see Retirement Benefits Schemes (Restriction on Discretion to Approve) (Small Self-administered Schemes) Regulations 1991 (SI 1991/1614)). The DSS has power to prescribe limits in relation to employer-related investments (see s. 112(2) of the PSA 1993 for the meaning of 'employer-related investments'). These are limited to 5 per cent (see Occupational Pension Schemes (Investment of Scheme's Resources) Regulations 1992 (SI 1992/246)).

2.1.4   Administrative regulation

Administrative regulation includes the resolution of disputes over both legal and factual issues. A number of mechanisms exist to resolve these issues and they include:

(a)   schemes' internal dispute resolution regimes,
(b)   the Occupational Pensions Advisory Service,
(c)   the Pensions Ombudsman,
(d)   industrial tribunals,
(e)   the courts.

In addition to the role of the OPB in relation to contracting-out provisions (see 2.1.2), the OPB's general remit includes modification of schemes and to advise schemes on their compliance with the rules relating to preservation of benefits. The Pensions Ombudsman is not directly concerned with the day-to-day regulation of schemes but provides part of the backdrop to the regulatory scene. The Pensions Ombudsman is empowered, *inter alia*, to investigate and/or determine complaints by a scheme member alleging injustice as a result of maladministration and disputes that arise between the member complainant and the trustees or managers of the scheme. The powers of the Ombudsman have been enlarged by PA 1995.

2.1.5 Criticism

Five broad criticisms could be made of the regulatory system before the PA 1995. First, in the 'administrative' sphere, there was a lack of cohesion. Though there was regulation it was fragmented and there was a lack of an overall regulator. Second, there were identifiable omissions of regulatory powers in areas of the framework. For example, allied to the lack of clear statutory duties relating to the activities of pension fund trustees, the OPB was never vested with powers to regulate and enforce duties relating to the activity or inactivity of scheme personnel and to take remedial action to secure scheme assets. Third, and a corollary of the first and second, there was a lack of powers to investigate and resolve particular aspects of both potential and actual disputes in the scheme which undermined the security for scheme members. Fourth, in a sense the framework perpetuated the escalation of misunderstanding and dispute between scheme members and trustees and managers of the scheme (for example, no requirement for some form of alternative dispute resolution mechanism, and provisions that require only a paucity of information to be disclosed to scheme members). Fifth, there was potential for duplicity of effort between the bodies identified above and in general their goal was not the cohesive regulation of pension schemes. With this in mind, one of the most significant aspects of the Act is the establishment of the Occupational Pensions Regulatory Authority.

2.2 THE OCCUPATIONAL PENSIONS REGULATORY AUTHORITY (OPRA)

The recommendation for a pensions regulator made by the Goode Committee was embraced by the government (see the White Paper, *Security, Equality, Choice: The Future of Pensions* (Cm 2594-II), para. 1.37) and the regulator has been established and given powers primarily in ss. 1 to 15 of and sch. 1 to the PA 1995. OPRA's powers and functions are not exactly as recommended by the Goode Committee but are a manifestation of the government's view of the role the regulator shall have. The Minister of State, Lord Mackay of Ardbrecknish stated that it will be:

an independent statutory body, fully accountable to Parliament. It will have the powers necessary to enforce compliance with the law. It will act swiftly and incisively to protect scheme members and to sanction and remove wrongdoers. And it will have a wide range of investigatory powers to act wherever it has reason to suspect that something is amiss, even where no formal report has been made.' (Hansard HL, 7 February 1995, col. 109.)

It is hoped by the government that OPRA will be up and running in April 1997.

The Act abolishes the OPB (s. 150) and provides for its property, rights and liabilities to be taken over by the Secretary of State. Most of the OPB's functions will be transferred to OPRA but some (for example, provisions relating to contracting out) will remain in accordance with s. 150 with the Secretary of State to be exercised by the Contributions Agency.

The government has a particular ideological stance to the conduct of public administration and the way it is financed. Unsurprisingly then, OPRA is created as a body corporate (s. 1), will be funded by schemes itself (s. 165 inserting a new s. 175 into the PSA 1993 relating to the funding levy) which means being in essence financially remote from the public purse except for start-up costs, and will have as an employee for day-to-day management a chief executive. This means that OPRA will not, at least on a constitutional footing and in terms of perception, be assimilated within, or an extension of, one of the existing departments of State. Further, despite the provisions of sch. 1 which eschews OPRA being regarded as a servant or agent of the Crown, it should not be supposed that OPRA is anything other than part of the *public regulation* of occupational pension schemes. This view is reinforced by, amongst other things, the extensive control exercised by the Secretary of State over the constitution of OPRA and that OPRA falls under the jurisdiction of the Parliamentary Commissioner for Administration (sch. 1, para. 10).

2.3   OPRA'S CONSTITUTION

The Secretary of State will appoint the members of OPRA which will consist of not less than seven members. The Secretary of State will appoint one of the members as full-time chairman but the other members will be part-time.

One member must be appointed after consultation by the Secretary of State with 'organisations appearing to him to be representative of employers' (s. 1(3)(a)) and another after like consultation with employees' organisations (s. 1(3)(b)). This requirement of consultation undoubtedly seeks to require a balance between employers' groups (for example, the CBI) and employees' groups (for example, trade unions), though there is no requirement that the members appointed as a result of the consultation process necessarily emanate from or represent these 'organisations'. A further member of OPRA will be a person who appears to the Secretary of State to have 'experience' of, and to have shown capacity in, the management or administration of occupational pension schemes.

An oddly drawn criterion for membership of OPRA appears in s. 1(3)(c) and (e). Paragraph (c) requires one member to be 'knowledgeable' about life assurance business and para. (e) similarly requires two members to be 'knowledgeable' about occupational pension schemes. Whether these members are 'knowledgeable' in their respective fields is to be decided by the Secretary of State which seems at first glance an incongruous criterion. If these persons had been required to be 'representative' of the life assurance business and occupational pension schemes, this might have appeared to have sectionalised OPRA and turn its members into delegates which clearly runs counter to the concept of OPRA. Arguably though, if the government does not wish OPRA to be viewed as containing sectional interests it could have extended the consultation requirements to a broader range of bodies. OPRA will accordingly draw its membership from a wide variety of backgrounds, experience and expertise.

Unfortunately an obvious omission is a requirement that one member of OPRA be appointed as a result of consultation with organisations who appear to be representative of pensioner groups. It cannot be suggested that pensioners do not have personal and financial interest in the security and management of schemes. This alone, notwithstanding any symbolic gestures to the community of interest in the role of the regulatory authority, should have been a basis for extending the statutory consultation requirements.

There is a residual power given to the Secretary of State to appoint one or more others to make up the membership. The Act does not prescribe any qualities for these appointments.

Lord Mackay stated that the members of OPRA would not serve in a representative capacity, eschewing any vested interests (Hansard, HL, 7 February 1995, col. 117). In terms of perception, however, the 'shepherding' role that OPRA will undertake is undermined by the current requirements. A further argument that seeks to justify the constitution of OPRA is that it follows a model adopted for the OPB. With respect this misses the point. The OPB, despite its good work, was never created as, had the powers to be or held out as the type of public regulator that OPRA is envisaged as.

The length of a member's term of office will be set by his or her instrument of appointment (sch. 1, para. 3). It may be altered by the Secretary of State if the member is appointed chairman or on vacation of the office of chairman (para. 4). Schedule 1 does nothing to undermine our view as to the 'publicness' of OPRA. Provisions in sch. 1, para. 6, enable the Secretary of State to remove the chairman at any time by written notification, which will also terminate his or her membership of OPRA. Unusually for an office of this type, the Act does not stipulate any grounds for removal. The Secretary of State also has power to remove a member who is not the chairman, though only on the grounds specified in para. 7, namely, where the Secretary of State is satisfied, that a member:

(a) has been absent from meetings for more than three consecutive months without OPRA's permission;

(b) is unable or unfit to fulfil the duties of office; or

(c) has become bankrupt or made an arrangement with his or her creditors or, in Scotland, has been sequestrated or has made a trust deed for the behoof of his or her creditors or a composition contract.

OPRA will, subject to reference to the Secretary of State, employ staff and one of the employees will be chief executive (para. 11). The Secretary of State shall appoint the first chief executive but any subsequent reappointment or appointment of a new chief executive shall be made by OPRA with the approval of the Secretary of State. As the chief executive is referred to in para. 11, under the heading of 'staff', it is clear that he or she is to be regarded as an employee of the authority and not of any department of State. The terms and conditions as to remuneration of other employees require the approval of the Secretary of State and employees will be members of a civil service pension scheme to avoid the anomalous position of being members of and regulating their own scheme. As originally drafted the Bill required staffing and resourcing to be approved by the Treasury but under greater Departmental budgetary autonomy, this was deleted but in this respect it is the Treasury who ultimately have its hand on the 'financial tiller'.

OPRA and its members and employees cannot be liable in damages for any action or inaction in the exercise of its functions under PA 1995 or the PSA 1993 unless it can be demonstrated that the action or inaction was in bad faith (PA 1995, s. 1(4)). However, as the Act clearly states that OPRA shall not be regarded as servants or agents of the Crown, this does mean that they are susceptible to remedies that would ordinarily not be available against the Crown, such as injunctive relief.

Finally, if emphasis needs to be given of the 'publicness' of OPRA, the obligation to keep proper accounts, records in relation to accounts and to prepare a statement of accounts for each financial year is combined with a duty to send copies of the statement to both the Secretary of State and the Comptroller and Auditor General. The latter must examine and report on each statement and lay copies of the statement and report before Parliament (sch. 1, para. 16).

Section 2 of the Act requires OPRA to report annually to the Secretary of State on each successive year's activity. The Secretary of State must lay before each House of Parliament a copy of this report.

2.4   OPRA'S PROCEEDINGS

Regulations made by the Secretary of State will govern the procedure to be followed by OPRA in the exercise of its functions (PA 1995, sch. 1, para. 13). The regulations will provide, in particular, for OPRA to conduct certain of its functions in a quasi-judicial fashion, such as by way of formal hearing and having all the significant attributes of a tribunal. Regulations may provide for:

(a)   taking evidence and the hearing of parties;
(b)   the manner in which parties before OPRA may or are to be represented;
(c)   summoning persons to give evidence, including that given on oath;
(d)   requiring documents to be produced to it for these purposes.

Accordingly, amendments made by sch. 3 to the Tribunals and Inquiries Act 1992 will include OPRA in the supervisory jurisdiction of the Council on Tribunals in relation to the conduct of hearings and reviews.

2.5   OPRA'S POWERS

The nature and extent of OPRA's powers was a contentious issue during the passage through Parliament of the Bill. Initially, the Goode Committee had sought to recommend an authority with wide powers of supervision, powers to make spot checks of schemes, powers which would enable it to carry out detailed investigations and to receive information about actual or suspected irregularities in a scheme and about persistent non-compliance with regulations (see Goode Report, para. 4.10.56). These powers would have laid the basis for an authority with sufficient armament to play an effective role. The general consensus within the 'pensions industry' is that the regulator should have these powers but conduct its functions proactively. Goode had envisaged a regulator that was 'less proactive' than its counterparts in the financial services sector. Whilst embracing the concept of a regulatory authority, the government sought to suggest that it would be 'actively responsive' (White Paper, para. 1.38). In essence this meant that it would not have powers that would enable it to act proactively. Further, the White Paper suggested that the authority would 'sit and wait' for scheme problems or general problems to come to it. This combined with the fact that other provisions of the Act place a statutory duty upon certain persons connected with a scheme to make any problems with the scheme known to the regulator (see chapter 3), suggested a less full role than intended by the Goode Committee. It is right to say that the tenor of the White Paper in relation to the activities of the proposed regulator gave little hint of this (see App. 3). It broadly suggested that the regulator would enforce general statutory obligations and, importantly, might become involved in *problem cases*, i.e., cases where the problem has in some way already manifested itself. The establishment of the regulator's role in this fashion was and is thought in some quarters, insufficient to meet the degree of scheme security required. On balance, though, the Goode Committee itself did not seek to suggest a regulator that would be actively monitoring every scheme by some mandatory reporting requirement placed upon them. It suggested:

> It would . . . be quite impracticable for the Regulator to keep all schemes under active review. . . . Of necessity, the Regulator's intervention will normally come about as a result of complaints made to [it] about scheme solvency or administration rather than from investigations which the Regulator undertakes on [its] own initiative.' (Goode Report, para. 4.19.24.)

During the Act's passage through Parliament, the opposition unsuccessfully tabled amendments during both committee stages which sought to empower the regulator with more dynamic supervisory qualities; powers that involved, *inter alia*, a process of scheme monitoring allied to mandatory annual financial reporting to OPRA by schemes and an ability to intervene in scheme administration when OPRA believed the assets of the scheme to be in jeopardy (see Hansard, HL, 3 February, col. 106 and Commons Standing Committee D, 2 May, cols. 6–27). However, the government signalled that in its opinion this was to require too much of the regulator and of schemes. During debate on the proposed amendment in the House of Lords, Lord Mackay stated that, simply because the regulator is called the Occupational Pensions Regulatory Authority, one should not think they should, can be or will be some sort of 'all-singing, all-dancing act' (Hansard, HL, 7 February, col. 109).

The powers of OPRA can be broadly divided into five main heads:

(a) trustee supervision;
(b) scheme wind-up;
(c) scheme asset protection;
(d) information gathering;
(e) resolution of disputes.

2.6 TRUSTEE SUPERVISION

2.6.1 Prohibition and removal

Section 3 PA 1995 provides for OPRA to 'prohibit' a person by order from being a trustee of a particular scheme. Allied to this power is a power in s. 4 to suspend a person from acting as trustee pending consideration of prohibiting him or pending resolution of other prescribed proceedings. In its original form in the Bill, s. 3 provided only for the removal of a trustee in limited circumstances. The revised provisions forming the current basis of OPRA's power were introduced at a relatively late stage in the proceedings, during the Bill's report to the House of Lords (Hansard, HL, 13 March 1995, cols. 575–82). Prohibiting a person from acting as trustee has, where the person is acting in that capacity, the effect of removing him (s. 3(3)).

These statutory powers are a further layer of supervision to that provided under the general law of trusts (though it should be noted that OPRA does not have power to enforce the latter), and do not purport to amend, vary or nullify the general law. The legal obligations of trustees are enhanced by PA 1995 (see chapter 3) and it is the statutory duties and functions of trustees under PA 1995 and PSA 1993 to which the powers granted to OPRA of prohibition, suspension and removal of trustees under s. 3 and s. 4 are aimed.

If a person has been prohibited from acting as trustee of a particular scheme under s. 3 then OPRA can also prohibit a company of which that person is a director from being a trustee of that scheme (s. 3(2)(c)). Similarly a Scottish partnership in which a prohibited person is a partner can be prohibited (s. 3(2)(d)). This precludes the possibility of circumventing the prohibition of the director by appointing the company as trustee. Prohibition of a person under s. 3 is only from being a trustee of a particular scheme, but it can lead to OPRA making an order under s. 29(3) prohibiting the person being a trustee of *any* scheme (see 3.2).

Under s. 3, OPRA may by order prohibit a person from being a trustee of a trust scheme to which the Act applies when OPRA is itself satisfied that the trustee is in *serious or persistent breach* of any of his duties under Part I except ss. 51 to 54 (indexation), 62 to 65 (equal treatment provisions) and 110 to 112 (the Compensation Board). A prohibition order may also be made if the trustee is in *serious or persistent breach* of duty under provisions of the PSA 1993 relating to registration under s. 6, transfer values and rights to cash equivalent under Chapter IV of Part IV, provision of information under s. 113 and the levy funding under s. 175.

The deliberate omission of the provisions relating to indexation and equal treatment under the Act from the sanction powers of OPRA appears anomalous given that, on the one hand, they are obligations under the Act and yet, on the other, OPRA have no means of enforcing them. The situation is justified on the basis that such issues, where raised, fall readily under the jurisdiction of the Pensions Ombudsman.

There are two distinct issues in a determination by OPRA to prohibit a person being trustee:

(a)   whether the trustee in question is in breach of duty;
(b)   whether the breach is also either *serious* or *persistent*, which OPRA must determine as a factual issue.

There is no guidance in the Act as to what 'serious or persistent' may mean. 'Serious' is a qualification of the breach of duty in question and would not necessarily refer to the consequences of the breach though it is difficult to ignore the consequences of a breach when ascertaining whether it is serious. Moreover, it is suggested that a serious breach of duty should not be limited to finding dishonesty or other moral turpitude, but should include all relevant acts or omissions. 'Persistent' clearly envisages some repetition or continuance of the same breach or series of breaches. Some support for this view can be found, albeit in different contexts, in the following examples. The Company Directors Disqualification Act 1986, s. 3, permits a court to disqualify a person from acting as director for being 'persistently in default' of companies legislation requiring certain matters to be delivered to the registrar of companies. By s. 3(2), conviction of three defaults in five years is conclusive proof of persistent defaulting, but this is without prejudice to other means of proof. See also *Re Arctic Engineering Ltd (No. 2)* [1986] 1 WLR 686, considering 'persistently in default' in the forerunner to s. 3 of the 1986 Act. Also in *R v Tuck* [1994] Crim LR 375, the Court of Appeal in considering s. 32 of the Sexual Offences Act 1956 (an offence relating to persistent importuning or solicitation of a male in a public place for an immoral purpose) suggested that persistent meant some degree of repetition — in this context — by more than one invitation to a person.

PA 1995, s. 3(2)(a) appears to countenance that breach of one or more of the prescribed statutory duties by a trustee will not lead to that trustee's prohibition where the breach cannot be deemed serious or is one which is not persistent. In any event, even where the breach can be said to be serious or persistent, the power to prohibit is expressed in permissive terms and not mandatory. However, there would be cause for concern where OPRA found that a trustee was in serious or persistent breach of duty and did not act to prohibit the person from being trustee.

OPRA's statutory powers to prohibit a trustee are extended by s. 3(2)(b) to embrace other faults on the part of a trustee. This is a confusing and poorly drafted provision. In many provisions throughout Part I of the Act, s. 3 is specifically identified as being applicable (in ss. 15, 21, 28, 31 32, 35, 36, 37, 40, 47, 49, 57, 58, 59, 60, 73, 76, 77, 81, 87 and 88) to a trustee who, though not necessarily in breach of a duty as required by s. 3(2)(a), has defaulted, for example, by failing 'to take all such steps as are reasonable to secure compliance' with the provision. When OPRA are satisfied that s. 3 has applied to a person by virtue of any of these provisions (or, reading s. 3(2)(b) in its broadest sense, provisions of regulations made under Part I), while the person was trustee of a scheme, then it may, under s. 3(2)(b), prohibit the person from being trustee of that scheme. This, in a sense, introduces as a minimum a negligence requirement for the prohibition order. Failure to take steps is the most common form of fault required in these provisions to invoke the power to prohibit. However, in ss. 21(2), 28(4) and 47(3), there is no requirement of failing to take reasonable steps. For example, merely acting as auditor or actuary to a scheme while being trustee of the scheme renders the trustee susceptible to prohibition (s. 28(4)). Likewise, trustees who rely upon the advice of a legal adviser not appointed by the trustees or managers, in the exercise of any of their functions, are susceptible to prohibition (s. 47(3)). This is so whether the advice is good, bad, given or sought in good faith or given in appropriate contexts.

It may be that s. 3(2)(b) was inserted due to an over-abundance of caution as at times, the 'fault' on the part of the trustee would be sufficient, where the relevant provision can be construed as placing a duty on the trustees, for the power in s. 3(2)(a)(i) — serious and persistent breach of duty — to be exercised. What in essence subsection (2)(b) purports to do is to extend the power to prohibit a trustee beyond the enforceable duties envisaged by subsection (2)(a)(i). This view finds some support in the explanatory and financial memorandum that accompanied the Bill which referred to the power to prohibit as being exercisable for serious or

persistent breach of duty or for failure 'to comply with certain requirements'. This
may be the desired effect, but it is respectfully suggested that the drafting could have
made the requirements clearer. We have noted that at times the power in subsection
(2)(b) could arguably overlap with the power to prohibit in subsection (2)(a)(i),
where the provision in question can be construed as placing a duty upon the trustees.
Section 3 becomes applicable in certain circumstances, generally, serious or
persistent breach of duty or failure to take reasonable steps to secure compliance.
The question then is, if there is a duty on the trustees to secure compliance (for
example, to ensure that arrangements and rules for member-nominated trustees are
in place — s. 16(1)), and this is breached by failure to take reasonable steps
(s. 21(1)), is this breach (of duty) by failure to take reasonable steps to secure
compliance required to be *serious or persistent* (s. 3(2)(a)(i)), or is simple *failure to
take reasonable steps* enough? If the former view is correct then four conditions
must be fulfilled before a person can be prohibited for failure to take steps:

(a)   that the trustee has failed to take the requisite steps to secure compliance,
(b)   that the failure is as a result of no steps being taken or where taken were
not reasonable to secure compliance,
(c)   that the trustee is in breach of duty, and
(d)   that such a breach is serious and persistent.

If the latter view prevails, steps (c) and (d) are unnecessary as, for the purposes of
subsection (2)(b), a breach of duty, though it may follow, is rendered otiose.

The difficulties do not necessarily arise where there is no requirement of any
'fault' in those sections identified above and the four-stage approach is inapplicable. Further, it is a moot point whether, for example, in relation to considering
whether to prohibit a person being a trustee by reason of him acting as auditor to
the scheme, OPRA would need necessarily to consider whether the trustee is in
serious or persistent breach of duty, as it is the essence of the Act that this state
of affairs should not occur. Concluding that this state of affairs exists should be
sufficient to activate the power and it is suggested that all that should be required
is that OPRA is acting *intra vires* and bona fide for them to prohibit the person as
trustee relying on the general power in subsection (2)(b).

Other grounds that exist for prohibition are:

(a)   that the person who is to be prohibited is a director of a company which
has itself been prohibited by reason of circumstances falling within s. 3(2)(a) or (b);
(b)   and the acts or defaults giving rise to those circumstances were committed
with the person's consent or connivance or are attributable to neglect on his part; or
(c)   other grounds prescribed by regulations.

Section 5 attempts to imbue the process leading to prohibition under s. 3 with
some basic notions of procedural fairness. OPRA must, before making an order
under s. 3 without the trustee's consent, give the trustee at least one month's notice,
which may be by post, of their proposal to remove him. There is no general
requirement as to what the notice must contain other than an invitation to the
trustee to make representations as to this proposal within a stipulated time. As

drafted, there would seem nothing to prohibit this notice being given orally, though as we have noted the notice may be given by post and s. 5(5) refers to it being delivered to the trustee, being left at his proper address or being sent in the post. Where the trustee cannot be found or has no known address, there is no obligation to provide a notice of the proposal (s. 5(1)).

There is no requirement that the representations of the trustee, where given, be given in writing or orally though it is likely that regulations under sch. 1 will require them to be given in written form. Having invited representations — and having received them within the stipulated period — OPRA must take them into consideration — see s. 5(2).

Where OPRA has made its decision to remove the trustee, before it makes the order it must give notice of its intention to remove the trustee to the other trustees of the scheme, except those that cannot be found or have no known address (see s. 5(3)). Not all parties who have an interest in the administration of the scheme are required to be given notice of the proposal to remove the trustee and the most obvious omission from this is the employer. The obligation to invite representations does not extend to the other trustees of the scheme but relates solely to the trustee under consideration. That said, it is open to OPRA to obtain evidence from the other trustees of the scheme for the purposes of the prohibition order.

2.6.2 Suspension

Section 4 PA 1995, again added at a relatively late stage to the Bill, permits OPRA to suspend a trustee of a scheme in specific circumstances. Circumstances above in themselves may call into doubt the fitness of the trustee to act for the scheme and it is sensible that while these doubts are in some way in issue, OPRA may order the trustee to desist from acting. However, it may seem at times that the suspension order has an element of 'overkill' in its nature and extent but it must be noted that it does not automatically follow on the occurrence of the prescribed circumstances. Before turning to the circumstances in which OPRA may suspend a trustee, it is suggested that an obvious omission from them is when the Pensions Ombudsman is conducting an investigation into alleged maladministration of a scheme. Maladministration is a broad concept and acts or omissions which may constitute it can amount to serious dishonesty.

OPRA may, under s. 4(1)(a), suspend a trustee of a scheme while it is giving consideration to prohibiting him under s. 3(1). Section 4 also stipulates a variety of other circumstances in which a suspension order may be issued against a trustee and these are:

(a) where the person has proceedings instituted against him for an offence involving dishonesty or deception and the proceedings have not been concluded;

(b) where a petition for bankruptcy or sequestration has been presented against the person and the petition proceedings have not been concluded;

(c) in the case of a corporate trustee, where a petition to wind up the company has been presented and the proceedings have not been concluded;

(d) where an application has been made to disqualify the person as a director under the Company Directors Disqualification Act 1986 and the proceedings have not been concluded; or

(e)   where the Trustee is a company or Scottish partnership and, if any director or partner were a trustee, OPRA would have power to suspend the director or partner under (a), (b) or (d) above.

The effect of a suspension order is to prohibit the subject of it for that period from exercising any functions as trustee of a particular scheme. The order may also have the wider effect of suspending the subject from a class of schemes or schemes in general (s. 4(3)). Suspending a trustee may of course affect the operation of the scheme which may be unworkable given the reduction in the number of trustees capable of acting. However, the order may provide for matters which arise from the suspension in terms of enabling any person to execute any instrument in the trustee's name or otherwise to act for him and it may also provide for an adjustment to the scheme rules to take the reduction into account (s. 4(6)).

Section 4(4) permits retrospective effect as the order may be made on the basis of (a) to (d) above, even if the proceedings in question were commenced before the commencement of s. 4(1).

The duration of a suspension order is, under s. 4(2), dependent upon the basis upon which it is made. Where it is made pending consideration of a prohibition order, then the initial duration is 12 months though this may be extended for a further 12 months. There is no power to extend beyond this second 12 month period where it is made on the basis of (a) to (e) above, it will last until the relevant proceedings have concluded.

A person subject to a suspension order may apply to OPRA to revoke the order. OPRA can determine whether to revoke the order in totality or, as applicable, in relation to a particular scheme or class of schemes and revocation of the order will not affect anything done before the time of revocation (s. 4(5)). The procedure that OPRA will adopt will be prescribed in regulations under the general power in sch. 1.

Where OPRA proposes to suspend a trustee from acting, it must give immediate notice of that fact to him. Unlike notice of a proposal of prohibition, there is no requirement that OPRA invite representations from the trustee concerned. OPRA must also give notice — though here the suggestion is of a more relaxed pace, 'as soon as reasonably practicable' — to the other trustees of the scheme except those who cannot be found or have no known address. Again, the employer is excluded from this requirement.

Section 6(1) is a corollary of ss. 3 and 4 and provides OPRA with coercive back-up by creating a number of criminal offences. Where OPRA has made an order to suspend or prohibit a trustee but the trustee purports to act notwithstanding the order then the trustee would be guilty of an offence and liable on summary conviction to a fine not exceeding the statutory maximum and, on indictment, to a fine and/or imprisonment. Where the trustee acted in relation to the scheme while suspended or prohibited by OPRA, s. 6 preserves the validity of that trustee's actions, though only in so far as things done by the trustee are not to be deemed invalid merely because the trustee was removed or suspended at that time. This of course would not provide for the validity of the trustees' actions in relation to the scheme where there are other grounds that may render such actions invalid, for example, where the trustee subject to a suspending order executes a trust instrument in his name *ultra vires* the scheme rules — suspension would not then be the sole reason for the act being invalid (s. 6(3)).

Section 6(4) makes it explicit that neither s. 3 nor s. 4 can be taken as affecting civil or criminal liability of any person as a result of actions or omissions of the trustee while purporting to act as trustee of the scheme.

2.6.3 Appointment

Section 7 PA 1995 contains multifarious provisions relating to the appointment of a trustee by OPRA to a trust scheme. Where OPRA has acted to prohibit a trustee under s. 3 or a trustee ceases to be a trustee by virtue of being disqualified from acting, OPRA may by order appoint another trustee (s. 7(1)). In exercising a power of appointment there is no explicit requirement that OPRA consult with any other party, for example, the other trustees, the employer or members of the scheme, or of the qualities that the appointee should have. Undoubtedly the appointment under subsection (1) will be made on an assessment of the best interests of the scheme and a relevant consideration may be the views of the other parties related to the scheme. More than this, OPRA would have to satisfy itself that, for example, the trustee has, or will continue to have, the knowledge and skill necessary for the correct administration of the scheme. This common-sense approach is no more than an application of the criteria for OPRA's consideration when appointing a trustee under s. 7(3) (see below).

Section 23(1)(b) confers a power to appoint a trustee to a scheme on an insolvency practitioner or official receiver in the circumstances set out in s. 22, and the conditions of ss. 22 to 26 apply to the appointee (see chapter 3). Where OPRA appoints a trustee under s. 7 to replace such a trustee, then similarly ss. 22 to 26 will apply to the replacement trustee (s. 7(2)).

There is a second power to appoint a trustee by order in s. 7(3) which can be exercised if OPRA is satisfied that appointing a replacement is necessary in order:

(a) to secure that the trustees as a whole have, or exercise, the necessary knowledge and skill for the proper administration of the scheme; or

(b) to secure that the number of trustees is sufficient for the proper administration of the scheme; or

(c) to secure the proper use or application of the assets of the scheme.

Section 7(3) would seem to leave determining the necessity of appointing a trustee to a scheme to the discretion of OPRA. The basis is its subjective assessment of the requirements of the scheme in terms of skill etc., that should be met by the trustees of the scheme and that there is a lacuna in the existing trustees' skill and knowledge. Whether that lacuna does exist is undoubtedly for OPRA to decide, but arguably a decision to appoint or not appoint a trustee to fill the 'skill and knowledge' lacuna in the scheme could be demonstrated to be wrong on objective criteria, for example, the performance of the scheme, or the omission to consider some relevant fact (based on the so-called 'Wednesbury principles': *Associated Provincial Picture Houses Ltd* v *Wednesbury Corporation* [1948] 1 KB 223). However, given the reactive role that OPRA will have, opportunities that would arise for this power to be exercised would naturally arise where a problem in the administration of the scheme has manifested itself and has been brought to OPRA's attention and any attempt to demonstrate that such a decision was wrong on that basis would be extremely difficult.

Where OPRA exercises the power to appoint a trustee by order under s. 7, it may, under s. 7(5):

(a)   determine the appropriate number of trustees for proper administration of the scheme;

(b)   require that any trustee so appointed by OPRA is paid fees and expenses from the scheme's resources; and

(c)   provide for the trustee so appointed to be removed or replaced.

Further detail may be added later by regulations under s. 7(4) and (6). The power to make regulations occurs at a great number of points throughout the Act and is perhaps a manifestation of a desire to streamline the primary provisions and allow for the minutiae to be added later. Thus, s. 7(4) provides for flexibility in the future by providing that the regulations may allow for trustees to be appointed in specified circumstances. This is a common-sense approach to the powers to appoint trustees under s. 7 where it is desirable to provide for future contingencies. Similarly, s. 7(6) enables regulations to be made relating to the descriptions of persons that OPRA may or may not appoint. Undoubtedly trustees appointed by OPRA will be required to have minimum standards of expertise and experience and OPRA will have to be satisfied of the putative trustee's integrity. The regulations under s. 7(6) will no doubt be no more than an expression of these requirements. The flexibility that regulations will provide is for a relaxation or tightening of the standards as a process of ongoing review.

A trustee appointed by OPRA will have the same powers and duties as the other trustees of the scheme (s. 8(3)). This may be varied, though, where the order appointing the trustee circumscribes the powers and duties, or provides for powers or duties to lie solely upon the appointee (s. 8(4)).

Though we noted earlier that the appointed trustee can be reimbursed from the scheme, the costs may in reality be borne by the employer. Section 8(1) provides that on order appointing a trustee under s. 7 may provide for any amounts paid to the appointee from the scheme, and which are not reimbursed to the scheme by the employer, to be treated as a debt due from the employer of an equivalent sum.

Where OPRA has exercised its power of appointment or removal under Part I, there may be problems vesting in, or transferring trust property to, the newly constituted trustees. Section 9 addresses this by providing for OPRA, where it has exercised its powers of appointment or removal, to have the jurisdiction and powers exercisable by the High Court or, where applicable, the Court of Session for vesting any scheme property in, or transferring it to, the trustees.

The powers of the High Court are contained in ss. 44 to 56 of the Trustee Act 1925 and are wide and multifarious.

However, OPRA's powers to vest or transfer property arise only as a direct consequence of powers exercisable under Part I of the PA 1995 and will not affect the vesting or transfer of property to the trustees where there is a reconstitution of the trustees by virtue of any other provision or method. Similar powers exist in relation to s. 30, where a trustee of a trust scheme becomes ineligible to act in that capacity by virtue of s. 29 (see chapter 3). Again, OPRA can exercise its power to vest or transfer property.

2.6.4 Directions

Provisions within PA 1995 relate to the separation of scheme moneys received by the trustees and this separation is achieved by the payment of those moneys into a separate bank account (see s. 49). Further, regulations made under s. 49(5) must provide for, *inter alia,* the employer to put into a separate account any payments of benefits not made to the members (see chapter 3). If an employer fails, in contravention of regulations made under s. 49(5), to pay benefit within the prescribed period and has not preserved it in a separate bank account then OPRA may direct the trustees of the scheme in writing to make appropriate arrangements for payment of the benefit (s. 15(1) and (3)).

Further powers to give directions to trustees of a trust scheme arise in relation to:

(a)   trust schemes which publish annual reports; and
(b)   trust schemes generally.

In the former case, OPRA may direct the trustees to include within the annual report a statement prepared by OPRA. In the latter, OPRA may direct the trustees to send to the members a copy of a statement prepared by them (s. 15(2)).

The rationale behind these powers is to seek to deter breaches of the Act or regulations by the threat of adverse comment or publicity. The publicity generated by the statements is in some circumstances likely to be of a limited effect given the restricted audience and there is no power to require the trustees to 'go public'. However, OPRA does of course have an ability to publish its own reports of its investigations (s. 103 and see 2.10.1.5). There is no limit placed in the Act upon the purposes or subject-matter of a statement to be disseminated under s. 15. However, it must be relevant to the powers and functions of OPRA under the Act and relate to some act or omission on behalf of some person connected with the scheme or some activity of the scheme in relation to which OPRA is empowered by primary or secondary legislation to act. The penalty provisions of both ss. 3 and 10 apply to any trustee where the above directions are not complied with and the trustee has failed to take all reasonable steps to secure compliance with the directions (s. 15(4)).

2.6.5 Sanction

The government was clear that OPRA would be provided with some wide powers to supervise scheme trustees and to enforce compliance with the requirements of the legislation (White Paper, app. 3). We have noted already the powers of prohibition and suspension. Additionally, to achieve this, s. 10 PA 1995 provides for OPRA to require *any person* (including scheme trustees) to pay a civil penalty. This requirement may arise in two different ways:

(a)   under s. 10(1) where OPRA is satisfied that, by reason of any act or omission, a provision of Part I of the Act has made s. 10 applicable (see, for example, the references to s. 10 in ss. 15, 17, 19, 21, 31, 32, 35, 36, 37, 40, 47, 48, 49, 50, 57, 58, 59, 60, 73, 76, 87 and 88);

(b)   under s. 10(3) where regulations made under Part I or under the new s. 168 inserted into the PSA 1993 by s. 155 PA 1995 include a requirement that any person who contravenes such regulations pay a civil penalty.

The level of penalty payable shall not exceed the 'maximum amount' and this is £5,000 in the case of an individual or £50,000 in any other case, such as a corporate trustee (s. 10(2)(a)), or such lower amounts as prescribed in each case (s. 10(2)(b)). The maximum amounts may be amended by the Secretary of State who may substitute *higher* amounts. Where the penalty provisions regulations apply the regulations must specify the maximum amount of penalty payable and must differentiate in terms of the maximum amounts payable by individuals and other cases. In any event, these maximum amounts may not exceed the maximum levels in subsection (2)(a) (s. 10(3)). The time period in which a person must pay a penalty is left to be set down in regulations made under subsection (1) or, in the case of subsection (3) or s. 168(4) of the PSA 1993, as prescribed in the relevant regulations. Any orders amending the maximum amounts in s. 10(2)(a) PA 1995 or in regulations will not affect any amounts recoverable against a person by virtue of an act or omission occurring before the change (s. 10(4)).

If a corporate trustee is liable to a penalty by reason of any act or omission then its officers will also be liable under s. 10(5) and (6) if they consented to or connived in the act or omission or if the act or omission was attributable to their neglect. In relation to a body corporate, the persons who may be liable are:

(a)   any director, manager, secretary or other similar officer of it or person purporting to act in those capacities; or
(b)   where its affairs are managed by its members, any member in connection with management functions.

This applies likewise to the partners of a Scottish partnership from which a penalty is recoverable. Where a penalty is recovered from a director etc., or partner, then OPRA cannot also recover a penalty from the corporate trustee or partnership in respect of the same act or omission (s. 10(7)). Liability of corporate officers and partners is fault-based.

OPRA is empowered to recover the penalties yet ultimately it is the public purse which is the recipient (see s. 10(8) and (9)).

2.7   SCHEME WIND-UP

Section 11 PA 1995 provides OPRA with statutory powers relating to winding up pension schemes. This power exists in addition to the established methods of winding up a scheme, for example, in accordance with the scheme rules. It is important to note that the power as manifested in the Act does not provide for the more extensive involvement of OPRA that is perhaps desirable (see chapter 6 for discussion). The power conforms to the 'reactive model' of OPRA's role and eschews any 'paternalistic' role for OPRA by the omission of any requirement to notify OPRA that a scheme is being wound up in any case where the winding up is not as a result of the power under s. 11. This may, albeit in rare circumstances, leave the interests of the beneficiaries exposed.

2.8 ASSET PROTECTION

Previous experience has shown that in some cases where there is a danger that scheme assets will or have been misused or misappropriated, the evidence that reflects these positions is either not known or, if known, is not acted upon by the trustees and officials. For members of the scheme, not having the relevant information invariably means that they cannot act to protect scheme assets and it is here that their rights and interests are at their most vulnerable. OPRA will be actively responsive to schemes which evidence problems. PA 1995 places statutory duties on scheme auditors and actuaries to notify OPRA immediately of any non-compliance with any duty placed by any rule of law on scheme trustees, employers or professional advisers (see chapter 3). It is a natural corollary of both these aspects that OPRA be given power to act to prevent or prohibit the misuse or misappropriation of scheme assets or, where this has not occurred, to act to avoid repetition of the same or similar acts which may have threatened them. This is, in essence, the position provided for in PA 1995, ss. 13 and 14.

Sections 13 and 14 provide OPRA with a permissive power to act to protect a scheme's assets and provides the court with power to grant the prescribed remedy. Section 13 allows OPRA to seek from the High Court a prohibitory injunction, or from the Court of Session an interdict of a similar nature, where it satisfies the court either:

(a) that there is a *reasonable likelihood* that any person (for example, the employer or a scheme employee) will do any act that amounts to a misuse or misappropriation of the scheme's assets; or

(b) where such a person has committed any such act, that there is a *reasonable likelihood* of continuation or repetition of the act, or that he will do a similar act.

Section 13 does not alter the general law relating to the available remedies. The Act introduces a relatively low threshold test of 'reasonable likelihood' of the prescribed circumstances for the grant of the remedy, but this would not, for example, alter the discretionary nature of the court's jurisdiction to grant injunctive relief.

It is not possible to guarantee the scheme assets from every attempt or concerted effort to misuse or misappropriate scheme funds. The provisions of ss. 13 and 14 do provide a measure of reactive security for pension scheme assets and this is to be welcomed. The Goode Committee fully considered, but refrained from recommending, compulsory measures relating to custodianship of scheme assets and designation of ownership of scheme investments (see Goode Report 4.10.37 and 4.10.55). It concluded that in themselves they would not provide for the security of assets and, to the extent that they did, would be outweighed by the disadvantages of inconvenience and cost. An attempt was made, however, during the passage of the Bill to introduce such measures. The Goode Committee wanted to encourage good practice with OPRA providing codes of practice relating to pension fund investment (see Goode Report recommendations 115 and 116). These matters are left to OPRA's general powers to facilitate its functions under the Act (see sch. 1). In the final analysis it is perhaps a question of priorities but by not introducing measures relating to, *inter alia,* custodianship and designation of ownership of scheme investments an opportunity was missed to shore up the safeguards for pension scheme assets.

Section 14 seeks to provide OPRA with a permissive power to act to protect scheme assets, by seeking restitution to a scheme of improper payments of surplus to the employer (s. 37), asset distribution to the employer (ss. 76 and 77) or employer-related investments (s. 40). The essence of restitution is to seek to restore the parties, where possible, to the position they were in before the challenged transaction took place. To this end, the High Court and the Court of Session are given jurisdiction to make an order requiring the employer, or any person knowingly concerned in the improper payments etc., to take such steps as the court requires for restoring the pre-transaction position — s. 14(1) and (2). OPRA may seek such an order and must satisfy the court that either:

(a)   the power to make the payment, or distribute assets, to the employer was exercised in contravention of s. 37, 76 or 77; or

(b)   that any act or omission of the trustees or managers of the scheme has resulted in 'employer-related investments' in contravention of s. 40.

2.9   RESOLUTION OF DISPUTES

The function of resolving disputes under PA 1995 rests on different grounds to that of the Pensions Ombudsman. Broadly speaking the Ombudsman investigates and resolves disputes that arise as a result of complaints made to him. The area of complaint is broad, is not restricted to the provisions of PA 1995 and is concerned with problems arising out of specific relationships, for example, beneficiary and manager of the scheme or scheme co-managers (see chapter 7). However, OPRA's dispute investigation and resolution function arises from its general purview of obligations provided by or under the Act or in specific instances of the PSA 1993. For example, it would arise as a result of investigating an alleged breach of duty under PA 1995 by a trustee, and a determination that such a breach is, in accordance with s. 3, 'serious and persistent'. This, as we have seen, activates the power to prohibit the person being trustee. In both cases, determinations of fact and law are required though there are differences in the methods of enforcement of the respective determinations. So OPRA's dispute-resolution function relates primarily to resolving any disputed issues between OPRA and the subject(s) of investigation.

However, a dispute may not end there and a person subject to a determination by OPRA, say to prohibit him from acting as trustee, may wish to challenge it. Accordingly, PA 1995 attempts to obviate any doubts that it is for OPRA to determine the issues that arise for resolution under the Act. It does this by stating that any determination by OPRA of any question which is within their functions under the Act is to be final (s. 96(1)). Attempts to preserve the sanctity of the decision-making powers of public bodies have long been vulnerable to circumvention by the courts and in many cases have been ineffective for their purpose (see, for example, *Re Plowright* (1686) 3 Mod 94 and *Anisminic Ltd* v *Foreign Compensation Commission* [1969] 2 AC 147). However, the use of such wording strongly suggests that the ordinary remedies of the court would be unavailable, unless the determination was *ultra vires*. Where statute has provided an alternative to the court review to a determination, as PA 1995 does, the courts usually require a person questioning a determination to use the alternative procedure (where, for example, the persons who will make the review under that procedure have specialist skill and/or knowledge). The statutory remedy may impliedly exclude ordinary remedies obtained via the courts. There are occasions, however, where the court has provided exceptions to this approach (see, for example, *Pyx Granite Ltd* v *Ministry of Housing and Local Government* [1960] AC 260).

We have seen that OPRA may determine to prohibit a person from the office of trustee of a scheme (s. 3), require a person to be subject to a civil penalty (s. 10 PA 1995; s. 168(4) PSA 1993), or disqualify a person from being a trustee of any trust scheme (s. 29(3) and (4) PA 1995). We have also seen that the Act purports to render such determinations final. However, OPRA is empowered to review these decisions. By PA 1995, s. 96(2), OPRA must, where it receives an application by any person (referred to as 'the applicant'), review any determination under ss. 3, 10 or 29(3) and (4) of PA 1995 or s. 168(4) of the PSA 1993. The applicant has to be the person who has been removed, disqualified or required to pay a penalty, as the case may be.

Section 96(3) deals with the review of other determinations by OPRA. A determination which is not one of those covered by s. 96(2) may be reviewed by OPRA:

(a)   within six months from the date of determination, or longer if OPRA allow, on any ground;

(b)   at any time if the Authority has satisfied itself that there has been:

(i)   a subsequent and relevant change in circumstances; or

(ii)   a mistake made as to a material fact or based upon ignorance of a material fact; or

(iii)   an error of law.

For the purpose of initiating a review under s. 96(3), there is a less restrictive approach to standing than in s. 96(2). A review of a determination under s. 96(3) can be initiated by an application to OPRA by a person who appears to OPRA to be an interested person. It is hoped that OPRA will not unduly restrict the class of persons whom it deems to have sufficient 'interest', but there must be some filter to avoid unnecessary repetition of the exercise of powers which will increase delay and cost. This would also seek to eradicate applications for review from the officious or meddlesome with no or only a remote interest in a determination. Regulations may provide for criteria to guide the 'sufficiency of interest' consideration. They may also specify how OPRA will conduct its proceedings on review. This could be done under a general power to make regulations concerning procedure on an application and the Secretary of State's wide powers to make regulations concerning OPRA's functions generally (see s. 96(5) and sch. 1, para. 13). OPRA may of its own volition review a previous determination without the necessity of an application (s. 96(6)).

It is of vital importance that the regulations concerning procedural aspects are imbued with fairness. This can be addressed by the regulations providing for, for example, whether and in what circumstances a party may be entitled to a hearing and whether the party may be represented and the manner of representation. There is a fine balance to be achieved between administrative efficacy and cost-effectiveness and procedural fairness. Depending upon the nature of the function in question, the balance can be achieved by the provision of simple safeguards. However, some functions require that the balance be addressed by more elaborate means. This may mean, for example, requirements that the party knows what material is being considered by OPRA, is permitted to comment upon the material and have representations made either personally or by a representative — perhaps orally — and is not otherwise unduly prejudiced simply by the quest for efficiency and cost.

In conducting reviews under s. 96, OPRA will be acting in a quasi-judicial manner. Accordingly it was thought desirable to place OPRA under the supervision of the Council on Tribunals. This is achieved by an amendment to the Tribunals and Inquiries Act 1992 (PA 1995, sch. 3, para. 21). This is welcome but, unfortunately, like the OPB, OPRA is not subject to all provisions of the Tribunals and Inquiries Act (e.g., s. 10, obligation to furnish reasons for a decision on request).

In conducting a review under s. 96(2) and (3), OPRA may deal with matters as if they had arisen on the original determination and may deal with the original decision by varying or revoking it or substituting a different determination or order. They may also, where necessary, make savings and transitional provisions (s. 96(4)).

Questions of law will invariably arise for determination by OPRA, whether in the exercise of any of its functions under Part I of the Act or, where it undertakes to review their earlier decisions. The Act provides for OPRA to *refer* such issues to the High Court or where applicable the Court of Session for determination. In certain circumstances, an 'aggrieved' person may *appeal* to the court on a question of law.

OPRA's power to refer exists only in connection with a question of law that derives from any matter that has arisen for OPRA's determination under Part I or from a review of an earlier determination, including questions that have arisen from either a 'requested review' under s. 96(2) and (3) or a 'self-initiated review' under s. 96(6) (s. 97(1)). Whether OPRA refers the question or not is for it to decide as it thinks fit. This limits an aggrieved person's opportunity to seek a determination of the court unless the decision to refuse can itself be shown to be wrong in law. This would be extremely difficult.

The right of appeal granted by the Act to aggrieved persons is limited to two circumstances. Section 97(3) refers to a person 'aggrieved' by:

(a)   a determination given on a review by OPRA; or
(b)   a refusal by OPRA to review a determination.

A person aggrieved in either of these ways is granted a right to appeal on a question of law that derives from the determination, though in both cases this is dependent upon OPRA failing to refer the question to the court under s. 97(1). It should be understood that in seeking an appeal by virtue of point (b), the question of law that is to be appealed must not be concerned with the *refusal to review* the determination but with a question of law *germane to a determination* that is not reviewed. However, the mechanism is triggered by the person being aggrieved by the refusal.

The potential class of persons from which an 'aggrieved' person could be drawn may be wider than the class of persons who are deemed to have interest to initiate a review provided they have some connection with the decision. This may encompass, for example, a member seeking to appeal an issue of law that was germane to OPRA determining not to remove a trustee. There is no suggestion as to how the person demonstrates that he or she is 'aggrieved' nor to what extent they are 'aggrieved', though it is anticipated that regulations will provide for procedural requirements.

We can illustrate how a decision of OPRA or a related question of law can be reviewed by OPRA, referred or appealed to the court by the following examples.

Example 1 OPRA determines to remove a trustee. The trustee considers that in reaching the determination, OPRA has erred in law. The determination can be reviewed or the related question of law referred by:

(a) the trustee applying to OPRA to review the determination, which it must do — s. 96(2);
(b) OPRA undertakes to review the decision of its own volition — s. 96(6);
(c) OPRA refers the question to the court — s. 97(1)(b);

or appealed by the trustee as an 'aggrieved' person where:

(d) there has been a review by OPRA under s. 96 and the question of law is not referred to the court by it — s. 97(3)(a); or
(e) OPRA refuses to review the decision and fails to refer the question of law to the court — s. 97(3)(b).

Example 2 OPRA determines that a scheme should be wound up. The trustees consider that in reaching this decision OPRA has erred in law. The determination can be reviewed or the question of law referred or appealed by:

(a) the trustees seeking a review by OPRA, which it may carry out — s. 96(3):
(b) OPRA undertakes to review the decision of its own volition — s. 96(6);
(c) OPRA refers the question to the court — s. 97(1)(b);

or appealed by the trustees as 'aggrieved persons' where:

(d) there has been a review by OPRA under s. 96 and the question of law is not referred to the court by it — s. 97(3)(a); or
(e) OPRA refuses to review the decision and fail to refer the question of law to the court — s. 97(3)(b).

Example 3 Before its determination of the questions of law in examples 1 or 2, OPRA may refer the question to the court to seek the court's ruling — s. 97(1)(a).

In examples 1 and 2, where the dispute involved a factual issue, say, that the determination was made in ignorance of some material fact, then the referral or appeal mechanism to the court is inapplicable and the determination may be reviewed by 'requested review' (s. 96(2) or (3)) or by 'self-initiated review' (s. 96(6)). This does not of course rule out judicial review proceedings.

Certain parties are required to be given notice in writing of OPRA's intention to refer a question of law to the court. Notice must be given to the applicant where the question has arisen on an application to review and in any case to those persons who appear to OPRA to be concerned with the question. Depending on the question at hand, this could involve a small or large class of persons (s. 97(2)). Where the question is the subject of a reference or appeal, which in the latter case does not require OPRA's fiat, then OPRA is given the right to appear and to be heard (s. 97(4)).

The Act provides the court with power to order OPRA to pay the other party's costs irrespective of whether the decision of the court is in that party's favour or OPRA appears at the hearing (s. 97(7)). This is welcomed as in some instances questions of law will require an authoritative resolution and the stumbling point for the parties should not of itself be the impecuniosity of one side. However, it should not be thought that these provisions countenance endless litigation and delay. The procedures will be subject to, *inter alia*, time limits within which appeals must be brought under rules of the court (s. 97(5)). This point is further enhanced by s. 97(6), which makes it clear that the decision of the court on a reference or appeal will be final.

2.10   INFORMATION GATHERING AND DISCLOSURE

As a necessary corollary to OPRA's role, it will require wide-ranging powers to enable information to be obtained and, at times, disclosed to other bodies. Accordingly, wide powers are given to OPRA for the purposes of gathering information relevant to its functions. The powers contained in ss. 98 to 109 implement the recommendations of the Goode Committee (see Goode Report, para. 4.19.39).

2.10.1   Information gathering

2.10.1.1   General   Trustees, managers, professional advisers, employers and any other person who appears to OPRA to be a person who either holds, or will hold, information that is relevant to the discharge of OPRA's functions must, when OPRA requires them to, produce any relevant document to it (PA 1995, s. 98(1)). Documents for these purposes (and for the purposes of ss. 99 to 101), include material recorded in any form and would include, for example, computer-held material or any other form of record. Where information is not recorded in legible form, then a reference to production is to production in a legible form (s. 98(3)).

Where OPRA requires a person to produce a document they must do so in writing and specify the manner, place and period within which the document must be produced (s. 98(1) and (2)).

There will be occasions where OPRA's functions can only be facilitated by more direct and coercive means. Powers of this nature are, within proper limits, no more than can be expected to be held by an effective public regulatory body. OPRA may appoint an inspector to carry out functions that require the inspector to enter premises at any reasonable time to inquire whether the statutory provisions are being complied with (s. 99). Section 99 is ambiguous as it appears on first reading to grant the inspector a right of entry to premises with or without the occupier's consent. However, it is suggested that the better view is that while it permits OPRA to carry out spot checks, the consent of the occupier is required for entry. This view is substantiated by comparing the powers and functions of the inspector whilst on the premises — which do not suggest that any threat or immediacy of danger to documentation or information is required for entry — and the grounds for obtaining a warrant to secure entry to premises under s. 100, where some reasonable belief in such a threat is a prerequisite (see 2.10.1.2). Additionally, the terms of s. 99(4) refer to an inspector 'applying for admission to any premises'.

Premises that are liable to inspection are those that the inspector on reasonable grounds believes that:

(a)   members of an occupational pension scheme are employed there; or
(b)   documents that are relevant to the scheme administration are kept there; or,
(c)   the administration of the scheme is being carried out there; or
(d)   work that is connected in some way with the scheme administration is being carried out there.

Private dwellings are excluded from the potential range of premises where they are not used by or with the permission of the occupier for the purposes of a trade or business (s. 99(3)). The next question is: what may the inspector do while on the premises?

These provisions are broadly drafted so as to allow latitude in the carrying out of the inspector's functions. These would include the questioning of personnel and documentary examination. While on the premises the inspector may, under s. 99(1):

(a)   examine or inquire to the extent necessary for the purposes of the inspection;
(b)   require any person there to produce, or secure the production of any relevant document;
(c)   examine, or require the examination of any person there whom the inspector has reasonable cause to believe is able to give information that is relevant to compliance with the regulatory provisions.

Section 99(2) provides that an inspector's entry of premises must be for investigating compliance with:

(a)   provisions of Part I other than ss. 51 to 54, 62 to 65 and 110 to 112;
(b)   provisions of s. 6, Chapter IV of Part IV, or ss. 113 or 175 of the PSA 1993; or
(c)   any corresponding provisions in force in Northern Ireland.

Examination may be undertaken either alone or in the presence of another person, but it is unclear whether the person examined for these purposes may require some other person to be present (see s. 99(1)(c)). Ostensibly, the provisions here are drafted so as to leave the manner of the examination at the inspector's discretion.

2.10.1.2   Warrant to enter premises   Section 100 PA 1995 provides for a justice of the peace, or justice in Scotland, where satisfied by evidence given on oath, to issue a warrant to secure entry by the inspector of any premises named in the warrant in prescribed circumstances. The magistrate must, before issuing the warrant, be satisfied that there are reasonable grounds for believing:

(a)   that documents required by virtue of s. 98(1), s. 99(1)(b) or similar provisions in force in Northern Ireland, are on the relevant premises and have not been produced in accordance with OPRA's request;

(b)   that documents which may potentially be required for production are on the premises and if required would be removed, hidden, tampered with or destroyed (s. 100(1)(a) and (b)).

There is no indication of the degree of likelihood of removal or tampering etc., but it is suggested that this should not be a difficult threshold to cross, provided that OPRA acts in good faith and presents objectively verifiable evidence, given that immediate preservation of information or evidence may be vital to uncover non-compliance and serious wrongdoing within a scheme.

Section 100 also takes the issue of securing and protecting information a step further. The information here is required for different purposes. A magistrate may issue a warrant that authorises an inspector to enter any premises specified in the warrant where there are reasonable grounds for believing that there are on the premises documents which are relevant to establishing whether:

(a)   an offence has been committed under PA 1995, the PSA 1993 or similar provisions in force in Northern Ireland;

(b)   a person is subject to liability under the civil penalty provisions of PA 1995, s. 10, the PSA 1993, s. 168(4) or similar provisions in force in Northern Ireland (s. 100(1)(c)).

The inspector may, by virtue of the warrant, use such force as is reasonably necessary to secure entry, search the premises and take possession of any document relevant to the reason for him being on the premises, and take any other necessary steps which will secure the documents' preservation or prevention from interference. Alternatively the inspector may copy documents or require a person named in the warrant to provide him with an explanation of the contents or where the documents may be found (s. 100(2)). The documents that the inspector takes possession of under the warrant may be retained for either six months or, if they relate to criminal proceedings under any of the above provisions, until such proceedings are concluded.

2.10.1.3   Sanctions   The 'teeth' of the information-gathering provisions are contained in PA 1995, s. 101, which creates a number of criminal offences, for example, obstruction of an inspector exercising the powers discussed above. Similarly, offences are created for failure to meet certain obligations, for example, to produce documents where required by ss. 98 or 99. There are also a number of specific offences relating to action or non-action.

Where a person is required by virtue of s. 98 to produce a document and does not do so by either neglect or refusal, without reasonable excuse, then he is guilty of an offence (s. 101(1)). The onus is on the defendant to provide a reasonable excuse for the failure. It is an offence under s. 101(2):

(a)   intentionally to delay or obstruct an inspector exercising any of the powers in s. 99,

(b)   to neglect or refuse to produce or secure the production of any document when required to do so under s. 99, or,

(c)   to neglect or refuse to answer a question or to provide information when obliged to.

These offences are triable summarily and punishable by a fine of a maximum of level 5 on the standard scale (s. 101(4)).

Two further offences are created by subsections (5) and (6) of s. 101 which relate to deceiving OPRA. These offences are marked with sentences that are commensurate with their greater degree of seriousness than those above. It is an offence under s. 101(5) for a person knowingly or recklessly to provide information which is false or misleading in a material particular:

(a)   in purported compliance with s. 99; or

(b)   though not for the purposes of s. 99, in circumstances in which the person intends, or could reasonably be expected to know, that it would be used by OPRA for the purposes of its functions under the Act.

It is an offence under s. 101(6) for a person who is required by s. 98 or 99 to produce to OPRA any document to alter, suppress, conceal or destroy that document intentionally and without reasonable excuse.

These offences are punishable on summary conviction with a fine not exceeding the statutory maximum and on indictment, to imprisonment or a fine or both (s. 101(7)).

2.10.1.4   Privilege   The provisions relating to gathering information in ss. 98 to 101 do not undermine or circumscribe an individual's right not to incriminate either him or herself or his or her spouse (s. 102(1)). Also, nothing in these sections requires a person to produce documents where that person is entitled to refuse production in legal proceedings on the basis that such documents are covered by legal professional privilege or, in Scotland, that it contained a confidential communication made by or to a solicitor or advocate acting in that capacity (s. 102(2)). As a further measure of protection, where a person has a legal claim to a document, its production to OPRA under ss. 98 or 99 does nothing to prejudice that claim (s. 102(3)).

2.10.1.5   Reports of investigations   Publicity can be a potent tool in the hands of a regulator. It may be the only way that members of a scheme can be informed of any problems with the scheme in the absence of litigation. Where OPRA has undertaken an investigation for the purpose of discharging any of their functions under Part I of the Act, it may, where it considers it appropriate to do so, publish a report of its investigation and the result, in any manner or form. This would include OPRA's decision to 'go public' by publishing a report of its investigation and result in some form of publicly available material (s. 103(1)). This is fortified by subsection (2) which protects OPRA from potential defamation action by enveloping such reports in absolute privilege.

2.10.2 Disclosure of information

OPRA will as part of its everyday functions require interaction with various other public or private bodies, both within and without the United Kingdom. However desirable it is that there be cooperation and a free flow of information between these bodies for OPRA to discharge its functions, such disclosure should be trammelled by proper criteria. This is because the nature of the information may relate to an employer's or individual's personal and business affairs. Unrestricted disclosure may have direct and indirect detrimental consequences for an employer or individual. The Act seeks to address these issues by:

(a) providing for disclosure by OPRA in general terms;
(b) restricting the type of information that may be disclosed;
(c) restricting the class of recipients of this information;
(d) restricting the recipients of certain types of information from disclosing it;
(e) providing for the creation of criminal offences relating to unauthorised disclosure;
(f) restricting disclosure of tax information.

2.10.2.1 General disclosure   OPRA may in general terms disclose information where necessary. This necessity may occur where OPRA wishes to seek professional opinion on some issue or desires to disclose information to a public body to facilitate its own functions. Though nothing in PA 1995 specifically provides for this, there is in sch. 1 provision for OPRA to do anything that facilitates the discharge of its functions. Also, information may be disclosed via OPRA's power to publish reports (see 2.10.1.5).

Sections 106 to 108 provide for a certain type of information to be disclosed in limited terms. This is referred to as 'restricted information' (see 2.10.2.2) — but this implies that information which cannot be classed as 'restricted information' is not subject to these provisions and the restrictions therein other than disclosure being made *intra vires*.

2.10.2.2 The types of information that may be disclosed   In general terms there is no restriction on the type of information that may be disclosed. The caveat of course is that a decision taken to disclose information *ultra vires* could be susceptible to challenge, but given the broad nature of the powers and functions of OPRA, this would be difficult to show. However, by PA 1995, s. 104(1), 'restricted information' must not be disclosed by OPRA or any person receiving the information either directly or indirectly from OPRA, except where:

(a)   the person to whom it relates and, if different, from whom it is obtained, consents to the disclosure; or

(b)   disclosure is permitted by the Act.

The latter point effectively allows disclosure to a wide class of recipients (see 2.10.2.3).

'Restricted information' is information which is obtained by OPRA in the exercise of its functions, which:

(a)   relates to the business or other affairs of any person (this could, for example, include information relating to other trusteeships, directorships or relationships with companies for consultancy purposes, whether a person is or has been adjudged bankrupt, or has been convicted of any criminal offences, or personal or business tax affairs) (s. 104(2));

(b)   is supplied to OPRA by some body which exercises functions outside the UK similar to those of OPRA (there is no requirement that this information specifically relates to the business or other affairs of any individual) (s. 105(1));

(c)   is tax information received by OPRA (s. 109(3) — see 2.10.2.6).

Though information may relate to the business or other affairs of a person it ceases to be 'restricted information' where:

(a)   at the time of disclosure, it is or has already been placed in the public domain by other means; or,

(b)   it is provided in summary form or in a collection in such a way that the information does not enable any particular person to be ascertainable (s. 104(2)).

2.10.2.3   The class of recipients 'Restricted information' may be disclosed where:

(a)   There is consent.

(b)   Disclosure is for the purposes of 'enabling or assisting' OPRA to discharge its functions (s. 106(1)).

(c)   Advice is sought by OPRA from a qualified person on a matter of law, accountancy, valuation or other matter that requires the exercise of professional skills and the information appears to OPRA to be necessary to ensure that the person from whom the advice is sought is properly informed with respect to the matters on which the advice is sought (s. 106(2)). Seeking the advice must be considered by OPRA to be necessary to enable or assist it properly to discharge its functions.

(d)   The disclosure is to any of the persons identified in column 1 of the table in s. 107(1), and OPRA consider that disclosure of this information will 'enable or assist' the recipient of the information to carry out the functions identified in column 2. This table may be amended by the Secretary of State by adding or removing persons, removing or altering the functions or restricting the circumstances in which disclosure is permitted or imposing conditions (s. 107(1) and (2)).

(e)   Disclosure is to the Secretary of State or the Department of Health and Social Services for Northern Ireland and it appears 'desirable or expedient' in the interests of members of occupational pension schemes or in the public interest (s. 108(1)).

(f)   Disclosure is for the purposes of enabling the detection, investigation or prosecution of a number of criminal, regulatory or disciplinary matters referred to in s. 108(2)(a) to (f) including any proceedings for breach of trust in relation to an occupational pension scheme.

(g)   Disclosure is for 'enabling or assisting' authorities outside the UK exercising similar regulatory functions, (s. 108(2)(g)).

(h)   Disclosure is in pursuance of a Community obligation (s. 108(2)(h)).

(i)   Disclosure is to the Director of Public Prosecutions, the Director of Public Prosecutions for Northern Ireland, the Lord Advocate, a procurator fiscal or a constable (s. 108(3)). Though this subsection refers in more general terms to 'information' and not 'restricted information', it should be understood as referring to the latter as s. 104 only precludes disclosure of 'restricted information'.

None of this applies to information which is restricted by virtue of being provided to OPRA by an authority which exercises in a foreign country functions corresponding to OPRA's functions. By s. 105, such information may be disclosed only:

(a)   when permitted by s. 104 (i.e., (i) by consent; (ii) where the information is already public; or (iii) in summary form);

(b)   for the purpose of enabling or assisting OPRA to discharge its functions under the Act; or

(c)   with a view to the institution of criminal proceedings.

2.10.2.4   Restricting the recipient   Any person who receives, directly or indirectly, restricted information obtained by OPRA must not disclose it (s. 104(1)). This is broad enough to cover any person to whom restricted information has been properly or improperly disclosed. However, the information itself may, as we have noted, lose the quality of being 'restricted' where at the time of the disclosure, though it is unclear which disclosure, the information is public. Though s. 104 places a restriction on disclosure of restricted information, s. 108 provides for a number of exceptions to this. We noted in 2.10.2.3 that persons specified in s. 108(3) (e.g., the DPP) may be the recipients of restricted information. Those persons are not subject to the prohibition in s. 104(1) where the disclosure by them is in accordance with the consent of OPRA (s. 108(4)). This exception also extends to persons specified in column 1 of the table in s. 107(1), where:

(a)   disclosure is with the consent of OPRA; and

(b)   it is for the purpose of 'enabling or assisting' that person to discharge functions under provisions specified in column 2 (s. 108(5)).

Though it is not obliged to give its consent under s. 108(4) or (5), OPRA is under a duty in both cases to consider the representations of the persons seeking to make the disclosure as to the 'desirability of the disclosure or the necessity for it' (s. 108(6)).

2.10.2.5   Criminal offences   Section 104(3) stipulates that any person who discloses restricted information in contravention of the section shall be guilty of an offence. To mark the gravity of this offence, a person can, on conviction on indictment, be liable to be imprisoned or fined or both. Similarly, on summary conviction, the person shall be liable to a fine up to the statutory maximum.

2.10.2.6   Tax information   Information that relates to the tax affairs of any person, corporate or natural, will undoubtedly be relevant to OPRA for discharging its functions. For example, it may be relevant in determining whether a trustee is in breach of a duty prescribed by the Act and thus relevant to any decision to issue a prohibition order under s. 3. It may also be an indicator of problems or potential problems with a scheme's management.

PA 1995 permits the tax authorities to divulge to OPRA 'tax information' (s. 109(1)). This is broadly referred to as information relevant to tax or duty in the case of an identifiable person which is held by a person for the purposes of 'tax functions'. Tax functions is given the same meaning as s. 182 of the Finance Act 1989 and this broadly concerns functions relating to tax or duty carried out by the Inland Revenue or Customs and Excise or any person employed by or providing services to these, including the General and Special Commissioners or any VAT tribunal. Accordingly, no duty under s. 182 of the Finance Act, or in broader terms, as to secrecy placed on those exercising tax functions prohibits disclosure of tax information where it is for the purposes of 'enabling or assisting' OPRA to discharge its functions. PA 1995, s. 109(3) confirms that tax information is restricted information, and is subject to the restrictions imposed by s. 104. Sections 106 to 108 are inapplicable. OPRA may only disclose tax information in two circumstances:

(a)   to, or with the proper authority of, the Inland Revenue or Customs and Excise; or
(b)   where the information is disclosed for the purposes of, or with a view to the institution of criminal proceedings under, PA 1995, the PSA 1993 or similar provisions in force in Northern Ireland.

Chapter 3
Role and Responsibilities of Pension Fund Trustees

3.1 INTRODUCTON

The vast majority of occupational pension schemes are set up under an irrevocable trust and therefore the trustee plays a vital role in the administration of the pension scheme. The initial trustees are appointed in the trust deed itself and, until the introduction of the PA 1995, were generally, though not necessarily, chosen by the employer. Their office is an onerous one, 'there is much to be said about the duties and obligations of a trustee, but little of his rights' (Law Reform Committee, *23rd Report,* Cmnd 8733, 1982). They must act in the interest of the trust, observe a high standard of integrity, a reasonable standard of business efficiency in the management of the fund, and are subjected to liability if they fail to reach a certain standard.

The law governing their appointment and removal, their powers and duties and their liabilities has four main sources:

(a)   the pension scheme documents;
(b)   the rules and principles developed by the courts;
(c)   statute law which is applicable to all types of trusts, such as the Trustee Act 1925 and the Trustee Investments Act 1961; and
(d)   statute law and regulations which are applicable only to occupational pension scheme trusts.

3.2   WHO MAY BE A TRUSTEE OF AN
OCCUPATIONAL PENSION SCHEME

Before the PA 1995, in theory at least, any individual person could be appointed to the office of pension fund trustee, but clearly in practice there were limitations to this.

Section 29 of the PA 1995, however, introduces a statutory disqualification for certain persons from acting as a trustee of an occupational pension scheme. The section in the main reflects the proposals contained in the Goode Committee Report on the disqualification of trustees and represents nothing more than common-sense. Disqualification under s. 29 can be either mandatory or discretionary.

The following persons are now *automatically* disqualified from becoming a trustee:

(a)   Anyone who has been convicted of an offence involving dishonesty or deception, whether the conviction occurred before or after s. 29 came into force. If the conviction is spent for the purposes of the Rehabilitation of Offenders Act 1974, however, the person is not disqualified from so acting.

(b)   Anyone who has been adjudged bankrupt or whose estate has been sequestrated, if, in either case, the person has not been discharged. A person is disqualified from acting as a trustee whether the adjudication of bankruptcy or award of sequestration occurred before or after the section came into force.

(c)   A person who has made a composition agreement, contract or a trust deed with his creditors and who has not been discharged in respect of it. The section applies whether the composition agreement or contract was made or trust deed granted before or after the section came into force.

(d)   A person who is subject to a disqualification order under the Company Directors Disqualification Act 1986 or subject to an order made under s. 429(2)(b) of the Insolvency Act 1986. The disqualification order could be made before or after the coming into effect of s. 29.

The Company Directors Disqualification Act 1986 covers the disqualification of a person in the following circumstances:

(i)   where a person is convicted of an indictable offence in connection with the promotion, formation, management, liquidation or striking off of a company, or with the receivership or management of a company's property — s. 2 Company Directors Disqualification Act 1986;

(ii)   where it appears that the person has been persistently in default in relation to provisions of the companies legislation requiring any return, account or other document to be filed with, delivered or sent, or notice of any matter to be given, to the registrar of companies — s. 3 Company Directors Disqualification Act 1986;

(iii)   if during the course of the winding up of a company it appears that the person has been guilty of fraudulent trading under the Companies Act 1985, s. 458, or has been guilty of any fraud in relation to the company or any breach of his duty as an officer, liquidator, receiver or manager — s. 4 Company Directors Disqualification Act 1986;

(iv)   if the person is convicted in consequence of a contravention of, or failure to comply with, any provision of the companies legislation requiring a return, account or other document to be filed with, delivered or sent, or notice of any matter to be given, to the registrar of companies and, including the present offence, there have been three instances within the past five years of conviction for such offences — s. 5 Company Directors Disqualification Act 1986;

(v)   if the person is or has been a director of a company which has become insolvent, while he was a director or subsequently, and his conduct as a director of that company makes him unfit to be concerned in the management of a company — s. 6 Company Directors Disqualification Act 1986;

(vi)   where it appears to the Secretary of State that it is in the public interest that a disqualification order be made against a person who is or has been a director or shadow director of any company, after a report has been made by inspectors under s. 437 Companies Act 1985 — s. 8 Company Directors Disqualification Act 1986;

   (vii)   where a person is disqualified for wrongful trading or fraudulent trading under the Insolvency Act 1986.

   (e)   Where the trustee is a trust corporation then the corporation is disqualified from acting as a trustee if any director of the company is disqualified under the PA 1995, s. 29.

A person *may* be disqualified from acting as a trustee of an occupational pension scheme in the following circumstances:

   (f)   Where OPRA, in its opinion, think that it is undesirable for the person to act as a trustee of the scheme where the trustee is prohibited from being a trustee of a trust by an order of OPRA under s. 3 or he has been removed as a trustee of a trust scheme by an order of the High Court because:

   (i)   of his misconduct in or mismanagement of the administration of a scheme for which he was responsible or to which he was privy; or
   (ii)   his conduct contributed to or facilitated such misconduct or mismanagement (s. 29(3) PA 1995).

   (g)   Where in OPRA's opinion the person is incapable of acting as a trustee by reason of mental disorder (s. 29(4)(a) PA 1995). The term 'mental disorder' has the same meaning as in s. 1(2) of the Mental Health Act 1983. This section says that mental disorder means a mental illness, an arrested or incomplete development of the mind, a psychopathic disorder and any other disorder or disability of the mind.

   (h)   Where the person is a company and has been disqualified by OPRA under s. 29(4)(b) because it has gone into liquidation within the meaning of s. 247(2) Insolvency Act 1986. This subsection says that a company 'goes into liquidation' either at the moment it passes a resolution for voluntary winding up, or when an order for winding up is made by the court at a time when the company has not gone into liquidation by passing a resolution to do so.

A person who is disqualified by virtue of s. 29 may apply to OPRA to have the disqualification waived if the disqualification falls within categories (a) to (e) above, or revoked by order if it falls within categories (f), (g) or (h). If OPRA decide to waive the disqualification they must inform the applicant in writing of this fact — s. 29(5). The notice or revocation is not retrospective — s. 29(6). Where a person acting as a trustee of a scheme becomes disqualified while so acting, he ceases to be a trustee of the scheme — s. 30(1).

The Act introduces criminal penalties for a person who acts as a trustee of a trust scheme while being disqualified under s. 29. Such a person on summary conviction is liable to a fine not exceeding £5,000 and on conviction on indictment to a fine or imprisonment or both — s. 30(3). Nothing in the Act, however, affects the liability of the disqualified trustee under the general law of trusts for acts or omissions carried out by him while acting when disqualified — s. 30(6). Thus a disqualified trustee remains personally liable for any breach of trust he has committed. Any acts performed by the disqualified trustee in relation to the trust are not invalidated merely because the trustee is disqualified — s. 30(5).

The Act imposes an obligation on OPRA to keep a register of persons who are disqualified from acting as trustees under s. 29(3) or (4). OPRA must disclose, if requested to do so, whether the name of a person specified in a request is included in the register — s. 29(7).

3.2.1 The auditor and actuary as trustee

The employer as the instigator of an occupational pension scheme may select any person he wishes to act as a trustee. There is no reason why a trustee should have any business connection with the employer but in practice some of the trustees will because there is an advantage to making such an appointment since such trustees will have an intimate knowledge of the business environment they are dealing with. Occupational pension schemes are becoming increasingly complex and therefore the employer may think it desirable to appoint a professional person to the panel of trustees. While most professional advisers are governed by their own professional body's code of practice, such appointments can cause a conflict of interest since the existence of the professional relationship with the scheme is incompatible with the office of trusteeship. The adviser may feel a sense of divided loyalty, believing he has a duty to the employer in his professional capacity and to the trustee board as trustee. Furthermore, the introduction of the role of auditors and actuaries as 'whistle blowers' (see 3.6) would make it inconsistent for them to act as trustees.

Section 27 PA 1995 states that a trustee of a trust scheme, and any person who is connected with, or an associate of, such a trustee is ineligible to act as an auditor or actuary of the scheme. The phrase 'connected with or an associate of' is to be given the same meaning as in ss. 249 and 435 Insolvency Act 1986 — s. 123 PA 1995. Section 249 Insolvency Act 1986 says that a person is 'connected with' a company if either he is a director or shadow director of the company or an associate of such a director or shadow director or he is an associate of the company. Section 435 is an elaborately drafted section and says that a person is an associate:

(a)   of an individual if that person is the individual's husband or wife, or is a relative, or the husband or wife of a relative, of the individual or of the individual's husband or wife;

(b)   of any person with whom he is in partnership, and of the husband or wife or a relative of any individual with whom he is in partnership;

(c)   of any person whom he employs or by whom he is employed.

For the purposes of s. 435 Insolvency Act 1986 a person is a relative of an individual if he is a brother, sister, uncle, aunt, nephew, niece, lineal ancestor or lineal descendant of the individual and any relationship of the half blood is treated as a relationship of the whole blood. Stepchildren and adopted children are treated as a child of that person and an illegitimate child treated as a legitimate child of the mother and reputed father. The term husband or wife includes a former husband or wife and a reputed husband or wife. The interrelation between s. 27(1) PA 1995 and ss. 249 and 435 Insolvency Act 1986 is a somewhat convoluted way of prohibiting a firm from acting as an auditor or actuary of a trust scheme if any person who is a partner or connected with, or an associate of the firm is a trustee of the occupational pension scheme in question. However, s. 27(2) PA 1995 then excludes a director, partner or employee of a firm of actuaries (but not auditors) from being ineligible to act as an actuary of an occupational pension scheme just because another employee, director or partner of the firm is a trustee of the scheme. It is difficult to know why s. 27(2) allows this exception to s. 27(1) in the case of actuaries.

Regulations can also be made to prescribe other exceptions from ineligibility under s. 27(1). Neither the lawyer nor the scheme administrator is ineligible under s. 27, however, although the Goode Committee did state that as a matter of 'good practice' the scheme administrator should not be a trustee.

A person who contravenes s. 27 is guilty of a criminal offence and liable on summary conviction to a fine not exceeding £5,000 and on conviction on indictment to imprisonment or a fine or both — s. 28(1). Any acts done by an actuary or auditor who is ineligible to act are not invalid merely because of that fact — s. 28(3).

Section 28(4) says that s. 3 of the Act applies to a trustee who acts as an auditor or actuary of the scheme and a person who acts as an auditor or actuary of a trust scheme when he is ineligible to do so by reason of being connected with or an associate of a trustee of the scheme.

3.2.2 Member-nominated trustees

The employer as drafter of the scheme will retain a power to appoint and approve trustees and this has resulted in the employer controlling the composition of the board of trustees. It has been a long-held view that member-nominated trustees should, by law, be appointed to the board of trustees. (See the Occupational Pension Board in their report in 1975, *Solvency, Disclosure of Information and Member Participation in Occupational Pension Schemes* Cmnd 5904.) The main reasons for this view are that:

(a)   member-nominated trustees can ensure that the interests of the member-beneficiaries are kept in mind;

(b)   members are less likely to view decisions taken by the board of trustees with suspicion if they know that trustees they have appointed are involved with the decisions of the board;

(c)   the member-nominated trustees can ensure that employer-appointed trustees do not allow themselves (whether innocently or otherwise) to be influenced by the wishes of the employer; and

(d)   the presence of member-nominated trustees would overcome, in part at least, the problems of lack of access of information available to members (see 3.5).

Despite there having been no statutory requirement for the election of member-nominated trustees to the board of trustees, many pension schemes have voluntarily installed a system for member-nominated trustees. In 1991, for example, 3,000 occupational pension schemes had elected member trustees, 500 had trade-union-nominated trustees and 7,700 had other member-nominated trustees.

Section 16 of the PA 1995 introduces new measures requiring that individual member-nominated trustees be elected to the board. Section 16(1) places a requirement on the existing trustees of the scheme to ensure that arrangements and rules are made and implemented for persons selected by the members of the scheme to become trustees of it. The arrangements must provide for a person nominated and selected in accordance with the 'appropriate rules' to become a trustee of the scheme by virtue of his selection — s. 16(3)(a). Such a person can be removed by the agreement of all other trustees — s. 16(3)(b).

When the position of a member-nominated trustee is not filled because of lack of nominations, then the rules must provide for the filling of the vacancy, or for the vacancy to remain open until the expiry of the next period in which a person may be nominated and selected in accordance with the appropriate rules — s. 16(4). This period should be contained in the appropriate rules (see p. 42). This subsection could result in the number of member-nominated trustees being less than the statutory requirement if the members fail to make sufficient nominations. The members do, however, have an opportunity to make sufficient nominations at a later date, but in the meantime fewer member-nominated trustees will be represented on the board.

There should be periodic changes to the composition of the board, since, as the Goode Report said, 'New blood helps to inject fresh ideas into the thinking of the trustees, as well as reducing the risk of impropriety' (para. 4.5.45). But there must be some continuity to their appointment in order for them to develop a greater understanding of their role and acquaint themselves with the rules and general investment strategy of the scheme. The Act therefore allows the rules to provide for the member-nominated trustees to hold their office for a period of three to six years, although the trustees are eligible for reselection at the end of the period — s. 16(5).

An area that has caused controversy is whether a minority or majority of the trustees should be member-nominated. If only a minority are member-nominated this may redress the balance of power slightly in favour of the members and lead to greater access of information for them, but in a situation that allows for different views to be taken, then the majority employer-nominated trustees can win the vote. This may be of importance where, for example, there is a discretion over the investment of scheme funds, and the member-nominated trustees wish to choose the safer yet possibly lower-yield investments, whereas the employer-nominated trustees wish to invest in investments that carry a greater risk yet higher yield. If a majority of the board are member-nominated this means that the individuals whose lives may be substantially affected by trustee decisions will be given a greater role in administering the scheme. Despite there being a great debate over the issue in both Houses of Parliament, the government has taken the view that a minority of trustees should be member-nominated and the Act, therefore, says that the rules must provide for there to be at least two member-nominated trustees (or at least one if the scheme has less than 100 members) *and* for at least one third of the total number of trustees to be member-nominated — s. 16(6). The employer can, however, allow for a greater proportion of member-nominated trustees if it wishes.

There appears to be no obligation in s. 16 to ensure that at least one of the member-nominated trustees be a pensioner — in fact there appears to be no requirement imposed by s. 16 that at least one or more of the member-nominated trustees is necessarily a member of the scheme, although in practice it is likely this will be so. Pensioner trustees have a special knowledge and experience of how their scheme works. Issues regarding eligibility of new members, which may 'dilute' schemes, changes in benefits for contributions or changes in accrued rates may all add to the liabilities of the scheme and are therefore matters that are of particular concern to pensioners. The pensioners' interests, however, may be contrary to the interests of active members but their membership of the board becomes particularly important when there are more retired members than active ones.

The functions of the member-nominated trustees should be no different from those of any other trustees although for the purposes of s. 16 any provision made by an order under s. 8(4) (see 2.6.3) and s. 25(2) (see 3.2.4) is to be disregarded — s. 16(7). Where a member-nominated trustee was a member of the scheme when he was appointed but ceases to be a member of the scheme then he also ceases to be a trustee — s. 16(8).

Section 16 does not apply in certain situations, namely:

(a)   Where an occupational pension scheme is a non-trust scheme. Many public-sector occupational pension schemes are not set up under a trust, for example, local government schemes. These schemes will not therefore have to meet the requirements for member-nominated trustees. These bodies are already exempted from certain regulatory requirements, for example, registration under the Financial Services Act 1986. The government has again seen fit to exempt them from further regulatory measures. There are about 5.25 million members of 180 public-sector schemes which hold about 40 per cent of pension fund assets and it is difficult to see why such schemes should constantly be exempted in such a manner, although the government would argue that they are adequately protected by other means.

(b)   Where a trust falls within a prescribed class. This is an open-ended provision and it is thought that small self-administered schemes will come within the provisions of this subsection. These are schemes which have less than 12 members and are self-invested. Such schemes are similar to individual pension arrangements, but they are subject to additional approval requirements, including the appointment of a pensioneer trustee, who is an individual or body who has given an undertaking to the PSO that he will not consent to any termination of a scheme of which he is a trustee other than in accordance with the approved terms of the winding-up rule (see the present regulations contained in the Retirement Benefit Schemes (Restriction on Discretion to Approve) (Small Self-Administered Schemes) Regulations 1991 (SI 1991/1614). The reason that such schemes are exempted is that the cost and practical difficulty of requiring member-nominated trustees outweigh the benefits.

(c)   Where there is already an approved procedure for selecting and appointing trustees to the scheme, or the employer proposes to implement new arrangements for selecting trustees — s. 17(1). Section 17(1)(b) says that the proposed arrangements should be approved or rejected under the statutory consultation procedure, which is to be prescribed in regulations. These it is thought will contain details and instructions to employers which will ensure that members are consulted effectively and the statutory consultation procedure will provide that eligible members will be consulted afresh every six years. The trustees will also have to consider whether further consultation is appropriate following, for example, mergers or bulk transfers. Members would also be given a right to request or conduct a further consultation exercise at any time. A problem is that if the employer has failed to conduct a statutory consultation procedure the Act does not provide the arrangement for declaring that trust board to be invalid.

The civil penalties introduced by s. 10 can be imposed upon an employer who makes a proposal for the continuation of an existing arrangement or the adoption of a new arrangement but who fails to give effect to the statutory consultation procedure.

There is a problem, however, with the interrelation between s. 16 and s. 17(1). The reason for this is that s. 17(1) begins by saying, 'Section 16 does not apply . . .'. Therefore none of the provisions in s. 16 apply including s. 16(8) which states that the functions of member-nominated trustees should not be different from those of any other trustee. If interpreted literally this could result in member-nominated trustees in schemes falling outside the provisions of s. 16 being disenfranchised from having full involvement with the scheme.

Where s. 17(1) applies and the employer's proposal is adopted then the duty is on the trustees to ensure that the proposed arrangements are made and implemented — s. 17(2).

(d)   Where the trustees of the scheme consist of all the members then s. 16 does not apply to it — s. 17(4)(a).

The corporate trustee is playing an increasing role in the administration of occupational pension schemes and ss. 18 and 19 extend the scope of ss. 16 and 17 to include corporate trustees. Subsections (1) and (6) of s. 18 say that where the trustee is a company and the employer is connected with the company, or any prescribed conditions are satisfied, then the company must ensure that arrangements are made to provide that the number of member-nominated directors is (a) at least two (or at least one if the scheme comprises less than 100 members), and (b) at least one third of the total number of directors. The company must ensure that such arrangements and the appropriate rules are implemented. The employer can if he so wishes allow for a greater number of member-nominated directors to be appointed.

The arrangements must provide for any person who has been nominated and selected in accordance with the appropriate rules to become a director by virtue of his selection. The removal of such a director will require the agreement of all other directors — s. 18(3).

As in s. 16, where the position of a member-nominated director is not filled because of lack of nominations then arrangements must be made to provide for the filling of the vacancy, or for the vacancy to remain open until the expiry of the next period in which persons can be nominated and selected in accordance with the appropriate rules — s. 18(4). As with s. 16 this can result in there being fewer member-nominated directors during this time period. Section 18(5) provides that the arrangements should allow for member-nominated directors to hold their office for a period of three to six years. The arrangements should provide that where a member-nominated director who was a member of the scheme when he was appointed to the position ceases to be a member of the scheme, then he also ceases to be a director by virtue of that fact — s. 18(7).

Where a company is a trustee of two or more trust schemes and is a wholly owned subsidiary of a company which is the employer in relation to those schemes then ss. 18, 20 and 21(8) apply as if the schemes were a single scheme and the members of each scheme were members of that scheme — s. 18(8). The term 'wholly owned subsidiary' is given the same meaning as it is in s. 736 of the Companies Act 1985.

The requirement of s. 18 does not apply in the following circumstances:

(a)   Where the occupational pension scheme is not a trust scheme.

(b)   Where a company which is a trustee of a trust scheme falls within a class to be prescribed in regulations — s. 19(4).

(c)   Where a proposal has been made by the employer for the continuation of existing arrangements, or the adoption of new arrangements for the selecting of directors of a company, and the arrangements are for the time being approved under the statutory consultation procedure and such other requirements as prescribed by regulation are satisfied — s. 19(1).

Where a scheme falls within the provisions of s. 19 then the company must ensure that the proposed arrangements are made and implemented.

Civil penalties under s. 10 can be imposed upon an employer who makes a proposal for the continuation of an existing arrangement or adoption of a new one, but who fails to give effect to the statutory consultation procedure.

The same problem exists with the interrelation of ss. 18 and 19(1) as with the interrelation of ss. 16 and 17(1).

The 'appropriate rules' for the purpose of ss. 16 to 21 must provide for the following:

(a)   the procedure for nomination and selection of a person to fill a vacancy as member-nominated trustee;

(b)   for the member-nominated trustees to be eligible for reselection at the end of the term of office;

(c)   for determining, when a vacancy is not filled because of insufficient nominations, the next period in which persons may be nominated and selected in accordance with the rules, being a period ending at a prescribed time;

(d)   for selection as a non-member as a member-nominated trustee to be conditional on the employer's approval, where the employer so requires.

The appropriate rules may in addition determine the conditions required for a person to fill a vacancy.

As well as providing for the above, the rules must also be approved under the statutory consultation procedure, or if no rules are being so approved then the rules must be rules prescribed under regulations. The statutory consultation procedure is the procedure which will be prescribed by regulations for obtaining the views of members of the scheme. The approval of the appropriate rules or arrangement under the statutory consultation procedure must be given by active and pensioner members of the scheme and such deferred members as the trustees may determine and must be 'taken as a whole'. There is clearly ambiguity in the phrase 'taken as a whole' and it is only to be hoped that the regulations will clearly spell out the meaning of this phrase.

Section 21(4) allows regulations to be made to prescribe appropriate timescales and the government hopes that member-nominated trustees who are selected pursuant to s. 16 should be in place within six months of the Act coming into force. Similar arrangements are proposed for s. 17.

Section 21(5) provides that regulations may determine when the arrangements for selecting trustees shall cease to have effect; these arrangements can be those chosen under the member-nominated trustee requirement or those proposed by the employer. Members will have a right to a periodic review of the arrangements for selecting trustees and therefore an employer opt-out can only last for a maximum of six years or, if earlier, until the employer or trustees want a change. Trustees must review the decision to opt out in the event of a takeover, merger or bulk transfer and should be able to consider a review on any other occasion if, in their opinion, the circumstances warrant it.

Section 21(6) gives the Secretary of State an extraordinarily wide power to modify ss. 16 to 20 in cases prescribed in regulations. It is envisaged that regulations will allow for the statutory requirements to be modified in cases where there would be considerable practical difficulties in implementing them, for example, centralised schemes where there is more than one unassociated partici-pating employer.

Where the trustees, or the company which is the trustee, fail to make arrange-ments for the nomination and selection of member-nominated trustees, or member-nominated directors, or where such arrangements or rules are not implemented, then OPRA may:

(a)   prohibit a trustee of the scheme from acting as such if it is satisfied the trustee is in serious or persistent breach of his duty under s. 16 or 18 (for the meaning of 'serious or persistent breach' see 2.6.1); or

(b)   suspend an existing trustee from exercising his functions over other trustees for a period of not more than 12 months (which may be extended for a further 12 months), pending consideration being given to his prohibition; or

(c)   by notice in writing, require the offending trustee to pay a penalty not exceeding a prescribed amount — s. 10.

3.2.3   Time off for trustees

The Goode Committee emphasised the need to raise the general level of knowledge amongst trustees (Goode Committee Report, para 4.5.65), and the government has recognised that training is essential to the performance of the trustees' duties. Trustees can incur penalties if they fail in any aspect of their duties, for in addition to the liability imposed on them under the general law of trusts, the PA 1995 introduces 12 offences that could result in suspension or removal of a trustee from the office of trustee, 14 offences that could result in a fine being imposed on the trustee and five that carry the possibility of criminal charges being brought against the trustee. Section 42 thus makes provision for time off for trustees for the performance of their duties and for training. The employer must permit any employee who is a trustee of the scheme to take time off during his working hours for the purpose of performing his duties as a trustee of the scheme or undergoing training which is relevant to the performance of those duties — s. 42(1). The amount of time off that an employee is permitted to take must be reasonable in all the circumstances, particular regard being had to:

(a)   how much time off is required to perform the duties of trustee and the undergoing of relevant training, and how much time off is required for performing a particular duty or for undergoing the particular training; and

(b)   the circumstances of the employer's business and the effect the employee's absence will have on the running of that business.

Where an employer has failed to allow an employee to take time off as required by s. 42 the employee may bring a complaint to an industrial tribunal.

Where an employer allows an employee time off then under s. 42 he must pay him for this time. The employee must receive his normal rate of pay — s. 43.

If the employee has a complaint under ss. 42 or 43 then it must be presented to the industrial tribunal either within three months of the date when the failure occurred or, where the industrial tribunal is satisfied it was not reasonably practical for the complaint to be presented within that period, within such period as the tribunal considers reasonable — s. 44.

Where the tribunal finds a complaint under s. 42 to be well-founded, it must make a declaration to that effect. It may also make an award of compensation to the employee to be paid by the employer. The amount of compensation to be paid to the employee is such as the tribunal considers 'just and equitable in the circumstances', regard being made to the employer's default in failing to permit the employee to take time off and to any loss sustained in matters complained of — s. 45(1) and (2).

Where a tribunal finds an employer has failed to pay an employee in accordance with s. 43, it must order the employer to pay the employee the amount due.

Thus the tribunal has a discretion to award compensation where s. 42 is breached, but it must award compensation to the employee where s. 43 applies.

Section 46 introduces measures to provide protection for a member-nominated trustee against victimisation by the employer for any activities performed during the trusteeship. The law at present allows the employee to claim compensation or reinstatement for wrongful dismissal, but the burden of proof falls on the employee. In addition the employee needs two years' qualifying service. Section 46 is designed to make dismissal automatically unfair in the case of trustees and requires no qualifying service. It strengthens the protection given by the Employment Protection (Consolidation) Act 1978.

It is important that member-nominated trustees feel free to act in the best interests of the scheme members without any form of pressure. Thus s. 46(1) says that an employee should not be subjected to any detriment by his employer on the ground that the employee performed or was going to perform any function as a trustee of a trust scheme which relates to his employment. Clearly, however, he can be dismissed for other legitimate grounds.

Section 46(5) says that an employee is unfairly dismissed for the purposes of Part V of the Employment Protection (Consolidation) Act 1978 if the reason or principal reason for the dismissal is that the employee performed or is about to perform his functions as member-nominated trustee. Unfair dismissal covers dismissal for redundancy where the following conditions are met:

(a)   the circumstances of the redundancy applied equally to more than one employee and the position held by the member-nominated trustee is similar to that of those other employees but they have not been dismissed by the employer; and

(b)   the reason the employee was selected for redundancy was because he performed or was about to perform an act in relation to the trust as member-nominated trustee — s. 46(6).

Subsections (5) and (6) of s. 46 apply to employees regardless of their period of employment with the employer and regardless of their age. Any clause in the contract of employment or any other agreement which attempts to exclude or limit the operation of s. 46 or preclude any person from presenting a complaint to an industrial tribunal is void — s. 46(8). Section 46(8) does not apply, however, to an agreement to refrain from preventing or continuing with a complaint where a conciliation officer has taken action under s. 133(2) or (3), or s. 134(1), (2) or (3) of the Employment Protection (Consolidation) Act 1978 or the conditions regulating compromise agreements under s. 140(3) Employment Protection (Consolidation) Act 1978 are satisfied.

3.2.4   Exercise of powers by member trustees

Section 39 PA 1995 deals with the exercise of powers by member trustees. The section is aimed to protect member trustees who have to make discretionary decisions from which they themselves may benefit. As Lord Hershell said in *Bray* v *Ford* [1896] AC 44, 51,

It is an inflexible rule of a Court of Equity that a person in a fiduciary position . . . is not, unless otherwise expressly provided, entitled to make a profit; he is not allowed to put himself in a position where his interest and duty conflict. It does not appear to me that this rule is, . . . founded upon principles of morality. I regard it rather as based on the consideration that, human nature being what it is, there is danger in such circumstances, of the person holding a fiduciary position being swayed by interest rather than duty, and thus prejudicing those who he was bound to protect. It has therefore been deemed expedient to lay down this positive rule. But I am satisfied that it might be departed from in many cases, without any breach of morality, without any wrong being inflicted, and without any consciousness of wrongdoing.

Thus there can be an inherent conflict in an occupational pension scheme where trustees who are members of the scheme seek to improve benefits for members. In *Manning* v *Drexel Burnham Lambert Holdings Ltd* [1994] PLR 75, Linsay J thought that a trust which is a pension trust may amount to a special circumstance which could form an exception to the general rule. He went on to say at p. 84,

If the 'managing' of conflicts is frequently to involve, . . . argument before and a decision of the court, time and money will be spent on legal processes which many would, with some justice, think unnecessary and undesirable. When the legislature considers how far and in what terms to embody the report of Professor Goode . . . I commend to it consideration of the creation of a clear exception to the so-called 'general rule of equity' so that in appropriate cases the administration of pension trusts by trustee-beneficiaries might safely proceed without the expense and delay of proceedings.

Thus the new section ensures that trustees who take decisions prudently and in good faith will be protected under s. 39.

3.2.5 Independent trustee

Sections 22 to 26 of the PA 1995 re-enact, with certain amendments, ss. 119 to 122 of the PSA 1993. Sections 22 and 23 of the PA 1995 require that a person acting as:

(a)   an insolvency practitioner in relation to a company which is the employer in relation to the scheme; or
(b)   an official receiver who becomes the liquidator or provisional liquidator of a company which is the employer in relation to the scheme; or
(c)   a receiver and manager or trustee of the estate of a bankrupt who is the employer in relation to the scheme;

must ensure that at least one of the trustees is an independent person.

This duty is a continuing one. If there is no independent trustee then the insolvency practitioner or official receiver must appoint or secure the appointment of an independent trustee as soon as reasonably practicable and if a period is prescribed by regulations then within that period.

There had been some uncertainty surrounding the earlier law which stated that the rules only applied to an occupational pension scheme which was 'constituted by trust deed'. Thus it appeared that a scheme established under a resolution of a board would not be subject to the rule. The new s. 22 replaces the phrase 'constituted by trust deed' by 'in relation to a trust scheme', and the earlier uncertainty is remedied.

Regulation 6 of the Occupational Pension Schemes (Independent Trustee) Regulations 1990 (SI 1990/2075), which came into force on 12 November 1990, says that s. 119 of the PSA 1993 (which was the corresponding provision to s. 22 PA 1995) did not apply to:

(a)   small self-administered schemes;
(b)   money-purchase schemes;
(c)   schemes solely providing death-in-service benefits;
(d)   schemes under which all the benefits to be provided are secured by insurance policies that are earmarked for certain members.

This is still the case.

Section 23(3) of the PA 1995 lays down the criteria for establishing whether a person is 'independent'. A trustee is 'independent' if he has 'no interest in the assets of the employer or of the scheme, otherwise than as trustee' and he is not connected with or an associate of the employer, the insolvency practitioner or the official receiver. The terms 'connected with' and 'associate of' the employer are to be given the same meaning as in ss. 249 and 435 Insolvency Act 1986 (see s. 3.2.1 where this was discussed in relation to the actuary or auditor of the scheme). The Occupational Pension Schemes (Independent Trustee) Regulations 1990 (SI 1990/2075) reg. 2, provides additional requirements that the independent trustee must fulfil. These are:

(a)   the trustee must not have provided any services to the trustees or managers of the scheme or the employer with regard to the scheme less than three years before the provision started to apply to the scheme; and
(b)   the trustee must be neither an associate of nor connected with:

(i)   a person who has an interest in the assets of the employer or of the scheme, except as a trustee of the scheme, or
(ii)   a person to whom (a) above applies.

The meaning of the term 'independent' was examined in the recent case of *Clark* v *Hicks* [1992] PLR 213. Here Rengredal established a pension scheme for its employees of which Investment Capital Pension Trustees Ltd (ICPT) was the sole trustee. Rengredal went into liquidation and on 20 December 1991 a liquidator was appointed. The liquidator in compliance with his duty under s. 57C of the Social Security Pensions Act 1975 (now s. 23 PA 1995) appointed Mr Clark to fulfil the role of independent trustee on 31 January 1992. ICPT remained the trustee of the scheme, but the effective administration of the scheme was vested solely in Mr Clark.

Mr Clark was a solicitor and partner in the firm of Clarks, and following his appointment he set about various tasks such as identifying and securing the assets of the scheme. In order to carry out these tasks he obtained the assistance of a number of people in the firm of Clarks. The firm also acted for the trustee, ICPT.

Section 57C(2) of the Social Security Pensions Act 1975 said that where an insolvency practitioner acts in relation to a company at least one of the trustees of the scheme should be an independent person at all times. Subs. (3) then described when a person is independent (and this section is in substantially the same terms as s. 23(3) PA 1995) and required that the person satisfy such requirements as may be prescribed by Reg. 2 of the Occupational Pension Schemes (Independent Trustee) Regulations 1990 (SI 1990/2075).

The issue was whether Mr Clark satisfied the requirement of s. 57C. The court first had to determine whether the test for independence under this section was a once-and-for-all test to be applied at the date the independent trustee was appointed, or whether the test was a continuing one. Mervyn Davies LJ said the latter view was to be preferred because the wording of s. 57C(2) (and of s. 23(1) PA 1995) said, 'If and so long as this section applies to a scheme, it shall be the duty of the practitioner or official receiver— (a) to satisfy himself *that at all times* at least one of the trustees of the scheme is an independent person' (emphasis added).

The next question the court had to determine was whether Mr Clark met these criteria. The court recognised that a sole practitioner who is an independent trustee could use his own assistants, clerks etc., without losing his independence. Such people would not provide services to the fund but to the independent trustee. However, if in the course of his office an independent trustee were to act for himself (and his co-trustee) in the course of litigation, then it could be said that he is providing services to the trustees.

Mr Clark was in partnership and thus reg. 2(3) required him not to be a partner of a person to whom reg. 2(2) applied. Mervyn Davies J thought that there was difficulty in reconciling reg. 2(3) with reg. 2(2) since reg. 2(2) refers to a person not providing services. However, reg. 2(3) is difficult to understand unless the reference is to someone who *does* provide services. The judge said that it was a fact that Mr Clark's partners had provided services to the trustees and were acting in litigation proceedings. Furthermore, a bill of costs showed that Clark had carried out work for the trustees and therefore the judge concluded that Mr Clark did not satisfy the joint requirements of paras (2) and (3) because he was an associate within s. 435 Insolvency Act 1986 of a person who had provided services to the trustees. An independent trustee cannot promote his own firm to provide services to the fund or trustees without losing his independence.

The case, however, leaves several issues unresolved (and the PA 1995 has failed to address them):

(a)   Mervyn Davies J said that the date at which Mr Clark ceased to be an independent trustee was 1 June 1992 when the bill of costs was submitted. It is difficult to see why the judge chose this and not the date when Mr Clark started to carry out the work in question, which was clearly before the date of the bill of costs.

(b)   Section 57D(2) of the Social Security Pensions Act 1975 states that if a trustee who has been appointed under s. 57C(2)(b) ceases to be an independent trustee, then he ceases to be a trustee of the scheme. Therefore a question remains as to the legality of Mr Clark's actions in relation to the trust after 1 June 1992.

(c)   Section 57C(3) allows an independent trustee to deduct his reasonable fees from the assets of the scheme. For the period after 1 June 1992 Mr Clark could not do this. This could prove to be a problem where the period between ceasing to be an independent trustee and the discovery of this fact is of any length of time.

Section 24 PA 1995 gives the members of the scheme a power to apply to the court where an insolvency practitioner or official receiver 'neglects or refuses to discharge any duty imposed on him by s. 23(1)'. The court in such a case may issue an order requiring the insolvency practitioner or official receiver to discharge the duties imposed on him under s. 23(1).

Section 25 contains further provisions regarding the appointment and powers of independent trustees. Section 25(1) says that if the employer is the only trustee at the time an independent trustee is appointed, then it ceases to be a trustee at the time of the appointment of the independent trustee.

Section 25(2) says that when the independent trustee is appointed, any power vested in the current trustees of the scheme and exercisable at their discretion may be exercised only by the independent trustee. The independent trustee may also exercise any power vested in the employer and exercisable at his discretion as trustee of the power. Where there is more than one independent trustee the powers vested in them shall be exercisable with the consent of at least half the independent trustees — s. 25(2)(b).

It should be noted that any existing trustees of the scheme are not automatically removed by the appointment of an independent trustee. No provision in the scheme rules or documents may provide for the removal of an independent trustee — s. 25(3). Where a trustee ceases to be independent then he should give written notice of that fact to the insolvency practitioner or official receiver immediately, and he will cease to be a trustee of the scheme — s. 25(4). He will not cease to be a trustee where s. 25(4) applies if there is no other trustee of the scheme, until another independent trustee is appointed.

A trustee who is appointed as an independent trustee is entitled to payment of his fees from the scheme and this statutory charging provision overrides any scheme rules — s. 25(6).

While s. 22 of the PA 1995 applies to a scheme, the insolvency practitioner or official receiver must provide the trustees with any information which they may reasonably require for the purpose of the scheme. This must be done as soon as practicable after the receipt of a request — s. 26.

3.3   DUTY OF THE TRUSTEES TO ACT UNANIMOUSLY

Under the general law of trusts the principle is that, subject to any contrary provision in the trust instrument, only the joint exercise by the trustees of their powers and discretions is valid — see *Luke* v *South Kensington Hotel Co.* (1879) 11 ChD 121, 125. This can be illustrated by the following example: if one of the trustees enters into a contract to sell trust property, whether he is purporting to act as an absolute owner or on behalf of himself and his co-trustees, then the sale cannot be enforced against the trust fund unless it is later ratified by the other trustees. Nevertheless occasionally one of several trustees alone may be authorised to receive income where it is practical to do so. The rationale for this general rule is to make the trustees more wary and cautious in the exercise of their powers and duties.

This principle has often been subject to a contrary provision in the case of a pension scheme and frequently a scheme will allow for decisions to be made by a majority of the trustees. The reason for this exception in the case of pension schemes is usually one of practicality.

Section 32 PA 1995 reflects this position and states that decisions of the trustees may be taken by the agreement of a majority of the trustees. The scheme rules can provide otherwise. This section can result in the views of the member-nominated trustees being virtually ignored. In cases where the decision of the trustees may be taken by the agreement of the majority of them, they may, by determination under s. 32(2) (unless the scheme documents provide otherwise), require a certain minimum number of trustees specified in the determination to be present when any decision is taken — s. 32(2)(a). Notice of an occasion at which the decisions may be so taken must be given to each trustee to whom it is reasonably practicable to give such notice — s. 32(2)(b) unless the occasion falls within a class or description to be detailed in regulations. Notice within s. 32(2) must be given in a prescribed manner not later than the beginning of a period to be prescribed in regulations — s. 32(3).

Where s. 32(2)(b) is not complied with then ss. 3 and 10 apply to a trustee who has failed to take reasonable steps to secure the compliance thereof.

Section 32 is subject to the provisions in s. 8(4)(b) (see 2.6.3), 16(3)(b) (removal of member-nominated trustees) and 25(2) (exercise of powers where an independent trustee is appointed).

3.4 INVESTMENT BY A TRUSTEE

3.4.1 General

Any trustee is under a duty to invest money that is in his hands: this means that he must employ the money to purchase something from which a profit or interest can be expected. The trustee must make investments either within the terms of the Trustee Investments Act 1961 or, more usually in the case of an occupational pension scheme, within a broader express power of investment contained in the trust deed. Without an express power of investment, the trustees are restricted to making investments within the terms of the Trustee Investments Act 1961. If the trustees are investing under the Act then they must divide the trust fund into two parts. One called the narrower-range part and the other called the wider-range part. A maximum of one half of the fund can be invested by the trustees in the wider-range part, although if they so desire they can invest the whole of the fund in the narrower range. The narrower-range investments divide into:

(a) those not requiring advice (sch. 1 Part I of the Trustee Investments Act 1961), including Defence Bonds and National Savings Certificates; and

(b) those requiring advice (sch. 1 Part II Trustee Investments Act 1961), including government and public authority fixed-interest securities, debentures, deposits with building societies within the Building Societies Act 1986, mortgages of freehold property in England and Wales and Northern Ireland and of leasehold property with more than 60 years left to run and loans on heritable security in Scotland, authorised unit trusts within s. 468(1) Income and Corporation Taxes Act 1988.

Wider-range investments include unit trusts within the meaning of the Financial Services Act 1986, shares in a building society within the meaning of the Building Societies Act 1986 and shares in UK companies provided that the following provisions are met:

(i)   the company must be incorporated in the UK and its securities registered in the UK;

(ii)   it must have total issued and paid-up share capital of more than £1 million;

(iii)   the shares must be quoted on a recognised investment exchange within the meaning of the Financial Services Act 1986;

(iv)   the shares must be fully paid up or required to be fully paid up within nine months of their issue;

(v)   the company has for each of the five preceding years paid a dividend on all its shares ranking for dividends.

Note that these provisions also apply to investments in debentures under Part II of Schedule 1.

The trustees can if they wish invest the whole of the fund in narrower-range investments, no division of the fund being necessary in such a case. If, however, the trustees wish to invest in wider-range investments then they must divide the fund into two parts of equal value, and only one part can be invested in wider-range investments. There is no need for the trustees to ensure that the two halves remain of equal value, but all additional money coming to the fund must be divided into two halves.

The Trustee Investments Act 1961 makes provision for 'special-range investments', i.e., those specifically authorised by a clause of the trust deed. The powers conferred by the Act always give way to this clause and it is usual in an occupational pension scheme for this clause to contain all the powers of investment of the trustees. To the extent that the clause does not contain all the trustees' investment powers, the provisions of the Trustee Investments Act 1961 apply. In such a situation the fund will be divided into two parts, one to be invested in special-range investments and one to be invested under the provisions of the Trustee Investments Act 1961.

3.4.2   Duty of the trustee in choosing investments

The duty of the trustee in an occupational pension scheme in choosing investments has, until the advent of the PA 1995, been governed principally by the same rules as apply to investments under trust law generally. The trustees must ensure not only that their chosen investments are authorised (either under the provisions of the Trustee Investments Act 1961 or the express investment clause), but also that they are selected in accordance with the standard of the prudent man of business. The duty was restated in the case of *Learoyd* v *Whiteley* (1887) 12 App Cas 727 (HL). In the Court of Appeal (sub nom. *Re Whiteley* (1886) 33 ChD 347) Lindley LJ said, at p. 355:

The duty of the trustee is not to take such care only as a prudent man would take if he had only himself to consider; the duty rather is to take such care as an ordinary prudent man would take if he were minded to make an investment for the benefit of other people for whom he felt morally bound to provide.

The matter arose for discussion again in the case of *Cowan* v *Scargill* [1985] Ch 270. Here a mineworkers' pension fund with large assets and wide powers of investment was managed by 10 trustees, of whom five, including the defendant, were appointed by the NUM. The trustees were aided in their investment decisions by an advisory panel of experts. An investment plan was submitted but the NUM trustees refused to accept it on a matter of policy. The NUM trustees wanted no increase in the number of overseas investments, that those already made be withdrawn and that no further investments be made in energies that were competing with coal. The court held that they were in breach of their duty if they refused to adopt the investment strategy.

Megarry V-C listed several factors that the trustees must bear in mind when considering the exercise of their investment powers (whether under the authority of the special investment clause or under the Trustee Investments Act 1961). These factors can be summarised as follows:

(a)   The trustees' paramount concern should be the benefit of the present and future beneficiaries. Normally this means their financial benefit, but if the beneficiaries were adult and had strong views against, for example, alcohol, it might be construed as being to their benefit to avoid investment in companies involved in the sale of alcohol even though it may be to the beneficiaries' financial advantage.

(b)   The trustees must put to one side their own personal interests, views and prejudices. (See *Martin* v *City of Edinburgh District Council* 1988 SLT 329, where it was held that a breach of duty had been committed by a local authority which had adopted a policy of disinvestment in companies which had interests in South Africa, without considering whether this investment strategy was in the best interests of the beneficiaries.)

(c)   the trustees must consider the need for diversification of investments. Section 6(1) of the Trustee Investments Act 1961 expressly provides that, whether the trustees are exercising their power of investment under the Act or under a special investment clause they must:

(i)   Consider the need for diversification of investments in so far as it is appropriate to the circumstances of the trust. In a small fund there would be little diversification of investments and the only type that would normally be made would be the purchase of insurance policies.

(ii)   Have regard to the suitability to the trust of the description of investment proposed. For example, if the proposed investment is in a food company the trustees should consider whether food company shares in general are suitable shares for the trust fund to hold.

(iii)   Have regard to the suitability of the investment proposed, as an investment of that description. For example, if the trustees have decided that food company shares are a suitable investment, is, for example, investment in Allied-Lyons the most suitable food company investment to make.

If the trustees are exercising their power of investment under the Trustee Investments Act 1961 to invest in narrower-range investments requiring advice wider-range investments, they are required to obtain and consider 'proper advice' in regard to the investment being satisfactory having regard to (i), (ii) and (iii) above. The term 'proper advice' is defined in s. 6(4) of the Trustee Investments Act 1961 as being the advice of a person reasonably believed by the trustees to be qualified by his ability and practical experience of financial matters, for example, a stockbroker or a chartered accountant. The proper advice must be given or confirmed in writing — s. 6(5). In addition trustees who retain a narrower range investment requiring advice or a wider-range investment must determine at what intervals the circumstances, and particularly the nature of the investment make it desirable to obtain advice on the question of whether the investment continues to be satisfactory, and the trustees must then obtain and consider advice accordingly.

These provisions do not apply to trustees where one of the trustees is giving proper advice to his fellow trustees — s. 6(6).

Section 36(2) of the PA 1995 reiterates s. 6(1) of the Trustee Investments Act 1961 (which is also the third requirement expounded by Megarry V-C in *Cowan v Scargill*) and says that the trustees or fund manager must have regard to diversification of investments in so far as appropriate to the circumstances of the scheme and to the 'suitability to the scheme of investments of the description of investment proposed and of the investment proposed as an investment of that description.' The corresponding provisions under the Trustee Investments Act 1961 and the general law of trusts were applicable to pension fund trustees before the passing of the Act, but the PA 1995 makes them specifically applicable to pension fund trustees. Section 36(3) of the PA 1995 restates s. 6(2) of the Trustee Investments Act 1961 and requires the trustees to obtain and consider 'proper advice' on the question of whether an investment is satisfactory having regard to the matters mentioned in s. 36(2) of the PA 1995 and the principles contained in the statement under s. 35 (see 3.4.3) before making the investment. This requirement does not apply however where the trustee is investing in narrower-range investments not requiring advice. A trustee retaining investments must determine at what intervals the circumstances and nature of the investment make it desirable to obtain proper advice, and he must obtain and consider such advice accordingly — s. 36(4). Such advice must be given or confirmed in writing — s. 36(7).

Whether advice is 'proper advice' for the purposes of s. 36 depends on whether giving the advice constitutes carrying on investment business.

Where the giving of the advice constitutes carrying on investment business in the UK, within the meaning of the Financial Services Act 1986, advice is proper advice if:

(a) It is given by a person who is authorised under Chapter III of Part I of the Financial Services Act 1986. The Financial Services Act 1986, s. 7, defines an authorised person as being a person who is a member of a recognised self-regulating organisation. A self-regulating organisation is a body which regulates investment business by enforcing rules which are binding on people who are carrying on the business of investment. Such people will either be members of that body or subject to its control. Examples of recognised self-regulating organisations are the PIA and IMRO.

(b) It is given by a person exempted under Chapter IV of the Financial Services Act 1986, who, in giving the advice is acting in the course of the business in respect of which he is exempt.

(c) It is given by a person where, by virtue of para 27 of sch. 1 to the Financial Services Act 1986, para. 15 of that schedule does not apply to the giving of such advice. What this does is to exempt advice given by an overseas person to a trustee in the United Kingdom provided the trustee took the initiative in seeking the advice or was approached by the overseas person without any breach of the Financial Services Act 1986, s. 56 (unsolicited calls) or s. 57 (restrictions on advertising).

(d) It is given by a person who by virtue of reg. 5 of the Banking Coordination (Second Council Directive) Regulations 1992 (SI 1992/3218) may give advice though not authorised to do so as mentioned in (a) above.

In any other situation the provider of the advice must be reasonably believed by the trustees to be qualified by his ability in and practical experience of financial matters *and* to have the appropriate knowledge and experience of the management of the investments of trust schemes — s. 36(6) PA 1995.

A trustee who has obtained and considered advice is not *required* to act on it. Nor is he entitled to reject it just because he disagrees with it, *unless* in so doing he is acting as an ordinary prudent man would act — see *Cowan* v *Scargill* [1985] Ch 270. The trustee is not necessarily protected from breach of trust if he follows the advice, but it is thought that he would obtain relief under s. 61 Trustee Act 1925 if he relied on the advice in good faith. Liability for breach of a trustee's obligation to take care or exercise skill in the performance of his investment functions cannot be excluded or restricted in any way — s. 33(1)(a) PA 1995.

A trustee who has failed to take reasonable steps to secure compliance with s. 36 may be prohibited or suspended under the provisions of ss. 3 and 4 and subject to civil penalties imposed by OPRA (see chapter 2). This is clearly in addition to any general remedies for breach of trust that are applicable under the general law of trusts.

3.4.3 Investment principles

A further requirement that is placed on the trustee in relation to investment is that his power of investment must be exercised with a view to giving effect, as far as is reasonably practicable, to the principles contained in the statement made under s. 35 of the PA 1995.

Section 35 requires trustees to prepare and maintain a written statement of the principles governing their decisions regarding the scheme investments. Certain matters must be covered in the statement. These matters are specified in s. 35(2) and (3) as being:

(a) the trustees' policy for securing compliance with ss. 36 and 56;
(b) the trustees' policy about the following:

    (i)   the kinds of investments to be held;
    (ii)   the balance between different kinds of investments;
    (iii)   the risk;
    (iv)   the expected return on investments;
    (v)   the realisation of investments; and
    (vi)   such other matters as the Secretary of State may prescribe from time to time.

Before the statement is made or revised the trustees must obtain and consider the advice of a person who is reasonably believed by them to be qualified by his ability in and practical experience of financial matters and to have the appropriate knowledge and experience of the management of the investments of such schemes and consult with the employer — s. 35(5).

There must be no restrictions in the deed or statement imposed on the power to make investment by requiring the consent of the employer before such investments are made — s. 35(4).

Where a trustee fails to prepare or maintain a statement or fails to obtain and consider advice then the trustee can be removed or suspended under s. 3 and may also have civil penalties imposed on him by s. 10. It is also thought that failure to comply with s. 35 will result in the trustees being liable under the general law of trusts for breach of trust.

Section 35 does not apply to schemes which are not operated under a trust deed and/or are regulated under other statutes, for example, local authority schemes.

3.4.4 Delegation and investment

If the trustees are carrying out the investment of the fund themselves then they must be authorised as investment managers by the Investment Management Regulatory Organisation (IMRO) as an occupational pension scheme that can manage the investments itself (see DTI, *Guide to the Financial Services Bill* (1985), p. 29). If the trustees are not authorised then the investment management will have to be delegated to an investment manager authorised by IMRO under s. 191 Financial Services Act 1986 or the trustees of the scheme will pass the contributions to an insurance company to invest under a management contract.

There are a number of types of investment advisers available to the trustees — merchant banks, stockbrokers (although since they do not charge a fee and rely on gaining a commission as a means of obtaining remuneration there may be a greater amount of buying and selling of shares than is necessary), specialist firms which have been set up to look after pension fund moneys, and investment advisory services which are offered by firms of actuaries and accountants. In larger pension funds a professional investment manager is appointed and he meets with the trustees to discuss investment matters. Alternatively an investment management subcommittee may be formed, which would meet every six months to report on the implementation of policy.

3.4.4.1 General law of delegation The original law in the area of delegation regarded the trustees as taking upon themselves the management of the trust property for the benefit of others and therefore having no right to delegate their duty to any one else — *Turner v Corney* (1841) 5 Beav 515, 517. This is a highly impractical attitude to take to the role of the trustee and thus it became established that delegation was allowed if the trustees had authority to do so. The authority to delegate trusteeship can arise from a number of different sources:

(a)   Where the trust instrument itself confers a power to appoint agents.
(b)   Under s. 23(1) Trustee Act 1925, which provides:

Trustees or personal representatives may, instead of acting personally, employ and pay an agent, whether a solicitor, banker, stockbroker, or other person, to transact any business or do any act required to be transacted or done in the execution of the trust . . . and shall be entitled to be allowed and paid all charges and expenses so incurred . . .

By this section a trustee is no longer required to perform the actual work himself but he may employ an agent to do such work, whether there is any necessity for this or otherwise — see per Maugham J in *Re Vickery* [1931] 1 Ch 572.

(c)   There are also narrower powers of delegation in the Trustee Act 1925, for example, the power to appoint agents to deal with property abroad — s. 23(2).

Under s. 23 Trustee Act 1925 the extent of the agent's authority is limited. The trustees must take the basic decisions themselves, but they can employ agents to implement such decisions and to carry out the routine administration of the trust. However, s. 25 Trustee Act 1925, as substituted by the Powers of Attorney Act 1971, allows a trustee to delegate the power to make decisions. This can only be done, however, for a period not exceeding 12 months during the trustee's absence abroad.

3.4.4.2   Liability for the defaults of the agent   Section 25(5) Trustee Act 1925 makes a trustee who delegates authority to a fund manager under s. 25 liable for the fund manager's acts or defaults as if they were the acts and defaults of the trustee.

The liability of a trustee for any loss that occurs for the default of an agent appointed under s. 23 Trustee Act 1925 is slightly uncertain because of the inconsistency that exists between two statutory provisions. The first is s. 23(1) Trustee Act 1925 which says that trustees 'shall not be responsible for the default of any such agent if employed in good faith' and the second is s. 30 of the same Act which says that a trustee shall be accountable only for his own acts, receipts, neglects or defaults and not for those of anyone else with whom any trust money may be deposited 'unless the same happens through his own wilful default'. The issue arose for discussion in the case of *Re Vickery* [1931] 1 Ch 572, where it was held that loss occasioned by the behaviour of a solicitor who had been employed to wind up an estate did not amount to wilful default on the part of the executor. This was despite the fact that after appointing the solicitor the executor became aware that the solicitor had been suspended from practice at one time. Maugham J said, at pp. 584–5:

It is essential in this case to guard oneself against judging the conduct of the defendant in the light of subsequent events. To have employed a new solicitor as soon as the defendant became aware that H.H. Jennens [the absconding solicitor] was a person with a tarnished reputation for honesty would certainly have meant further costs. It might have proved quite unnecessary even on the supposition that Jennens was a rogue. Even a man of the world might have thought that the sum involved . . . was far too small to make it probable that the solicitor would be likely — unless, indeed, in the case of stern necessity — for such a sum to expose himself to the orders of the court and to the action of the Law Society. Nor must it be forgotten that upon the facts as I find them it was not till the month of September 1927 [one year after Jennens's employment commenced] that the defendant had any real reason for suspecting that Jennens was unworthy of confidence; and it seems that after that date he kept on pressing for an immediate settlement and kept on being assured that a settlement would immediately take place. . . . I have come to the conclusion that the defendant was on any view of the facts guilty only of an error of judgment, and this, in the case of a loss occasioned by the defalcations of a solicitor, does not amount to wilful default on the part of the executor. The action accordingly in my judgment fails.

3.4.4.3 Delegation under the Pensions Act Before the PA 1995 a pension fund trustee delegated investment decisions by means of s. 23 Trustee Act 1925 or more usually a wider power of delegation contained in the trust deed. The problem was that unless the trust deed authorised the trustees to appoint a fund manager to engage in discretionary management the manager could only advise and execute purchase and sell orders. Section 34(2)(a) PA 1995 allows the trustee of an occupational pension scheme to delegate any discretion to make a decision regarding investments (but only delegation of investments) to a fund manager who falls or is treated as falling within s. 191(2) Financial Services Act 1986.

Section 34(2)(b) says that trustees must not otherwise delegate any such discretion except under s. 25 Trustee Act 1925 or s. 34(5) PA 1995. Section 34(5) PA 1995 permits the trustees of the scheme (subject to anything to the contrary in the trust deed or rules) to authorise two or more of the board of trustees to exercise the board's power to make investments — s. 34(5)(a). The effect of this subsection is that member-nominated trustees can legitimately be prevented from sitting on the investment subcommittee, while nevertheless remaining liable for any decisions of that subcommittee. This subsection really goes against the spirit of s. 16 which says that the role of member-nominated trustees should be no different from other trustees. The trustees may also, under s. 34(5)(b), delegate any decision regarding investment to a fund manager who is not an authorised person for the purposes of s. 191 Financial Services Act 1986 provided that any decision about investment would not be regarded as investment business in the UK for the purposes of the Financial Services Act 1986.

Section 34(2)(b) says that trustees must not otherwise delegate any such discretion except under s. 25 Trustee Act 1925 or s. 34(5) PA 1995. Section 34(5) PA 1995 permits the trustees of the scheme (subject to anything to the contrary in the trust deed or rules) to authorise two or more of the board of trustees to exercise the board's power to make investments — s. 34(5)(a). The effect of this subsection is that member-nominated trustees can legitimately be prevented from sitting on the investment subcommittee, while nevertheless remaining liable for any decisions of that subcommittee. This subsection really goes against the spirit of s. 16 which says that the role of member-nominated trustees should be no different from other trustees. The trustees may also delegate any decision regarding investment to a fund manager who is not an authorised person for the purposes of s. 191 Financial Services Act 1986 provided that any decision about investment would not be regarded as investment business in the UK for the purposes of the Financial Services Act 1986 — s. 34(5)(b).

Section 33 PA 1995 does not prevent the trustee excluding or restricting libility for any acts or defaults of a fund manager who has exercised his discretion under s. 34(5)(b), where the trustees (or the person who has made the delegation on their behalf) have taken all such steps as are reasonable to satisfy themselves that the fund manager has the appropriate knowledge and experience to manage the investments of the scheme and that he is carrying out his work competently and complies with s. 36.

The PA 1995 expressly outlines the liability of the trustee for the acts of the agent. If the trustees delegate their power of investment under s. 34(2)(a) then they are not responsible for any act or default of the agent if they have taken all such steps as are reasonable to satisfy themselves that the agent:

(a) has the appropriate knowledge and experience for managing the investments of the scheme: and
(b) carries out his work competently; and
(c) complies with s. 36 when choosing investments.

In other cases, however, the trustees will remain liable for the acts and defaults
of their agent. The provisions contained in ss. 33, 34, 35 and 36 also apply to a
duly appointed agent.

The provisions contained in s. 34 override any inconsistent provision imposed
by any rule of law or statute other than one contained in Part I of the Act itself or
the PSA 1993.

3.4.5 Exclusion of the duty of care in relation to investment

Section 33 of the PA 1995 provides that the liability of a trustee or an agent of the
trustee for breach of trust of an obligation to take care and exercise skill when
investing trust funds cannot be excluded or restricted by the trust deeds. Exclusion
has a wide meaning and includes:

(a) making the liability or enforcement subject to restrictive or onerous
conditions;
(b) excluding or restricting rules of evidence or procedure;
(c) excluding or restricting liability any right or remedy regarding liability, or
subjecting a person to prejudice as a result of pursuing his right or remedy.

Section 33 overrides any restriction which is inconsistent with the provision
which may be imposed by any rules of law or by or under any enactment. The Act
does not, however, define what the phrase 'exercise skill' means. Reference must
therefore be made to the general law of trusts as to the meaning of the phrase. It
is thought however that following a series of cases culminating in the case of
Speight v *Gaunt* (1883) 9 App Cas 1, a higher level of skill will be expected from
paid trustees and, by inference, from others with relevant professional expertise in
specific fields compared to say lay member-nominated trustees. Section 33(3)
provides for regulations to make exemptions in relation to certain types of trust
schemes and certain types of exclusion or restriction. It is expected that s. 33 will
not apply to, for example, local authority schemes or non-trust schemes. Section
34(6) also allows trustees to be exempted by the trust deed or an agreement from
liability for the acts and defaults of a fund manager in exercise of a discretion
delegated to him under s. 34(5)(b) provided that the trustees have taken all such
steps as are reasonable to satisfy themselves that:

(a) the fund manager has the requisite knowledge and experience of managing
pension fund investments; and
(b) he is carrying out his work competently and complying with the provision
of s. 36.

3.4.6 Self-investment

In order to obtain Inland Revenue approval, and thus qualify for tax advantages, most occupational pension schemes must be set up under an irrevocable trust. Where a scheme is contracted-out, the trustee must establish scheme accounts which are separate from the employer's. The object of such rules is to ensure that the funds of the pension scheme are separate from the assets of the employer, so that they will not be available to the employer's creditors.

Until recently, however, the trustees could invest part of the pension fund in the sponsoring employer. In such a case the assets would cease to be segregated and would become part of the employer's assets. Thus the trustees would lose the legal title to the assets and acquire instead a right against the employer. The argument in favour of self-investment is that self-investment in an up and coming company can produce good returns. There had for many years been Inland Revenue restrictions on the powers of self-investment in relation to small self-administered schemes, but no such requirement existed in relation to other types of occupational pension schemes until March 1992. The legislation was on the statute book at the time the Maxwell scandal broke since that case was not the first where self-investment went wrong — examples can also be found with the Burlington International Group and the Lewis Group — and the Occupational Pension Schemes (Investment of Scheme's Resources) Regulations 1992 (SI 1992/246) limited self-investment to 5 per cent of the scheme resources. This was designed to reduce the risk of loss to the occupational pension schemes that could result from an employer's insolvency.

Clearly there needs to be a restriction on self-investment, otherwise the purpose of establishing the trust as the basis of the scheme in order to separate scheme assets from the employer would be defeated. Nevertheless the Goode Committee Report did not consider that a blanket exclusion covering associated companies was practical for two reasons. The first was that many large schemes track the market and to disentangle certain investments in the sponsoring company would be difficult. The second reason was that if an employer comprises of part of a large corporate group it is difficult to see how the trustees in proposing to make a small investment in a particular company could be expected to ensure the company was not a parent, or subsidiary of the employer, or engage in a monitoring service to ensure that it does not later become one. Thus the Goode Committee recommended that the 5 per cent bar remain. In practice, however, it is difficult to know whether the 5 per cent has been exceeded. The government have missed an opportunity for policing the 5 per cent limit by allowing OPRA to receive annual reports and assess what is happening in the scheme.

To this extent s. 40 PA 1995 re-enacts, with some amendments, s. 112 of the PSA 1993 (which was originally enacted in the Social Security Act 1990). By s. 40(1) the trustees or the managers of an occupational pension scheme must ensure that the scheme complies with any prescribed restrictions on employer-related investments that are in force. The Occupational Pension Schemes (Investment of Scheme's Resources) Regulations 1992 (SI 1992/246) say that not more than 5 per cent of the current market value of resources of the scheme may be invested in employer-related investments, although there are some exceptions to this in the case of bank accounts and resources derived from AVCs. The

Regulations apply only to approved schemes which have at least one member in the UK, or have one or more trustees in the UK.

Section 40(2) says that 'employer-related investments' means:

(a)   shares or other securities issued by the employer or any person who is connected with, or an associate of, the employer;
(b)   land occupied by or used by or subject to a lease in favour of the employer or any such person;
(c)   property (other than land) which is used for the purposes of any business carried on by the employer or any such person;
(d)   loans to the employer or any such person;
(e)   any other prescribed investment.

'Securities' means any asset, right or interest falling within para. 1, 2, 4 or 5 of sch. 1 to the Financial Services Act 1986.

Section 40(3) PA 1995 provides that outstanding debts and contributions owed to the occupational pension scheme by the employer should be regarded as loans made to the employer by the trustees or manager and that such debts will count as part of the limit on loans as employer-related investments.

The Occupational Pension Schemes (Investment of Scheme's Resources) Regulations 1992 deal with occupational pension schemes which were holding investments in their employer companies at the time that the Regulations came into force, i.e., at 9 March 1992. Employer-related loans and listed shares could be retained until 8 March 1994. Employer-related investments which are traded in a second-tier market of a recognised stock exchange on 9 March 1992 can be retained until 8 March 1997. Any other employer-related investment can be retained without limit of time.

Where the provisions of s. 40 are not complied with then any trustee who fails to take steps that are reasonable for compliance with this section can be prohibited or suspended under ss. 3 and 4 and subject to civil penalties under s. 10 of the PA 1995 (see chapter 2). If s. 40(1) PA 1995 is not complied with then a trustee or manager who has failed to take all such steps as are reasonable is guilty of a criminal offence and liable to a fine not exceeding £5,000 on summary conviction or a fine and/or imprisonment on conviction on indictment.

3.5   PROVISION OF DOCUMENTS FOR MEMBERS

In practice many schemes supplied members with information before any statutory regulations were introduced to guarantee them information. The Occupational Pension Schemes (Disclosure of Information) Regulations 1986 (SI 1986/1046, the Disclosure Regulations) introduced a statutory obligation on trustees to provide members and potential members of a pension scheme with information. Further statutory measures regarding the auditing of pension schemes were introduced in the Occupational Pension Schemes (Auditors) Regulations 1987 (SI 1987/1102), and as a result of the recommendations made by the House of Commons Select Committee on Social Security (*The Operation of Pension Funds* (House of Commons Papers, Session 1991–92, 61-II) the Occupational and Personal Pension Schemes (Miscellaneous Amendments) Regulations 1992 (SI 1992/1531) were passed to strengthen the requirements for disclosure still further.

The object of these regulations has been to:

(a)   make scheme members aware of where they can obtain independent advice on their rights and benefits;

(b)   provide more information to those who have left employment and have retired;

(c)   ensure the information is made available within a reasonable timescale;

(d)   give greater protection to members where schemes are being wound up or merged.

The Disclosure Regulations apply to all schemes which are approved by, or seeking approval from, the Inland Revenue, even public-sector schemes. But they do not apply to unapproved schemes. The Regulations detail:

(a)   the information to be provided;

(b)   the persons to whom the information is to be provided;

(c)   the time and frequency of disclosure;

(d)   the form that disclosure must take.

The information to be provided comprises the following:

(a)   The formal scheme documentation, including the trust deed and rules and any supplemental deeds, which must be made available for inspection or copies supplied on request (though only one request in every 12 months need be complied with). This information must be made available to prospective members of the occupational pension scheme, existing members and their spouses, other beneficiaries and independent trade unions recognised to any extent for the purposes of collective bargaining — PSA 1993; Occupational Pension Schemes (Disclosure of Information) Regulations 1986 (SI 1986/1046).

(b)   Basic information about the scheme, which must be given to new members automatically within two months of joining the scheme, and to existing members, prospective members, their spouses and beneficiaries and trade unions on request within one month. The information should not be requested more than once in any 12-month period — PSA 1993, s. 113; Occupational Pension Schemes (Disclosure of Information) Regulations 1986 (SI 1986/1046). The information to be supplied is set out in Sch. 1 of the Regulations and includes, *inter alia,* details of eligibility, membership, contributions, the tax-approval status of the scheme, benefits payable under the scheme and the funding status.

(c)   Information to which the member and his beneficiaries are entitled must be supplied as of course when the benefit has become payable to the individual and in other cases on request. Schedule 2 to the Regulations says that the information to be supplied includes information about the benefits the member is to receive on retirement, on death, on leaving service, on transfer and on winding up. The Regulations distinguish between information that must be made available to members of final salary schemes and money-purchase schemes.

On winding up the trustees must notify all the members and beneficiaries as soon as practicable that the scheme is wound up and the members must be told of the amount of the benefits which have been secured for them and who will be responsible for paying them the benefit — PSA 1993, s. 113; Occupational Pension Schemes (Disclosure of Information) Regulations 1986 (SI 1986/1046).

(d)   An annual report which must be made available to the members under reg. 9. Schedule 5 lists the things that the report must contain. The annual report must contain a copy of the audited accounts and actuarial statement (see below) and the annual report must be made available no later than one year after the scheme year ends — PSA 1993, s. 113; Occupationl Pension Schemes (Disclosure of Information) Regulations (SI 1986/1046).

The responsibility for providing or making available the above information rests on the trustees or the scheme manager.

Section 41 PA 1995 (which replaces s. 114 PSA 1993) specifies other information that should be obtained and made available to members, prospective members, their spouses and beneficiaries, and independent trade unions recognised to any extent for the purposes of collective bargaining. The section is in substantially the same terms as s. 114 PSA 1993 which it replaces. The information that should be obtained at prescribed times is as follows:

(a)   The audited accounts of the scheme. Regulation 7 of SI 1986/1046 says that trustees must obtain audited accounts every scheme year. The regulation sets out who can be an auditor and what the contents of the accounts ought be (see 3.6).

(b)   An actuary's statement about the contributions to the scheme. This should confirm the content of the accounts, and say whether the contributions that were due to be paid during the scheme year have been paid in accordance with the recommendation of the actuary — s. 41(2)(b) PA 1995.

(c)   A valuation by an actuary of the assets and liabilities of the scheme and a statement concerning such aspects of the valuation as the regulations may prescribe — s. 41(2)(c). Regulation 8 of SI 1986/1046 says that such a valuation should be prepared in accordance with the guidelines published by the Institute of Actuaries and Faculty of Actuaries (Retirement Benefit Schemes — Actuarial Reports (Guidance Note 9)). The valuation must contain a statement of the scheme's future contribution rates and funding levels. The valuation must be prepared by an actuary who is a Fellow of the Institute of Actuaries, or a Fellow of the Faculty of Actuaries or such person as the Secretary of State may approve — s. 41(5) PA 1995.

The documents that should be made available to the members, their spouses etc., referred to in s. 41(4) are:

(a)   any valuation or certificate which must be prepared under s. 57 or 58 by the actuary of the scheme,

(b)   any report prepared by the trustees or managers under s. 59(3) (see chapter 5).

The PA 1995, however, has done nothing to change the law (with the exception of disclosure in relation to minimum solvency requirements) in this area, despite there being several problems with regard to disclosure. The first problem was highlighted by a survey carried out by Social and Community Planning Research (commissioned by the Goode Committee) which said that there was 'widespread ignorance among members of the details of their scheme including fundamental issues' (para. 4.12.13). Members recorded a general feeling of powerlessness when it came to the provision of information. Employees did not know what questions to ask nor did they know what to do with the information they received. Goode therefore suggested a need for a simple format in disclosing information to employees together with the use of 'plain English'. This, however, is difficult to legislate for.

The second problem is that although the nature of the information given to members allows them to monitor the security of their benefits and their value, it provides them with no information about how the scheme is administered (with a few exceptions like the Occupational and Personal Pension Schemes (Miscellaneous Amendments) Regulations 1992, reg. 5, which requires self-investment in excess of 5 per cent to be disclosed), and why certain decisions are taken by the trustees. In order to obtain documents relating to these issues before any litigation has been commenced the members have to rely on the principles in the general law of trusts and the decision in *Re Londonderry's Settlement* [1965] Ch 918 (followed in *Wilson* v *Law Debenture Corp.* [1994] PLR 141, for disclosure of occupational pension scheme documents). In *Re Londonderry's Settlement* the Court of Appeal said that beneficiaries have the right to see all documents relating to the trust that can be classed as 'trust documents'. It might have been thought that all documents connected with the administration of the trust are prima facie trust documents, but the court held that the trustees did not have to disclose documents relating to the trustees' deliberations on how they should exercise their powers or disclosing the reasons for the exercise of such powers, or the material upon which the reasons were based. Salmon LJ suggested that for a document to be regarded as a trust document it should possess three characteristics:

(a) it should be a document in the possession of the trustees *qua* trustees; and

(b) it should contain information about the trust which the beneficiaries are entitled to know; and

(c) the beneficiaries should have a proprietary interest in the document and be entitled to see it accordingly.

It is difficult to see how (a) and (b) assist in determining whether a document is a trust document or not given their circularity of reasoning.

Should a document pass the 'Salmon test' the Court of Appeal held that the beneficiaries may still be prevented from seeing the document. In essence there was a convergence of views that disclosure should be discouraged unless it was positively shown that there had been bad faith or an improper exercise of discretion by the trustees. This argument has an air of circularity about it since disclosure may be necessary to determine where the discretion has been exercised bona fide or not.

3.6 PROFESSIONAL ADVISERS

There has been an increasing need for professional advisers in occupational pension schemes, because of the ever-increasing complexity of the legislation and benefit structures. There have been concerns, however, as to whether the role of the professional adviser is adequately defined and whether there is enough interaction between the various advisers. The Goode Committee thought that although 'the bulk of evidence . . . indicated that . . . most professional advisers to occupational pension schemes are governed by codes of practice issued by their respective professional bodies, there is still a need for their roles, duties and responsibilities to be clearly set out in client agreements and made known to all interested parties' (para. 4.8.9). The Committee also said that there was concern about the accountability of professional advisers and the terms upon which they discharge their duties, and that there was an increasing role for advisers in monitoring scheme administration.

Actuaries play a central role in earnings-related schemes and it is a statutory requirement that actuarial advice be obtained and valuations, statements and certificates prepared by the actuary. It has been thought that the actuary has a responsibility to both the employer and the trustees and is required to have regard to the interests of scheme members and others who may rely on his advice. The actuary depends on the receipt of relevant information to perform his task and one of the problems was that prior to the PA 1995 there was no explicit statutory duty upon anyone to provide any information to the actuary. Furthermore if the actuary found any irregularities there was no one to whom he had a duty to report this.

The auditor's role is to carry out such work as is necessary to form an opinion as to whether the accounts the trustees have prepared are accurate. It has not always been clear who appoints the auditor and to whom the auditor is responsible.

Section 47 therefore deals with the appointment, role and responsibilities of professional advisers (i.e., auditors, actuaries, fund managers and legal advisers). The trustees or managers of the scheme are required to appoint an individual or firm as an auditor and an individual as an actuary — s. 47(1). Section 47(2) places a responsibility on the trustees or manager to appoint a fund manager where the scheme has investments within the meaning of the Financial Services Act 1986. Clearly the trustees could themselves act as fund manager if authorised to do so under the Financial Services Act 1986. Section 47(3) says that ss. 3 and 10 PA 1995 apply to any trustee who, in exercising any of his functions, places reliance on the skill or judgment of any person who is appointed, other than by the trustees or managers, to exercise prescribed functions, or who is appointed as fund manager or legal adviser, and s. 10 applies to a manager who places reliance on such a person. The prescribed functions could include those carried out by a custodian or a pension consultant. It is difficult to see in what circumstances a fund manager, for example, could be appointed to the scheme by someone other than the trustees. Apparently this subsection gives OPRA the power to sanction any trustee who places reliance on the skill or judgment of advisers appointed other than by the trustees, but apparently the government has said that it is not intended that such appointments will be made! The intention is to catch any situation in which someone may have purported to appoint an adviser other than via the trustees and to ensure that the trustees do not rely on advice from such a person. Trustees have no defence for their actions if they have relied on an adviser they have not appointed.

Section 47(5)(a) says that regulations may be made to allow exceptions to the requirements under s. 47(1)(a) and (b) to appoint an individual or firm as an auditor or an individual as an actuary. Regulations made under this subsection will exempt schemes from the requirement of appointing an auditor if they are not required to obtain audited accounts under the PSA 1993 and the Occupational Pension Schemes (Disclosure of Information) Regulations 1986 (SI 1986/1046). Under reg. 7 of SI 1986/1046 the trustees of any scheme shall obtain, as soon as reasonably practicable and in any event not more than one year, after the end of each scheme year audited accounts for that scheme year, but the regulation does not apply to public-service pension schemes. Any regulations made under s. 47(5)(a) PA 1993 will also exempt defined-contribution schemes from having to appoint a scheme actuary, since such schemes do not have to obtain actuarial valuations.

Section 47(5)(b) allows regulations to be made which specify the qualifications and experience, or approval required for appointment of a professional adviser. Regulations 7(3) and 8(6) of SI 1986/1046 are currently the regulations that specify the qualifications required by persons who are appointed to prepare the audited accounts and actuarial valuations. An auditor must be a person who is eligible for appointment as a company auditor under s. 25 of the Companies Act 1989 or a person approved by the Secretary of State. The auditor must not be a member or a trustee of the scheme he is auditing, nor can he be a person employed under a contract of service by the trustees of the scheme, nor the employer of any member of the scheme who is in relevant employment. Where such an employer is a company, the auditor cannot be a person who is ineligible by virtue of s. 27 Companies Act 1989. An actuary must be a fellow of the Institute of Actuaries or Faculty of Actuaries, or a person with other actuarial qualifications who is approved by the Secretary of State at the request of the trustees. The power to make the regulations was contained in s. 114 PSA 1993 but that was repealed by the PA 1995 in which s. 47(5)(b) gives power to the Secretary of State to make similar provisions to those in the Disclosure Regulations, but these provisions apply to all professional advisers.

Section 47(6)(a) allows regulations to be made about the manner in which the trustees of a trust scheme may appoint and remove professional advisers. The regulations will require that the trustees draw up clear terms of engagement for professional advisers and that these terms will define the role and responsibility of the employer, the trustees and the adviser. Section 47(6)(b) allows regulations to be made specifying the terms on which the trustees of a trust scheme may appoint professional advisers, including the manner in which such advisers can resign.

Section 47(9)(a) permits regulations to be made to place a duty on employers and their auditors, and actuaries engaged by the employer, to disclose information to the trustees or managers and professional advisers of the scheme. Section 47(9)(b) says that regulations can be made to impose a duty on the trustees or managers to disclose information and make documents available to the scheme's professional advisers.

Where no auditor or actuary has been appointed to the scheme under s. 47 then ss. 3 and 10 apply to any trustee who has failed to take all such steps as are reasonable to secure such appointment and s. 10 applies to a manager who has failed to take all such steps to secure compliance — s. 47(8) (see chapter 2). Subsections (10) and (11) of s. 47 ensure that employers pass relevant information to trustees and that trustees pass relevant information to their advisers. OPRA can impose a civil penalty under s. 10 on an employer, or anyone acting as an auditor or actuary to an employer who fails to disclose information to the trustees or the scheme's professional advisers. The subsections also allow OPRA to impose a fine and disqualification on any trustee or a fine on any manager who fails to disclose information to the scheme's professional advisers. The information that must be disclosed will be set out in regulations under the powers contained in s. 47(9). The information is that which the trustees or professional advisers will need to carry out their duties under the Act.

Section 48 places a duty on the actuary or auditor of any trust scheme to report any irregularities ('blow the whistle') to OPRA if he has reasonable cause to believe that any duty relevant to the administration of the scheme has not been or is not being complied with and the failure to comply is likely to be of material significance in the exercise by OPRA of any of its functions. The report must be in written form. However, the meaning of the phrases 'reasonable cause' and 'material significance' in s. 48(1) is unclear. 'Reasonable cause' does suggest that the actuary or auditor must have a degree of knowledge which can be either actual or constructive. The term 'material significance' is even more difficult to define as it is attempting to distinguish between cases where there is a minor breach and those where there is a serious breach. Presumably further guidance on this may be provided by the Institute and Faculty of Actuaries and the accountancy institutes. The section fails to lay down a time limit for this written report. Section 48(1)(a) says that regulations may prescribe persons, in addition to the trustees or managers, the employer and any professional adviser, who should be reported to OPRA if they fail to comply with any duty in relation to the administration of the scheme. The duty of client confidentiality is relieved by s. 48(3), so that neither the auditor or actuary who 'blows the whistle' will be in breach of that duty.

Section 48(7) says that any actuary or auditor who fails to comply with s. 48 can face civil penalties under s. 10.

OPRA also has power under s. 48(8) to disqualify an auditor or actuary from being an auditor or actuary of any scheme which it specifies in an order where the auditor or actuary has failed to comply with s. 48(1) or (2). The order that OPRA can make under s. 48(8) may just refer to the scheme to which the failure relates, all schemes falling within a certain class or description or all occupational pension schemes — s. 48(9).

OPRA may, where a disqualified person makes an application, revoke the order made under s. 48(8) where OPRA are satisfied that he will comply with s. 48(1) in future — s. 48(10).

A person who purports to act as an auditor or actuary of an occupational pension scheme specified in the order while he is disqualified is guilty of a criminal offence and is liable to a fine of no more than £5,000 on summary conviction and a fine or imprisonment or both on conviction on indictment — s. 48(12). The overall effect of this section on the role of the actuary and auditor of the scheme, it is believed, is to make such individuals proactive in ascertaining any problems that the scheme might have and such a role is essential to the overall effectiveness of the Act.

Section 48(1) imposes a duty on the actuary or auditor to whistle-blow and this should be contrasted with the discretion that is placed on others to whistle-blow under s. 48(4) and (5) (see below). One of the reasons for such a distinction is that actuaries and auditors are involved in certifying the health of the scheme both for the members and for outsiders and as such their position is very different from others involved with the scheme and hence a duty to whistle-blow should be placed on them.

Subsections (4) and (5) of s. 48 encourage others involved in occupational pension schemes to whistle-blow and strengthens the Act's whistle-blowing provisions to a wider group of people. Section 48(4) says that in an occupational pension scheme any professional adviser (other than the auditor or actuary), any trustee or manager or any person involved in the administration of the scheme *may* report if he has reasonable cause to believe any duty relevant to the administration of the scheme is breached and failure to comply is likely to be of material significance in the exercise by OPRA of any of its functions. Section 48(5) says that no duty to which the adviser, manager or trustee is subject is regarded as contravened merely because of any information contained in a report under this section. This provision ensures that those involved in running the scheme will be protected from being sued for breach of confidentiality if they report a matter to OPRA. Such a section is necessary to protect individuals who may be employees of the employer sponsoring the scheme and whose contract of employment may contain confidentiality clauses which might otherwise inhibit them from reporting matters of concern to OPRA. The section does not apply to any information disclosed in a report by the legal adviser of an occupational pension scheme if he is entitled to refuse to produce a document containing the information in any proceedings in court on the ground that it is the subject of legal professional privilege. Thus by this provision solicitors are specifically exempted from the function of whistle-blowing under legal professional privilege. The reason for this is that those involved in the running of occupational pension schemes are entitled to expect lawyers to treat their exchanges in confidence.

3.7 RECEIPTS, PAYMENTS AND RECORDS

Section 49 of the PA 1995 imposes requirements in relation to the administration of trust schemes. These requirements are as follows:

(a) Contracted-out schemes are already required to set up a separate bank account but many small funds which are not contracted out do not have a separate pension scheme bank account. The Goode Committee said, 'We can see no reason for any distinction between contracted-out and non-contracted-out schemes' and went on to say '. . . we believe that trust funds should be protected regardless of a scheme's position in relation to the State scheme' (para. 4.8.75). Section 49(1) reflects this proposal and says that trustees are required, except in certain prescribed circumstances, to keep money they receive in a separate account at a bank, building society or institution authorised under the Banking Act 1987. Regulations will exempt certain schemes where, for example, the employer pays money directly to an insurance company where the existence of a separate bank account would be unnecessary.

(b) There is a duty under the general law of trusts that trustees must keep a proper set of accounts. This has been supplemented in the case of occupational pension schemes by the Accounting Standards Committee's Statement of Recommended Practice (SORP 1) and SI 1046/1986.

When something goes wrong with the pension fund administration, however, it is often found that the accounts and other records are seriously inadequate or defective. Therefore s. 49(2)(a) allows regulations to be made to require the trustees of an occupational pension scheme to keep records of their meetings (including meetings of any of their number). Section 48(2)(b) allows regulations to be made requiring the trustees of any trust scheme to keep books and records relating to any prescribed transaction. Where the requirements of subsection (1) and (2) are not complied with then ss. 3 and 10 apply to a trustee who has failed to take all such reasonable steps as are reasonable to secure compliance (see chapter 2).

Section 49(3) allows regulations to be made requiring the employer and any prescribed persons (for example, a fund manager) acting in connection with the scheme to keep, in a prescribed manner, books and records relating to any prescribed transaction. Section 49(4) says that regulations may be made which prescribe the form and manner in which the books and records in s. 49(2) and (3) are to be kept. Where the requirements of subsection (3) are not complied with then s. 10 applies.

(c)   Section 49(5) confers power to make regulations prescribing the time limit within which employers must pass on the payment of benefits made on behalf of trust schemes to members. Where such a payment is not made within the prescribed time limit employers must place the fund into a separate account with a bank, building society or institution authorised under the Banking Act 1987.

(d)   Section 49(8) allows regulations to be made to prescribe time limits within which employers who have deducted employees' contributions from earnings must pay them over to the trustees or managers of the scheme. Where this is not done then the employer is guilty of an offence and is liable on summary conviction to a fine not exceeding the statutory maximum and on conviction indictment to imprisonment or a fine, or both.

3.8   SCHEDULE OF PAYMENTS IN MONEY PURCHASE SCHEMES

In a money purchase scheme the pension is linked to the amount of the contributions paid into the scheme, and timely payment of contributions is essential to the proper running of the scheme. The Goode Committee recommended that a schedule for due dates of payments should be agreed between the employer and the trustees so that the trustees could monitor timely payment and pursue non-payment or late payment. Section 87 PA 1995 requires the trustees or fund managers of money purchase schemes to ensure that there is in place a payment schedule and that it is revised from time to time. (There is a corresponding provision in s. 58 of the Act, for defined benefit schemes). Section 87(1) allows regulations to be made to exempt some schemes, for example, some small self-administered schemes. Section 87(2)(a) requires contributions to the scheme to be shown on the schedule. Section 87(2)(b) allows regulations to be made requiring other amounts which are payable to the scheme to be shown on the payment schedule. Included in this payment schedule will be levy payments to be made by trustees under s. 165 (see 4.6). Section 87(2)(c) requires the schedule to show the dates on or before which the payments of the contributions are to be made. Section 87(3) requires the payment schedule to satisfy prescribed requirements. Regulations will be made which will require schemes that are contracted out by virtue of satisfying s. 9(3) PSA 1993 to state the amounts for employees' maximum payments (as defined in s. 8(2) PSA 1993) separately in the payment schedule.

Section 87(4) leaves the trustees in no doubt about how the matters in the payment schedule should be determined. The matters shown in the payments schedule, to the extent that the scheme makes provision for their determination, must be so determined and where the scheme makes no such provision they must be matters that are either previously agreed between the employer and the trustees or managers of the scheme or if there is no such agreement matters determined by the trustees or managers of the scheme.

Section 87(5) says that where s. 87 is not complied with s. 3 applies to a trustee who has failed to take such steps as are reasonable to secure compliance and s. 10 applies to a trustee or scheme manager who has failed to take such steps (see chapter 2).

Section 88 requires the trustees or managers of a fund to which s. 87 applies in circumstances where any amounts payable in accordance with the payment schedule have not been paid on or before the due date, to give notice of that fact, within a prescribed period, to OPRA and to the members of the scheme.

It is hoped that the prescribed period will be fairly short because of the nature of money purchase schemes.

Section 89 says that where money purchase schemes fall within a certain class or description then regulations may prescribe for the provision of ss. 56 to 60 to apply in a modified form.

Section 90 inserts a new subsection (3A) into s. 124 PSA 1993 which clarifies the application of s. 124 in the case of a money purchase scheme. The section provides that where an employer becomes insolvent and there are unpaid contributions to the scheme then an application can be made to the Secretary of State for payment of the amount due to the scheme within certain limits. It applies to money purchase and final salary schemes and the amendment clarifies the way in which the amount claimed is limited when the scheme is a money purchase scheme.

The original s. 124 was designed to protect the public purse and prevent the payment of claims for unpaid contributions which would result in the production or increase of a surplus in the scheme. The limit within s. 124 is the smallest of the following:

(a) the unpaid contributions relating to the 12 months before the date of the insolvency;
(b) the amount certified by an actuary as necessary for the scheme to meet its liability on dissolution of payment of benefits to or in respect of the employees; or
(c) an amount equal to 10 per cent of the remuneration paid or payable to the employees concerned for the 12 months preceding the employer's insolvency.

Many actuaries have felt unhappy about completing a certificate under (b) above because, given the design of a money purchase scheme, the extra amount needed to allow the scheme to meet its liabilities would be nil. Hence the amendment omits the second of the three amounts.

3.9   MISCELLANEOUS PROVISIONS

Section 31 of the PA 1995 bars a trustee from being indemnified from scheme assets for any fine imposed for an offence of which he is convicted, or a civil penalty under s. 10 of the Act or s. 168(4) PSA 1993. Where a trustee is reimbursed out of fund assets for a fine or penalty and he knows or has reasonable grounds to believe that he has been reimbursed as such he is guilty of an offence — s. 31(4). The trustee is then liable to a fine not exceeding the statutory maximum on summary conviction or imprisonment or fine or both on conviction on indictment.

Section 115 PA 1995 deals with offences by corporate bodies, partnerships and unincorporated associations. Where an offence has been committed with the consent or connivance of, or is attributable to the neglect of, a director, manager, secretary or other similar officer of a body corporate then the person so acting as well as the body corporate is guilty of an offence. This deals with the situation where the trustees themselves are directors of a trust company.

Section 155 PA 1995 amends s. 168 PSA 1993 and inserts penalties for failure to provide information to the Registrar or knowingly or recklessly providing the Registrar with incorrect information.

Chapter 4
The Pensions Compensation Board

4.1 INTRODUCTION

The provision of compensation in the UK, whether by relief provided as a measure of legal redress, State or industry-backed initiatives, can at best be described as piecemeal and lacking in coherence. In one sense, the provision of a financial compensation mechanism for losses incurred by occupational pension schemes is evidence of this and this is demonstrated by the 'disaster relief' approach to the losses incurred by Maxwell schemes (Goode Report, para. 4.1).

There are powerful arguments in the pensions field for a compensation scheme to cover losses incurred to schemes in certain circumstances. Sections 78 to 86, 110 to 114 of and sch. 2 to the PA 1995 establish and delineate the powers of a compensation mechanism, the Pensions Compensation Board (the PCB). The scope for the PCB's operation will hopefully be limited given the Act's broader aims relating to scheme regulation and funding levels. Nevertheless, opportunities will always remain for the dishonest removal or negligent erosion of scheme assets. Before the PA 1995, there could be no redress for losses to a scheme by way of compensation for the ultimate benefit of the members. A member's recourse was through the general law and this is not an entirely satisfactory situation.

One argument for combating the opportunity for such losses would be to require members to exercise greater involvement and vigilance in their schemes, for example, where active or deferred members transfer the value of their accrued rights to some other basis of pension provision. Further, the involvement of professional advisers and the integrity of the trustees themselves would ensure that the risk of loss was reduced and this is bolstered by the Act in relation to the duties placed upon trustees and professional advisers. This simple, yet attractive view underestimates the degree of protection that would be provided. For example, for members with pensions in payment, there is no way of transferring the pension value elsewhere. In any event, it must be conceded that no system will or can be foolproof. Rather than substitute greater scheme protection for a compensation scheme, the ethos of the Act is to provide a financial safety net in those (hopefully rare) situations when loss occurs.

From the employer's perspective, the existence of a compensation scheme may have a number of unfortunate side-effects. It may undermine the role of the employer in ensuring scheme security and in some instances facilitate the exercise of the employer's influence over the trustees in terms of the manner of investment as there may be a willingness to take greater risks with investment to seek higher returns — with the knowledge that a compensation scheme exists to cover the losses. However, the strength of these arguments is diminished given the Act's provisions relating to minimum solvency and trustees' and professionals' duties. A number of the side-effects of a compensation scheme were recognised by the Goode Committee (see Goode Report, paras. 4.11.13 to 4.11.26), which nevertheless went on to recommend the establishment of a compensation scheme (recommendation No. 120). This recommendation was embraced by the government in its White Paper (paras 1.40 and 1.41).

All of the issues considered in relation to the PCB overlap, but in broad terms we can consider the compensation mechanism established by the Act under a number of heads:

(a)   The PCB; constitution, procedure and powers.
(b)   Risks and schemes covered.
(c)   The amount of compensation.
(d)   The raising of funding.

4.2   THE PCB: CONSTITUTION, PROCEDURE AND POWERS

4.2.1   Constitution

Section 78(1) PA 1995 establishes the PCB which, like OPRA discussed in chapter 2, is established as a body corporate and is in terms of perception distanced from any department of State by being denied the status, privilege and immunities of Crown servants or agents. Additionally the PCB's property is not regarded as property held by or on behalf of the Crown (sch. 2, para. 1).

The PCB will consist of not less than three members all appointed by the Secretary of State, one of whom will be appointed as chairman (s. 78(2)). The government's White Paper envisaged that the compensation scheme would be administered by the Pensions Ombudsman (see para. 1.40), and whilst this is not specifically provided for in the Act, it remains theoretically possible for the Pensions Ombudsman to be made a member and be appointed chairman of the PCB. The strain and diversification of roles that this would place on the office of Ombudsman would, however, tend to militate against this approach.

In its original form, s. 78(3) only required of the Secretary of State that he consult with the chairman in relation to appointing other members to the PCB and did not require any prerequisites in terms of appointees emanating from, or as a result of consultation with, various representative bodies. Subsection (3) in its current form significantly enhances the consultative procedure for appointment of members. One member of the PCB must be appointed as a result of consultations between the Secretary of State and organisations who appear to him to be representative of employers' groups. Similarly, a further member must be appointed as a result of the Secretary of State's consultation with organisations appearing to him to be representative of employees. In both cases, the Secretary of State must also consult with the chairman. As with OPRA, pensioner groups are excluded from the consultation process. Other appointments to the PCB shall be as a result of the Secretary of State's consultation with the chairman (s. 78(3)). Members will hold or vacate office subject to the terms of the appointing instrument (sch. 2, para. 3). Where a member ceases to be or becomes chairman the Secretary of State may vary the terms of the appointing instrument so as to alter the date of vacating office (para. 4). This could be done, for example, to facilitate a transition between appointments. Resignation from membership of the PCB must be by written notice, signed by the resigning member, to the Secretary of State (para. 5). The chairman or any member of the PCB may be removed at any time by the Secretary of State by giving him written notice (para. 6). There is immense latitude given to the Secretary of State in the removal of the chairman or 'ordinary' member of the PCB as there are no requirements that the chairman or member be given any reasons for his removal from office or that particular conduct or inactivity will be a condition of removal, unlike members of OPRA.

The PCB, its members and its employees will not be liable in damages for anything done or omitted to be done by it in the exercise of its statutory functions, unless the relevant acts or omissions are done in bad faith (s. 78(7)).

Like OPRA, irrespective of the fact that the PCB is distanced from any department of State or Crown authority, it will be noted that in the constitution of the PCB, there is extensive State involvement. That involvement is enhanced by the provisions relating to remuneration of the members, appointment of staff to the PCB and their conditions of service which all require the determination or approval of the Secretary of State and, like OPRA, the PCB will be subject to the jurisdiction of the Parliamentary Commissioner for Administration (sch. 2, para. 9).

Public scrutiny of the financial performance of the PCB is ensured by an obligation placed on it that copies of its annual statement of accounts must be sent to the Secretary of State and the Comptroller and Auditor General within the specified timescale (sch. 2, para. 17(1) (c)). The accounts must contain information that has been prescribed by the Secretary of State with the approval of the Treasury (para. 17(2)). Once the Comptroller and Auditor General has examined the financial statement, he must certify and report as to his findings, and lay copies of each statement and of his report before Parliament (para. 17(3)). Furthermore, the PCB must prepare an annual report on its previous 12 months' activities which must be submitted to the Secretary of State, who is obliged to lay a copy of the report before Parliament (s. 79).

4.2.2 Procedure

Regulations may provide for procedure generally and the manner in which the functions of the PCB will be exercised (sch. 2, para. 12). However, the PCB must meet at least once in the first 12-month period. Thereafter meetings will be at the PCB's discretion, subject to an obligation to meet at least once in each successive 12-month period but the timetabling and frequency of meeting may of course be prescribed in regulations under the general power in para. 12. Paragraph 14(1) provides that the functions of the PCB may be exercised by any of their members as they determine but, by para. 14(2) they may not delegate the power:

(a) to determine whether s. 81 applies to an application under s. 82 (so that compensation may be payable);

(b)   to determine the amount of compensation payable under s. 83;

(c)   to determine whether any payment should be made or the amount of such payment under s. 84; or,

(d)   to exercise any functions prescribed in regulations.

The PCB may determine the quorum for its meetings and regulate its own procedure (para. 14(3)). Decisions must be by majority of members present (para. 14(4)). The PCB's freedom to regulate its own procedure is subject to any regulations promulgated under para. 12 and of course its proceedings must be consistent with its powers under the Act and the general law which may apply in particular circumstances, such as a duty to act with fairness (for example, by an application of the *audi alteram partem* principle; see Wade and Forsyth, *Administrative Law,* 7th ed., pp. 494–575, for a general discussion of its application to public bodies, though it should be noted that there are different strands to the principle, which differ in their application in this context). The PA 1995 provides for some aspects of fairness to be met by obliging the PCB, where it notifies a person of its decision on any matter that it may determine by formal hearing or on review, to provide a written statement of the reasons for the decision which will form part of the record of the PCB (para. 15). This can be compared with the procedure of OPRA in sch. 1, which does not impose such an obligation expressly, though it is right to point out that both OPRA and the PCB are subject to the supervision of the Council on Tribunals (see sch. 3, para. 21).

No vacancy in the membership of the PCB or defect in the appointment of any member will render any of its proceedings invalid (sch. 2, para. 16).

Any determination made by the PCB within its functions, for example, whether a scheme is eligible for compensation under the Act or the amount and terms upon which compensation is to be given, is final (s. 80(1)). We noted in relation to OPRA a similar provision and considered the view that such terms do not necessarily render such decisions inviolate. Notwithstanding this, the PCB may review any determination they have made either of their own volition or on application by a person whom the PCB consider has sufficient interest in the decision (which is flexible enough to permit bodies acting on behalf of persons — for example, trade unions) (s. 80(2) and (5)). The PCB may review the determination or any earlier review under s. 80(2)(a) if satisfied that there has been:

(a)   a relevant change in circumstances since the determination; or

(b)   the determination was made in ignorance of a material fact; or

(c)   it was based on a mistake as to a material fact; or

(d)   was erroneous in point of law.

It may also review a determination on any ground within a three-month period which it may extend (s. 80(2)(b)). The powers of the PCB on review extend to varying or revoking the earlier determination and substituting a different decision and it may deal with the issues as if they had arisen on the earlier determination. Accordingly, it is not bound by facts found by it on the earlier decision (s. 80(3)). Regulations will 'flesh out' the procedure to be adopted on review, including the application itself and may, for example, delineate time limits and the form that the application should take (s. 80(4)).

4.2.3 Powers to gather information

The PCB has powers to ensure that a two-way flow of information will be possible to facilitate its functions. These powers are similar in some respects to those provided to OPRA, but they do not provide for the PCB to obtain relevant information in the same coercive manner. This is entirely consistent with the role of the PCB but where necessary, criminal offences have been created to ensure that information properly requested by them is provided.

In relation to *any* trust scheme (though this should be understood to relate to any occupational pension scheme established under a trust — s. 124), documents relevant to the discharge of the PCB's functions held by a trustee, professional adviser, employer or any person who appears to the PCB to be a person who holds or is likely to hold relevant information, must be produced to the PCB where it gives written notice of this requirement (s. 110(1)). To comply with subsection (1), the documents must be produced in such manner, place and period as the notice may specify (s. 110(2)). If a document is not in legible form, then it must be produced in legible form (s. 110(3)).

A number of criminal offences are created in s. 111 in an attempt to enforce the requests of the PCB for documents under s. 110. To invoke these offences the requisitioned documents must be *relevant to the discharge* of the PCB's functions. There is nothing in the Act to suggest that, for example, the trustees of a scheme are required to establish that requisitioned documents are *not relevant* to those functions before deciding not to produce them. Whilst relevancy should not be difficult to establish, it is suggested that, given that the only sanction for non-production is the imposition of a criminal penalty and that nothing in the wording of the section seeks to require otherwise, it is for the PCB to establish the relevancy of a requisitioned document to its functions.

A person who, without reasonable excuse refuses or neglects to produce a document when required to do so will be guilty of an offence. This is triable summarily and on conviction, punishable by a fine not exceeding level 5 (s. 111(1) and (2)). There is nothing in the Act to suggest that the burden of establishing whether the non-production was without reasonable excuse is placed upon the relevant trustee etc. It is of course open for such a person to demonstrate that he had a reasonable excuse for not producing the document by, for example, demonstrating that the document was subject to legal professional privilege or would incriminate himself in accordance with the saving provisions in s. 112.

More serious offences may be committed where a person;

(a) knowingly or recklessly provides the PCB with false or misleading information where that information is provided in circumstances where he:

(i)   intends; or,
(ii)   could reasonably be expected to know

that it would be used by the PCB for the purpose of discharging its functions under the Act; or

(b) intentionally and without reasonable excuse, alters, suppresses, conceals or destroys any document which he has been required by the PCB under s. 110 to produce.

A person committing one of these offences will be subject, on summary conviction, to a fine up to the statutory maximum, or on conviction on indictment to imprisonment, a fine, or both.

Where the PCB has undertaken an investigation to discharge any of its functions under Part I, then it may publish a report (s. 113(1)). There is no specified rationale for the exercise of this power, other than that the PCB considers it appropriate in the case. It is hoped that this power will be used as part of a general policy of keeping members and interested parties informed. It is further hoped that in such situations the PCB will not be reluctant to place such material in the public domain given that such reports are, for the purposes of the law of defamation, absolutely privileged (s. 113(2)).

In general terms, the PCB will, like OPRA, interact closely with other statutory bodies. Accordingly, the PCB will, as a corollary of its functions, be required to both receive and disclose information received or obtained by it as part of its statutory role. The following provisions delineating these powers apply to the receipt and disclosure of information as permitted under s. 114 and do not affect or prejudice other methods of obtaining and disclosing information. Where it is necessary for the PCB to obtain information as part of the discharge of its functions, s. 114(1) contains a broad permissive power to enable certain persons in receipt of information as part of a statutory function to disclose this information to the PCB. This does not require such information to have been solicited. The disclosure must be for the purpose of 'enabling or assisting' the PCB with its functions. At this point it should be noted that unlike the powers relating to the receipt and disclosure of information by OPRA, there is no classification of information as 'restricted information' (see 2.10.2.2) and no restriction on the *type* of information that is disclosed either to or by the PCB. The determinant for disclosure broadly relates to the *purpose* for which information is received or disclosed (see also s. 114(3)).

One variation to the general authority to disclose information to the PCB relates to information that is held by the Inland Revenue or its officers and relates to any tax within the Commissioners' general responsibility. Such information can be disclosed to the PCB only in accordance with an authorisation given by the Commissioners of Inland Revenue (s. 114(2)).

The PCB is empowered by s. 114(3) to disclose information to certain persons whether received or gathered by them under any statutory provision, where that disclosure is for:

(a) any purpose connected with the discharge of their functions; or
(b) enabling or assisting the recipient to discharge any of his functions.

However, by s. 114(5), this does not apply to information obtained from the Inland Revenue. Such information may not be disclosed by the PCB unless:

(a) to, or with the authorisation of the Commissioners of Inland Revenue or Customs and Excise; or,
(b) with a view to instituting criminal proceedings under, or otherwise for the purposes of, the PA 1995, the PSA 1993 or similar provisions in force in Northern Ireland.

Information may be received by the PCB subject to some restriction on its use or subject to a total or partial restriction on its disclosure to any or a specified person. This restriction is not without force notwithstanding the statutory provisions referred to above, and the PCB is bound by the terms of such a restriction irrespective of the purpose for the disclosure (s. 114(4)).

The persons who can disclose information to the PCB under s. 114, or to whom the PCB can disclose include all the persons referred to in s. 114(7), which is broadly drafted to include, for example, any department of the government. This list may be extended where regulations prescribe other persons to whom the provisions relating to disclosure will apply.

4.3   RISKS AND SCHEMES COVERED BY THE COMPENSATION PROVISIONS

4.3.1   Risks

The Goode Committee considered at length what risks and what schemes should be covered by a compensatory mechanism. It was open to the Committee to consider that the mechanism should apply to losses caused to a scheme by any risk, including investment under-performance (see para. 4.11.28). This would, from a scheme member's perspective, be patently attractive. For an earnings-related scheme, this would provide an absolute safety net for the terms of the pension promise for losses however caused and to the extent of the shortfall in the entitlement. However, given provisions in the PSA 1993 that would require such shortfalls to be a debt due from the employer, an all-risks scheme would be rendered otiose for an earnings-related scheme. This view is of course subject to the employer's capacity to fulfil the debt. The Goode Committee concluded that the all-risks approach 'clearly [could not] apply to money purchase schemes'. This is on the basis that the investment risk is borne by the member. While this may be correct, given that the Committee was considering a mechanism for losses, including investment under-performance, it is not so obvious why on this view such a mechanism clearly could not apply.

Alternatively, compensation could be limited to loss caused by misappropriation covering fraud, theft and other misappropriation of scheme assets) and other breach of fiduciary duty. Losses to a scheme as a result of misappropriation are inevitably difficult to counter and, given the deleterious effects on scheme assets, can cause losses that are catastrophic to the scheme. Losses caused by a non-fraudulent breach of fiduciary duty can occur, for example, where the trustees are induced by the employer to make loans on a non-commercial basis or to invest in some form, beyond permissible limits, in the employer. The Goode Committee described this as 'more insidious' than deliberate loss through criminal activity. However, due to the controls on self-investment (see 3.2.6), and controls over trustees both under the general law and the measures under the Act, this type of loss should be minimalised. Nevertheless, the possibility remains that the trustees may, in making decisions of this nature, be induced, or themselves place, the survival of the employer to the fore. Though recognised by the Committee, this was seen as a legitimate trade-off for active members to make. This view is unfortunate. Perhaps given the context of the provisions relating to employer-related investments, the provisions under the Act relating to the composition and accountability of trustees and non-commercial or imprudent commercial loans, such a scenario is now better characterised as remote and not 'legitimate'.

The final option considered by the Committee was compensation for losses to a scheme caused solely by misappropriation. There was a general consensus that a compensation scheme must cover this type of loss, despite provisions of the PA 1995 which seek to make this type of loss difficult or, if attempted, discoverable at an earlier stage.

The Goode Committee commented, that none of these approaches is self-evidently the right one. However, if a compensation scheme is to be acceptable to a broad range of interests, it must provide a minimum level of safety for members at a minimum cost to the pensions industry and government. So the Goode Committee recommended a scheme that covered losses caused by misappropriation alone (see Goode Report, paras 4.11.37 and 4.11.38). The White Paper adopted this approach by limiting compensation to losses caused by:

> the dishonest removal of assets from a pension fund (including fraud, theft and other misappropriation) in cases where the employer is insolvent and unable to make good the loss (para. 1.40).

4.3.2 Schemes covered

All trust schemes are included within the compensation provisions of the PA 1995 as in principle there is no obvious reason why a particular type of scheme should be singled out and excluded. This point is given extra weight by the limitation of compensation payable to losses resulting from misappropriation and not, for example, losses from the under-performance of investments. On this basis, money purchase schemes are included within the provisions. However, regulations may be made to exclude schemes and the government is considering whether insured schemes should be excluded because they are already covered by the Policyholders Protection Act 1975. This cover does not, however, extend to losses caused by fraudulent diversion of contributions away from the insurance company or the monetary benefits remitted by the insurance company to a third party as paying agent. There is no obvious reason to exclude insured schemes.

4.4 APPLICATIONS FOR COMPENSATION

4.4.1 Procedure

An application for compensation is made under s. 82 PA 1995, which should be read in conjunction with s. 81. The application must be made in a manner and provide all the information that the PCB will require (s. 82(2)). Amongst other things, information will be required that is relevant to the PCB's determination of whether the compensation provisions are applicable and the amount of compensation payable. Two issues arise from this section; first, who may apply and second, the relevant time period for applications.

4.4.2 Who may apply?

This, like many other facets of the Act, will be determined by regulations (s. 82(1)).

4.4.3 Time limits

The application must be made in what the Act refers to as the 'qualifying period' (s. 82(3)). This is the period of 12 months, which may be extended by the PCB, that begins from the later of:

(a) the insolvency date — that is the date upon which the employer became insolvent;

(b) when the auditor, actuary or trustees of the relevant scheme knew or ought reasonably to have known that a reduction in the value of the scheme assets has occurred and which there are reasonable grounds for believing is attributable to an act or omission which makes up a prescribed offence (see s. 82(4) which incorporates by reference s. 81(3) and (1)(c) respectively).

The definition of prescribed offence is left to regulations, but it is envisaged that this will relate to the fairly broad notion of misappropriation covering fraud, theft and other misappropriation of scheme assets that was envisaged by the Goode Committee (see Hansard, HC Standing Committee D, 13 June 1995, cols. 529–530). These provisions will not apply to schemes which sustain losses by misappropriation before the commencement of the section as in each case the relevant qualifying periods noted above will be a period after the 'appointed day', that is, the day on which the section is brought into force (see s. 82(4) and 81(3)(b)).

4.4.4 Scheme eligibility

Whether a scheme is eligible for compensation is to be determined by application of the criteria in s. 81, all of which must be met in the relevant circumstances. To emphasise the limitations that may be placed upon the type of scheme that is eligible, ss. 81(2) and 86 provide for regulations to prescribe exceptions to the provisions for certain types of scheme and for the modification of the provisions as they may apply to certain schemes. Nevertheless, s. 81 is drafted in seemingly broad terms (subject of course to regulations) to provide for a scheme to be eligible for compensation if:

(a) it is a trust scheme;

(b) the employer is insolvent (applying the meaning of insolvency in s. 123 of the PSA 1993 — see s. 81(8));

(c) the value of scheme assets has been reduced and there are reasonable grounds for the PCB to believe that this was attributable to an act or omission that constitutes a prescribed offence;

(d) where the scheme is a salary related scheme immediately before the date of the date of the application for compensation, the value of the scheme is less than

90 per cent of the amount of the liabilities of the scheme (i.e., below the minimum solvency level);

and, as an overriding feature of the PCB's determination of whether these provisions apply even if the above are met:

(e)   it is reasonable in all the circumstances that the members of the scheme should have assistance by the PCB paying such amounts as is determined in accordance with the compensation provisions.

The trustees cannot rest and rely on compensation from the PCB, they must attempt to mitigate the scheme's losses themselves. The trustees have an obligation to obtain any 'recoveries of values', provided this can be done without disproportionate cost and in a reasonable time (s. 81(5)). This may not necessarily obviate the trustees from securing an increase in the scheme assets by legal action but is designed as a 'longstop' provision to preclude such action being a prerequisite of compensation payments. 'Recovery of value' means any increase in the value of the assets attributable to any payments received by the trustees (other than from the PCB) in respect of any act or omission reasonably believed to constitute a prescribed offence to which the reduction in the value of the scheme assets for which compensation is sought is attributable (s. 81(3)(f)). The Act makes it clear that it is the PCB who may determine whether the payment received is a recovery of value as defined above (s. 81(4)).

4.4.5   Anticipatory payments

Section 84 of the PA 1995 sensibly allows the PCB to make anticipatory payments to schemes where there has been an application for compensation under s. 82. This is desirable not only to secure the level of scheme assets so that pensions in payment can be maintained but also over a period of time it will allow the PCB to asses the scheme properly and identify losses accurately. Additionally, given that the PCB may make payment on such terms and conditions as are appropriate (see s. 78(4)), it could as a condition of anticipatory payment (or final), require, for example, the trustees to take specific steps to recover lost assets. Such steps would, however, have to be proportionate in terms of cost and time.

Before making an anticipatory payment the PCB must consider that the criteria for applicability of the compensation scheme under s. 81 apply or may apply to the application, and that the trustees would not otherwise be able to meet liabilities that fall into a prescribed class (s. 84(1)). An anticipatory payment cannot be made unless the PCB has not at that time determined the 'settlement date' (s. 84(1)). This is the date that the PCB considers, after consulting with the trustees of the scheme, to be a date after which further recoveries of value (see 4.4.4) are unlikely to be obtained without a disproportionate cost or within a reasonable time (s. 81(3)(d)). The amounts of anticipatory payments payable will be determined in accordance with regulations (s. 81(2)).

The caveat to these anticipatory payment provisions is that in certain circumstances the PCB may recover some or all of the payment as they consider to be appropriate (s. 84(3)). This may arise where the PCB subsequently form the opinion that:

(a) section 81 does not apply to the application; or
(b) that the amount of payment was excessive.

In any event, the payments to the scheme will form part of the trust and the PCB may only seek recovery from the scheme.

4.5 THE AMOUNT OF COMPENSATION

Section 83 of the PA 1995 specifies the amount of compensation that may be paid by the PCB either as a one-off payment or a series of payments to the trustees. The PCB must have determined that s. 81 applies to an application for compensation under s. 82.

Section 83(2) provides for the amount of compensation to be determined in a manner prescribed under regulations. The government intends that the regulations will also specify the way in which compensation payments are to be calculated. The payments must take account of any anticipatory payments made under s. 84. The PCB is required to give a written notice of their determination to the person who has made the application for payment and (if different) to the trustees.

Section 83(3) makes provision for the amount of the payment or payments. The maximum amount payable is 90 per cent of the loss at the date of the application (plus interest to the settlement date), subject to a maximum for salary-related schemes of an amount required for the fund to meet the 90 per cent solvency level at the 'settlement date' (see 4.4.5). For example, in the case of a salary-related scheme, the fund has £200m assets and £150m worth of liabilities on the statutory solvency basis. £100m of assets are stolen leaving the fund with £100m. The fund needs assets of £135m to be 90 per cent funded on the statutory solvency basis. Therefore the compensation scheme pays £35m.

4.6 RAISING OF FUNDING

It was never the intention at any of the formulative stages of the Act to require the taxpayer to fund the compensation scheme (see the Goode Report, para. 4.11.67 and the White Paper, para. 1.43). A fundamental objection to this was that the general taxpayers would be supporting schemes in which they had no interest, rights or benefits. Schemes should be the source of compensation funds irrespective of the manner of funding chosen as in the Goode Committee's view 'there were two principal advantages to looking to schemes to fulfil [the funding role]'. First, schemes were more readily identifiable for this purpose, especially as the contributions would need to be based on the size of the pension fund or its membership. Second, in balance of cost schemes where ultimately the employer would pay, the amount of payment would be automatically smoothed over a number of years as part of the process of setting the general rate of contributions (Goode Report, para. 4.11.70). Indeed the White Paper expressed the government's concerns in keeping employers' and schemes' costs to the minimum and of achieving its policy objectives for a compensation scheme combined with lower costs to businesses (see para. 1.46 and app. 5, Draft Compliance Cost Assessment, para. 46). Therefore, whatever funding system that was embraced by the Act, it would be schemes which would be liable for funding. There were a number of options that could be taken and it is illuminating to consider these:

(a) Pool funding. The PCB could build up and manage a pool of money, raised by powers to levy schemes and by using its own borrowing and investment powers. This would provide for some predictability but as the Goode Committee pointed out, there are, *inter alia,* difficulties in quantifying the future risks relating to demands on the funds and thus the appropriate size of the fund.

(b) An annual levy. An annual levy of schemes and employers would be raised by the PCB to meet its expected expenditure for the forthcoming year. Where there was a surplus at the end of the year in the funds held by the PCB, this could be redistributed among the contributors. The difficulties that exist in relation to pool funding, apply equally here.

(c) Post-event levy on schemes. This is the method of funding of the compensation scheme that was suggested be chosen (see generally, s. 165 PA 1995 inserting new provisions in the PSA 1993). The evident attraction to this method is that the level of contribution can be set accurately to meet the expenditure of the scheme. Additionally, rather than pay contributions that may or may not be utilised, contributions could continue to be properly managed and invested by the scheme until required.

One related issue remains: upon what basis is the amount of levy to be set? The Goode Committee had sought to recommend a system that was 'liability based'. This meant that it would be based upon the proportion of the value of a scheme's liabilities required to meet its minimum funding requirement rather than the size of its assets. The alternative was a contribution based on the size of a scheme's membership. 'Liability based' was suggested as a better option because, first, the size of a scheme's membership is arbitrary in that it takes no account of funding levels; second, for the purposes of liability-based funding, the better funded scheme would pay a smaller proportion of its assets than would a scheme that is less well funded (see, for example Goode Report, para. 4.11.74). In money purchase schemes, it was suggested that contributions from the pension scheme to the compensation mechanism would be matched by the employer paying an additional contribution equivalent to the payment.

In any event, the government was not persuaded by these arguments and announced in its White Paper that the levy would be based on total scheme membership. This, it argues, will facilitate combined collection of levies (for funding both the PCB and OPRA), and would keep administrative burdens on schemes to a minimum (see para. 1.42). It also intends to levy for the compensation scheme on the basis of a flat rate per head across schemes. Accordingly, the funding of the compensation scheme will arise out of the general levy requirements of the new s. 175 of the PSA 1993 which in this respect will be payable to the PCB. Regulations will prescribe rates, times and deal generally with the minutiae of the funding provisions. To counter any shortfalls in its funds, the PCB is provided with power to borrow from any institution authorised under the Banking Act 1987 the sums it requires in the exercise of its functions, and such amounts may be capped by regulations (s. 78(5) and (6)). As a corollary of this, sch. 2, para. 2 permits the PCB to do anything that is calculated to facilitate the discharge of its functions, or is incidental or conducive to discharging them. In this respect, this may mean giving indemnities, guarantees or making any agreement or arrangement with or for the benefit of any person.

Where the PCB has a surplus in the funds it holds, the Secretary of State may, after consulting with the PCB, order that the surplus be distributed among occupational pension schemes. This power is exerciseable where the Secretary of State considers that such funds exceed that which is reasonably required for the PCB's purpose and the distribution may be made in a prescribed manner and subject to prescribed conditions (s. 85(1) and (2)). However, before this time, it is open to the PCB to invest any funds it holds (whether they are surplus to its purposes or not) in:

(a)   any investments at that time falling in Parts I, II or III of sch. 1 to the Trustee Investments Act 1961; or

(b)   in any prescribed investment.

Chapter 5
Minimum Funding Requirement

5.1 THE GOODE COMMITTEE AND THE MINIMUM SOLVENCY REQUIREMENT

Before the advent of the PA 1995 there was no general requirement to fund a scheme and hence no minimum level of funding for a funded scheme — although some schemes, such as local authority schemes, did have a requirement to be fully funded. Many arguments were advanced to the Goode Committee for *not* introducing any form of minimum solvency standard. These include:

(a)   A minimum solvency standard is unnecessary where the solvency of the employer is no way in doubt. If a scheme is wound up in deficit the employer has a statutory liability to make good the deficit — PSA 1993 s. 144 which was implemented by the Occupational Pension Schemes (Deficiency on Winding Up etc.) Regulations 1992 (SI 1992/1555). Nevertheless the fortunes of the employer may change over the lifetime of the scheme and the Goode Committee thought that the only way in which the risk of insolvency would be fully eliminated is if the scheme liabilities are fully underwritten by the State.

(b)   To insist on full funding at all times may place an overwhelming financial difficulty on the employer or make an adverse financial situation worse. Despite there being some force to this argument the Goode Committee said that to leave scheme members exposed to uncontrolled decisions of employers, which may be arbitrary, as to what accrued liabilities they could or could not afford at any given time, would be to 'drive a coach and horses' through a funding requirement. The Committee acknowledged that there may be times when the requirement should be relaxed but any relaxation of the funding requirement should be at the discretion of a pensions regulator.

(c)   There is no obligation on an employer to set up a scheme and therefore he should be free to decide the level of funding. While the setting up of a scheme is indeed a purely voluntary act the Committee thought that once a scheme was set up the pension promise should be properly secured.

(d)   The promise is to pay benefits to individual members at pension age and it is not necessary that there be sufficient assets to meet future as well as current needs at every point in time. This argument means that if the scheme is wound up at a given point in time when the employer is insolvent, future pension rights that have already accrued by service would be unsecured.

(e)   The act of setting up a minimum solvency standard would rapidly result in that becoming the maximum level to which employers would fund and this may result in less security for schemes. The Committee thought, however, that even though no minimum solvency requirement is required above that needed to secure guaranteed minimum pensions (GMPs), the majority of schemes are funded to a level sufficient to meet their accrued liabilities.

Despite these arguments the Goode Committee concluded in their report that it was desirable for a minimum solvency standard to be introduced for all funded schemes in the UK. The Committee said that whenever there was a risk, however small, of an employer's insolvency then the funding of the scheme will only meet the requirements of the benefit security if at all times the assets of the scheme are sufficient to cover its liabilities. A minimum solvency standard is necessary to ensure that the rights of scheme members are adequately protected against the insolvency of the employer when the scheme is in deficit. This minimum solvency requirement (MSR) should ensure that, irrespective of what is happening to the employer, the fund will have enough money to meet the value of members' accrued rights which will therefore be protected. Funding is a necessary condition of security but it will only be adequate if the funding process is flexible enough to respond to changes in both assets and liabilities (Goode Report, para. 4.4.9).

The subsequent White Paper endorsed the Goode Committee's view that a minimum solvency standard be introduced. The White Paper said that a minimum solvency requirement would not only reinforce confidence that accrued rights will be protected but also provide a basis and a yardstick for setting a schedule of contributions to maintain an appropriate level of funding, thus providing a key measure for trustees in maintaining and managing the scheme and for giving clear information to members regarding the health of the scheme.

Throughout the Act's passage through Parliament the problems of the type of MSR envisaged by Goode and the White Paper were highlighted. These problems include the following:

(a)   The solvency of a scheme on an ongoing basis and the solvency of the scheme on the basis of immediate discontinuance are totally different. A scheme's solvency on an ongoing basis is defined by the relationship between the assets of the scheme and the projected benefits for service to date, i.e., its liabilities. The scheme's assets will usually include a substantial investment in equities, which, although subject to fluctuation and hence a degree of risk, have provided a return greatly exceeding the return on other assets over the last several decades. In the case of a scheme's winding up and discontinuance, its solvency is defined as the cost of buying an insured non-profit annuity for pensioners and deferred pensioners. Hence the ongoing scheme is evaluated in terms of equity and the discontinuance scheme in terms of insured non-profit annuities.

The Goode Committee recognised this dilemma. It said:

Schemes which are comfortably funded on an ongoing basis may well have insufficient assets to meet their discontinuance liabilities by the purchase of annuities. In an ongoing fund even sharp fluctuations in the price of equities at a particular time are of little significance, since the values are based on the anticipated income stream of a notional portfolio over the life of the scheme. But where an ongoing scheme has to be valued for testing its solvency on a discontinuance basis, the relevant figure is the market value of the particular investments at the time of the valuation. If there has been a sharp fall in the market, the solvency of the scheme will be correspondingly reduced. At the same time, the cost of purchasing annuities is not responsive to variations in the market value of the equity-orientated portfolio of a typical ongoing scheme. (Goode Report, Cm 2342-I, para 4.4.30.)

(b)   The market for the purchase of annuities with insurance companies is extremely limited. Firms of actuaries have, even in cases where the assets are of the order of £100m, been able to find only three companies willing to give a quote.

(c)   The object of the MSR, as envisaged by Goode, was to ensure that schemes are solvent on discontinuance. If schemes are required to be truly solvent, however, and this means have sufficient assets to purchase insured annuities to cover benefits, then this could cause serious economic problems for the pensions industry. For in such a situation MSR:

> could force intrinsically healthy schemes to reduce benefits and increase contributions substantially in order to meet liabilities on a hypothetical discontinuance which in the ordinary way would be very unlikely to occur. A scheme's investment managers might feel constrained to move from an equity-based to a fixed-interest or index-linked portfolio so as to be certain of covering its wind-up liabilities, with the likelihood that over the long term, it would lose both income and the prospects of capital growth, and the benefits would go down. (Goode Report, Cm 2342-I, para. 4.4.31).

Thus a true MSR would result in higher costs and lower benefits. The CBI calculated that the cost to employers of the Goode Committee's proposals would be at least £1.2 billion per annum over the 12-year implementation period.

The problem with the Goode Committee proposal is that it tried to achieve two objectives that were incompatible. It argued for there to be assets to meet long-term commitments, while at the same time arguing for immediate protection against the possibility of disaster. The test was too onerous for the first objective and too weak for the second. As a result the MSR introduced by the PA 1995 represents a somewhat watered-down version of a true MSR, allowing for, *inter alia,* an equity base for younger members and a gilts base for those approaching retirement. In addition both the Institute of Actuaries and the Faculty of Actuaries in Scotland have objected to the use of the term MSR — for a solvency requirement that is not based in gilt yields cannot be a true solvency test. Hence the government have changed the term MSR to minimum funding requirement (MFR).

5.2   FUNDING TEST

MFR is intended to provide security for members so that whatever happens to the sponsoring employer, the members can expect pensions in payment to continue and younger members can expect to receive a fair actuarial value of their accrued rights.

It is important to note that MFR interrelates with other parts of the Act in several different ways:

(a)   It interrelates closely with the compensation scheme. Without an agreed funding requirement, it is difficult to operate a fair compensation scheme as it is difficult to know how much compensation to pay to schemes.

(b)   It interrelates with the Act's provisions on contracting out. The changes to contracting out remove the guaranteed minimum pension and the solvency test on which contracting-out schemes were assessed. The new MFR therefore relates to the whole of the pensions promise.

(c)   It interrelates with the increased role of member-nominated trustees who need a benchmark by which to judge schemes.

(d)   It interrelates with the duty of the actuary in relation to a scheme who must provide a schedule of the contributions that has to be met and thus it interrelates with the duty of the regulator who must ensure that this happens.

The Act contains surprisingly little detail about MFR. Only six sections in the Act deal with the concept. The Act merely lays down a framework for MFR which will be expanded by subsequent regulations. Section 56 PA 1995 says that every occupational pension scheme to which the section applies is subject to the MFR, i.e., 'that the value of the assets of the scheme is not less than the amount of the liabilities of the scheme' — s. 56(1). The provisions for MFR do not come into effect until 1997 and will not be fully in place until 2007. The section does not apply to money purchase schemes (see subsection 12) or to schemes exempted by regulations. This means that regulations will exempt schemes which provide benefits above the Inland Revenue limits or the earnings cap and schemes such as the local authority schemes which have a guarantee at least as good as the MFR. The section, however, hides the fact that an actuary can make a diversity of assumptions when choosing to calculate the funding level.

Section 56(3) allows regulations to be made which will set out the method of valuing the scheme's assets and liabilities for the purposes of the MFR. It is unclear which method of valuing the assets and liabilities will be chosen. In the White Paper a cash-equivalent approach for all members was suggested. Thus in the case of active and deferred members funding liabilities will be valued as the sum of the cash-equivalent transfer values, excluding the value of any discretionary benefits. In the case of pensioners, funding liabilities will be the value of providing pensions in payment; this would be based on appropriately dated gilts with a margin to account for the administration costs of running the scheme as if it had become closed. This method of valuation will provide a cash equivalent that is equity based for younger members, moving to a gilts base for pensioners and those approaching retirement. The value of any self-investment up to the legally permitted level is also included. Thus if a scheme which includes employer-related investments is forced to wind up because the company is going out of business then the proportion of the fund in employer-related investments would not be available to pay pensions due under the scheme, but it is used to calculate the MFR and counted among the assets of the scheme.

The assets of the scheme will be valued by reference to market values. Both the Goode Committee and the White Paper envisaged the assets and the liabilities of the scheme being calculated on a particular day. To do this makes the test particularly volatile, however, and may either create the need for unnecessary cash injections or give members a misleadingly optimistic view of their scheme. Therefore, the government has allowed for 'averaging', i.e., the solvency of a scheme is averaged over a period in order to smooth out the peaks and troughs and to present a more accurate picture.

One of the major problems with the cash-equivalent test chosen by the government is that it is likely to produce many undesirable changes in investment strategy — i.e., higher contributions and lower benefits. The reason for this is that the MFR is likely to result in a change in the pattern of investments from equities to gilts. Pension fund investments in the UK stock market account for nearly half of all equity investment. A significant swing to investment in gilts away from equities, even if made over the transition period, is likely to cause a significant fall in the value of UK equities, with all the likely repucussions on the UK economy. The government has conceded that large schemes may allow for a proportion (25 per cent) of equity investment when valuing the pension liability. This would make the test much easier to meet if a large part of the scheme liabilities relates to pensioners and the assets of the scheme are heavy in equities. Under the proposals in the White Paper such a scheme would have had to hold a margin above 100 per cent solvency to provide a cushion against a fall in equities relative to gilts. This margin is now less necessary. However, without such a margin there is a greater risk if the scheme is wound up that the assets of the scheme will be insufficient to meet pensioners' benefits.

5.3   SCHEMES AFFECTED BY THE MFR

A consultation exercise was conducted by the DSS to test the impact of the introduction of the new MFR as at 31 March 1993, on the assumption that schemes had to meet the test on that day. The DSS surveyed 500 company pension schemes and found that 86 per cent of those who participated should meet the MFR, and 96 per cent of all schemes who participated were more than 90 per cent funded.

The policy of most occupational pension schemes is to maintain a fund with regard to active members which is sufficient to cover the value of their accrued benefits based on earnings projected to retirement or even earlier. Discretionary benefits are also frequently funded in advance. Thus for most schemes the normal target fund will be in excess of that required to meet the MFR and most schemes will comfortably pass the MFR. The reason for this is that:

(a)   the MFR is based on the cash equivalents of early-leaver benefits, which are based on current earnings;
(b)   the MFR does not include the value of discretionary benefits; and
(c)   funding targets are frequently based on prudent assumptions.

If, however, a scheme were to adopt a less prudent funding target then that together with the requirement that deferred pensions to be increased in line with inflation up to a 5 per cent limit during the period of deferment and legislation requiring schemes to guarantee pension increases on benefits for service completed after 5 April 1997 may mean that the MFR would not be as comfortably attained as at first thought.

5.4 MONITORING SOLVENCY

Sections 57 and 58 PA 1995 introduce measures which enable the funding of a scheme to be monitored. These measures can be divided into:

(a) more frequent actuarial valuations;
(b) the keeping of schemes of contributions;
(c) annual funding checks.

Section 57 PA 1995 requires the trustees to obtain written valuations and certificates assessing the funding of the scheme from the scheme's actuary. Section 57(1)(a) allows regulations to be made specifying by when and at what subsequent intervals the trustees or managers of the scheme must obtain written valuations. Before the PA 1995, schemes were allowed up to three and a half years between valuations, but the White Paper recommended that the full actuarial valuation reports be made at intervals of no more than three years and an annual certificate of funding be provided in inter-valuation years. Section 57(1)(b) contains a power for regulations to be made specifying the occasions on which the trustees or managers of the scheme must obtain a certificate stating whether or not the contributions are adequate for the purpose of securing the minimum funding requirements throughout the period prescribed in the regulations, which is likely to be five years.

If the actuary in his certificate says that the contributions payable towards the scheme are not sufficient for the purpose of securing that the MFR is met throughout the prescribed period, or if the MFR is not met, then the trustees or scheme managers must obtain an actuarial valuation within a period of six months beginning with the date on which the certificate was signed — s. 57(2)(a) and 57(4)(a). Section 57(2)(b) allows regulations to be made specifying the circumstances in which the trustees or the scheme managers are required to obtain an emergency valuation. This valuation must be made within a prescribed period. This subsection will enable regulations to be made to require a valuation if, for example, the trustees or the scheme managers become aware of a sudden unexpected increase in the liabilities of the scheme which the employer has not previously agreed to fund through an increase in contributions due according to the schedule.

Any valuation or certificate obtained under s. 57 must be made in such manner, give such information and contain such statements as regulations will prescribe — s. 57(5).

Where a valuation or certificate is obtained under s. 57 the trustees or scheme managers must make it available to the employer within seven days of receiving it — s. 57(6).

If subsections (1), (2) or (6) of s. 57 are not complied with then ss. 3 and 10 apply.

Section 58 deals with the operation of the schedule of contributions, which is central to ensuring that schemes are funded at least to the level of the MFR, and the section also provides a means whereby the trustees can monitor the funding of the scheme. Section 58 places a duty on the trustees or the scheme managers to ensure that there is a schedule of contributions which shows:

(a) the rates of contributions payable towards the scheme by the employer and members; and
(b) the dates on or before which such contributions are to be paid.

Section 58(2) allows for regulations to be made specifying the detail of what should be shown in the schedule of contributions in addition to or in expansion of (a) and (b) above.

Section 58(3) enables regulations to specify the time limit for preparing the schedule of contributions. This is expected to be within two months of the date on which the actuarial valuation is signed. The schedule of contributions may be revised from time to time where the revisions are previously agreed by the trustees or the scheme managers and the employer and any revision is certified by the scheme actuary. It must be revised before the end of a prescribed period beginning with the signing of each subsequent actuarial valuation.

Normally the employer and the trustees would agree the rates of contributions to be entered in the schedule and hence s. 58(4) says that the matters included in the schedule of contributions must either be matters previously agreed by the trustees or the scheme managers and the employer. The section also provides for a fail-safe in the event of the employer and trustees being unable to agree on the rates of contributions.

Nevertheless the trustees should not be given a free hand to expose the employer to financial risk by misusing the power to set the contribution rate. Section 58 limits their discretion so that they cannot prescribe a rate that is more than adequate to comply with the MFR. Thus where no agreement about contribution rates exists, s. 58(4) provides that the schedule should show rates of contributions determined by the trustees or managers, being such rates as, in their opinion, are adequate for the purposes of securing that the MFR will continue to be met throughout the prescribed period or, if it appears to them that it is not met, will be met by the end of that period and any other matters determined by the trustees or managers.

In any case the contributions shown must be certified by the actuary of the scheme. Section 58(5) enables regulations to be made to specify the period in which an agreement must be reached between the employer and the trustees about the matters to be included in the schedule.

Section 58(6) relates to an actuary certifying the rates of contribution shown in the schedule of contributions. Where the last preceding actuarial valuation shows that the MFR was met on the date of the valuation, the actuary may not certify the rates of contributions shown in the schedule of contributions unless he is of the opinion that the rates are adequate for the purpose of securing that the requirement will continue to be met throughout the prescribed period, i.e., the period specified in s. 57(1)(b) of five years commencing with the previous valuation. In any other situation the actuary may not certify the rates of contributions shown in the schedule of contributions unless he is of the opinion that the rates are adequate for the purpose of securing that the requirement will be met at the end of that period.

Where the last preceding actuarial valuation shows that the MFR was not met on the effective date of the valuation, the actuary may not certify the rates of contributions shown in the schedule unless he is satisfied that each rate is such that, if subsequent rates were maintained at the same level, the requirement would be met at the end of the prescribed period — s. 58(6).

Section 58(7) allows regulations to be made to prescribe the circumstances in which OPRA may extend the time limits for the employer to restore the MFR.

Where s. 58 is not complied with then ss. 3 and 10 apply (s. 58(8)).

The role of the schedule of contributions is an important one. It has a purpose for well-funded schemes, as well as for those that might experience a shortfall from time to time. It will show clearly the amounts of the contributions and when they are due and the document will allow trustees and auditors to check that contributions are paid on time. It is important in that not only does it state the agreed rate at which a scheme should be funded but it also provides a means of monitoring the health of the scheme.

Section 59 provides for the enforcement of the schedule of contributions. Except in circumstances prescribed by regulations, where the amount payable by or on behalf of the employer or members in accordance with the schedule of contributions has not been paid on or before the due date the trustees or scheme manager should give notice of this, within the prescribed period, to OPRA and to the members of the scheme. It is thought that OPRA must be informed within one month and, if payment is still not made after three months, the members must be informed.

Any amounts which for the time being remain unpaid shall be treated as a debt due from the employer to the trustees or scheme manager, even if it is not so apart from by means of s. 59.

Where a scheme fails to achieve the MFR at the end of a period covered by its schedule of contributions then a report must be prepared by the trustees or scheme managers which will give information about the failure to meet the MFR. The information to be given will be prescribed by means of regulations and will be available to members.

If a scheme fails to comply with s. 59(1) or (3) then ss. 3 and 10 apply (s. 59(4)).

5.5 RESTORING FUNDING

The PA 1995 introduces a two-tier approach in cases where a scheme falls short of the funding levels. The two standards are first where the shortfall is less than 10 per cent, i.e., where the scheme is more than 90 per cent funded; and secondly where the shortfall is more than 10 per cent, i.e., where the scheme is less than 90 per cent funded. The problem with the MFR is that funding margins fluctuate and there is nothing necessarily wrong with that. In a well-managed fund they can fluctuate over a period of time between 85 per cent and 150 per cent without there being any threat to the fund. In the last quarter of 1987 portfolios lost up to 30 per cent of their value over a period of a few days and in 1994 the share index fell about 10 per cent over the course of a year. None of these events would prove a threat to a scheme that is well run — indeed they may provide the fund with an excellent opportunity to buy shares which will result in an overall gain to the fund at a later date.

Where a scheme is more than 90 per cent funded, ss. 58 and 59 say that the trustees must arrange a full actuarial valuation and agree with the employer a contribution schedule which is designed to restore the scheme to 100 per cent funding within a period of five years. These sections anticipate that in such a case the shortfall will be made up by an increase in contributions including employee contributions.

Section 60 deals with the position where the scheme falls below 90 per cent funding. In the White Paper it was proposed that the employer would have to make a cash injection to restore the scheme to at least 90 per cent solvency within three months. Such a proposal caused great controversy. The reason for this is that such a proposal demands a great injection of cash over a short period of time when the employer may not be in a financial position to make such an injection. The government therefore changed the time limit for restoring funding to 90 per cent in this case from three months to one year, and clearly after that ss. 51 and 52 apply to restore the scheme to 100 per cent funding. The extension of the period makes sense for two reasons. The first is that it gives the employer a greater amount of time to arrange the finance, and the second is that if the fall in funding is as a result of a depressed stock market then the longer period of time gives the market an opportunity to recover.

Section 60(2) contains a power to make regulations to provide for methods, other than cash injection to be used to restore a scheme to 90 per cent funding. Such options would include a bank guarantee or 'ring-fencing' unencumbered assets from other creditors in the event of an employer's insolvency.

If the 90 per cent funding is not achieved by the time limit of one year in s. 60(3) then s. 60(4) provides that the trustees or the scheme managers must notify OPRA and the scheme members within 14 days (which may be extended by regulations). Any shortfall shall, if not a debt due from the employer to the trustees or scheme managers apart from by virtue of s. 60, be treated as such.

Section 60(6) allows regulations to be made to determine the value of an increase in assets where this has been secured by an alternative method, such as a bank guarantee.

Section 60(7) contains a power allowing regulations to be made to prescribe the circumstances in which OPRA can extend the time limits for the employer to restore the scheme to 90 per cent solvency.

If s. 60(4) is not complied with then s. 3 and 10 apply (s. 60(8)).

Chapter 6
Winding up, Surpluses, Modification and Forfeiture

6.1 WINDING UP

6.1.1 Methods of winding up

The winding up of an occupational pension scheme can take place in a number of ways, namely:

(a) By means of ss. 11 and 12 PA 1995.
(b) By the collective agreement of all the beneficiaries if all are *sui juris* and entitled to the trust property — see *Saunders* v *Vautier* (1841) 4 Beav 115.
(c) By a court order.
(d) By means of a power contained in the trust deed and rules.

6.1.1.1 Pensions Act 1995, sections 11 and 12   Section 11 of the PA 1995 allows OPRA to direct or authorise an occupational pension scheme to be wound up. Before the advent of the PA 1995 the Occupational Pensions Board had similar powers to those contained in s. 11. One of the following conditions must be satisfied before s. 11 can apply:

(a) the scheme, or part of it, ought to be replaced by a different scheme; or
(b) the scheme is no longer required; or
(c) it is necessary in order to protect the interests of the generality of the members of the scheme that it be wound up.

Section 11(3) specifies the persons who can apply for an order on grounds (a) and (b) above. They are:

(a) the trustees or managers of the scheme; or
(b) any person other than the trustees or managers of the scheme who has the power to alter any of the rules of the scheme; or
(c) the employer.

OPRA should only need to direct the winding up of a scheme as a last resort. The power contained in s. 11 is there to prevent a bad situation from getting worse.

OPRA should not step in to wind up a scheme unless it is in difficulty and winding up is the only option available to protect scheme members' interests.

Section 11(2) says that an order can only be made by OPRA under s. 11(1)(a) or (b) in the following circumstances:

(a) if the winding up can only be achieved by means of that order; or
(b) the winding up could be achieved only by using an unduly complex or protracted procedure or one that involves the obtaining of consents which cannot be obtained; or
(c) the winding up could be obtained only with undue delay and difficulty.

Furthermore it must be reasonable in all the circumstances to make the order.

A direction to wind up may include directions with respect to 'the manner and timing' of the winding up — s. 11(4).

Section 11(6) says that winding up under s. 11 overrides any rule of law or clause in the trust deeds to the contrary.

Section 11(7) says that in an order to wind up public service pension scheme can only be made where necessary to protect the interests of the generality of the members of the scheme, i.e., on the grounds in s. 11(1)(c). Such an order may, if OPRA think it appropriate, adapt, amend or repeal any enactment in which the scheme is contained.

Section 12 re-enacts s. 143 PSA 1993. This permits the appropriate authority (i.e., the Minister or government department with responsibility for the scheme) to wind up a public service scheme that is being replaced or is no longer needed, if the scheme itself does not have an adequate wind-up power. In the absence of such a provision schemes would possibly have to be maintained when there are no longer active members, or indeed no members at all. It is pragmatic in such a situation to allow the appropriate authority to wind up the scheme and allow alternative provision to be made for any remaining deferred or pensioner members.

6.1.1.2   The rule in Saunders *v* Vautier   The rule in *Saunders* v *Vautier* is of little use in the case of an occupational pension scheme since the rights of the members are contingent.

6.1.1.3   Winding-up power in the trust deed or rules   The most common method of winding up an occupational pension scheme is to rely on the winding-up provisions contained in the trust deed and rules. The rules will usually give the employer the right to stop contributing to the scheme by giving notice of his discontinuance of contributions to the scheme and this may occur whether the employer is solent or insolvent. A solvent employer may wish to stop paying contributions in the case so as to cut costs, to merge the scheme with other schemes or to offer a different form of pension provision, for example, moving from a final salary scheme to a money purchase scheme.

On the cessation of a scheme the trustees usually have the option (given to them in the trust deeds and rules) to make the scheme a 'paid-up' (or frozen) scheme or to wind up the scheme. Very few schemes continue as paid-up schemes since there will be no employer's contributions to such a scheme and this will affect the prospect of continuing to run the scheme, unless, of course, it is in massive surplus.

Although technically the trustees have the power to wind up a scheme, it is the employer who has the actual power, since it is the employer who ceases to pay contributions to the scheme. This power of the employer to control the winding up of a scheme is a useful economic tool. The employer can choose the time of winding up to coincide with a time when the scheme is in substantial surplus and then claim to be entitled to the surplus. This point was discussed by the Goode Committee which was recognised that winding up can:

(a) act to defeat the expectations of the employees who believe that the scheme will continue up to, and beyond, their retirement; and
(b) fail to secure members' rights adequately.

Despite this the Committee said that employees cannot realistically assume that the scheme will continue until they retire, any more than they can assume that they will remain with the same employer until retirement. Furthermore it was said that the rights of members are now adequately protected by means of the newly introduced minimum funding requirement (see chapter 5).

6.1.2 Priorities

It is usual for a scheme to state the order of priority of benefits on winding up. This becomes very important where the scheme does not have sufficient assets to meet liabilities. Section 73 of the PA 1995 makes provision for applying the assets of a salary related scheme which is being wound up (provided that the minimum funding requirements apply to the scheme) to the discharge of specified preferential liabilities. The object of the section is to ensure that the liabilities covered by the minimum funding requirement (see chapter 5) are, so far as possible, secured and that the purpose behind the minimum funding requirement is not frustrated by any priority rules in a scheme allowing the assets to be distributed differently. Therefore the requirement of the scheme to meet the preferential liabilities in the section will ensure that a scheme which meets the statutory minimum funding requirement will, on winding up, attribute to each member the actuarial value of his or her accrued rights, including the right of indexation.

The section also deals with the situation where schemes wind up with less than the minimum funding requirement, or are otherwise unable to meet their liabilities in full. The priority order in that case attempts to ensure that there is a just distribution of assets.

By s. 73(3) the following liabilities must be satisfied first and in the following order:

(a) any liability for benefits or pensions which in the opinion of the trustees are derived from the payment by any member of the scheme of voluntary contributions;

(b) where a person's entitlement to payment of pension or other benefit has arisen, liability for that pension or benefit and for any pension or other benefit which will be payable to dependants of that person on his death but excluding increases to pensions;

(c) any liability for pensions which have accrued or any liability for the return of contributions to members with less than two years' pensionable service;

(d)   any liability for increases to pensions referred to in (b) and (c).

It may seem rather suprising that AVCs are ranked above increases in benefit levels. However, AVCs are made voluntarily and are an addition to normal pension payments. The government therefore believed that members making such payments should receive the benefit of them. If the contrary were so members whose rights are higher in the list of priorities would in effect receive the benefit of voluntary contributions paid by members whose rights are given a lower priority.

Section 73 overrides any contrary provision in the scheme documents — s. 117 PA 1995. Where the liabilities in any one of the categories (a) to (d) above cannot be satisfied in full, then the liabilities within that category must be satisfied in the same proportions — s. 73(2)(b) PA 1995.

Section 73(5) contains a power to prescribe in regulations the method of calculating and verifying liabilities. Section 73(4) says that any assets left over after satisfying the statutory priorities should be distributed according to the scheme rules.

Regulations may under s. 119 provide for the detailed actuarial valuation method and assumptions to be used and these are currently contained in Guidance Notes issued by the Institute of Actuaries and Faculty of Actuaries (Guidance Note GN 19).

Section 73(9) allows regulations to be made modifying s. 73 where only part of a scheme is being wound up, for example, by the sale of a subsidiary company.

Regulations may also be made to modify s. 73(3). The section does not apply to an occupational pension scheme which falls within a prescribed class or description.

If a scheme confers a power on anyone, other than the trustees or managers of the scheme, to apply the assets of the scheme in respect of pensions or other benefits then such a power cannot be exercised by that person, but may be exercised instead by the trustees or managers — s. 73(5).

Section 3 applies to a trustee who has failed to take all such steps as are reasonable to secure compliance with s. 73 and s. 10 applies to a trustee or scheme manager who has failed to take all such steps. (s. 73(6)).

There are several difficulties with s. 73. The first is how its provisions will interrelate with priorities in respect of GMPs. Although GMPs are to be phased out (see 9.2.2), schemes will still have to continue to provide for pre-1997 GMPs. It would seem that the GMP payment will continue to have a degree of priority on winding up, still behind AVCs but ahead of deferred and active pensioners. Future increases and revaluations of GMPs will, it seems, have a lower priority even if as a result of s. 73(4) the determination of liabilities reverts back to the scheme rules.

The second problem is that s. 73 fails to provide adequate protection for existing pensioners as it fails to provide for any increases in pensions in payment in line with any prescribed arrangement. Once pensions in payment have begun the only opportunity a pensioner usually has to improve his financial position is by means of increases to his pension in line with a formula prescribed in the scheme. The Act does, however, give the pensioner priority over active members and hopefully his position will be further strengthened by the fact that the actuarial valuation basis to be used in the calculation of liabilities under s. 73 will be consistent with MFR so that liabilities relating to pensioners will have to be valued by reference to the return on gilts.

Section 74 is a modified re-enactment of s. 95 PSA 1993 and deals with the discharge of liabilities on winding up. It gives the trustees greater flexibility if the liabilities of the scheme cannot be fully satisfied. In the past older schemes have merely provided for the discharge of liabilities solely by means of the purchase of annuities and this may not necessarily be the best way of securing a member's pension rights. The Act gives trustees several options for discharging liabilities. These are:

(a) The acquisition of transfer credits allowed under the rules of another occupational pension scheme which satisfies any prescribed requirements and whose trustees or managers are able and willing to accept payment in respect of the member. The present requirements are contained in the Occupational Pension Schemes (Transfer Values) Regulations 1985 (SI 1985/1931).

(b) The acquisition of rights under a personal pension scheme which satisfies any prescribed requirements and trustees or managers who are able and willing to accept payment in respect of the member's accrued rights. These requirements are at present contained in the Personal Pension Schemes (Transfer Payments) Regulations 1988 (SI 1988/1014).

(c) The purchase of one or more annuities which satisfy any prescribed requirements from one or more insurance companies chosen by the member which are able and willing to accept payment on account of the member from the trustees or managers. The prescribed requirements are currently those contained in SI 1985/1931.

(d) Subscription to other pension arrangements which satisfy any prescribed requirements. This caters for the possibility of a new form of pension vehicle which may arise at a future date.

By s. 74(2) the liability to a member is treated as being discharged if the trustees or managers of the scheme have, in accordance with the prescribed arrangements, provided for the discharge of the liability in one or more ways specified in s. 74(3). If the assets are insufficient to satisfy all the liabilities in respect of pensions and other benefits as calculated in accordance with the rules of the scheme, then the reference in s. 74(2) to providing for the discharge of any liability in one or more of the ways mentioned in s. 74(3) is to be read as applying any available amount (in accordance with s. 73) in one or more of those ways.

Section 74(5) provides that regulations may be made to modify the effect of s. 74 in relation to parts of benefit rights and in particular classes or descriptions of schemes. Section 74(1) provides a power to exempt particular classes or descriptions of scheme from s. 74. Secondary legislation will provide that individual members will have six months in which to consider the trustees' proposals, take advice and suggest an alternative if they wish.

Section 75 is a restatement (in essence) of s. 144 PSA 1993 and provides that when the scheme is in the process of being wound up or the employer is becoming insolvent, the deficiencies of the scheme are to be regarded as a debt owed by the employer to the trustees. The original s. 144 was introduced as a result of the Maxwell scandal and the deficiencies discovered in those schemes. With the minimum funding requirements in place there should hopefully be less need for schemes to resort to these provisions.

Section 75(5) contains a power for regulations to be made to prescribe a method of calculating the scheme's assets and liabilities. The intention is that such a method will be based on the method used to calculate the minimum funding requirement under s. 56(3). The regulations may, by s. 119, provide for the method to be to be in accordance with a Guidance Note produced by the Faculty of Actuaries and the Institute of Actuaries. Currently this is contained in *Retirement Benefit Schemes — Deficiency on Winding up* (GN 19). Section 75 does not apply to occupational pension schemes failing within a prescribed class or description — s. 75(9).

6.2   SURPLUSES

Where the totality of the assets of the scheme exceed the totality of the liabilities then an actuarial surplus exists. There is a difference between the computation of a surplus in an ongoing scheme and one that is being wound up.

The valuation of assets and liabilities of a continuing scheme involves a number of long-term assumptions and projections. The present value of an estimated future income is compared with an estimated value of future liabilities. Actuarial assumptions have to be made regarding earnings increases, price increases and return on investments. Demographic assumptions have to be made regarding mortality rates, rates of entry to and withdrawal from the scheme and the rates of early retirement.

The valuation of a scheme being wound up represents a 'snapshot' of the assets and the liabilities of the scheme at a point in time. The current value of the assets and the current cost of buying immediate annuities for pensions in payment and deferred annuities for active members have to be compared.

The existence and amount of a surplus in either situation will depend on the funding objective and the funding method which can vary from scheme to scheme. A surplus may result from using one actuarial method or set of assumptions, but may appear as a deficit if another method is used — see *LRT Pension Fund Trustee Co.* v *Hatt* [1993] PLR 227.

The courts have found it difficult to decide who should receive the surplus. The question depends on the view taken of the nature of the pension bargain between the employer and the employee. The employee would claim that a pension represents a form of deferred pay and there is some judicial support for this argument — see *Barber* v *Guardian Royal Exchange Assurance Group* (case C-262/88) [1991] 1 QB 344. There would also seem to be empirical evidence in the Committee of Inquiry into the Value of Pensions, *Report*, Cmnd 8147 (1981), to suggest that there is a downward adjustment in wages which is made to compensate for the contribution that the employer has to make towards the pension. The employer, however, would claim that there is an obligation on him to pay sufficient contributions to meet the liabilities of the scheme and if the scheme is in deficit then he will have to make good the deficit. So where the fund is in surplus he has overpaid the fund and thus the surplus should revert to him. There is also some judicial support for this view. Millett J in *Re Courage Group's Pension Schemes* [1987] 1 WLR 495 at pp. 514–15 seems to support this view, for there he said:

Such surpluses arise from what, with hindsight, can be recognised as past overfunding. Prima facie, if returnable and not used to increase benefits, they ought to be returned to those who contributed to them. In a contributory scheme, this might be thought to mean the employer and the employees in proportion to their respective contributions. That, however, is not necessarily, or even usually, the case. . . . Employees are obliged to contribute a fixed proportion of their salaries or such lesser sum as the employer may from time to time determine. They cannot be required to pay more, even if the fund is in deficit; and they cannot demand a reduction or suspension of their own contributions if it is in surplus. The employer, by way of contrast, is obliged to make such contributions if any as may be required to meet the liabilities of the scheme. If the fund is in deficit, the employer is bound to make it good; if it is in surplus, the employer has no obligation to pay anything. Employees have no right to complain if, while the fund is in surplus, the employer should require them to continue their contributions while itself contributing nothing. If the employer chooses to reduce or suspend their contributions, it does so ex gratia and in the interests of maintaining good industrial relations.

In deciding how a discretion over a surplus is to be exercised the courts are influenced by three factors:

(a)   The terms of the trust deed.

(b)   The fact that the beneficiaries of a pension scheme are not volunteers in the sense that the beneficiaries under a traditional trust are. In *Mettoy Pension Trustees Ltd* v *Evans* [1990] 1 WLR 1587, Warner J said at p. 1610:

[The members'] rights have contractual and commercial origins. They are derived from the contracts of employment of the members. The benefits . . . have been earned by the service of the members under those contracts and, where the scheme is contributory, *pro tanto*, by their contributions.

(c)   Whether the surplus exists in relation to a continuing scheme or one which is being wound up.

The PA 1995 has done very little to change the general principles of law relating to the distribution of surpluses, but has introduced new provisions for cases where a power is given to a person in the trust deeds to deal with surpluses but that person is not the trustee of the scheme. There are different provisions in the case of a scheme which is being wound up and a scheme which is not being wound up.

6.2.1   Surpluses on winding up

The PA 1995 s. 76 provides that if a scheme is being wound up and a power is conferred on the employer or trustees to distribute assets to the employer on winding up then the power cannot be exercised unless subsections (3) and (4) of s. 76 are satisfied. In order for s. 76 to apply the scheme must be an exempt approved scheme within the meaning of s. 592(1) ICTA 1988.

Section 76(3) sets out the conditions that must be met before a return of the assets to the employer. These conditions are:

(a)   The liabilities are fully discharged.

(b)   After the discharge of those liabilities, where there is a power in the scheme rules to distribute the assets to any person other than the employer, the power has been exercised or it has been decided not to exercise it.

(c)   The annual rates of pensions under the scheme which have commenced are increased by the appropriate percentage and this means the percentage specified in the last revaluation order made before the increase is to take effect as the valuation percentage for the last revaluation period of 12 months. The term 'pension' in this context does not include any GMP or increase in GMP or money purchase benefit as defined in s. 181(1) PSA 1993.

(d)   Notice has been given in accordance with prescribed requirements to the members of the scheme of the proposals to exercise the power.

(e)   Any additional prescribed requirements are satisfied.

Section 76(4) says that OPRA must be of the opinion that any prescribed requirements are satisfied and that the requirements of subsection (3) are satisfied.

Section 76(8) says that regulations may prescribe that s. 76 will not apply to certain schemes or will only apply to them with modification.

Where s. 76 applies to a trust scheme and if the trustees purport to exercise the power in s. 76(1)(c) without complying with the requirements of the section, then ss. 3 and 10 apply to any of them who have failed to take all such steps as are reasonable to secure compliance. Where a person other than a trustee purports to exercise the power without complying with the requirements of s. 76 then s. 10 applies to him.

Section 77 deals with cases of winding up when there is no power under the scheme rules to distribute the assets to the employer. Section 77 applies to a trust scheme satisfying the following conditions:

(a)   It is exempt approved under s. 592(1) ICTA 1988.

(b)   It is being wound up.

(c)   Any liabilities have been discharged.

(d)   Where the scheme contains a power to distribute surpluses to anyone other than the employer the power has been exercised or a decision has been made not to exercise the power.

(e)   Assets remain undistributed.

(f)   The scheme prohibits the distribution of assets to the employer in those circumstances.

In such a case the trustees must use the surplus to provide additional benefits or increase the value of any benefits subject to the prescribed limits, and then the trustees may distribute any excess assets to the employer.

The requirements of s. 3 apply to any trustee who has failed to take all such steps as are reasonable to secure compliance with s. 77.

6.2.2   Surpluses not on winding up

Section 37 PA 1995 provides that where (apart from by s. 37) a power is conferred on any person, other than the trustees, to make payments to the employer out of the scheme funds, the power cannot be exercised by that person, but can be exercised instead by the trustees. Any restriction imposed by the scheme on the exercise of the power shall, so far as capable of doing so, apply to its exercise by the trustees.

The scheme must meet certain conditions:

(a)   It must be one to which sch. 22 ICTA 1988 applies. This says that schemes must, as a condition of their approval, obtain an actuarial certificate giving information regarding any surplus based on the Inland Revenue's prescribed actuarial method and assumptions. If the actuarial value of the scheme's assets exceeds 105 per cent of past service liabilities worked out on the Inland Revenue's formula, the Inland Revenue will regard the surplus as excessive. Then contribution reductions or benefit improvements should have the object of eliminating surpluses over a period of five years. Before a return of the surpluses to the employer is considered the surpluses can be used for the following:

(i)   to provide benefit improvements;
(ii)   to provide a contributions holiday for the employer or the employees. Such a holiday should not be for a period in excess of five years unless a longer period is appropriate under reg. 11 of the Pension Scheme Surplus (Validation) Regulations 1987 (SI 1987/412);
(iii)   to make payments to the employer.

The administrator of the scheme is required to make proposals to the Inland Revenue to eliminate at least the excess of the surplus over 5 per cent.

The proposals to bring the surplus within the 5 per cent margin should be effective within either six months where (i) or (iii) above is used or up to five years where (ii) above is used.

Refunds are not permitted which reduce the surplus to less than 105 per cent.

(b)   The scheme is not one that is being wound up.

The power to exercise a discretion over surpluses under s. 37(1)(a) cannot be exercised unless the requirements of s. 37(4) are satisfied. These requirements are:

(a)   The Inland Revenue must have approved the proposals — s. 37(4)(a).
(b)   The trustees must be satisfied that it is in the interest of the members that the power be exercised in the manner proposed — s. 37(4)(b).
(c)   Where the power over surpluses is conferred on the employer, the employer must have asked for the power to be exercised, or consented to it being exercised in the proposed manner — s. 37(4)(c).
(d)   Pensions in payment must be increased by the appropriate percentage — s. 37(4)(c).
(e)   Prescribed notice must have been given to the members — s. 37(4)(d).

OPRA must be of the opinion that any requirements in s. 37(3) and (4) are satisfied — s. 37(5). Section 37(8) says that if the trustees purport to exercise the power referred to in s. 37(1)(a) without complying with the requirements of the section, ss. 3 and 10 apply to a trustee who has failed to take all such steps as are reasonable to secure compliance. If a person other than the trustee purports to exercise the power referred to in s. 37(1)(a) then s. 10 applies to him.

Section 37(10) gives a power to the Secretary of State to prescribe that s. 37 does not apply to certain schemes or that it will apply to them with prescribed modifications, for example, it may be modified when applying to industry-wide schemes with different employers so that each section is treated as a scheme in its own right.

Section 38 PA 1995 allows trustees to decide to allow a scheme to continue even where the scheme rules require it to be wound up. The rules of a scheme can require the trustees to wind it up when certain conditions are met, such as the insolvency of the employer, even though it may not be in the best interests of the members for this to occur. Many schemes stipulate that the liabilities with regard to the members must be discharged by the purchase of annuities, even when this would be prohibitively expensive and would result in members receiving much less than their entitlement. The trustees might prefer to wait and get a better financial deal for their members. Section 38 will allow them to do this.

If the trustees of a properly funded scheme allow it to continue then they should be able to discharge their liabilities gradually, as and when they crystallise. The trustees should continue the scheme as a frozen scheme only where it is in the best interests of the members to do so, and this means their decision to defer winding up would have to be constantly under review and they would have to wind up when it was no longer in the best interests of the members to continue.

Section 38 allows trustees to decide not to admit new members to the scheme, and to limit its continuing operation to the benefit of existing members. The trustees cannot, however, waive any provisions regarding indexing scheme benefits in order to make more funds available for all scheme members — s. 38(2).

Section 38 does not apply to a money purchase scheme, or a scheme falling within a prescribed class or description. This latter category would cover, for example, small self-administered schemes.

6.3   AMENDMENTS TO AN OCCUPATIONAL PENSION SCHEME

There are six ways in which an amendment to an occupational pension scheme can be made. They are:

(a)   By means of an express power of amendment.
(b)   ICTA 1988, s. 610.
(c)   Under the powers given to OPRA.
(d)   An amendment by the court.
(e)   Pension Act 1995, s. 68.
(f)   The rule in *Saunders* v *Vautier*.

6.3.1   Express power of amendment

It is usual when drafting an occupational pension scheme trust deed to include an express power of amendment in the deed. This is nothing more than common sense, since the circumstances in which the scheme is operating are changing, and the scheme may need to change to accommodate these circumstances. This power of amendment should be drafted as widely as possible and should include the ability to make amendments with retrospective force.

There are nevertheless a number of limitations on such a power of amendment:

(a)   Frequently there is an express proviso to the power of amendment which prevents the alteration of the main object or purpose of the scheme — see *Bullard* v *Randall* (unreported 22 March 1989).

Even if there is no such express proviso the courts seem to suggest that one is implied. See *Re Courage Group's Pension Schemes* [1987] 1 WLR 495, at p. 505, where Millett J said:

> The next question is whether the plaintiffs are entitled, if so minded, to join in executing the amending deeds. They may do so only if the proposed amendments are within the power to amend the trust deeds and rules, and can properly be made. They must not infringe the provisos to the rule-amending power, particularly the express prohibition to be found in all three schemes against altering the main purpose of the schemes, namely, the provision of pensions on retirement at a specified age for members. This is a restriction which cannot be deleted by amendment, since it would be implicit anyway. It is trite law that a power can be exercised only for the purpose for which it is conferred, and not for any extraneous or ulterior purpose. The rule-amending power is given for the purpose of promoting the purposes of the scheme, not altering them.'

The time for testing the legality of the change is the time of the proposed alteration, not the time when the original rules were drafted — see *Thellusson* v *Viscount Valentia* [1907] 2 Ch 1.

(b)   Section 519B(2) ICTA 1988 provides that where an alteration is made to an occupational pension scheme then no approval which has been given will continue to apply unless the alteration is now approved by OPRA, or the scheme is of a kind and the alteration of a type which does not require the approval of OPRA. Copies of the amendment must be forwarded to the PSO and approval obtained from the PSO.

(c)   The PSA 1993, s. 72, says that a scheme cannot contain any rule which results (or can result) in a member being treated less favourably for any purpose relating to short-service benefit than his corresponding treatment for long-service benefit. Thus no amendment to the scheme rules can be made to contravene s. 72.

(d)   The PSA 1993, s. 37, provides that the rules of a contracted-out occupational pension scheme may not be altered if the alteration will affect the provisions relating to the certification of occupational pension schemes, the effect on a member's State scheme rights and duties or the protection of increases in the GMP. Any such purported changes are void.

(e)   The PA 1995, s. 67, provides that a power to amend the scheme cannot be exercised on any occasion in a manner which 'would or might' affect any entitlement or accrued right of any member of the scheme which has been acquired before the power is exercised, unless certain requirements are satisfied. These requirements are:

(i)   The trustees must be satisfied that certain prescribed requirements have been met so that the power is not exercised in any manner which would in the opinion of an actuary affect the member of the scheme (unless he gives his consent) in respect of his entitlement before the power is exercised.

(ii)   Where the power is exercised by a person other than the trustees, the trustees must have approved the exercise of the power in that manner on that occasion.

Section 67 is not applicable to a public-service pension scheme.
The purpose behind s. 67 is twofold:

(a)   It is designed to provide protection against amendments to the scheme which would detrimentally affect the accrued rights of members. Therefore no amendments can be made without either an actuarial certificate stating that the amendment is not detrimental or the consent of each individual member is given.

(b)   It provides a practical measure to enable trustees to overcome the difficulty of untraceable members where the scheme rules require the consent of all the members.

The problem with s. 67 is the meaning of the term 'accrued rights'. Does it in a final salary scheme cover only benefits based on past service and current salary or does it include benefits based on past service and eventual final salary? It would seem that the government intend accrued rights, in this context, to mean only early-leaver rights.

6.3.2   ICTA 1988, s. 610

Section 610(3) ICTA 1988 states: 'In the case of a scheme which contains no powers of amendment the administrator of the scheme may, with the consent of all the members of the scheme, and of the employer (or each of the employers), make any amendment to which this section applies.'

The amendments to which section applies are set out in s. 610(1) of the Act and cover amendments that are necessary in order that the scheme qualifies for approval or provides the maximum permitted benefits.

6.3.3   Powers given to OPRA

Before the passing of the PA 1995, the Occupational Pensions Board was vested with various powers to authorise the modification of a scheme in order to achieve various purposes. With the abolition of the OPB, various powers have now been vested in OPRA with regard to the amendment of schemes.

Section 69 PA 1995 permits OPRA on an application 'by persons competent to do so' to modify schemes (except public-service schemes) for certain purposes. Regulations may be made under s. 69(2) to make provision about the manner of dealing with such applications.

Section 69(3) sets out the purposes for which OPRA is empowered to modify a scheme. OPRA may make an order under s. 69(3)(a) to modify a scheme to allow a payment to be made to the employer to reduce or eliminate a surplus. This power can only be exercised where s. 37(4) and any other prescribed requirements apply, see 6.2.2. OPRA may, under s. 69(3)(b), make an order to modify a scheme which is being wound up to enable the assets remaining after the liabilities of the scheme have been fully discharged to be distributed to the employer if prescribed requirement are met. Section 69(3)(c) allows a modification order to be granted to enable a scheme to meet contracting-out requirements. The reason for this is that some schemes which before the Act were contracted-out schemes, will not now qualify to contract out under the new requisite benefit test, and they do not have a sufficiently wide power of amendment. Thus OPRA is given the power to authorise the amendment of such schemes to allow them to comply with the new contracting-out provisions. This power will apply for a transitional period and regulations will be made to specify this.

The only persons who are competent to make an application for modification of the scheme are those specified in s. 69(4). In relation to amendments being made under s. 69(3)(a) and (b) they are the trustees of the scheme. In relation to amendments being made under s. 69(3)(c) the persons include the trustees or managers of the scheme, the employer, and persons other than the trustees or managers who have power to alter the rules of the scheme.

Section 69(6) allows provision to be made for s. 69 not to apply to certain schemes.

Section 70 provides that the s. 69 procedure can only be used where the result could not be achieved by any means other than by s. 69, or could only be achieved in accordance with a procedure which is likely to be 'unduly complex or protracted' or would involve 'the obtaining of consents which cannot be obtained or can only be obtained with undue delay or difficulty' — s. 70(1)(b). The extent of OPRA's powers to make an order under s. 70 is not limited 'in relation to any purposes for which they are exercisable, to the minimum necessary to achieve those purposes' — s. 70(2).

Section 71 provides that the power to modify under s. 69 can be applied to a scheme retrospectively — s. 71(1). An order may also be made despite any enactment, scheme rule or rule of law which operates to prevent the modification being made — s. 71(3)(a).

Section 72 empowers the 'appropriate authority' to make such modification of a public service scheme as could be made by an order of OPRA under s. 69(1)(b) to schemes other than public service schemes. The 'appropriate authority' means such Minister or government department as may be designated by the Treasury as having responsibility for the particular scheme in question — s. 72(2). Any order made under s. 72 may contain such supplementary and transitional powers as are appropriate.

This section brings forward powers currently contained in s. 143 PSA 1993, although it provides more restricted powers of modification than existed under the PSA. This is because most public service schemes are presently contracted out of SERPS and presumably will continue to remain so when the new contracting-out regime comes into effect. Such schemes would have no difficulty in meeting the new requirements without any amendment and hence the power to modify for contracting-out purposes will be rarely used.

6.3.4 Amendments by the court

A detailed discussion of this topic can be found in any standard work on trust law and is beyond the scope of this book. Amendments by the court may be made in one of the following ways:

(a)   Under the inherent jurisdiction of the court.
(b)   By the Variation of Trusts Act 1958.
(c)   By the Trustee Act 1925, s. 57.

6.3.4.1   Inherent jurisdiction   In the case of *Chapman* v *Chapman* [1954] AC 429 Lord Simonds LC said, at p. 445:

> There is no doubt that the Chancellor (whether by virtue of the paternal power or in the execution of a trust, it matters not) had and exercised the jurisdiction to change the nature of an infant's property from real to personal estate and vice versa, though this jurisdiction was generally so exercised as to preserve the rights of testamentary disposition and of succession. Equally, there is no doubt that from an early date the court assumed the power, sometimes for that purpose ignoring the direction of a settlor, to provide maintenance for an infant, and, rarely, for an adult, beneficiary. So, too, the court had a power in the administration of trust property to direct that by way of salvage some transaction unauthorised by the trust instrument should be carried out. Nothing is more significant than the repeated assertions by the court that mere expediency was not enough to found the jurisdiction. Lastly, and I can find no other than these four categories, the court had power to sanction a compromise by an infant in a suit to which that infant was a party by next friend or guardian *ad litem.*

It is highly unlikely that this jurisdiction will be used in relation to occupational pension schemes in any situation other than where there is an emergency in relation to the assets of the scheme.

6.3.4.2   Variation of Trusts Act 1958   Section 1(1) of the Variation of Trusts Act 1958 says that the court may:

> if it thinks fit by order approve on behalf of—
>
> (a)   any person having, directly or indirectly, an interest, whether vested or contingent, under the trusts who by reason of infancy or other incapacity is incapable of assenting, or
>
> (b)   any person (whether ascertained or not) who may become entitled, directly or indirectly, to an interest under the trusts as being at a future date or on the happening of a future event a person of any specified description or a member of any specified class of persons, so however that this paragraph shall not include any person who would be of that description, or a member of that class, as the case may be, if the said date had fallen or the said event had happened at the date of the application to the court, or
>
> (c)   any person unborn, or
>
> (d)   any person in respect of any discretionary interest of his under protective trusts where the interest of the principal beneficiary has not failed or determined, any arrangement (by whomsoever proposed, and whether or not there is any other person beneficially interested who is capable of assenting thereto) varying or revoking all or any of the trusts, or enlarging the powers of the trustees of managing or administering any of the property subject to the trusts:

Provided that except by virtue of paragraph (d) of this subsection the court shall not approve an arrangement on behalf of any person unless the carrying out thereof would be for the benefit of that person.

6.3.4.3 *Trustee Act 1925* The Trustee Act 1925 s. 57 provides:

(1) Where in the management or administration of any property vested in trustees, any sale, lease, mortgage, surrender, release, or other disposition, or any purchase, investment, acquisition, expenditure, or other transaction, is in the opinion of the court expedient, but the same cannot be effected by reason of the absence of any power for that purpose vested in the trustees by the trust instrument, if any, or by law, the court may by order confer upon the trustees, either generally or in any particular instance, the necessary power for the purpose, on such terms, and subject to such provisions and conditions, if any, as the court may think fit and may direct in what manner any money authorised to be expended, and the costs of any transaction, are to be paid or borne as between capital and income.

(2) The court may, from time to time, rescind or vary any order under this section, or may make any new or further order.

(3) An application to the court under this section may be made by the trustees, or by any of them, or by any person beneficially interested under the trust.

This section may be used where a transaction is not authorised in a deed, but the transaction is one that is expedient for the beneficiaries and concerns the trust fund.

6.3.5 Section 68 PA 1995

Section 68 PA 1995 is a necessary introduction because some scheme rules, as currently constituted, prevent trustees from modifying schemes in any way. In the absence of this section many trustees would be unable to comply, or would have great difficulty in complying, with the requirements of the Act. The section gives the trustees a power to modify schemes by resolution to achieve certain purposes.

These purposes are listed in s. 68(2) and include:

(a) extending the class of beneficiaries who can receive benefits under the scheme on the death of a member of the scheme;

(b) enabling a scheme to conform with s. 16(1) or 17(2) (see 3.2.2);

(c) enabling the scheme to comply with any terms and conditions imposed by the PCB in relation to a payment made by them under s. 83 or 84 (see chapter 4);

(d) allowing a scheme to conform with s. 37(2) (see 6.2.2), s. 76(2) (see 6.2.1), s. 91 (see 6.4.1), or s. 92 (see s. 6.4.2);

(e) any other purpose prescribed by regulations.

A modification made under category (a) above requires the consent of the employer.

Section 67 does not apply to schemes falling within a prescribed class or description. This provision is specifically designed to cover two existing British

Coal pension schemes which will become closed schemes and which can only be modified by the Secretary of State, although clearly the provision can cover other schemes in future.

6.3.6   The rule in *Saunders* v *Vautier*

See 6.1.1.

6.4   ASSIGNMENT AND FORFEITURE OF PENSION RIGHTS

6.4.1   Assignment

In a traditional trust the beneficiary usually has the right to deal with his interest in any way he wishes and he can, for example, assign it or use it as security in order to obtain a loan. The position is modified in the case of a pension fund trust by statute (see for example, s. 159 PSA 1993, which says that any assignment, or charge, and any agreement for an assignment or charge with regard to GMPs and entitlements to payments giving effect to protected rights are void. See also PSA 1993, s. 77) and express clauses in the trust deed or rules which prevent a member from using his interest in this way. Where a member does attempt to use his pension right in such a manner, the benefits will cease to be payable, except at the discretion of the trustee.

The main reason why there is a prohibition against the member dealing with his pension rights during his lifetime is that the purpose of a pension scheme is not to build an assignable asset but to provide a means of economic support for the member upon his retirement and for his dependants on the member's death. If a person fails to build up such pension rights then the State may have to provide economic support in retirement. Therefore approval of a scheme by the Inland Revenue is conditional on a provision in the trust deed or rules preventing the assignment or surrender of a pension except within certain limits allowing for commutation of the pension or an allocation of the pension to provide for a widow, widower or dependant.

Other jurisdictions, such as Canada, for example, have recognised the fact that pension rights should only be used for the purposes for which they were established and have provided in their legislation (see s. 65 Ontario Pension Benefits Act) that every transaction purporting to assign, charge, anticipate or give as security money payable under a pension plan is void — although there are certain statutory exceptions. The PA 1995 has followed the example of such jurisdictions and s. 91 provides that, except in certain circumstances, where a member is entitled to a pension or has an accrued right under an occupational pension scheme then such an entitlement or right cannot be assigned, commuted, surrendered, charged or have a lien exercised in respect of it and no set-off can be exercised over it. The section gives effect to the Goode Committee's recommendation that the immunity from creditors currently conferred on contracted-out benefits should be extended to cover all occupational pension entitlement or accrued right to pension benefits. However, once pension benefits are payable they can be accessed by creditors in the same way as other income. GMPs and payments giving effect to protected rights are the exception to this. An agreement altering the effect of s. 91 is unenforceable — s. 91(1).

Section 91(3) provides that where a bankruptcy order is made against a person, any entitlement or right of his which by virtue of s. 91 cannot, except by subsection (5), be assigned, is excluded from his estate for the purpose of Parts VIII to XI of the Insolvency Act 1986.

Section 91(5) lists the situations in which s. 91(1) does not apply and these are as follows:

(a) an assignment in favour of the member's widow, widower or dependant;
(b) A surrender, at the option of the member, for:

(i) providing benefits for the member's widow, widower or dependant; or
(ii) acquiring for the member entitlement to further benefits under the scheme.

(c) A commutation:

(i) of the member's benefit at or after normal pension age or in exceptional circumstances of serious ill-health;
(ii) in circumstances prescribed by regulations of any benefit for the member's widow, widower or dependant;
(iii) in any other circumstances as may be prescribed.

(d) Subject to s. 91(6), a charge or lien on, or set-off against the member's pension entitlement (except to the extent that it includes transfer credits), or accrued rights, for the purpose of enabling the employer to discharge some monetary obligation due to the employer by the member and arising out of a criminal, negligent or fraudulent act or omission by the member.

(e) Subject to s. 91(6), except in prescribed circumstances, a charge or lien on, or set-off against, the member's entitlement or accrued right to pension for the purpose of discharging some monetary obligation due from the person to the scheme and arising either out of a criminal, negligent or fraudulent act or omission by him or, in a trust scheme of which the person is trustee, arising from a breach of trust by him.

Without this provision s. 91 could override the principle in trusts law of impounding a beneficiary's interest, i.e., recovering trust debts from the beneficiary, where the beneficiary has caused a breach of trust or by a criminal, negligent or fraudulent act or omission.

The words arising out of a criminal, negligent or fraudulent act or omission' mirror the existing words in s. 79 PSA 1993. If there is any dispute about the amount of the debt and the circumstances surrounding it the dispute will have to be settled by a court or an arbitrator. Generally an arbitrator can only get involved where both parties agree, although some trust deed rules contain an arbitration clause.

Despite s. 91 the court may still make either an attachment of earnings order under the Attachment of Earnings Act 1971 or an income payments order under the Insolvency Act 1986 (s. 91(4)). Section 91(6) contains a power to specify how the value of a member's pension entitlement or accrued rights under a scheme should be determined for the purposes of s. 91(5)(d) or (e). The amount of the charge, lien or set-off should not be greater than the amount of the monetary obligation in question or, if less, the value of the member's pension entitlement or accrued right and the member must be given a certificate showing the amount of the charge, lien or set-off and how it affects his benefits. If there is a dispute about the amount of the charge, lien or set-off then such a charge, lien or set-off cannot be exercised unless it becomes enforceable under an order of a competent court. The powers contained in this section replace those of ss. 21(1) and 77(5) of the PSA 1993.

6.4.2 Forfeiture

Usually the trust deed or scheme rules will contain a forfeiture clause which provides that pension rights are forfeited on an attempted alienation or bankruptcy of the member or his misconduct, and this misconduct can be totally unrelated to the employment. The clause can even provide for the pension rights of an ex-employee to be forfeited. The clause will also contain a proviso to allow the trustees in the case of an attempted alienation to make pension payments to the member's spouse or dependant. Such a clause is valid provided that it goes no further than limiting the conditions in which future entitlements arise and does not confer a power to forfeit pension rights that are already in payment. See *Brandon* v *Robinson* (1811) 18 Ves 429; *Edmonds* v *Edmonds* [1965] 1 WLR 58. The reason why most schemes contain such a clause is to ensure that pension rights are not treated as a disposable asset.

A measure of protection is given to GMPs and short-service benefits. GMPs can only be forfeited where the scheme member is convicted of treason or an offence under the Official Secrets Acts 1911 to 1989 for which he has been sentenced to at least 10 years' imprisonment. HM Forces pension schemes have extended forfeiture of GMPs to cover the situation where a member has committed an act which is gravely prejudicial to the defence, security or other interests of the State in the opinion of the Secretary of State. In private-sector schemes forfeiture of short-term benefits is governed by similar rules to forfeiture of GMPs generally. In public-service schemes a benefit can be forfeited if a member is convicted of an offence if the offence was committed before the benefit became payable where a Minister of the Crown certifies that the offence was gravely injurious to the State or liable to lead to a serious loss of confidence in the public service.

The scheme rules may, however, allow an employer to exercise a charge or lien against a member's short-service benefits (except to the extent that it includes transfer credits) in order to obtain a discharge of a monetary obligation due to the employer by the employee, if such an obligation arises from a criminal, negligent or fraudulent act or omission by a member — PSA 1993 s. 79(2).

Employers do not set up occupational pension schemes to benefit creditors of members and so most schemes will contain a clause which provides for pensions not in payment to cease if an attachment of earnings order or bankruptcy order is made against the member. Therefore there is no asset or pension capable of being attached and made available to creditors. If, however, the pension is one that has already come into payment then the income in the hands of the scheme member is available to creditors, except to the extent that it is either in the form of GMPs and protected rights which cannot pass to a trustee in bankruptcy (PSA 1993, s. 159) or GMPs which cannot be the subject of an attachment of earnings order (Attachment of Earnings Act 1971, s. 24(2)(f)).

Section 92 PA 1995 provides that, except in certain circumstances, an entitlement or accrued right to a pension cannot be forfeited. The section basically extends the protection given to GMPs, protected rights and short-service benefits to 'long-service benefits'. The section does not prevent forfeiture where the bankruptcy of the person entitled to the pension or whose right to it has accrued has occurred whether this occurred before or after the pension has become payable, or where a transaction or purported transaction under s. 91 is of no effect — s. 92(2) PA 1995.

Where an act of forfeiture mentioned in s. 92(2) occurs, any pension which was or would be payable if the forfeiture had not occurred may at the discretion of the trustees or scheme manager be paid to any or all of the following:

(a)   a member of the scheme to whom the pension was or would become payable;
(b)   a spouse, widow or widower of the member;
(c)   a dependant of the member;
(d)   any other person falling within a prescribed class.

Section 92(4) provides that forfeiture is allowed where certain offences have been committed if they are committed before the pension becomes payable. These offences are:

(a)   offences of treason;
(b)   offences under the Official Secrets Acts 1911 to 1989 if the member has been sentenced to a term of at least 10 years;
(c)   any additional offences that may be prescribed by regulations.

Section 92(6) contains a power to specify other circumstances where forfeiture is allowed.

Section 92(1) PA 1995 (subject to subsection (2)) does not prevent a person's entitlement or accrued right to a pension being forfeited where the person has incurred a monetary obligation to the employer due to a criminal, negligent or fraudulent act or omission by that person. Such a right can only be forfeited to the extent that it does not exceed the amount of the monetary obligation in question — s. 93. Forfeiture of this kind can only take place where there is no dispute about the amount in question unless the monetary obligation became enforceable under a court order.

Section 95 PA deals with pension rights on bankruptcy. The object of the section is to prevent abuse by a bankrupt of the statutory protection offered to occupational pension rights under s. 92(2). The Act provides that all pension rights under occupational pension schemes will be protected from creditors. A trustee in bankruptcy acting on behalf of creditors can only gain access to the rights by applying to the court for an income payments order against income which is payable from the pension fund to the bankrupt.

Some debtors may use this statutory protection to defeat creditors. Such people may try to place the assets beyond the reach of creditors by putting them in an occupational pension scheme. Section 95 inserts a provision into the Insolvency Act 1986 which will enable a court, on application by a trustee in bankruptcy, to order recovery of some or all occupational pension contributions which have been made in the five years preceding the bankruptcy. The court can only make such an order when it believes the contributions were excessive in that they unfairly prejudiced the interests of the creditors. The court will have a discretion to decide whether contributions should be recovered and in so doing will be required to take into account certain criteria such as:

(a)   whether any of the contributions were made by or on behalf of the debtor for the purpose of putting them beyond the reach of his creditors;
(b)   whether the total amount of contributions made during the relevant period was excessive given the debtor's circumstances at the time of the payment;
(c)   whether the level of benefits under the scheme, together with those under any other occupational pension scheme to which the debtor is entitled or likely to become entitled is excessive.

The amount of recovery will usually be limited to the amount of contributions that are excessive. The court must, however, take account of any fall in the value of contributions to make sure that the scheme does not suffer any loss.

Section 94 contains powers to make regulations to modify or disapply ss. 91 to 93 in certain cases. Section 94(1)(a) contains a power to modify ss. 91 to 93 in the case of public service schemes and other prescribed schemes. Regulations under s. 91(1)(b) will only be made if there is confirmation that there are schemes which should be exempted from s. 91 to 93.

The Act has done nothing, however, to deal with the position that occurs when a scheme document contains a provision which allows the trustees to cease or reduce paying pensions to a member's widow or widower in the event of his or her remarriage or cohabitation — although the scheme rules cannot deprive a widow of her GMP on remarriage at, or after she has reached, the age of 60 (at present), or the remarriage of a widower of his GMP on remarriage at or after he has reached the age of 65. These provisions reflect the principle that the purpose of a pension scheme is to provide security in retirement for the member and his dependants. Nevertheless the Goode Committee thought that once a widow's or widower's pension had started to be paid it should continue, irrespective of remarriage or cohabitation. It said, 'Entitlement to a dependant's pension is a right which has been paid for and to which the surviving spouse's personal situation is irrelevant.'

6.4.3 Forfeiture and divorce

The law governing pensions and divorce until the provisions of the PA 1995 come into force (and according to s. 180 these provisions will come into force on a day chosen by the Lord Chancellor and will be brought into effect by statutory instrument) is contained in s. 25(2) Matrimonial Causes Act 1973. This section states that the court shall in particular have regard to the matters set out and para. (h) states: 'in the case of proceedings for divorce or nullity of marriage, the value to each of the parties to the marriage of any benefit (for example, a pension) which, by reason of the dissolution or annulment of the marriage, that party will lose the chance of acquiring'. Thus the court must take into account the fact that a divorced spouse's expectations and contingent rights will be lost. The court has done this in three ways. First the court has been able to ensure that the pensioner's spouse receives compensation for the loss. See, for example, *Milne* v *Milne* (1981) FLR 286 where the court ordered the husband to pay a deferred lump sum equal to half the amount which was ultimately received on retirement or death. See also *Richardson* v *Richardson* (1978) 9 Fam Law 86 where the court ordered the husband to pay the wife an enhanced lump sum to take account of her loss of expectations to pension benefits which her husband would be entitled to on retiring some three years after the divorce.

Secondly, the court has adjourned the application until the husband receives the retirement lump sum. The problem with this, however, is that such an adjournment is inconsistent with the 'clean-break' principle laid down in *Minton* v *Minton* [1979] AC 593. Therefore a court rarely orders an adjournment for more than two or three years.

Finally, the court may be influenced by the fact that an applicant is losing an opportunity of obtaining a pension even though the pension itself is not directly affected and thus makes an order reflecting this fact. See, for example *M* v *M* *(Financial Provision)* [1987] 2 FLR 1 where the courts were deterred from imposing the 'clean-break' solution because of the loss of the opportunity to gain a pension right.

The problem with the law before the PA 1995, however, has been that the court will not usually be able to make orders directly affecting the divorced spouses' rights to the pension. The reason for this is twofold. The first is that the beneficiaries' rights to a pension are often discretionary; and the second is because the assignment or commutation of benefits is prohibited. The latter point has caused great difficulties and resulted in inequalities with regard to pensions and divorce. It has resulted in many cases in the husband keeping the pension and the wife receiving the house. The pension may, however, in certain situations be the only major asset of any substantial value. This can occur, for example, where the couple have been in rented accommodation or where the debts attached to the matrimonial home are worth more than the equity that the couple have in the house. Many women do not have the chance to build up a decent pension of their own. They earn less during their lifetime and their career is often interrupted by having children. Yet if the parties divorce they rarely have any entitlement to the husband's pension rights. In the recent case of *Brooks* v *Brooks* [1995] 3 WLR 141, the wife won the right to part of her husband's pension and a dependant's pension when the husband dies. The husband and wife were married in 1977 and the husband set up his own company. The wife became a secretary to the company and a pension scheme was established to provide the husband with an income on retirement. He was the sole member and the scheme had a rule which allowed the husband on his retirement to choose to surrender a portion of his pension to provide a deferred pension for his spouse or any other person financially dependant on him from the date of his death. The scheme had a surplus of £166,000 over the cost of providing the husband's pension.

The couple split in 1989 and the wife petitioned for divorce. In the same year the company ceased trading. The district judge held, *inter alia*, that the husband's pension scheme was a post-nuptial settlement under s. 24(1)(c) Matrimonial Causes Act 1973, and that as such it could be varied in the wife's favour to provide her with an annuity of £2,618 and a deferred pension of £4,600 on the husband' death. The husband's appeal against the variation of the pension scheme was dismissed by the High Court and the Court of Appeal [1995] Fam 70. The Court of Appeal, however, was not unanimous in its decision and Hoffmann LJ said that the husband's pension scheme was not a post-nuptial settlement and that, even if it were, the surplus belonged to the company. The House of Lords held that the term 'any ante-nuptial or post-nuptial settlement' in s. 24(1)(c) of the Matrimonial Causes Act 1973 is to be given a wide meaning, and the court had jurisdiction on the dissolution of a marriage to vary the terms of the pension scheme, including an income provision which took the form of an obligation by one party to the marriage to make periodical payments to the other. Thus, as long as the pension fund constitutes a settlement made by the husband the court had power to vary it. A sole-member scheme which the husband entered with the intention that it provide financial support for himself and his wife on the husband's death was a disposition which fell within the meaning of marriage settlement in the context of matrimonial legislation. If, however, the benefits of the scheme were to be paid exclusively to the scheme member it could not be treated as a marriage settlement.

The surplus funds, however, belonged to the company, i.e., the husband in his capacity as owner of the company. This means that such property was never part of the settlement and therefore the court had no jurisdiction to vary its disposal. It is important to emphasise the wider aspects of this case for as Lord Nicholls said at p. 151:

> This decision should not be seen as a solution to the overall pensions problem. Not every pension scheme constitutes a marriage settlement. And even when a scheme does fall within the court's jurisdiction to vary a marriage settlement, it would not be right for the court to vary one scheme member's rights to the prejudice of other scheme members. . . . A feature of the instant case is that there is only one scheme member and, moreover, the wife has earnings of her own from the same employer which will sustain provision of an immediate pension for her.

The matter of pensions and divorce has been looked at on a number of occasions, first by the Law Commission in 1969 and again in 1977; by the Occupational Pensions Board in 1978; by the Lord Chancellor's Department in 1985 and by the Law Society Family Law Committee in 1991.

The PA 1995 s. 166 inserts new ss. 25B, 25C and 25D into the Matrimonial Causes Act 1973. The new s. 25B specifies more fully the duty of the court to take into account pension rights when considering financial provision on divorce. The court will also have to take into account any benefits under a scheme which a party would lose the chance of acquiring on divorce. As a result of the amendments the Matrimonial Causes Act 1973 not only gives the courts power to offset pension rights against capital assets in divorce settlements but also to make maintenance and deferred maintenance orders. Legally s. 166 PA 1995 is very important as subsections (4) and (5) facilitate making deferred orders by providing that the new provisions override any statutory and other provisions preventing assignment and preventing orders being made restraining a person from receiving anything which he is prevented from assigning.

The court can also direct trustees or the scheme managers of an occupational pension scheme, or a personal pension scheme or an arrangement with the same purpose, to make a maintenance payment to the former spouse from a pension when it is due to a scheme member. The payment may be a one-off lump sum or periodic payments.

The new provisions also include regulation-making power with regards to the person to whom the trustees or managers will make the payment. Further regulation-making powers are provided in relation to valuation of pension rights. Parties often rely on the cash equivalent transfer valuation which is available to the scheme member, but different methods can produce different results. That can cause work for the court and the scheme and may give scope for a continuing dispute between the parties. Regulations therefore will prescribe the basis of valuation for divorce settlement purposes. This will provide consistency of approach in dealing with pensions and divorce, and it is anticipated that the basis of the valuation will be the cash equivalent basis.

The new s. 25D Matrimonial Causes Act 1973 also contains a power permitting regulations to be made which will allow a scheme to recover the administrative costs of providing the pension valuation and paying the sum under the order to the ex-spouse. Schemes should, as far as is practicable, recover their costs from divorcing parties. The main cost involved in such a case will be that in operating deferred maintenance orders, because of the need to keep records and to make payments to people who move throughout the country.

The court still has a power of variation, discharge etc. under s. 31 Matrimonial Causes Act 1973.

Section 166 PA 1995 does not result in the former spouse becoming a member of the pension scheme in his or her own right as a result of an order of the court. The order would be made against the divorcing scheme member and the direction to the trustees to pay would be a means of enforcing the paying rather than giving the former spouse rights in the pension scheme in his or her own right.

All payments into pension schemes are to be treated in the same way, regardless of whether they are compulsory payments, FSAVCs or personal pensions. Together they form the assets that the court has to consider. An attachment order can be made against an occupational pension scheme, a personal pension scheme or a FSAVC.

As a result of new provisions, the courts have been given power to give effect to pension rights in divorce proceedings in two main ways. The first is by means of offsetting. The courts in this case would be able to offset, against the pension of the scheme member, other assets such as the matrimonial home. This method is employed by the courts at present but is found to be ineffective where there are insufficient assets to offset against the pension and the pension is worth more than the rest of the assets. Furthermore even where the material and pension assets balance each other out, the courts have to set immediate assets against long-term assets. Thus the member is stripped of his 'short-term' assets in order to enjoy a pension which he may never live to enjoy.

The second method is earmarking. This represents a form of deferred mainten-ance, and the pension is divided at the point of retirement. There are several difficulties with this method however:

(a)   It delays the final settlement of property rights until retirement unless of course the member is in receipt of a pension at the time of divorce.

(b)   It is unclear whether earmarking applies when a member leaves one job for another. Does earmarking just apply to the job that the member was in at the date of the divorce or does it apply to a succession of jobs?

(c)   It can result in several spouses each having a charge on the pension but not knowing what they will receive.

The Pensions Management Institute favoured pension splitting. This method involves the cash value of the pension that has accrued being worked out precisely (just as it is now when pension rights are transferred when a member changes his job) and the cash value divided. The government, however, did not favour this method.

Chapter 7
Resolution of Disputes

An important aspect of the PA 1995 is its provisions relating to dispute resolution. Disputes may be between individuals — where the complaint is raised by an individual member against the trustees or between individual trustees. Alternatively, disputes can be as a result of some collective response to a particular issue or where some commonality of issue arises in relation to, for example, a number of members or as between the trustees and the employer. Each of these types raises very different issues and constructing some mechanism to deal satisfactorily with each type is extremely difficult. For example, a dispute between a member and the scheme as to the way the benefits have been calculated may require the dispute settling forum to have different characteristics than a forum for settling a dispute between the trustees and the employer. That said, there are some issues common to all types of forum which the Act could seek to address — accessibility, speed, efficiency, effectiveness and cost.

There are marked differences of approach between the Goode Committee and the government's response as manifested in the White Paper and the Act. The Goode Committee's approach could be described as a campaign across a broad front, while the government's was a three-pronged attack.

7.1 DISPUTE RESOLUTION BEFORE THE PENSIONS ACT 1995

7.1.1 Occupational Pensions Advisory Service

The Occupational Pensions Advisory Service (OPAS) is a non-statutory organisation that provides a basis for dispute settlement. Its status and work will remain untouched by the Act's provisions. It provides a service to individual members of the public and the typical dispute that it deals with is concerned with benefits on leaving the service of the employer. These commonly are as a result of misunderstandings, or poor-quality or insufficient information being supplied to the member, and are dealt with informally and expeditiously. It is right to point out that the majority of pension disputes are dealt with by OPAS. Whilst OPAS can deal with disputes or provide a negotiation or conciliation service, there are limits and it has no decision-making powers and cannot conduct a case on behalf of the individual. There is an important relationship between OPAS and the Pensions Ombudsman whereby many inquiries of the Ombudsman and complaints to him are redirected to OPAS (see for example, the 1994/95 Report of the Pensions Ombudsman). The Occupational Pension Scheme (Disclosure of Information) Regulations 1986 (SI 1986/1046 as amended) require members to be given notice that OPAS is available to them to resolve difficulties in relation to the scheme which they have failed to resolve with the scheme's trustees or administrators. Though PA 1995 enhances the information that must be supplied to members (see chapter 3), the failure to address the issue of supplying information relevant to scheme administration may mean that disputes which have as an element misunderstandings based upon poor-quality or insufficient information are likely to continue.

7.1.2   Industrial tribunals

Industrial tribunals have some jurisdiction over pension related disputes. European law issues under art. 119 of the Treaty of Rome (equal treatment) and the Acquired Rights Directive (transfer of undertakings) fall within the purview of industrial tribunals. Also, where an unfair dismissal claim involves a pension or retirement issue, such matters fall within the tribunal's reach.

7.1.3   Courts

Disputes relating to pension schemes are almost invariably brought, in England and Wales, in the Chancery Division of the High Court. In Scotland such matters are dealt with under the procedure of the Court of Session.

Proceedings in the Chancery Division may involve contested issues of law and fact or may be conducted on the basis that the parties jointly seek a ruling of the court on some question of law or on a point of construction of scheme documents. In contested matters, where it is the trustees who are instituting or defending the proceedings, the court may order that the costs of the trustees and the other party, where successful, be borne by the pension fund. However, a prohibitive point for parties instituting proceedings against the trustees (including the members of the scheme), is that costs may have to be borne personally — though it was held in *McDonald* v *Horn* [1994] PLR 155 that the court may make a pre-emptive order that the costs be borne by the fund.

Where the proceedings are 'amicable' in the sense that there is a commonality of interest in the ruling of the court, normally the trustees agree to pay the costs from the scheme funds or obtain a '*Beddoe* order' (*Re Beddoe* [1893] 1 Ch 547) directing that costs be paid from the scheme funds. Litigation in relation to schemes is further complicated by the fact that different classes of membership may have conflicting interests which require separate representation and this increases costs. In any event, litigation is almost invariably a drain on the fund.

The Goode Committee looked at a number of proposals which it thought would go some way to alleviate some of the difficulties associated with this type of litigation (Goode Report, para. 4.13.52). It thought that there were three issues that it could address:

(a)   multiple representation;
(b)   the volume and complexity of documents;

(c)   the range of issues to be dealt with at the hearing.

Conceding that in the nature of an adversarial procedure each party strives to ensure that its interests are put with 'sufficient vigour and determination', it was forced to suggest tentatively that it was important to keep the number of interests separately represented to a minimum commensurate with justice being done. A pre-trial review procedure would, it thought, provide some basis for concentrating the range of issues, documents on which construction was agreed and the documents that would form the basis of an agreed core for the purposes of the trial. Further, the parties should be 'encouraged' to narrow the issues as far as is possible. These measures, plus the possibility of utilising skeleton opinions which would detail in outline the arguments on each issue and an agreed bundle of documents, both lodged with the judge, would go some way to ameliorate the current difficulties. Smaller schemes could be considered in the context of a simplified and faster procedure. These principles were embraced in one recommendation that 'urgent attention' be given to ways of reducing costs, expediting matters and alleviating the position of individual litigants (see recommendation No. 158).

The PA 1995 has not attempted to address any of these issues though these recommendations have been accepted by the government in principle.

7.1.4   Pensions Ombudsman

The Social Security Act 1990, s. 12(1) and sch. 3 inserted a new s. 59B into the Social Security Pensions Act 1975 establishing the office of the Pensions Ombudsman. The provisions concerning the establishment and powers of the Ombudsman now reside in ss. 145 to 151 of the PSA 1993. It is right to say that before the statutory provisions, there was, and still remains, a school of thought that the disputes that the Ombudsman would undertake to investigate and resolve could be best carried out by a pension tribunal (see, for example, the OPB report, *Protecting Pensions: Safeguarding Benefits in a Changing Environment* (Cmnd 573) and Hansard, HC Standing Committee D, 20 June 1995, cols 749–58). It was felt by the OPB that disputes may be between groups with a common interest (e.g., groups of trustees or the trustees and the employer) rather than individuals. It was argued that the Ombudsman system was best suited to disputes involving individuals. Also the Ombudsman may lack the necessary specialty and diversity of skills required where issues required the convergence of legal, actuarial and accountancy expertise. A tribunal system would be better suited to such disputes. Finally, the sums involved in the dispute may be of such a scale as to militate against the Ombudsman regime. The alternative in the absence of a tribunal was that these disputes would be dealt with by the court.

Nevertheless, the government persisted in the establishment of the office of Ombudsman which had already shown itself to be a success in other areas. The PA 1995 enlarges the original jurisdiction of the Pensions Ombudsman to some extent embracing the recommendations of the Goode Committee, and the basis and scope of the Ombudsman's powers will be discussed below when we consider the Act's provisions (see 7.2.2).

7.2 DISPUTE RESOLUTION UNDER THE PENSIONS ACT 1995

The PA 1995 deals with dispute resolution in three ways — first, by a requirement that schemes must establish internal dispute settling regimes, second by enlarging the jurisdiction of the Pensions Ombudsman and third by the dispute resolution functions of OPRA discussed in chapter 2.

7.2.1 Internal dispute resolution regime

The Goode Committee recommended that all schemes should be required to establish a dispute resolution regime which would have to be approved by the new regulator. Small schemes would be excluded (Goode Report, recommendation No. 148). It envisaged 'small schemes' as those where there were 50 or less active and pensioner members (Goode Report, para 4.5.22), though it is open to include small self-administered schemes within this class. The government adopted this recommendation and signalled early in the formative stages of its legislative proposals that it envisaged a dispute resolution mechanism would be a prescriptive requirement under the Act. Indeed, this was to be one aspect of a programme that would, where possible, attempt to divert disputes from the courts (see White Paper, para. 1.30). In the government's view, though, small schemes with less than 12 members, all of whom are trustees, would be exempted from this requirement.

The PA 1995, s. 50(1) requires a dispute resolving mechanism to be embraced under the Act by placing a duty on the trustees or managers of every occupational pension scheme to make and implement arrangements for some system for the resolution of disputes. Regulations may exempt certain schemes and issues from the requirement (s. 50(7)). The disputants will not necessarily include all persons directly or indirectly interested in the scheme, as those persons who will be able to utilise the scheme will be prescribed by regulations. It is hoped that the regulations will not draw the class of eligible persons too tightly. The duty will be enforced by OPRA by the application of the civil penalties in s. 10 where the arrangements for a dispute resolution mechanism have either not been made or, where made, not implemented and the trustees or managers have failed to take all reasonable steps to secure this (s. 50(6)). There is no requirement for the proposed regime to be approved by OPRA but it is hoped that OPRA will provide some guidance for schemes which are arranging for dispute resolution for the first time. Some features of a workable and accessible dispute resolution system are highlighted in the guidance issued by ACAS in its *Employment Handbook*. These include:

(a) speed of resolution — the system should aim to settle a dispute fairly, quickly and as closely to the point of origin as is possible;

(b) communication of the procedures available — details of the regime should be clearly communicated to the relevant parties in order that they are aware of the steps that need to be taken to have the dispute heard;

(c) an opportunity to appeal;

(d) a right for the complainant to be accompanied — though this right is dependent upon the level that the complaint is heard at;

(e) reasonable time limits to each stage of the process;

(f)   training for those involved in determining disputes.

Section 50 does prescribe some general requirements for each regime. The dispute resolution arrangements must have a person who can provide a decision on a dispute on the application of the complainant (s. 50(2)(a)). This may effectively end the issue. However, there is nothing to suggest that this person will act as, or will be, some sort of appeal forum and must necessarily have powers to reverse or confirm the original decision. The arrangements must also provide for the trustees or managers, after a decision has been made under s. 50(2)(a), to reconsider the issue on the application of the complainant and either confirm this earlier decision or give a new one in its place (s. 50(2)(b)). Both the applications and the decisions must be in writing (s. 50(4)). A number of issues spring from these provisions. First, there is no requirement that the person who is to fulfil the dispute resolution role be either intimately or remotely connected with the scheme or indeed be unconnected. Further, there is no requirement of the qualities that should be reposed in this person. It is of course open to OPRA to issue guidance or a code of practice in relation to these aspects and without minimum standards of fairness or competence it would be likely that the Act's requirements would be complied with as a matter of form alone as such arrangements could not carry the parties' confidence. However, both the context of these requirements should be understood and the issues that such arrangements would address. The Act is not attempting to require that schemes adopt formalised quasi-judicial proceedings. Second, where the trustees or managers are asked to reconsider the issue where there has been a decision under s. 50(2)(a), which has, for example, stated that their original decision was incorrect, a new decision in its place may in effect be simply reverting to the original. This problem, perhaps more a threat than real, is more insidious where the trustees or managers were party to the original decision.

Regulations made under s. 50(3) may provide for certain procedural aspects and these relate to:

(a)   applications for decisions under the dispute resolution arrangements;
(b)   the procedure for reaching and giving the decisions;
(c)   the timescale that may apply to applications made under the arrangements and decisions given.

Existing schemes must have arrangements complying with s. 50 in place on the commencement of the section (s. 50(5)) which will be appointed by order of the Secretary of State.

7.2.2   Pensions Ombudsman

The Goode Committee recommended four significant modifications to the statutory provisions concerning the Ombudsman. Most of these were adopted by the government and make their way into the PA 1995. These include:

(a)   the expansion of the Ombudsman's jurisdiction to include disputes between the trustees themselves and also between the employer and trustees (No. 150); and
(b)   that the Ombudsman be provided with sufficient resourcing for the expanded role (No. 155).

However, some recommendations, even though bolstered by the Ombudsman's own views, were not given statutory effect as it was thought that they were incompatible with the neutral role of the Ombudsman or that such power as existed sufficiently dealt with the issue. These include:

(a) a power to direct that compensation payments should include a reasonable sum to reflect any distress, delay and inconvenience caused as well as financial loss (No. 152);

(b) the power to enforce his decisions directly (No. 151); and

(c) a power to require papers to be given to OPAS and where it has obtained a settlement between trustees and the claimant which is intended by them to be a binding agreement, they should have the power to request that the Ombudsman incorporates this agreement in a formal determination.

A number of the recommendations of the Goode Committee did not require legislative intervention and have been adopted by the current Ombudsman, Dr Farrand, as part of his investigative powers, albeit in a small number of cases (see, for example, the recommendation (No. 153) relating to informal inquisitorial hearings).

It has been the practice of the Ombudsman to refer some complainants initially to OPAS for attempted resolution. Indeed OPAS is a most successful body for the resolution of pension-related disputes. There is no reason to suggest that this will alter.

Before considering the provisions of the PA 1995, it is worth noting that the roles of OPRA and the Ombudsman will need at times to interact (see 7.2.3.3 concerning the flow of information). Given the potentially broad nature of the jurisdiction which PA 1995 gives to the Ombudsman, there is scope for duplication of effort. As there is a fundamental difference between the respective roles of OPRA and the Pensions Ombudsman, the government proposes that regulations (made under s. 146 of the PSA 1993) will specifically exclude from the Ombudsman's jurisdiction the following matters, which are better suited to investigation by OPRA:

(a) cases involving payments from surplus to the employer;

(b) failures to meet the minimum funding requirement;

(c) failures to comply with the audit requirement; and

(d) procedures for the appointment of member-nominated trustees and the scheme actuary.

See Hansard, HL, 14 March 1995, col. 836.

7.2.2.1 *Resources* PA 1995, s. 156, amends s. 145 of the PSA 1993 by substituting new subsections (4A), (4B) and (4C) for the existing subsection (4). As a corollary of the enhanced jurisdiction that the Act bestows upon the Ombudsman, the new subsections purport to provide for greater flexibility in the appointment and secondment of staff and the provision of facilities to enable the Ombudsman to fulfil his role. Thus, it is the Ombudsman who may appoint staff, subject to the approval of the Secretary of State, as he may determine.

Additionally, the Secretary of State may make additional staff and facilities available to the Ombudsman. The new provisions continue to make it clear that it is the Ombudsman himself who is to determine complaints made and disputes referred to him.

7.2.2.2 *Jurisdiction*

Subsections (1) to (4) of PSA 1993 s. 146, are replaced by provisions providing for an enhanced jurisdiction (PA 1995, s. 157(2)).

The Ombudsman may investigate and determine the following complaints or disputes made or referred to him in writing:

(a)   A complaint by or on behalf of an actual or potential beneficiary of an OPS or personal pension scheme who alleges that he or she has sustained injustice in consequence of maladministration in connection with an act or omission of a person responsible for the management of the scheme (PSA 1993, new s. 146(1)(a)).

There are two points to note here. First, the change in nomenclature from 'authorised complainant' in the PSA 1993 to 'actual or potential beneficiary'. This should have no significant impact as s. 146(7) (defining who are authorised complainants for this purpose) remains unaltered save the change in title to actual or potential beneficiary (see PA 1995, s. 157(3)). Second, the reference to 'a person responsible for the management of the scheme'. These are, in the case of an OPS, the trustees or managers and the employer and in the case of a personal pension scheme, a trustee or manager (see PSA 1993, new s. 146(3) and (3A)). This widens the scope of the jurisdiction to embrace a potential complaint of, for example, an OPS member who alleges injustice caused by maladministration in relation to the scheme by the employer. Additionally, these provisions may be extended by regulations to include persons or bodies who, though not trustees, managers or employers, are concerned with the financing or administration of, or the provision of benefits under, the scheme (new s. 146(4)). This power could bring within the ambit of the Ombudsman's jurisdiction external administrators and, for example, insurers. It is worth noting in this context that the references to 'trustees or managers' should be read given the ordinary natural meaning and should not be read as including within the jurisdiction of the Ombudsman, the managers of a scheme where there are no trustees. Thus, this includes within the jurisdiction the persons involved in the day-to-day running of a scheme, irrespective of the fact that such a scheme is established under a trust, see *Century Life plc* v *Pensions Ombudsman*, (1995) *The Times*, 23 May 1995. Whilst this case involved consideration of s. 146(1) of the PSA 1993 before it was amended by the PA 1995, such a construction is equally applicable here and the addition in the new s. 146(1) of the employer should not alter this. Third, the gravamen of a complaint under the new s. 146(1)(a) must be injustice in consequence of maladministration. This is broadly in the same terms as the original s. 146(1), which some suggested excluded revisiting trustees' decisions, presumably by interpreting it as narrowing the focus of the jurisdiction to investigate the *steps taken* to reach the decision (see the general note to s. 146(1) of the PSA 1993 in *Current Law Statutes Annotated 1993*, vol. 3). It is difficult to accept that the subsection requires such a construction and in any event this also suggests that a distinct line can be drawn between the substance of a decision and its form. This does not necessarily follow given that maladministration is a broad term (see below). The question may be, for example, injustice as a consequence of arbitrariness in the decision. That view would be in danger of allowing the substance of the decision, and the jurisdiction of the Ombudsman, to be a slave to form. Notwithstanding the theoretical objections, it is also suggested that this approach flies in the face of the role and *raison d'être* of the Pensions Ombudsman as an accessible form of dispute resolution. This view is largely on all fours with the procedure adopted by the current Ombudsman.

(b)   A complaint:

(i)   by or on behalf of a person responsible for the management of an OPS who alleges maladministration of the scheme by any act or omission of some other person responsible for the management of the scheme; or

(ii)   by or on behalf of the trustees or managers of an OPS who allege maladministration of another scheme by any act or omission of any trustee or manager of that other scheme (PSA 1993, new s. 146(1)(b)).

The first aspect encapsulates one of the principal recommendations for extending the jurisdiction, to include a complaint of maladministration of a scheme made, for example, by one trustee against another or as against the employer. The second aspect could cover collective inter-scheme disputes.

(c)   Any dispute of fact or law that arises in relation to an OPS or a personal pension scheme, referred to the Ombudsman by or on behalf of an actual or potential beneficiary, between a person responsible for the management of the scheme (as defined above) and the actual or potential beneficiary (PSA 1993, new s. 146(1)(c)).

Again, the extension here is to include, at least in relation to an OPS, potential disputes between the actual or potential beneficiary (as defined in s. 146(7)) and the employer as a person responsible for the management of the scheme.

(d)   Any dispute of fact or law which arises between the trustees or managers of an OPS and:

(i)   another person who is responsible for the management of the scheme; or

(ii)   any trustee or manager of another OPS,

which has been referred to the Ombudsman by or on behalf of the persons in (i) or (ii) above (PSA 1993, new a. 146(1)(d)).

A number of general points can be made. First, it was not a recommendation of the Goode Committee, nor referred to in the government's proposals that complaints between, for example, a member of an OPS and the employer should be considered by the Ombudsman and this is a significant extension. Second, it is not a requirement of s. 146(1)(b) that the complainant or any person connected with the scheme necessarily suffer injustice. Third, 'maladministration' as an element of the complaints in s. 146(1)(a) and (b), though not defined in either the PSA 1993 or the PA 1995 should be understood to be an expansive term. In the debates on the statutory provisions relating to the Parliamentary Commissioner for Administration, where the same term is used, maladministration as used in the Parliamentary Commissioner Act 1967 was described (though not exhaustively) as covering 'bias, neglect, inattention, delay, incompetence, inaptitude, perversity, turpitude, arbitrariness and so on' (Hansard, HC, 18 October 1966, col. 51). Fourth, the extension of the Pensions Ombudsman's jurisdiction to include any factual or legal disputes between, for example, trustees and trustees, trustees and managers or employers, is an attempt to divert the parties from seeking litigation which may be both costly and destructive to the fund. The rationale for these changes is that the Ombudsman can provide relatively speedy decisions, at no direct cost, in a forum that is not adversarial and provides more 'user-friendly' procedures. This is not to say that the office of Pensions Ombudsman can provide a panacea for all ills. Of course litigation is still an option for the parties and indeed the Ombudsman himself may refer such questions to the court (s. 150(7) of the PSA 1993). This diversion, allied to the decision of Dr Farrand to relax the self-imposed restrictions on investigating, for example, the exercise of trustees' discretions, reintroduces the concerns in some quarters (it must be said largely unfounded) about the lack of resources and expertise for complex disputes which are potentially best suited to resolution by a specialist tribunal. Indeed, the powers of investigation, determination of issues and enforcement of decisions (albeit through the courts) that are reposed in the office of Pensions Ombudsman render his role more analogous to a statutory tribunal. However, we shall have to wait for the implications of these changes to come to light over a period of time and it may be that regulations could exempt certain types of dispute from the jurisdiction. In any event, it should be remembered that the power to investigate and determine a complaint is expressed as a permissive power and the Ombudsman has a discretion, as long as this is properly exercised, whether to entertain a complaint or not.

7.2.3.3 Consequential changes There are a number of changes that the PA 1995 brings to the PSA 1993 as a corollary of the jurisdictional changes described in 7.2.2.2. These primarily deal with the changes in nomenclature from 'authorised complainant' to 'actual or potential beneficiaries' and references to 'a person responsible for the management of the scheme', in order that these terms are use consistently at various points in the provisions. Amendments for this purpose are made to ss. 146(7) (who are actual or potential beneficiaries), 147 (the death, insolvency or disability of the complainant), 148(5) (staying court proceedings), 149(1) (procedure on investigation — who shall be given opportunity to comment on the complaint or reference) and 151 (concerning the determinations of the Ombudsman — to whom notice must be given and upon whom the determinations are final and binding). Other amendments are to the procedures of the Ombudsman and significant among these are:

(a) Amendments to s. 149(3) relating to the payment of costs and expenses. Subsection (3) prescribes that regulations made governing procedure of the Ombudsman on investigation (under subsection (2)), may include provision for procedure relating to oral hearings and who is entitled to appear and be heard. This is amended to provide for regulations to include payment by the Ombudsman of travelling and other allowances to specified persons who attend any oral hearings held by him in connection with his investigation.

(b) The insertion of new subsections (5), (6) and (7) into s. 149, which permits the Ombudsman to disclose any information which he has obtained for the purposes of his investigation to persons or bodies prescribed in subsection (6) where he considers that the information would enable or assist that person or body to discharge any of their functions. Subsection (7) permits the Secretary of State to amend the list of persons or bodies stipulated in subsection (6) and to limit the circumstances of disclosure or impose conditions on the disclosure. These amendments go some way to meeting the government's acceptance of the recommendation of the Goode Committee that OPRA be empowered to rely on a determination by the Ombudsman as evidence of the facts found, though as far as the Act is concerned this is not specifically laid down. The disclosure of information under s. 149(5) is also cloaked with absolute privilege for the purposes of the law of defamation (new para. (aa) inserted into s. 151(7)).

(c)   Where the Ombudsman directs any person responsible for the management of a scheme to pay a benefit which ought to have been paid earlier, he may also order the payment of interest on the sum at the prescribed rate (PSA 1993, s. 151A inserted by PA 1995, s. 160). There is no stipulation as to the length of the period that the interest is to cover.

Chapter 8
Equal Treatment

8.1 GENERAL

Article 119 of the Treaty of Rome embodies the principle in European law that men and women should receive equal pay for work that is equal. Discrimination (direct or indirect) or unfavourable treatment of one sex over the other in the matter of pay, based solely upon the question of biological differences, is contrary to the article. The European Court of Justice (ECJ) has determined that occupational pensions are 'pay' within art. 119 and has ruled that this applies to contracted-in and contracted-out schemes (see *Bilka-Kaufhaus GmbH* v *Weber von Hartz* (case 170/84) [1987] ICR 110 and *Barber* v *Guardian Royal Exchange Assurance Group* (case C-262/88) [1991] 1 QB 344. For a compendious review of the case law in the area, see Nobles, *Pensions, Employment and the Law* (1993) ch. 9).

Prior to the *Bilka-Kaufhaus* and *Barber* cases and up to the provisions in the PA 1995, United Kingdom legislation had consistently ignored the requirement of equal men and women and where purporting to address such issues, the UK has dragged its feet by delaying the coming into force of statutory provisions (though equal access was addressed in the Social Security Pensions Act 1975 and see the Social Security Act 1989 implementing the 1986 Directive on equal treatment, 86/378/EEC) in relation to OPSs and the provision of equal benefits. UK law permitted, for example, differences in pensionable ages. As a result of developments in European law obligations, this can no longer be the case and, in general, benefits enjoyed by one sex must be enjoyed by the other (or 'levelled up'). Sections 63 to 66 of PA 1995 provide for the principle of equal treatment of men and women OPS members to be embraced by schemes (section 62), the modification of discriminatory terms, the modification of the effects of terms which differ in relation to men and women and the importation of the procedure for enforcement of the Equal Pay Act 1970 (PA 1995, ss. 62 and 63), exceptions to the rule (section 64), powers to make the necessary alterations to schemes (section 65) and consequential amendments to both the Equal Pay Act 1970 and the Sex Discrimination Act 1975 (PA 1995, section 66). Equal treatment in relation to Official Pensions is tackled in PA 1995, s. 171. The equalisation of pensionable ages under the State scheme is dealt with in chapter 9.

A salary related OPS which contracts out of SERPS is required to provide benefits which will equate, at the very least, to the GMP. This is to provide some substitute for the loss of SERPS. SERPS is linked to the State pension age and, as a result, the GMP for a man and woman member of an equal age will have, at present, different accrual rates and will become payable at different ages. Also, the indexation requirements for GMPs, currently up to a maximum of 3 per cent, may differ in relation to other aspects of the pension. Together, these may make it difficult for schemes to equalise benefits. As a result, it is the Government's intention to assist schemes in the equalisation of overall benefit levels by breaking the links between contracted-out salary related schemes and SERPS. Instead of providing GMPs, schemes will be required to meet a test of, in the Government's view, *quality* applied to the whole of the pensions relating to future service. This is necessary because as between a GMP and SERPS, there is a link to the State retirement age which is not due to be equalised until the year 2020. The abolition of the GMP is discussed at length in chapter 9.

8.2   PROCEDURE FOR ENFORCING THE EQUAL TREATMENT RULE

Before considering the obligation and effects of including an equal treatment rule into OPSs, it is worth noting some preliminary issues relating to the enforcement mechanisms and procedure.

The enforcement mechanisms established under the Equal Pay Act 1970, as amended (the EPA 1970), are incorporated into the provisions of PA 1995 (section 63). Examination of such measures is beyond the scope of this work, but are considered in for example, J. Bowers and S. Honeyball, *Textbook on Labour Law* 4th ed. (London: Blackstone Press, 1995). Section 63 provides for enforcement measures or claims to be brought before an industrial tribunal and the dispute and procedural provisions under section 2 and 2A of the EPA 1970 apply for the purposes of the equal treatment rule (PA 1995, section 63(4)) and accordingly, references therein to 'equality clause' should be contrued to refer to the equal treatment rule. It is against the trustees or managers of the scheme that the member or prospective member must bring proceedings (section 63(4)(b)). This is interesting because, for the purposes of a claim under art. 119, the potential defendants include trustees, managers *and* employers, but the restriction to trustees and managers is consistent with the prominence given throughout the Act to the role and responsibilities of trustees and professionals. However, s. 66(4) allows regulations to provide for, *inter alia*, contributions from the employer to equalise benefits.

A claim cannot be referred to an industrial tribunal unless the woman member has been in the employment to which the scheme relates within the six months preceding the date of the reference (new s. 4(2) of the EPA 1970 substituted by PA 1995, s. 63(4)(c)). The effect or modification of the provisions of the EPA 1970 as they apply to the equal treatment rule may be dealt with by regulations (PA 1995, s. 63(5)). Section 63(6) continues the limitation in respect of pensionable service applicable for the equal treatment rule (propounded in the *Barber* case) of service on or after 17 May 1990.

8.3   EQUAL TREATMENT RULE

Section 62(1) PA 1995 is of overriding effect and requires that an OPS which does not contain an equal treatment rule shall be treated as including one. This is consistent with the *Barber* case and does no more than bring domestic law into line with Community law. If the equal treatment rule is construed in line with *Barber,* then it will render invalid scheme provisions that provide for the *total benfit* to be of equal value but with elements of different value for men and women members. Accordingly, a pension scheme infringes the equal treatment rule if it provides a 'benefit to only one sex . . . or gives it subject to a condition which applies to one sex. . . . Equal pay does not mean total remuneration of equal capital value, it means giving equal payments (whether lump sums or income), to men and women who fulfil the same conditions' (Nobles, *Pension, Employment and the Law* (1993), p. 205).

Section 62(2) defines an equal treatment rule as a scheme rule which relates to the terms on which:

(a)   persons become members of the scheme; and
(b)   members of the scheme are treated (including the effect of such terms on members' dependants: s. 63(1)).

By s. 62(5), references in ss. 62(4) and 63 to 65 to the terms referred to in s. 62(2), or the effect of any of those terms, include:

(a)   terms which bestow upon trustees or managers of an OPS, or any other person, a discretion which in any of the situations in s. 62(3)(a), (b) or (c) (see below):

(i)   may be exercised in such a manner as to affect the way persons of one sex may become members of the scheme or the way in which such members are treated (including the effect of such terms on members' dependants: s. 63(1)); and
(ii)   may be exercised in a way less favourable to a woman than to a man; and

(b)   the effect of any exercise of such a discretion.

The equal treatment rule requires that a term within s. 62(5)(a) cannot be exercised in a way less favourable to the woman than to the man (s. 62(6)).

By s. 62(3), the equal treatment rule has the effect, subject to the Social Security Act 1989, sched. 5, paras 5 and 6 (maternity and family leave provisions), of modifying any of the terms of the scheme which relate to how women become members and the way they are treated where such terms are, or become, less favourable to women, where:

(a)   a woman is *employed on like work* with a *man in the same employment,*
(b)   a woman is employed on work *related as equivalent* with that of a *man in the same employment,* or
(c)   a woman is employed on work which, though not being equivalent in terms of (a) and (b) above, is in terms of the demands made on her, of *equal value* to that of a man in the same employment.

Also, where the effect of the terms on which persons become members and are treated differs according to their family or their marital status, the effect is modified by the requirement that this is compared with members of the opposite sex who share the same status (section 63(2)).

The PA 1995 attempts to marry certain of its concepts with those referred to (in the same terms) in the EPA 1970. Accordingly, section 1 of the EPA 1970 and section 62 of PA 1995 are to be construed as one (s. 63(4)).

8.3.1 Employed on like work

A woman is employed on like work with a man in the same employment if and only if:

(a) her work and the male comparator's is of the same or a broadly similar nature; and

(b) the differences (if any) between the things she does and the things the comparator does are not of practical importance in relation to the terms and conditions of employment.

and regard should be had to the frequency or otherwise with which such differences occur in practice, as well as the nature and extent of the differences (s. 1(4) of the EPA 1970).

Whether a woman's and a man's work is of a broadly similar nature depends on the nature of the work that is carried out, not the terms of the employment contract (see, for example, *Redland Roof Tiles Ltd* v *Harper* [1977] ICR 349, EAT). In any event, in deciding what constitutes like work, a broad approach should be taken and this includes the circumstances in which the work is done and the responsibilities involved in the respective work (see, for example, *Eaton Ltd* v *Nuttall* [1977] ICR 272 at p. 276).

8.3.2 Man in the same employment

For the purposes of the 1970 Act, a man is employed in the same employment as a woman, if he is employed by her employer or any associated employer at the same establishment or at establishments in Great Britain which include that one and at which common terms and conditions of employment are observed either generally or for employees of the relevant classes (s. 1(6) of the EPA 1970). 'Man' includes males of whatever age (s. 11(2) of the EPA 1970).

8.3.3 Rated as equivalent

Section 1(5) of the 1970 Act requires that the woman's work be rated as equivalent with that of the male comparator if her job has been given equal value (in terms of the demands made upon her under various headings such as effort, skill, decision) in a job evaluation study or would have been given equal value but for the system being based upon setting different values for men and women on the same demands. Such job evaluation studies must be 'thorough in analysis and capable of impartial application. . . . one does not satisfy this test and requires management to take a subjective judgement concerning the nature of the work . . . would seem to us not to be a valid study for the purposes of subsection (5)'

(*Eaton Ltd* v *Nuttall* [1977] ICR 272 and see the principal methods of job ranking set out as an appendix to the decision of the Employment Appeal Tribunal).

8.3.4 Equal value

This is intended to cover the situation where though there may be no comparator in terms of being employed in the same or like job, comparisons may be made with a male who it is claimed is employed in work of equal value in the sense that the demands upon the woman in terms of (for example) effort, skill and decision are broadly the same (see PA 1995, s. 62(3)(c)). An industrial tribunal cannot determine a dispute about whether any work is of equal value unless either it is satisfied that there are no reasonable grounds for determining that the relevant work is of equal value or it has commissioned an independent expert to prepare a report on this issue and has received that report (s. 2A(1) of the EPA 1970).

8.4 NON-OPERATION OF, AND EXCEPTIONS TO, THE EQUAL TREATMENT RULE

The equal treatment rule does not operate in relation to any terms where the differences between the man's and woman's case are not based upon differences of sex but genuinely due to a material difference between the cases. The burden of establishing that the difference is genuinely due to a material difference is placed upon the trustees or managers of the scheme (PA 1995, s. 62(4)).

Similar provisions exist in relation to pay differentials under the EPA 1970 (section 1(3)) and this allows not only circumstances or attributes unique to the relevant employees to be established, but can include such differences that are based upon the economics of the employment as this affects the efficiency of the business or on administrative efficiency, which may be established on objectively verifiable grounds (see *Rainey* v *Greater Glasgow Health Board* [1987] AC 224). In the pensions context, for example, women may sometimes be discriminated against by the definition of pensionable salary — where schemes may disregard earnings below the LEL and as women, as a general rule, earn lower salaries, a greater percentage of their salaries fail to earn pension benefits. Unless such differentials can be justified and proved to be due to a genuine material difference — say on an objectively verifiable economic basis — such measures will fall foul of the equal treatment rule. Potentially, such measures also fall foul of art. 119 of the EC Treaty (see *Bilka-Kaufhaus GmbH* v *Weber von Harz* (case 170/84) [1987] ICR 110). The equal treatment rule does not operate in relation to differences between males and females brought about by terms of the scheme where this is permitted by s. 64. These permitted exceptions are:

(a) Where men and women are eligible in prescribed circumstances to receive differing amounts by way of pension, and in prescribed circumstances the differences are attributable only to differences in the State pension scheme to which in prescribed circumstances they would be entitled (s. 64(2)).

Such differences in the State scheme will of course eventually disappear (see chapter 9) but the exception includes, for example, bridging pensions paid where a member retires before State pension age. Differences occur where males retire between 60 and 65 years and receive extra remuneration to make up for the fact that during this period men will not be in receipt of the basic State pension. Such practices have been held not to amount to discrimination (see *Roberts* v *Birds Eye Walls Ltd* [1991] ICR 43).

(b) By virtue of a permissive power where the difference is based upon:

(i) actuarial factors which fall within a prescribed class or description; or

(ii) actuarial factors which differ on the basis of gender to the determination of benefits falling within a prescribed class or description. Benefit includes any payment or benefit paid or payable (s. 64(3)).

This exception is consistent with the view of the ECJ that actuarial factors, as a basis for pension differentials between men and women (for example morbidity and mortality tables, demonstrating the greater longevity of women), are outside art. 119 (see *Neath* v *Hugh Steeper Ltd* [1991] PLR 91 and *Coloroll Pension Trustees* v *Russell* [1994] PLR 211).

Regulations may permit further variation or amend or repeal s. 64(2) and (3) and the regulations may have retrospective effect in relation to pensionable service on or after 17 May 1990 (s. 64(4)). Regulations may therefore include within the permissible exceptions, for example, single-sex schemes (see also *Coloroll Pension Trustees* v *Russell*).

8.5 POWERS OF AMENDMENT

Where the trustees or managers of a scheme do not have power to alter the scheme so to enable conform with the equal treatment rule, they may by resolution make the necessary alterations to the scheme under PA 1995 s. 65(1)(a). Similarly, they may make necessary alterations under s. 65(1)(b) where they do have such a power, but the procedure is:

(a) liable to be unduly complex or protracted; or

(b) involves obtaining consents which cannot be obtained or can only be obtained with undue delay or difficulty,

Any resolution enabled by this section may have retrospective effect (s. 65(2)).

Chapter 9
Changes in Benefit Levels

9.1 INTRODUCTION

The PA 1995 introduces many changes to the level of benefits. These changes are of three types: first those that affect the level of benefits in occupational pension schemes; second those that affect the level of benefits in personal pension schemes; and third those that affect the level of benefits under the State scheme.

The main changes affecting occupational pension schemes can be summarised as follows:

(a)   the introduction of limited price indexation (LPI);

(b)   the abolition of guaranteed minimum pensions (GMPs) and their replacement by a new contracted-out test;

(c)   the introduction of age-related rebates for contracted-out money purchase schemes (COMPS); and

(d)   changes in the requirement for the payment of transfer values.

The main changes affecting personal pension schemes are as follows:

(a)   age-related rebates for appropriate (i.e., contracted-out) personal pensions;

(b)   an increase in the limit of post-retirement increases required on appropriate personal pensions from 3 per cent to 5 per cent; and

(c)   giving the Secretary of State power to reject an individual's choice of appropriate pension scheme where the Secretary of State is of the opinion either that the scheme is one that does not comply with the PSA 1993, or that it is inexpedient to allow the scheme to be chosen by the individual.

The changes to the State scheme are as follows:

(a)   the progressive equalisation of State pension age at 65 over the period from 6 April 2010 to 5 April 2020;

(b)   the inclusion of family credit and disability working allowance in the calculation of State Earnings Related Pension Scheme (SERPS) benefits;

(c)   a change in the way that SERPS benefits are calculated such that the lower earnings level is deducted from the member's earnings each year before valuation rather than at the year of retirement;

(d)   an increase in the increment granted for those who defer receipt of State pension, in respect of every week of deferment from 1/7 per cent to 1/5 per cent;

(e)   changes to the dependants' benefits which are in the main due to the equalisation of State pensions;

(f)   the equalisation of graduated pensions.

9.2   CHANGES TO OCCUPATIONAL PENSION SCHEMES

9.2.1   Limited price indexation

Limited price indexation (LPI) imposes an obligation on an occupational pension scheme to provide an increase to pensions in payment and the object of LPI is to provide a degree of protection against inflation. LPI requirements were first introduced in the Social Security Act 1990, s. 11, but the requirements were never fully implemented because of the uncertainties surrounding the judgment in the case of *Barber* v *Guardian Royal Exchange Assurance Group* (case C-262/88) [1991] 1 QB 344 (see 8.1). The PA 1995 has attempted to reintroduce LPI. The difference between LPI under the Social Security Act 1990 and the LPI under the PA 1995 is that the latter will only apply to benefits that have accrued *after* the implementation date. The reason for this is that the introduction of LPI for pension rights that have accrued before the implementation date would impose a considerable burden of cost on occupational pension schemes. However, the fact that LPI is restricted in such a way clearly undermines the value of the pension promise.

Section 51 PA 1995 provides that all pension schemes which are approved under the ICTA 1988 and which are not public service pension schemes are required to increase pensions each year by 'at least the appropriate percentage'. Salary-related schemes, money purchase schemes or hybrid schemes are all included in the indexation provisions. The appropriate percentage is defined in s. 54(3) PA 1995 as being 'the revaluation percentage for the revaluation period the reference period for which ends with the last preceding 30th September before the increase is made'. A revaluation percentage and revaluation period are defined in para. 2 of sch. 3 to the PSA 1993 which broadly speaking says that revaluation must take place at the rate of increase in the retail prices index (RPI) in Great Britain or 5 per cent, whichever is the less. The Secretary of State publishes an annual revaluation table showing what the relevant revaluation percentage is for the period over which the benefits must be revalued. Some schemes already make provision at least equal to that in the PA 1995. Therefore s. 51(1)(b) allows such schemes to continue as they have done.

Public-sector schemes are excluded from s. 51 because such schemes already provide for a guaranteed increase under the Pensions (Increase) Act 1971, which provides a mechanism for uprating pensions payable in most public-sector schemes. Increases under the Pensions (Increase) Act 1971 are linked to the full increase in retail prices which actually provides a level of protection which is at least as good as that provided for by the PA 1995.

Section 51(5) PA 1995 contains a power for the Secretary of State to make regulations for the purpose of calculating the increase to enable a pension that is derived from notional service attributed to the member and supplementary credits awarded to the member to be included as pensionable service.

Section 51(6) provides that the provisions of the section do not apply 'to any pension or part of a pension which . . . is derived from the payment by any member of the scheme of voluntary contributions'. Presumably 'voluntary contributions' covers both AVCs and FSAVCs, although the original exclusion applied only to FSAVCs. It was difficult to justify why in-house and free-standing AVCs were treated differently and the new provision which excludes all AVCs is at least equitable.

Early retirement is becoming increasingly common and the object of s. 52 is to strike a balance between protection against inflation and the cost of providing that protection, which is borne by the scheme.

Section 52 restricts LPI where a member is under 55. No increase is required by statute to be paid to, or for, a member whose pension is in payment and who has not reached the age of 55 at the time the increase takes effect — s. 52(1). Clearly this implies that if the scheme wishes to provide LPI in such a case it can do so. Section 52 does not apply to disability pensions — s. 52(2). Section 52(3) says that the rules of a scheme may provide that where a member under the age of 55, in receipt of a disability pension which had been paid at an increased rate, ceases to suffer from the disability before he attains the age of 55, but continues to be entitled to the pension, then any increases taking effect under s. 51 shall not be paid to him. Once the member reaches the age of 55 the pension has to be increased to the rate it would have been had he been entitled to the increases. What this means is that between the date of retirement and the age of 55, unless he is entitled to disability pension he is not entitled to any increases by reason of LPI. The provisions in this section already apply to public-sector schemes.

Section 53 weakens the concept of indexation. It says that where, in any tax year, the trustees or scheme manager make an increase in a person's pension which is not required (or part of which is not required) to be made under s. 51 or under s. 109 PSA 1993 then they may but are not required to deduct the amount of the increase (or that part of the increase) from any increase they would be required to make in the following tax year. Section 109 PSA 1993 allows for an annual increase of GMPs. Under the present contracting-out system, in every tax year since 1988–9 GMPs must be increased in line with retail prices index up to a maximum of 3 per cent. If a scheme makes an increase above that level in a tax year, that can be offset against the 3 per cent increase in the following tax year. This will continue for GMPs that have accrued before April 1997. If the rules of a scheme already require full RPI indexation then there will be no offsetting calculation from one year to the next as the scheme is already complying with the statutory requirements in full.

Section 55 PA 1995, however, introduces provisions which will end the annual increase in GMPs, and the amendments introduced by s. 55 to s. 109 PSA 1993 will therefore restrict increases in a member's GMP to those earned between the tax years 1988–9 and 1996–7. After that, increases to occupational pension schemes will be made in accordance with s. 55 PA 1995.

The effect of s. 53 is that it can lead to an averaging downwards of overall pension increases. This can be illustrated by the following example. Before s. 53 inflation was at 8 per cent in a particular year and the trustees decide, having regard to the performance of the fund, to increase the payment of pensions by 8 per cent. In the following year, inflation is running at 5 per cent and the trustees increase the payment of the pension by the LPI of 5 per cent. That would, ignoring compound interest, give a 13 per cent increase over two years and would protect pensions against inflation. However, the effect of s. 53 would be that in the second year the trustees could offset the extra 3 per cent they gave in the previous year and give only 2 per cent. The pensioner in such a case would then only enjoy increases in line with LPI.

Clearly the object of these sections is to protect members against the potential loss of pension rights by inflation, but the above example illustrates that they may not be as effective as was hoped. How effective they will be will depend on several factors. The first factor is the rate of inflation. If the rate of inflation were to remain below 5 per cent in future then LPI would provide total protection against the ravages of inflation. However, higher periods of inflation will occur from time to time and then LPI will not be so effective a measure.

The second factor is whether year-by-year or averaged LPI is chosen. Year-by-year LPI is where the 5 per cent limit will apply individually to each year, whereas an averaged LPI is where the limit is compared over the whole period to which it applies. The PA 1995 has chosen the former. The difference that year-by-year and averaged LPI can make to a pension can be illustrated by the following example. In a consecutive two year period inflation is at 1 per cent in year 1 and 9 per cent in year 2. The annual increases that are required over this two year period under a year-by-year LPI would be 1 per cent and 5 per cent. Under an averaged LPI the increases required would be 1 per cent in the first year and 9 per cent in the second. It is interesting to note that taking the years since 1972 a marginally greater degree of protection would have been afforded by using averaged LPI rather than year-by-year LPI.

The final factor that will determine the measure of protection is the percentage ceiling chosen for LPI. The figure chosen by the Act is 5 per cent which is somewhat arbitrary. What is important is that reasonable protection of pensions is provided in times when inflation oscillates widely over a short period of time. If we take the figure chosen for LPI of 5 per cent and look to see how effective this would have been between 1987 and 1993 it transpires that the real value of a pension which has been increased in line with this figure would have fallen by 10 per cent.

If, however, the LPI had been increased to 10 per cent then the value of the pension would have been protected over that period. Had the period chosen been a time when inflation reached 20 per cent — as it has done at certain times in the past — then not even the figure of 10 per cent would have provided protection.

The obvious problem when choosing the ceiling is the cost. Rather surprisingly, however, an increased LPI ceiling would lead to little increase in the cost. The reason for this is that the annual increase in pensions is funded through equities, which, when there is a period of high inflation, yield higher investment returns. Thus there would be an increase in the scheme's assets as well as its liabilities. Schemes that normally accrue a surplus when inflation exceeds the 5 per cent ceiling would therefore accrue less of a surplus.

9.2.2   Abolition of GMPs

The second major change introduced by the PA 1995 to occupational pension schemes is the abolition from 1997 of guaranteed minimum pensions (GMPs) which is required where schemes contract out of SERPS. The Social Security Pensions Act 1975 introduced the concept of SERPS in 1978 and provided for an additional State pension, i.e., SERPS (in addition to the basic flat-rate pension) based on earnings which exceed the lower earnings limit (LEL). There is also a ceiling called the upper earnings limit (UEL) of approximately seven and a half times the LEL. Many employees who are in an occupational pension scheme are 'contracted out' of SERPS and this means that in such a case the occupational pension scheme undertakes to provide a benefit at least equal to that which would have been earned under SERPS.

Section 136 PA 1995 covers the new arrangements for the future of contracting out. It introduces five new subsections and four new sections into the PSA 1993 and it amends the definition of contracting out. In a nutshell the new subsections (2A) and (2B) of s. 7 PA 1993 provide for the transition from the current contracting-out arrangements. Section 8 is amended to give a revised definition of contracted-out employment. The new ss. 12A to 12D set out the requirements for the new scheme-based contracting-out test for contracted-out salary related schemes (COSRs).

Section 136 inserts new subsections (2A) and (2B) into s. 7 PSA 1993. The new section will allow regulations to be made which permit contracting-out certificates already in force to continue until they are cancelled. Regulations will provide for the cancellation of the certificates at the end of a prescribed period, or at any time within that period if the prescribed conditions are no longer met. The regulations may also provide that a certificate issued before the appointed day, having effect on or after the effective date by virtue of subsection (2A), is to be effective in relation to an earner's service on or after that date as if it had been issued on or after that date. These powers are necessary in order to allow for a smooth transition from the old contracting-out certification requirements to the new ones.

Section 136(3) PA 1995 substitutes a new s. 9(2) in the PSA 1993 and inserts new subsections (2A) and (2B). An occupational pension scheme satisfies the new s. 9(2) if it satisfies the new subsection (2A) in relation to service before the provisions took effect and (2B) in relation to service on or after the date the provisions took effect. Subsection (2A) requires a scheme to comply with ss. 13 to 23 PSA 1993, or, in such cases or classes of case as may be prescribed, with those sections as modified by regulations. Sections 13 to 23 PSA 1993 outline the requirements for certification of occupational pension schemes which provide GMPs. Subsection (2B) requires a scheme to comply with the following requirements:

(a) it must comply with the provisions of s. 12A PSA 1993;

(b) it must comply with the restrictions imposed under s. 40 PA 1995 on employer-related investments;

(c) it should not fall within a prescribed class or description;

(d) it must satisfy such other requirements as may be prescribed, which must include requirements regarding the amount of the resources of the scheme and may include a requirement that, if the only members of the scheme were those falling within a prescribed class or description the scheme must comply with s. 12A; and

(e) its rules must be drafted so as to comply with the relevant requirements.

A new s. 9(2C) PSA 1993 provides for modification to be made through regulations to the new s. 9(2B)(a) and (b). A new s. 12A is introduced by the PA

1995 and this says that an occupational pension scheme must, in relation to the provisions of pensions for members and their widows or widowers, satisfy the statutory standard. A scheme complies with the statutory standard if it provides pensions to the member and the member's widow or widower which are equivalent or better than those provided under the reference scheme (see below) — s. 12A(3) PSA 1993.

Section 136 PA 1995 also inserts new ss. 12B, 12C and 12D into the PSA 1993. These set out the arrangements for the new scheme-based contracting-out test which salary related schemes will have to meet from April 1997. Current GMPs will be replaced by this new test, but GMPs which have accrued before the new test comes into effect will continue to form part of the occupational pension and this means that the scheme administrator will need to run two schemes side by side for at least 40 years after April 1997 until there are no scheme members left in active employment who have periods of pensionable service before that date. The new provisions state that schemes that are contracted-out are required to provide benefits that are at least as good as those of a 'reference scheme' which is defined in the legislation. A scheme actuary will have to verify that this requirement is met. New section 12A(4) allows for regulations to be made to set the criteria for the comparison of scheme benefits to the reference scheme. The method of comparison may be explained by a guidance note prepared by a body prescribed by the Secretary of State, such as the actuarial profession (s. 12A(5)). A reference scheme is, by new s. 12B, one that provides:

(a)   a pension from the age of 65 which continues for life;

(b)   an accrual rate of 1/80th of the average qualifying earnings in the last three tax years preceding the end of service multiplied by the number of years' service — not exceeding such number as would produce an annual rate equal to half the earnings on which it is calculated;

(c)   a spouse's pension of 50 per cent of the member's actual or accrued pension; and

(d)   that an earner's qualifying earnings in any tax year must be 90 per cent of band earnings, i.e., earnings between the upper and lower earnings limit.

These requirements may be modified by regulations (s. 12B(6)).

Section 12C contains powers to prohibit or restrict the transfer of any liability, the discharge of any liability to provide pensions under a relevant scheme or commutation of part of the benefit into a lump sum except in prescribed circumstances or on prescribed conditions. The regulations which govern the transfer will be utilised to ensure that the liability for the payment of pensions, or accrued rights to pensions, can only be transferred to secure arrangements. The intention with regard to lump sums is to follow current Inland Revenue limits, with appropriate exceptions for public-sector schemes.

Section 12D provides a power to prescribe by regulations the age at which benefits become payable in the case of salary related contracted-out schemes where members have service which falls after the principal appointed day. These powers will enable detailed requirements on contracted-out schemes to be prescribed.

Section 140 PA 1995 is fundamental to the changes in the contracting-out arrangements. Section 140(1) inserts a new s. 48A into the PSA 1993. This provides that no additional pension entitlement under SERPS arises in future where an employed earner in contracted-out employment whose Class 1 contributions are reduced in accordance with ss. 41 and 42A or whose minimum contributions towards an appropriate personal pension scheme are payable under s. 45(1). Regulations made under s. 48A(1) will, however, provide for an additional pension entitlement to accrue where an employed earner is in two concurrent employments if one is contracted-out and the other is not. The new s. 48A(3) will enable regulations to be made to prescribe circumstances under which the Secretary of State may restore, in full or in part, the SERPS rights of an individual whose employment has been contracted out of the State scheme. Section 141 PA 1995 sets out the circumstances in which that will be permitted.

A new s. 48A(4) PSA 1993 permits regulations to be made to provide enhanced entitlement to SERPS through Home Responsibilities Protection (HRP) to those contracted out of SERPS. The object of this is to ensure that employees who are contracted out of SERPS receive HRP to which they would have been entitled had they been in SERPS. Any regulations made in pursuance of s. 48A(4) are subject to the exercise of the power to enhance SERPS by HRP which is contained in s. 45(5) Social Security Contributions and Benefits Act 1992. This section should be of benefit to those who have more than one job and to women who will benefit from HRP.

Section 140(2) PA 1995 affects widows or widowers of people who have been members of COMPS or had an appropriate personal pension and amends s. 48 PSA 1993.

The broad principles of these provisions are that from 1999 onwards, SERPS will be based on a person's average earnings from 1978 or the age of 16, if later, up to the year he reaches State pension age. The average will be calculated by reference to the number of years in that period (the denominator). That period is 21 years in the case of a person reaching State pension age in 2027 or later.

Section 45(5) of the Social Security Contributions and Benefits Act 1992 enables regulations to be made that would allow for the denominator to be reduced for years when a person qualifies for HRP, with the proviso that it cannot fall below 20. Before the PA 1995, HRP applied to the basic pension. The intention behind the PA 1995 is to extend HRP to SERPS. Regulations need not be made yet as they will only be necessary as we approach 1999 when other changes to SERPS occur.

People contracted out of SERPS will get the benefit of HRP as well as those who are contracted in. The aim is to give to those who are contracted out after 1997 the value of HRP enhancement of SERPS that those not contracted out will receive. Those who are contracted out will be given a notional SERPS entitlement as if they had been in SERPS. This will be increased because of HRP. The increase will be paid as SERPS entitlement.

Section 141 PA 1995 sets out the circumstances after the principal appointed day, in which the buy-back of accrued occupational pension rights into the State scheme will be possible. The section is necessary because of the break between SERPS and contracted-out occupational pension schemes from 1997. As a result, the retention of the facility to buy back into SERPS which could be done before the provisions came into force will not be practicable. There is no system either for buying back pre-1997 GMPs, which will remain unequal for men and women, into a SERPS system that will begin to be equalised in 2010 or for buying back an unequal element of the new equal scheme benefit that will remain until 2020. The facility to buy back accrued rights should not be necessary after 1997 as trustees will be able to discharge accrued liabilities for periods of COSRS service by a number of methods which are to be detailed by regulations. Individuals can buy personal pensions or transfer to other contracted-out schemes.

Paragraph 5(3) of sch. 2 PSA 1993 deals with deemed buy-backs which provides a safety net when schemes wind up insolvent. This provision allows, but does not require regulations to be made 'where there has been a failure to pay a premium and the failure is shown not to have been with the consent or connivance of, or attributable to any negligence on the part of, the person in respect of whom it is payable, for treating the premium as having been paid'.

Regulations were made under the PSA 1993 and the Maxwell case was handled under these regulations. Future cases will fall to be handled under s. 141 PA 1995. There has been much debate over the role of the Secretary of State under the new para. 5(3A) of sch. 2 to the PSA 1993, which uses the phrase 'if, in the opinion of the Secretary of State'. The government's desire however is that, as under the previous regulations, the Secretary of State will express no opinion as to whether an employee deserves to have his State-scheme rights restored. The Secretary of State's opinion will only relate to the resources of the scheme and whether there are sufficient or insufficient resources to meet the liability to pay cash equivalents.

The way in which the system of restoring State-scheme rights will differ in future is that the amount restored will be calculated in the same way for COSRS as for COMPS.

When SERPS was originally introduced in 1978 it was intended that a contracted-out scheme would have to satisfy two conditions. The first was the requisite benefits rule and was based on a 1/80th accrual rate (as in the reference scheme) and the second was the GMP rule. In 1988 the government dropped the requisite benefit test as it was thought to be too complex and ineffective. It is somewhat surprising that a test that was thought to be too complex and ineffective less than 10 years ago should re-emerge!

This leaves us asking the question, How effective is the reference scheme likely to be in protecting members' benefits? One problem is that it may provide lower benefits if, during a person's working life, there are periods of high inflation. This is because it does not provide an adequate level of inflation protection compared with GMP. The reference scheme provides benefits levels that are equal to those provided by a GMP *only* if inflation does not rise above 5 per cent. If inflation is greater than 5 per cent then GMPs can provide a better deal. SERPS is inflation-proofed and even when members contract out of SERPS they are still entitled to 'residual SERPS benefits'. However the PA 1995 has abolished residual SERPS benefits. Residual SERPS benefits arise because members of a contracted-out scheme still retain at least some SERPS benefits. SERPS retain the obligation to pay increases on GMPs which are above 3 per cent per annum. The obligation for this will now fall to the scheme and be subject to a limit of 5 per cent.

Members of contracted-out schemes could also suffer losses under the provisions of the Act which removes guaranteed protection which the DSS offered for GMP benefits. The value of this can be illustrated by the Maxwell affair where the pensioner members of the Mirror scheme had their GMPs restored immediately because of this guarantee.

Other provisions in the Act such as the requirement for a solvency standard and a compensation scheme will only partially compensate for the loss of GMPs.

9.2.3   Age-related rebates

It is the intention of the government to make both occupational pension schemes and personal pension schemes more attractive to a broader age range. Section 137 PA 1995 tries to achieve this by including provision for age-related rebates for contracted-out personal pensions (see 9.3.1) and money purchase occupational schemes. The new rebates reflect different levels of rebates that are needed to produce benefits equivalent to SERPS at different ages. Section 137(2) substitutes for s. 41(1) PSA 1993 a new s. 41(1) and (1A). Section 41(1) allows regulations to prescribe alternatives to the LEL and UEL for people who are not paid on a weekly basis.

Section 137(4)(c) PA 1995 provides that the contracted-out rebate is to be set out and amended by an order of the Secretary of State, who must lay before Parliament the draft order which must be approved by a resolution of each House. The reason for this provision is that at present it is not known what the rate of rebate will be.

Section 137(5) inserts new ss. 42A and 42B into the PSA 1993 and introduces arrangements for setting, calculating and paying contracted-out rebate to contracted-out money purchase schemes (COMPS). Members of such schemes and the employers will receive a reduction in the rate of national insurance contributions they pay, and may receive further rebates after the end of the tax year. The amount of the rebate will depend on the age of the scheme member.

The new s. 42A(4) provides a power to prescribe how and when the rebate may be made by the Secretary of State. It is intended that payments will be made after the tax year to which they relate has ended and employers' end of year returns are received.

The new s. 42B allows the Secretary of State to lay before Parliament a report by the government Actuary on what the level of rebate for the members of COMPS and their employers should be, and a draft order setting out the levels of rebate for up to five years. The levels of future rebates will only appear in secondary legislation.

Under this new system different levels of rebate will be set for each tax year for COMPS, one for each age at the beginning of the tax year. The order will also set the flat-rate levels to be received as a reduction in national insurance contribution liability by employees in COMPS and their employers for the five-year period. The order will contain many rates and those will be detailed in secondary legislation, but subject to affirmative resolution procedures.

The government has decided that the total rebate will be capped at 9 per cent. The reason for this is to limit the short-term effect on the National Insurance Fund were too many older employees to contract out on a money purchase basis over the next few years, during which time the rebate could be as high as 15.5 per cent. On a long-term basis the higher age rebate will fall as SERPS accrual falls with the growing maturity of a scheme.

It is difficult to see at present how the system will operate until the government indicates its objectives in setting the level of rebate. If the rebate is set at a fair level the result will probably be that at most ages there will be a lower rebate and this may lead to less contracting out than at present.

9.2.4 Transfer values

Section 152 PA 1995 amends s. 93 PSA 1993 and makes provision for the right to a cash equivalent to be extended to a member who left an occupational pension scheme before 1 January 1986. Before this amendment, pre-1986 early leavers from occupational pension schemes had no statutory rights of transfer, and most pre-1986 early leavers have pensions which are frozen, i.e., the pensions are not protected by the revaluation provisions which apply to those who left after 1 January 1986. Section 152 PA 1995 gives members with such frozen deferred rights the opportunity to transfer those rights to another occupational pension scheme or personal pension scheme. However, new s. 93(1)(a) PSA 1993 contains a power to except such members from the right to a cash equivalent, provided certain prescribed requirements are met. The intention behind this is that schemes that have fully protected the rights of pre-1986 early leavers by revaluing the deferred benefits at least in line with the retail prices index will be excluded, as will all members of public service schemes.

Section 153 inserts a new s. 93A into the PSA 1993 and gives members whose occupational pension schemes are not wholly money purchase schemes the right to request and be given a guaranteed statement of their cash equivalent at a guaranteed date. The guarantee date must be within a prescribed period beginning with the date of the application and within the prescribed period ending with the date on which the statement of entitlement is provided to the member. Previous law allowed a scheme two months to produce an estimate of a member's cash equivaient, but under that there was no requirement that the estimated level of the transfer value be guaranteed and therefore a slightly longer time period is going to be allowed under the new law.

Regulations may be made to specify how often a member may apply for a statement of entitlement.

If a statement of entitlement is not provided under s. 93A then s. 10 PA 1995 applies to a trustee or a scheme manager who has failed to take all such steps as are reasonable to secure compliance with the section.

Section 154 PA 1995 amends s. 94 PSA 1993. The amendment made by s. 154(2) says a member who has received his statement of entitlement can make a relevant application within three months beginning with the guarantee date in respect of that statement and thereby acquires a right to his guaranteed cash equivalent. This three-month guaranteed period does not commence, however, until the statement has 'been produced. A relevant application is one made under s. 95 PSA 1993 and not withdrawn. A member's cash equivalent pension right must be exercised in writing to the trustee or manager of the scheme. The cash equivalent can only be used in a number of ways and these are defined in s. 95(2) PSA 1993 to be:

(a)   for acquiring rights under a personal pension scheme;
(b)   for acquiring transfer credits allowed under the rules of another occupational pension scheme;

(c)   for purchasing annuity contracts;

(d)   for acquiring credits in a self-employed pension arrangement.

Section 154(5) PA 1995 inserts a subsections (3) into s. 94 PSA 1993 and provides that regulations can be made to modify a member's right to a guaranteed cash equivalent where, for example, the payment of the guarantee might seriously prejudice the interests of the other members of the scheme.

9.3   CHANGES TO PERSONAL PENSION SCHEMES

9.3.1   Age-related rebates for appropriate personal pension schemes

The PA 1995 has introduced age-related rebates in connection with appropriate personal pensions (APPs) and COMPS. Section 138 introduces new arrangements for setting and calculating the contracted-out rebate for members of appropriate personal pension schemes. The age-related rebates introduced by the Act are specifically intended to make personal pensions more attractive to a higher age group and to take more people out of SERPS. Before the Act was introduced it was generally thought that older people (anyone aged over 55) were better off either staying with SERPS or opting back if they were out of it. The flat-rate rebate structure that operated in appropriate personal pension schemes meant that holders of such pensions did not maintain their appropriate personal pension until retirement as economically it did not make sense to do so. The reason for this was that with the old system of rebates there was a fixed limit. This fixed amount when multiplied by the number of years that it was held in the fund gave different calculations at different ages. The older one gets the fewer years there are remaining to retirement. Under the new regime the rebate is varied according to age.

Section 138(2) substitutes a new s. 45(1) into the PSA 1993. This provides for the Secretary of State to make payments of age-related rebates to APPs. This replaces the existing arrangements whereby APPs receive a rebate at a flat rate set for COSRS with an addition for those aged 30 or more.

Section 138(5) inserts a new s. 45A into the PSA 1993. This requires the Secretary of State to lay before Parliament:

(a)   a report of the Government actuary of the level of rebate for members of appropriate personal pension schemes;

(b)   a report by the Secretary of State stating what he considers the percentages should be;

(c)   a draft of the order.

The order has the effect in relation to a period not exceeding five tax years and may specify different percentages in respect of earners by reference to their ages on the first day of the year.

The procedure is largely the same as at present but s. 42 PSA 1993 set an initial level of rebate and it was amended afterwards by order. Now the arrangements will set and amend the levels by order. The orders will require approval by resolution of both Houses of Parliament. The object of the section is that appropriate personal pension holders are to be paid a rebate specifically designed to provide the appropriate level of pension in place of SERPS. At present, there must be a clear tax year between the order being made and its coming into force.

It should be noted at this point that the age-related rebates for occupational pension schemes and personal pension schemes will be set at a different level by the Government Actuary under the PA 1995 for two reasons. The first reason is that occupational pension schemes are related to a particular employment and such schemes would be expected to incur lower expenses due to economies of scale. Personal pension schemes are individualised and therefore can be expected to incur greater expenses. Each holder's fund has to be administered separately. The rebates have to reflect this. The second reason is that members of money purchase occupational pension schemes and their employers receive part of the rebate during the course of the tax year as a reduction in national insurance contributions. The balance is then paid at the end of the tax year. In personal pension schemes, however, the whole of the rebate is paid at the end of the tax year and this means a loss of investment return on the rebate. Thus the rebate of occupational pension schemes should be set at a lower rate than that for personal pension schemes.

Section 139 inserts a new s. 45(B) into the PSA 1993. Section 45B(1) allows regulations to be made to prescribe how age may be verified and to ensure the correct payment of age-related rebates in money purchase and personal pension schemes.

9.3.2 Increase in limit of post-retirement increases

Sections 162 and 163 PA 1995 require APPs to provide a measure of protection against inflation. Pensions in payment which give effect to protected rights will be required to be increased by at least the rate of inflation up to 5 per cent a year (LPI). This is meant to provide an acceptable level of protection against inflation, thereby helping to maintain an adequate stream of income throughout the period.

Section 162 provides that a personal pension that is used to contract out of SERPS must, in relation to contributions made in respect of employment carried on on or after the appointed day, be increased annually by at least a specific percentage.

The first increase under s. 162 must take place no later than the first anniversary of the date on which the pension was first paid and subsequent increases must take effect at intervals of not more than 12 months.

Section 163(2) specifies how the first increase should be calculated where the pension has been in payment for less than 12 months.

9.3.3 Power to reject choice of appropriate personal pension schemes

Section 164 PA 1995 amends s. 44 PSA 1993 and allows the Secretary of State to reject a person's choice of appropriate personal pension scheme where he is of the opinion that the scheme does not comply with certain requirements of the Act or that it is inexpedient to allow the scheme to be chosen by the earner.

This will prevent personal pension providers from selling APPs if they fail to deliver certain standards of financial supervision and control. This includes matters such as allocating money properly to schemes dealing with transfers and having proper standards of record keeping.

Section 34 PSA 1993 already provides for the cancellation of appropriate scheme certificates if schemes fail to meet those standards. Those powers are to be retained, but the government thought that a less severe measure was needed because of the implications for existing investors if the right of a scheme to conduct its business were cancelled.

The new power is designed to prevent schemes from accepting new business until such time as the shortcomings have been remedied. Existing members would not be required to make alternative pension arrangements and would not therefore incur additional costs of administration. The government would attempt wherever possible to assist the providers to resolve areas of difficulty.

9.3.4 Monitoring personal pension schemes

Section 147 PA 1995 inserts a new s. 33A into the PSA 1993. This introduces a new requirement on any person acting as the auditor or actuary of an appropriate personal pension scheme to 'blow the whistle' to the Secretary of State if he has reasonable cause to believe that the scheme is not satisfying the requirement for continued appropriate scheme status. The section is designed to increase the amount of protection given to investors in personal pension schemes.

9.4   CHANGES TO THE STATE SCHEME

State provision for retirement falls into three basic categories:

(a)   the basic State pension;
(b)   SERPS; and
(c)   other social security benefits.

The basic State pension is paid in full to a person who has paid or been credited with contributions for at least 90 per cent of his or her working life. Prior to the PA 1995 this was 44 years out of 49 for a man and 39 years out of 44 for a woman. For those with incomplete records the pension is reduced proportionally until there is no entitlement if the pension is less than a quarter of the full rate. The basic pension is independent of the actual value of contributions made. SERPS is the additional earnings-related pension which is paid for by national insurance contributions (see 9.4.3). Other benefits may be payable to people over the State pension age who have a low income or particular needs.

9.4.1   Equalisation of State pension age

Schdule 4 and s. 126 PA 1995 equalise treatment given to men and women with regard to State pensions and other benefits. These amendments in the Act have resulted, in part at least, from the European Court of Justice's decision in *Barber* v *Guardian Royal Exchange Assurance Group* (case C-262/88) [1991] 1 QB 344. Several different options were mooted with regard to the age chosen for equalisation. Should it take place at 60, 63 or 65, or should there be a flexible decade of retirement allowing people to choose to take their pension at any time between the ages of 60 and 70. The government decided to equalise the State pension age to

65 and announced its intention in December 1993 in its White Paper entitled *Equality in State Pension Age* (Cmnd 2420). The reasons that this age was chosen were mainly demographic and financial. If the age for retirement had been 60 then there would be 15.3 million people of pensionable age in 2020, 17.9 million in 2040 and 17.5 million in 2050. With the age of retirement being selected as 65, however, these numbers fall significantly to 11.6 million in 2020, 14.7 million in 2040 and 14.0 million in 2050.

Section 126 introduces the common retirement age of 65. This change will be gradually phased in between the years 2010 and 2020 and sch. 4 para. 1 provides for this. Schedule 4, para. 1 says that the pensionable age is 65 for men and 60 for women born before 6 April 1950, 65 for women born after 5 April 1955. No woman born before 6 April 1950 will be affected. According to the table in sch. 4, para. 1, for every two months that passes between 6 May 2010 and 6 March 2020 one month is added to the retirement age. A female pensioner who was born on 6 October 1951 will attain pensionable age on 6 May 2013, when she is aged 61 years and 7 months. A female pensioner born on 6 November 1951 will retire on 6 July 2013 having attained the age of 61 years 9 months. From 2010 to 2020, therefore, women's retirement age will gradually move from 60 to 65. This 10-year phasing starts in 15 years' time.

9.4.2 Inclusion of family credit and disability working allowance in calculating SERPS→STATE EARNING PENSION SCHEME

Section 127 PA 1995 inserts into the Social Security Contributions and Benefits Act 1992 a new s. 45A. This sets out provisions which will enhance additional pension entitlement under SERPS in respect of years where family credit and disability working allowance have been paid — s. 45A(1). Section 45A(2) contains a power which allows the Secretary of State to prescribe which member of a couple receiving family credit should receive the enhanced pension. Usually family credit is paid to the female of a couple, but she may not be in employment and thus accruing an additional pension entitlement. It would be economically more advantageous for the main earner to benefit from the enhancement.

9.4.3 Changes in the way SERPS is calculated

When SERPS was introduced, the original intention was that it would represent 25 per cent of average revalued reckonable earnings over the best 20 years of a person's working life. It was conceded that the cost of the scheme would be too great and the Fowler reforms were introduced. These reforms were designed to curb the cost in the 21st century, and they reduced the accrual rate in stages for people retiring after April 1992 to 20 per cent for people retiring in 2010 and later. They also removed the best 20 years provision. The calculation would be based on reckonable earnings over the whole working life, i.e., 16 to State pension age. Currently SERPS would mature after 44 years for women and 49 for men. PA 1995 will eventually equalise it at 49 years for all.

Section 128 introduces a new subsection (5A) into s. 44 of the Social Security Contributions and Benefits Act 1992 and deals with the annualisation of SERPS. The new subsection amends the method of calculation of SERPS for those who qualify after 5 April 2000.

The present method for calculating SERPS revalues total earnings (up to the UEL) for each year in line with the increase in average earnings and then the annual LEL is deducted for the last complete tax year from each year's revalued earnings to give a surplus for each year. Since the LEL increases with prices, SERPS entitlements have been growing. The government never intended this to happen and therefore the introduction of annualisation will change the calculation so that the annual LEL is deducted before revaluation takes place, i.e., when looking back at a person's working life, in each year the amount which is used for revaluation calculation up to the date of retirement is the difference between the salary (if it is below the UEL) and the LEL. It will be the amount above the LEL only which will be revalued.

It would seem that the effect of this amendment to the value of SERPS will be to cut the value of SERPS by about 14 per cent by the year 2020. Its effect is going to be greatest on those who have a complete work history of earnings above the LEL since 1978 and will be least for those with a broken work history. The section will not affect anyone reaching pension age or qualifying for widow's benefits before 6 April 2000.

Thus the overall effect of PA 1995 is to reduce SERPS spending. This is achieved in three ways:

(a) The equalisation of the State pension age to 65 results in a delay in the payment of SERPS to women by five years compared to the pre-Act situation and it is estimated that it will reduce SERPS expenditure by £2.6 billion in the year 2050.

(b) The annualisation of SERPS under s. 128.

(c) The contracting-out changes which break the links between SERPS and contracting out and the introduction of age-related rebates for APPs.

9.4.4 Increase in the increment granted to those who defer receipt of State pension

Section 55 of and sch. 5 to the Social Security Contributions and Benefits Act 1992 provide for the deferment of retirement. During the first five years after the attainment of pensionable age a person is able to defer his or her right to a State pension. This results in a higher rate of pension once it is actually taken up.

Paragraph 6 sch. 4 PA 1995 introduces a degree of flexibility for those who wish to defer drawing their pensions until a later date. It increases the increment granted to those who defer receipt of State pension from 1/7 per cent to 1/5 per cent for every week of deferment and removes the upper limit on the number of years that a pension claim can be deferred.

9.4.5 Changes to dependants' benefits

Schedule 4 Part II PA 1995 provides equality for men and women in certain pensions and other benefits. Paragraph 2 of sch. 4 replaces ss. 83 and 84 of the Social Security Contributions and Benefits Act 1992 with s. 83A. This provides that increases of pensions shall be subject to the same rules for a dependent wife or husband from 6 April 2010 and thus removes the extra condition for entitlement which is currently only applicable to women, i.e., that the pensioner must be entitled to an increase in unemployment benefit or incapacity benefit immediately before the commencement of her entitlement to retirement pension. The paragraph also carries forward an amended delegated power which allows regulations to be made to provide that there shall be no increase in pension where the spouse has earnings. This refers to adult dependency increases.

Paragraph 3 sch. 4 PA 1995 inserts new ss. 48A, 48B and 48C in place of ss. 49 and 50 of the Social Security Contributions and Benefits Act 1992. Under s. 49 a married woman or widow could claim a State retirement pension (Category B) on the basis of her husband's contribution record, provided that she had attained pensionable age and complied with any of the circumstances set out in subsections (2) to (5) of that section. Section 50 dealt with the method of calculating the rate of retirement pension.

Paragraph 3 of sch. 4 PA 1995 now makes Category B State retirement pensions available to either spouse by means of the other's contribution record and to both widows and widowers, i.e., it equalises the conditions for paying category B pensions (derived right pensions) to men and women for people reaching pension age on or after 6 April 2010.

9.4.6   Equalisation of graduated pensions

Graduated retirement benefit is the precursor to SERPS. The right to such benefit was acquired up until 1975. It is paid as an increase in the weekly rate of retirement pension. In the case of a person who is entitled to graduated retirement benefit only, the law provides that it can be paid on its own. Section 36(7) of the National Insurance Act 1975 provides that a person is treated as if he or she had a nominal weekly rate of retirement pension. Thus the graduated retirement pension benefit is paid as an increase in a nil-rate retirement pension.

The current wording of s. 36(7) National Insurance Act 1975 is misleading and could be interpreted as allowing a person to forgo retirement pension and take graduated benefit only. Section 131 PA 1995 clarifies the legislation to ensure that the provision applies only to a person who claims, but is not entitled to, retirement pension because of a failure to satisfy the contribution condition, but who has some graduated retirement benefit entitlement.

Section 131 also amends ss. 150 and 155 of the Social Security Administration Act 1992 in order to clarify how graduated retirement benefit is to be uprated. There can be three elements to graduated retirement benefit:

(a)   the basic unit rate;
(b)   increments; and
(c)   inherited benefit.

Since 1978 graduated retirements benefit has formed part of the normal pensions uprating. The legislation provides for uprating of the basic unit rate and increments, but not of inherited graduated retirement benefit. The amendments to ss. 150 and 155 amend the law to put it beyond doubt that inherited benefits are incremented.

Paragraph 7 of sch. 4 PA 1995 amends s. 62(1) of the Social Security Contributions and Benefits Act 1992 which provides the power to amend certain parts of s. 36(2) of the National Insurance Act 1965. This extended power will allow for regulations to be made to equalise the cost of a unit of graduated retirement benefit so that the value is the same for men and women. The entitlement conditions for widows and widowers will also have to equalised.

9.4.7 Contributions paid in error

The structure of the national insurance scheme provides for slightly different levels of contributions and ranges of benefits depending on whether individuals are employees or self-employed. While employees qualify for the additional pension in the SERPS generally the self-employed do not. There is usually no difficulty in deciding whether a person is employed or self-employed, but occasionally there are cases where the individual is treated as an employee and Class 1 contributions are paid but subsequently it transpires that he or she is self-employed and Class 2 contributions are payable.

Section 133 PA 1995 is designed to help with difficulties that can occur in such a situation.

At present where it is discovered that an individual has been wrongly treated as an employee and thus has paid the wrong contributions, such contributions may be refunded but any benefits which have been paid out as a result of erroneous contributions must be recovered from the refund. Future benefit title will be established on the basis of an amended contribution record.

Where the error is discovered after a number of years and the contributor has been expecting that SERPS will accrue as a result of Class 1 contributions, a refund may fall short of the amount needed to purchase equivalent pension rights from, for example, a personal pension scheme. Some workers may have retired and would therefore lose part of their SERPS with no way of fully replacing the loss.

The object of s. 133 PA 1995 is to introduce flexibility into the national insurance scheme. It is designed to provide new powers which, in circumstances prescribed by regulations, would allow individuals to opt not to have their Class 1 contributions refund but to have their SERPS entitlement determined as if the contributions had been properly paid. Similar arrangements also apply to additional pension paid with widow's and incapacity benefits.

The section also allows for individuals on whose behalf contributions have been made to a personal pension scheme, on the basis that they are employees, to be treated as if they were employees for the period of miscategorisation.

The section does not prevent a refund of contributions being made to the person engaging the individual and this avoids disputes between individuals and their engagers.

9.4.8 Uprating of pensions increased under s. 52 Social Security Contributions and Benefits Act 1992

Section 52(3) Social Security Contributions and Benefits Act 1992 provides for a person's additional pension entitlement to be increased by reference to the late spouse's additional pension entitlement, thus creating a composite element entitlement. The intention is that where this composite entitlement arises between 6 April and a date in April when the annual uprating order takes effect, only that part of the additional pension entitlement which was pre-existing should benefit from uprating. The recently acquired part of the additional pension, which is derived from inflation-proofed earnings, will not. This situation could arise if a pensioner has been receiving his or her own Category A additional pension, is widowed and becomes entitled to a further additional pension based on the contributions of his or her deceased spouse, in which case the existing legislation provides that the newly acquired national pension will not be uprated on that particular occasion, although it will be in the future.

A problem with the law before PA 1995 was that it did not cover the converse situation, i.e., where a widow's benefit recipient is already in receipt of inherited additional pension and becomes entitled, on retirement, to her own additional pension. Section 130(1) PA 1995 substitutes a new s. 156 into the Social Security Administration Act 1992 so that in such circumstances only the existing additional pension should be uprated on that occasion.

9.5   EARNER EMPLOYED IN MORE THAN ONE EMPLOYMENT

Section 148 PA 1995 amends paragraph 1 of Schedule 1 to the Social Security Contributions and Benefits Act 1992. That paragraph says that earnings paid from different employments are aggregated to determine the national insurance contributions due. The rule is applied if an employee has more than one employment, either with the same employer or with different employers who carry on business in association with each other.

The provision will apply only if an employee with different pension arrangements has more than one employment with the same or associated employers, and the earnings from the employments have to be aggregated for the purpose of calculating contributions. Different pension arrangements attract different rates of contributions and rebates. Contributions and earnings between the LEL and UEL are the only contributions and earnings that count towards some pension arrangements. Where the earnings from different employments fall to be aggregated and these different employments give title to more than one type of pension scheme, it must be decided which pension should receive the benefit of the rebated contributions.

Section 148 will now enable people to build up rights to APPs if they hold such a plan, before any other type of pension scheme.

9.6   INTERIM ARRANGEMENTS FOR GIVING EFFECT TO PROTECTED RIGHTS

The Finance Act 1993 introduced new measures for allowing the purchase of an annuity to be deferred but cash payments to be taken from the fund in the meantime in the case of appropriate personal pension schemes. The intention behind this was to allow those who retire at times when investment conditions are unfavourable to wait until they are better. Section 143 PA 1995 inserts a new s. 28A into the PSA 1993. This enables members of APP schemes, instead of having to use the whole of their protected rights to purchase an annuity at pension age, to defer doing so, but to withdraw payments in the meantime under interim arrangements.

Small self-administered occupational pension schemes already had some flexibility in the timing of the purchase of their annuities and s. 145 PA 1995 extends the option to occupational pension schemess, including FSAVCs.

9.7   DISCHARGE OF PROTECTED RIGHTS ON WINDING UP

Section 146 PA 1995 introduces new options for contracted-out money purchase schemes that are winding up. Such schemes may experience difficulties in finding a home for every member's protected rights. This may be so because a transfer to another occupational pension scheme is inappropriate or the member cannot be traced. In such a situation the scheme will be unable to wind up for a number of years.

Section 146 inserts a new s. 32A into the PSA 1993 wich will enable schemes to secure a member's protected rights by an in-house transaction which makes the member the beneficiary of an appropriate insurance policy. Protected rights can also be bought out by another insurance company through an appropriate insurance policy. An appropriate insurance policy is one that will ensure that the normal rules that apply to protected rights will apply to the rights secured by a policy, for example, the rules on providing a pension and survivor's rights.

The member can reject the option offered by s. 32A and take out an appropriate pension or transfer to another COMPS on going to a new employer.

Appendix

This appendix lists sections and subsections of the PA 1995 that contain the power to make delegated legislation or where regulations touch or concern the subject matter of the section or subsection.

Section/ Subsection	Subject area
3(2)	Prohibition Orders
7(4)	Appointment of trustees
7(6)	Appointment of trustees
10(1)	Civil penalties
10(2)(b)	Civil penalties
10(3)	Civil penalties
10(4)	Civil penalties
17(1)(c)	Exceptions to requirement for member-nominated trustees
17(4)(b)	Exceptions to requirement for member-nominated trustees
18(1)	Corporate trustees: member-nominated directors
19(1)(c)	Corporate trustees: exceptions to s. 18
19(4)	Corporate trustees: exceptions to s. 18
20(1)(b)	Selection and eligibility of member-nominated trustees and directors
20(4)	Selection and eligibility of member-nominated trustees and directors
21(4)	Member-nominated trustees and directors: supplementary
21(5)	Member-nominated trustees and directors: supplementary
21(6)	Member-nominated trustees and directors: supplementary
21(7)	Member-nominated trustees and directors: supplementary
23(2)	Requirement for independent trustee
23(3)(c)	Requirement for independent trustee
27(3)	Trustee not to be auditor or actuary of scheme
27(5)	Trustee not to be auditor or actuary of scheme
32(2)(b)	Decisions by majority of trustees
32(3)	Decisions by majority of trustees
33(3)	Investment powers: duty of care
35(7)	Investment principles
37(3)	Payment of surplus to employer

Section/ Subsection	*Subject area*
37(4)(e)	Payment of surplus to employer
37(5)	Payment of surplus to employer
37(10)	Payment of surplus to employer
38(3)(b)	Power to defer winding up
40(1)	Restriction on employer-related investments
40(2)	Restriction on employer-related investments
41(1)	Provision of documents for members
41(2)(c)	Provision of documents for members
41(5)	Provision of documents for members
41(6)	Provision of documents for members
47(3)	Professional advisers
47(5)	Professional advisers
47(6)	Professional advisers
47(7)	Professional advisers
47(9)	Professional advisers
48(1)	Blowing the whistle
48(2)	Blowing the whistle
48(9)	Blowing the whistle
49(1)	Keeping of receipts, payments and records
49(2)	Keeping of receipts, payments and records
49(3)	Keeping of receipts, payments and records
49(4)	Keeping of receipts, payments and records
49(5)	Keeping of receipts, payments and records
49(8)	Keeping of receipts, payments and records
50(1)	Resolution of disputes
50(2)	Resolution of disputes
50(3)	Resolution of disputes
50(7)	Resolution of disputes
51(3)	Annual increase in rate of pension
51(5)	Annual increase in rate of pension
55(b)	End of increase in GMP
56(2)(b)	Minimum funding requirement
56(3)	Minimum funding requirement
57(1)	Valuation and certification of assets and liabilities
57(2)	Valuation and certification of assets and liabilities
57(4)	Valuation and certification of assets and liabilities
57(5)	Valuation and certification of assets and liabilities
58(2)	Schedules of contributions
58(3)	Schedules of contributions
58(4)	Schedules of contributions
58(5)	Schedules of contributions
58(6)	Schedules of contributions
58(7)	Schedules of contributions
59(1)	Determination of contributions
59(3)	Determination of contributions
60(2)	Serious underprovision

Section/ Subsection	Subject area
60(3)	Serious underprovision
60(4)	Serious underprovision
60(5)	Serious underprovision
60(6)	Serious underprovision
60(7)	Serious underprovision
61	Section 56–60: supplementary
63(5)	Equal treatment
64(2)	Equal treatment: exceptions
64(3)	Equal treatment: exceptions
64(4)	Equal treatment: exceptions
66(4)	Effect on terms of employment of equal treatment rule
67(3)	Restriction on power to alter schemes
67(4)	Restriction on power to alter schemes
67(5)	Restriction on power to alter schemes
67(6)	Restriction on power to alter schemes
68(2)	Powers of trustees to modify schemes by resolution
68(6)	Powers of trustees to modify schemes by resolution
69(2)	Grounds for applying modifications
69(3)	Grounds for applying modifications
69(6)	Grounds for applying modifications
73(3)	Preferential liabilities on winding up
73(7)	Preferential liabilities on winding up
73(8)	Preferential liabilities on winding up
74(1)	Discharge of liabilities by insurance
74(3)	Discharge of liabilities by insurance
74(5)	Discharge of liabilities by insurance
75(5)	Deficiencies in assets
75(9)	Deficiencies in assets
75(10)	Deficiencies in assets
76(2)	Excess assets on winding up
76(4)	Excess assets on winding up
76(8)	Excess assets on winding up
77(1)	Excess assets remaining after winding up
77(6)	Excess assets remaining after winding up
78(6)	The Compensation Board
80(4)	Review of decisions
81(1)	Cases where compensation provisions apply
81(2)	Cases where compensation provisions apply
82(1)	Applications for payments
83(2)	Amount of compensation
83(3)	Amount of compensation
84(1)	Payments made in anticipation
84(2)	Payments made in anticipation
84(3)	Payments made in anticipation
85(2)	Surplus funds
85(3)	Surplus funds

Section/ Subsection	Subject area
86	Modification of compensation provisions
87(1)	Schedule of payments to money purchase schemes
87(2)	Schedule of payments to money purchase schemes
87(3)	Schedule of payments to money purchase schemes
88(1)	Schedule of payments to money purchase schemes: supplementary
89(1)	Further provisions regarding money purchase schemes
89(2)	Further provisions regarding money purchase schemes
92(4)	Forfeiture of pension by virtue of prescribed offences
92(6)	Forfeiture of pension in prescribed circumstances
93(2)	Forfeiture by reference to obligation to employer: determination of monetary value of obligation
94(1)	Modifications of ss. 91–93
95(2)	Reduction in value of pension scheme assets: value of assets determination
96(2)	Review of decisions of OPRA: period for application
96(5)	Review of decisions of OPRA: procedure on application for review
107(2)	Disclosure for facilitating discharge of functions by other supervising authorities
114(7)	Disclosure of information by Compensation Board: persons to whom such information may be disclosed
116(1)	Breach of regulations: provision for same to be an offence and for penalty
118(1)	Power to modify Part I
118(2)	Power to disapply sections 22–26 and 117 to trust schemes
119	Power to make regulations under ss. 56(3), 73(3) or 75: values of liabilities/assets to be calculated with guidance from prescribed bodies
120	Regulations made under Part I: requirement for consultation and exceptions
125(1)	Occupational Pension Scheme: salary related if not falling within prescribed class or description
125(2)	Power to apply Part I with modifications to OPS which are not money purchase schemes but where some benefits are money purchase benefits
125(3)	Extension of meaning of employer
125(4)	Extend or restrict meaning of member, determine who is treated as prospective member and determine times at which person is treated as becoming or ceasing to be same
133	New provision inserted into Social Security Contributions and Benefits Act 1992: regulations relating to
135	Order under s. 180 may designate day of coming into force as principal appointed day for purposes of Part III
136(1)	Amendments to s. 7 PSA 1993: regulations relating to
136(3)	Amendments to s. 9 PSA 1993: regulations relating to

Section/ Subsection	Subject area
136(5)	Amendments to s. 12 PSA 1993: regulations relating to
137(2)	Amendments to s. 41 PSA 1993: regulations relating to
137(5)	Amendments to s. 42 PSA 1993: regulations relating to
138	Amendments to s. 45 PSA 1993: regulations relating to
139	Amendments to s. 45 PSA 1993: regulations relating to
140(1)	Amendments to s. 48 PSA 1993: regulations relating to
141(1)	Amendments to s. 55 PSA 1993: regulations relating to
141(2)	Amendments to sch. 2 PSA 1993: regulations relating to
142(3)	Amendments to s. 28 PSA 1993: regulations relating to
143	New s. 28A to PSA 1993: regulations relating to
145	Regulations providing for effect of ss. 141 to 143 and modification of same
146(1)	New s. 32A to PSA 1993: regulations relating to
149	Regulations relating to hybrid occupational pension schemes
150	Provision for functions, rights, liabilities and property of OPB to become functions, property, rights and liabilities of OPRA or Secretary of State
152	Amendments to s. 93 PSA 1993: regulations relating to
153	New s. 93A to PSA 1993: regulations relating to
154(5)	Amendments to s. 94 PSA 1993: regulations relating to
155	Penalties for breach of regulations under PSA 1993: regulations relating to
157(4)	Power to extend Ombudsman's jurisdiction to persons involved in day-to-day administration of the scheme
159(1)	Disclosing information
165	New s. 175 to PSA 1993: regulations relating to
166(1)	Pensions on divorce
167	Pensions on divorce in Scotland
168(3)	Effect of remarriage on war widows
172(1)	Information regarding public service schemes
172(2)	Information regarding public service schemes
172(3)	Information regarding public service schemes
172(4)	Information regarding public service schemes
172(5)	Information regarding public service schemes
174	Orders and regulations
175	Parliamentary control of orders and regulations
180	Commencement

SCHEDULE 1: OPRA

Paragraph	Subject area
13(1)	Proceedings
13(2)	Proceedings
13(3)	Proceedings
14(1)	Proceedings
18	Fees

SCHEDULE 2: PCB

Paragraph	Subject area
12	Proceedings
14(5)	Proceedings

SCHEDULE 3: AMENDMENTS CONSEQUENTIAL ON PART I

Paragraph	Subject area
22	Amendment to s. 6 PSA 1993

SCHEDULE 4: EQUALISATION

Paragraph	Subject area
2	Substitution to ss. 83 and 84 Social Security Contributions and Benefits Act 1992

SCHEDULE 5: AMENDMENTS RELATING TO PART III

Paragraph	Subject area
28	Amendment to s. 16 PSA 1993
33	Amendment to s. 25 PSA 1993
34	Amendment to s. 28 PSA 1993
35	Amendment to s. 29 PSA 1993
36	Amendment to s. 31 PSA 1993
37	Amendment to s. 34 PSA 1993
39	Amendment to s. 37 PSA 1993
45	Amendment to s. 50 PSA 1993
46	Amendment to s. 51 PSA 1993
47	Amendment to s. 52 PSA 1993
48	Amendment to s. 53 PSA 1993
49	Amendment to s. 54 PSA 1993
51	Amendment to s. 56 PSA 1993
70	Amendment to s. 170 PSA 1993
80	Amendment to s. 185 PSA 1993

SCHEDULE 6: GENERAL MINOR AND CONSEQUENTIAL AMENDMENTS

Paragraph	Subject area
5	Amendment to s. 98 PSA 1993
6	Amendment to s. 99 PSA 1993
9	Amendment to s. 158 PSA 1993

Pensions Act 1995

CHAPTER 26
ARRANGEMENT OF SECTIONS
PART I
OCCUPATIONAL PENSIONS

Occupational Pensions Regulatory Authority

Pensions Act 1995

1995 CHAPTER 26

An Act to amend the law about pensions and for connected purposes.

[19th July 1995]

BE IT ENACTED by the Queen's most Excellent Majesty, by and with the advice and consent of the Lords Spiritual and Temporal, and Commons, in this present Parliament assembled, and by the authority of the same, as follows:—

PART I
OCCUPATIONAL PENSIONS

Occupational Pensions Regulatory Authority

1. The new authority

(1) There shall be a body corporate called the Occupational Pensions Regulatory Authority (referred to in this Part as 'the Authority').

(2) The Authority shall consist of not less than seven members appointed by the Secretary of State, one of whom shall be so appointed as chairman.

(3) In addition to the chairman, the Authority shall comprise—

(a) a member appointed after the Secretary of State has consulted organisations appearing to him to be representative of employers,

(b) a member appointed after the Secretary of State has consulted organisations appearing to him to be representative of employees,

(c) a member who appears to the Secretary of State to be knowledgeable about life assurance business,

(d) a member who appears to the Secretary of State to have experience of, and to have shown capacity in, the management or administration of occupational pension schemes, and

(e) two members who appear to the Secretary of State to be knowledgeable about occupational pension schemes,

and such other member or members as the Secretary of State may appoint.

(4) Neither the Authority nor any person who is a member or employee of the Authority shall be liable in damages for anything done or omitted in the discharge or purported discharge of the functions of the Authority under this Part or the Pension Schemes Act 1993, or any provisions in force in Northern Ireland corresponding to either of them, unless it is shown that the act or omission was in bad faith.

(5) Schedule 1 (constitution, procedure, etc. of the Authority) shall have effect.

(6) In this section, 'life assurance business' means the issue of, or the undertaking of liability under, policies of assurance upon human life, or the granting of annuities upon human life.

2. Reports to Secretary of State

(1) The Authority must prepare a report for the first twelve months of their existence, and a report for each succeeding period of twelve months, and must send each report to the Secretary of State as soon as practicable after the end of the period for which it is prepared.

(2) A report prepared under this section for any period must deal with the activities of the Authority in the period.

(3) The Secretary of State must lay before each House of Parliament a copy of every report received by him under this section.

Supervision by the Authority

3. Prohibition orders

(1) The Authority may by order prohibit a person from being a trustee of a particular trust scheme in any of the following circumstances.

(2) The circumstances are—

(a) that the Authority are satisfied that while being a trustee of the scheme the person has been in serious or persistent breach of any of his duties under—

(i)   this Part, other than the following provisions: sections 51 to 54, 62 to 65 and 110 to 112, or

(ii) the following provisions of the Pension Schemes Act 1993: section 6 (registration), Chapter IV of Part IV (transfer values), section 113 (information) and section 175 (levy),

(b) that the Authority are satisfied that, while being a trustee of the scheme, this section has applied to the person by virtue of any other provision of this Part,

(c) that the person is a company and any director of the company is prohibited under this section from being a trustee of the scheme,

(d) that the person is a Scottish partnership and any of the partners is prohibited under this section from being a trustee of the scheme, or

(e) that the person is a director of a company which, by reason of circumstances falling within paragraph (a) or (b), is prohibited under this section from being a trustee of the scheme and the Authority are satisfied that the acts or defaults giving rise to those circumstances were committed with the consent or connivance of, or attributable to any neglect on the part of, the director;
or any other prescribed circumstances.

(3) The making of 'an order under subsection (1) against a person who is a trustee of the scheme in question has the effect of removing him.

(4) The Authority may, on the application of any person against whom an order under subsection (1) is in force, by order revoke the order, but a revocation made at any time cannot affect anything done before that time.

4. Suspension orders

(1) The Authority may by order suspend a trustee of a trust scheme—

(a) pending consideration being given to the making of an order against him under section 3(1),

(b)   where proceedings have been instituted against him for an offence involving dishonesty or deception and have not been concluded,

(c)   where a petition has been presented to the court for an order adjudging him bankrupt, or for the sequestration of his estate, and proceedings on the petition have not been concluded,

(d)   where the trustee is a company, if a petition for the winding up of the company has been presented to the court and proceedings on the petition have not been concluded,

(e)   where an application has been made to the court for a disqualification order against him under the Company Directors Disqualification Act 1986 and proceedings on the application have not been concluded, or

(f)   where the trustee is a company or Scottish partnership and, if any director or, as the case may be, partner were a trustee, the Authority would have power to suspend him under paragraph (b), (c) or (e).

(2)   An order under subsection (1)—

(a)   if made by virtue of paragraph (a), has effect for an initial period not exceeding twelve months, and

(b)   in any other case, has effect until the proceedings in question are concluded;

but the Authority may by order extend the initial period referred to in paragraph (a) for a further period of twelve months, and any order suspending a person under subsection (1) ceases to have effect if an order is made against that person under section 3(1).

(3)   An order under subsection (1) has the effect of prohibiting the person suspended, during the period of his suspension, from exercising any functions as trustee of any trust scheme to which the order applies; and the order may apply to a particular trust scheme, a particular class of trust schemes or trust schemes in general.

(4)   An order under subsection (1) may be made on one of the grounds in paragraphs (b) to (e) whether or not the proceedings were instituted, petition presented or application made (as the case may be) before or after the coming into force of that subsection.

(5)   The Authority may, on the application of any person suspended under subsection (1), by order revoke the order, either generally or in relation to a particular scheme or a particular class of schemes; but a revocation made at any time cannot affect anything done before that time.

(6)   An order under this section may make provision as respects the period of the trustee's suspension for matters arising out of it, and in particular for enabling any person to execute any instrument in his name or otherwise act for him and for adjusting any rules governing the proceedings of the trustees to take account of the reduction in the number capable of acting.

5.   Removal of trustees: notices

(1)   Before the Authority make an order under section 3 against a person without his consent, the Authority must, unless he cannot be found or has no known address, give him not less than one month's notice of their proposal, inviting representations to be made to them within a time specified in the notice.

(2)   Where any such notice is given, the Authority must take into consideration any representations made to them about the proposals within the time specified in the notice.

(3)   Before making an order under section 3 against a person, the Authority must give notice of their intention to do so to each of the trustees of the scheme, except that person (if he is a trustee) and any trustee who cannot be found or has no known address.

(4)   Where the Authority make an order under section 4 against a person, they must—

(a)   immediately give notice of that fact to that person, and

(b)   as soon as reasonably practicable, give notice of that fact to the other trustees of any trust scheme to which the order applies, except any trustee who cannot be found or has no known address.

(5)   Any notice to be given to any person under this section may be given by delivering it to him or by leaving it at his proper address or by sending it to him by post; and, for the purposes of this subsection and section 7 of the Interpretation Act 1978 in its application to this subsection, the proper address of any person is his latest address known to the Authority.

6.   Removal or suspension of trustees: consequences

(1)   A person who purports to act as trustee of a trust scheme while prohibited from being a trustee of the scheme under section 3 or suspended in relation to the scheme under section 4 is guilty of an offence and liable—

(a)   on summary conviction, to a fine not exceeding the statutory maximum, and

(b)   on conviction on indictment, to a fine or imprisonment or both.

(2)   An offence under subsection (1) may be charged by reference to any day or longer period of time; and a person may be convicted of a second or subsequent offence under that subsection by reference to any period of time following the preceding conviction of the offence.

(3)   Things done by a person purporting to act as trustee of a trust scheme while prohibited from being a trustee of the scheme under section 3 or suspended in relation to the scheme under section 4 are not invalid merely because of that prohibition or suspension.

(4)   Nothing in section 3 or 4 or this section affects the liability of any person for things done, or omitted to be done, by him while purporting to act as trustee of a trust scheme.

7.   Appointment of trustees

(1)   Where a trustee of a trust scheme is removed by an order under section 3, or a trustee of such a scheme ceases to be a trustee by reason of his disqualification, the Authority may by order appoint another trustee in his place.

(2)   Where a trustee appointed under subsection (1) is appointed to replace a trustee appointed under section 23(1)(b), sections 22 to 26 shall apply to the replacement trustee as they apply to a trustee appointed under section 23(1)(b).

(3)   The Authority may also by order appoint a trustee of a trust scheme where they are satisfied that it is necessary to do so in order—

(a)   to secure that the trustees as a whole have, or exercise, the necessary knowledge and skill for the proper administration of the scheme,

(b)   to secure that the number of trustees is sufficient for the proper administration of the scheme, or

(c)   to secure the proper use or application of the assets of the scheme.

(4)   The Authority may also appoint a trustee of a trust scheme in prescribed circumstances.

(5)   The power to appoint a trustee by an order under this section includes power by such an order—

(a)   to determine the appropriate number of trustees for the proper administration of the scheme,

(b)   to require a trustee appointed by the order to be paid fees and expenses out of the scheme's resources,

(c)   to provide for the removal or replacement of such a trustee.

(6)   Regulations may make provision about the descriptions of persons who may or may not be appointed trustees under this section.

8.   Appointment of trustees: consequences

(1)   An order under section 7 appointing a trustee may provide that an amount equal to the amount (if any) to which subsection (2) applies is to be treated for all purposes as a debt due from the employer to the trustees.

(2)   This subsection applies to any amount which has been paid to the trustee so appointed out of the resources of the scheme and has not been reimbursed by the employer.

(3)   Subject to subsection (4), a trustee appointed under that section shall, unless he is the independent trustee and section 22 applies in relation to the scheme, have the same powers and duties as the other trustees.

(4)   Such an order may make provision—

(a)   for restricting the powers or duties of a trustee so appointed, or

(b)   for powers or duties to be exercisable by a trustee so appointed to the exclusion of other trustees.

9.   Removal and appointment of trustees: property

Where the Authority have power under this Part to appoint or remove a trustee, they may exercise the same jurisdiction and powers as are exercisable by the High Court or, in relation to a trust scheme subject to the law of Scotland, the Court of Session for vesting any property in, or transferring any property to, trustees in consequence of the appointment or of the removal.

10.   Civil penalties

(1)   Where the Authority are satisfied that by reason of any act or omission this section applies to any person, they may by notice in writing require him to pay, within a prescribed period, a penalty in respect of that act or omission not exceeding the maximum amount.

(2)   In this section 'the maximum amount' means—

(a)   £5,000 in the case of an individual and £50,000 in any other case, or

(b)   such lower amount as may be prescribed in the case of an individual or in any other case,

and the Secretary of State may by order amend paragraph (a) by substituting higher amounts for the amounts for the time being specified in that paragraph.

(3)   Regulations made by virtue of this Part may provide for any person who has contravened any provision of such regulations to pay, within a prescribed period, a penalty under this section not exceeding an amount specified in the

regulations; and the regulations must specify different amounts in the case of individuals from those specified in other cases and any amount so specified may not exceed the amount for the time being specified in the case of individuals or, as the case may be, others in subsection (2)(a).

(4) An order made under subsection (2) or regulations made by virtue of subsection (3) do not affect the amount of any penalty recoverable under this section by reason of an act or omission occurring before the order or, as the case may be, regulations are made.

(5) Where—

(a) apart from this subsection, a penalty under this section is recoverable from a body corporate or Scottish partnership by reason of any act or omission of the body or partnership as a trustee of a trust scheme, and

(b) the act or omission was done with the consent or connivance of, or is attributable to any neglect on the part of, any persons mentioned in subsection (6), this section applies to each of those persons who consented to or connived in the act or omission or to whose neglect the act or omission was attributable.

(6) The persons referred to in subsection (5)(b)—

(a) in relation to a body corporate, are—

(i) any director, manager, secretary, or other similar officer of the body, or a person purporting to act in any such capacity, and

(ii) where the affairs of a body corporate are managed by its members, any member in connection with his functions of management, and

(b) in relation to a Scottish partnership, are the partners.

(7) Where the Authority requires any person to pay a penalty by virtue of subsection (5), they may not also require the body corporate, or Scottish partnership, in question to pay a penalty in respect of the same act or omission.

(8) A penalty under this section is recoverable by the Authority.

(9) The Authority must pay to the Secretary of State any penalty recovered under this section.

11. Powers to wind up schemes

(1) Subject to the following provisions of this section, the Authority may by order direct or authorise an occupational pension scheme to be wound up if they are satisfied that—

(a) the scheme, or any part of it, ought to be replaced by a different scheme,

(b) the scheme is no longer required, or

(c) it is necessary in order to protect the interests of the generality of the members of the scheme that it be wound up.

(2) The Authority may not make an order under this section on either of the grounds referred to in subsection (1)(a) or (b) unless they are satisfied that the winding up of the scheme—

(a) cannot be achieved otherwise than by means of such an order, or

(b) can only be achieved in accordance with a procedure which—

(i) is liable to be unduly complex or protracted, or

(ii) involves the obtaining of consents which cannot be obtained, or can only be obtained with undue delay or difficulty,

and that it is reasonable in all the circumstances to make the order.

(3) An order made under this section on either of the grounds referred to in subsection (1)(a) or (b) may be made only on the application of—

(a) the trustees or managers of the scheme,

(b) any person other than the trustees or managers who has power to alter any of the rules of the scheme, or

(c) the employer.

(4) An order under this section authorising a scheme to be wound up must include such directions with respect to the manner and timing of the winding up as the Authority think appropriate having regard to the purposes of the order.

(5) The winding up of a scheme in pursuance of an order of the Authority under this section is as effective in law as if it had been made under powers conferred by or under the scheme.

(6) An order under this section may be made and complied with in relation to a scheme—

(a) in spite of any enactment or rule of law, or any rule of the scheme, which would otherwise operate to prevent the winding up, or

(b) except for the purpose of the Authority determining whether or not they are satisfied as mentioned in subsection (2), without regard to any such enactment, rule of law or rule of the scheme as would otherwise require, or might otherwise be taken to require, the implementation of any procedure or the obtaining of any consent, with a view to the winding up.

(7) In the case of a public service pension scheme—

(a) an order under subsection (1) directing or authorising the scheme to be wound up may only be made on the grounds referred to in paragraph (c), and

(b) such an order may, as the Authority think appropriate, adapt, amend or repeal any enactment in which the scheme is contained or under which it is made.

12. Powers to wind up public service schemes

(1) The appropriate authority may by order direct a public service pension scheme to be wound up if they are satisfied that—

(a) the scheme, or any part of it, ought to be replaced by a different scheme, or

(b) the scheme is no longer required.

(2) Subsection (2) of section 11 applies for the purposes of this section as it applies for the purposes of that, but as if references to the Authority were to the appropriate authority.

(3) In this section 'the appropriate authority', in relation to a scheme, means such Minister of the Crown or government department as may be designated by the Treasury as having responsibility for the particular scheme.

(4) An order under this section must include such directions with respect to the manner and timing of the winding up as that authority think appropriate.

(5) Such an order may, as that authority think appropriate, adapt, amend or repeal any enactment in which the scheme is contained or under which it is made.

13. Injunctions and interdicts

(1) If, on the application of the Authority, the court is satisfied that—

(a) there is a reasonable likelihood that a particular person will do any act which constitutes a misuse or misappropriation of assets of an occupational pension scheme, or

(b) that a particular person has done any such act and that there is a reasonable likelihood that he will continue or repeat the act in question or do a similar act, the court may grant an injunction restraining him from doing so or, in Scotland, an interdict prohibiting him from doing so.

(2) The jurisdiction conferred by this section is exercisable by the High Court or the Court of Session.

14. Restitution

(1) If, on the application of the Authority, the court is satisfied—

(a) that a power to make a payment, or distribute any assets, to the employer, has been exercised in contravention of section 37, 76 or 77, or

(b) that any act or omission of the trustees or managers of an occupational pension scheme was in contravention of section 40,

the court may order the employer and any other person who appears to the court to have been knowingly concerned in the contravention to take such steps as the court may direct for restoring the parties to the position in which they were before the payment or distribution was made, or the act or omission occurred.

(2) The jurisdiction conferred by this section is exercisable by the High Court or the Court of Session.

15. Directions

(1) The Authority may, where in the case of any trust scheme the employer fails to comply with any requirement included in regulations by virtue of section 49(5), direct the trustees to make arrangements for the payment to the members of the benefit to which the requirement relates.

(2) The Authority may—

(a) where in the case of any trust scheme an annual report is published, direct the trustees to include a statement prepared by the Authority in the report, and published, direct the trustees to include a statement prepared by the Authority in the report, and

(b) in the case of any trust scheme, direct the trustees to send to the members a copy of a statement prepared by the Authority.

(3) A direction under this section must be given in writing.

(4) Where a direction under this section is not complied with, sections 3 and 10 apply to any trustee who has failed to take all such steps as are reasonable to secure compliance.

Member-nominated trustees and directors

16. Requirement for member-nominated trustees

(1) The trustees of a trust scheme must (subject to section 17) secure—

(a) that such arrangements for persons selected by members of the scheme to be trustees of the scheme as are required by this section are made, and

(b) that those arrangements, and the appropriate rules, are implemented.

(2) Persons who become trustees under the arrangements required by subsection (1) are referred to in this Part as 'member-nominated trustees'.

(3) The arrangements must provide—

(a) for any person who has been nominated and selected in accordance with the appropriate rules to become a trustee by virtue of his selection, and

(b) for the removal of such a person to require the agreement of all the other trustees.

(4)　Where a vacancy for a member-nominated trustee is not filled because insufficient nominations are received, the arrangements must provide for the filling of the vacancy, or for the vacancy to remain, until the expiry of the next period in which persons may be nominated and selected in accordance with the appropriate rules.

(5)　The arrangements must provide for the selection of a person as a member-nominated trustee to have effect for a period of not less than three nor more than six years.

(6)　The arrangements must provide for the number of member-nominated trustees to be—

(a)　at least two or (if the scheme comprises less than 100 members) at least one, and

(b)　at least one-third of the total number of trustees;

but the arrangements must not provide for a greater number of member-nominated trustees than that required to satisfy that minimum unless the employer has given his approval to the greater number.

(7)　The arrangements must not provide for the functions of member-nominated trustees to differ from those of any other trustee but, for the purposes of this subsection—

(a)　any provision made by an order under section 8(4), and

(b)　section 25(2),

shall be disregarded.

(8)　The arrangements must provide that, if a member-nominated trustee who was a member of the scheme when he was appointed ceases to be a member of the scheme, he ceases to be a trustee by virtue of that fact.

17.　Exceptions

(1)　Section 16 does not apply to a trust scheme if—

(a)　a proposal has been made by the employer for the continuation of existing arrangements, or the adoption of new arrangements, for selecting the trustees of the scheme,

(b)　the arrangements referred to in the proposal are for the time being approved under the statutory consultation procedure, and

(c)　such other requirements as may be prescribed are satisfied.

(2)　Where—

(a)　by virtue of subsection (1), section 16 does not apply to a trust scheme, and

(b)　the employer's proposal was for the adoption of new arrangements which, in consequence of subsection (1)(b), are adopted,

the trustees shall secure that the proposed arrangements are made and implemented.

(3)　For the purposes of this section, the arrangements for selecting the trustees of a scheme include all matters relating to the continuation in office of the existing trustees, the selection or appointment of new trustees and the terms of their appointments and any special rules for decisions to be made by particular trustees.

(4)　Section 16 does not apply to a trust scheme if—

(a)　the trustees of the scheme consist of all the members, or

(b)　it falls within a prescribed class.

(5)　Section 10 applies to any employer who—

    (a)   makes such a proposal as is referred to in subsection (1)(a), but

    (b)   fails to give effect to the statutory consultation procedure.

18.   Corporate trustees: member-nominated directors

   (1)   Where a company is a trustee of a trust scheme and the employer is connected with the company or prescribed conditions are satisfied, the company must, subject to section 19, secure—

    (a)   that such arrangements for persons selected by the members of the scheme to be directors of the company as are required by this section are made, and

    (b)   that those arrangements, and the appropriate rules, are implemented.

   (2)   Persons who become directors under the arrangements required by subsection (1) are referred to in this Part as 'member-nominated directors'.

   (3)   The arrangements must provide—

    (a)   for any person who has been nominated and selected in accordance with the appropriate rules to become a director by virtue of his selection, and

    (b)   for the removal of such a person to require the agreement of all the other directors.

   (4)   Where a vacancy for a member-nominated director is not filled because insufficient nominations are received, the arrangements must provide for the filling of the vacancy, or for the vacancy to remain, until the expiry of the next period in which persons may be nonminated and selected in accordance with the appropriate rules.

   (5)   The arrangements must provide for the selection of a person as a member-nominated director to have effect for a period of not less than three nor more than six years.

   (6)   The arrangements must provide for the number of member-nominated directors to be—

    (a)   at least two or (if the scheme comprises less than 100 members) at least one, and

    (b) at least one-third of the total number of directors;

but the arrangements must not provide for a greater number of member-nominated directors than that required to satisfy that minimum unless the employer has given his approval to the greater number.

   (7)   The arrangements must provide that, if a member-nominated director who was a member of the scheme when he was appointed ceases to be a member of the scheme, he ceases to be a director by virtue of that fact.

   (8)   Where this section applies to a company which is—

    (a)   a trustee of two or more trust schemes, and

    (b)   a wholly-owned subsidiary (within the meaning of section 736 of the Companies Act 1985) of a company which is the employer in relation to those schemes,

the following provisions apply as if those schemes were a single scheme and the members of each of the schemes were members of that scheme, that is: the preceding provisions of this section, section 20 and section 21(8).

19.   Corporate trustees: exceptions

   (1)   Section 18 does not apply to a company which is a trustee of a trust scheme if—

    (a)   a proposal has been made by the employer for the continuation of existing arrangements, or the adoption of new arrangements, for selecting the directors of the company,

(b)   the arrangements referred to in the proposal are for the time being approved under the statutory consultation procedure, and

(c)   such other requirements as may be prescribed are satisfied.

(2)   Where—

(a)   by virtue of subsection (1), section 18 does not apply to a company which is a trustee of a trust scheme, and

(b)   the employer's proposal was for the adoption of new arrangements which, in consequence of subsection (1)(b), are adopted,

the company must secure that the proposed arrangements are made and implemented.

(3)   For the purposes of this section, the arrangements for selecting the directors of a company include all matters relating to the continuation in office of the existing directors, the selection or appointment of new directors and the terms of their appointments and any special rules for decisions to be made by particular directors.

(4)   Section 18 does not apply to a company which is a trustee of a trust scheme if the scheme falls within a prescribed class.

(5)   Section 10 applies to any employer who—

(a)   makes such a proposal as is referred to in subsection (1)(a), but

(b)   fails to give effect to the statutory consultation procedure.

20.   Selection, and eligibility, of member-nominated trustees and directors

(1)   For the purposes of sections 16 to 21, the appropriate rules are rules which—

(a)   make the provision required or authorised by this section, and no other provision, and

(b)   are for the time being approved under the statutory consultation procedure or, if no rules are for the time being so approved, are prescribed rules;

and the arrangements required by section 16 or 18 to be made must not make any provision which is required or authorised to be made by the rules.

(2)   The appropriate rules—

(a)   must determine the procedure for the nomination and selection of a person to fill a vacancy as a member-nominated trustee, and

(b)   may determine, or provide for the determination of, the conditions required of a person for filling such a vacancy.

(3)   The appropriate rules must provide for a member-nominated trustee to be eligible for re-selection at the end of his period of service.

(4)   Where a vacancy for a member-nominated trustee is not filled because insufficient nominations are received, the appropriate rules must provide for determining the next period in which persons may be nominated and selected in accordance with the rules, being a period ending at a prescribed time.

(5)   The appropriate rules must provide that, where the employer so requires, a person who is not a member of the scheme must have the employer's approval to qualify for selection as a member-nominated trustee.

(6)   Where section 18 applies to a trust scheme, references in this section to a member-nominated trustee include a member-nominated director.

21.   Member-nominated trustees and directors: supplementary

(1)   If, in the case of a trust scheme—

(a) such arrangements as are required by section 16(1) or 17(2) to be made have not been made, or

(b) arrangements required by section 16(1) or 17(2) to be implemented, or the appropriate rules, are not being implemented,

sections 3 and 10 apply to any trustee who has failed to take all such steps as are reasonable to secure compliance,

(2) If, in the case of a company which is a trustee of a trust scheme—

(a) such arrangements as are required by section 18(1) or 19(2) to be made have not been made, or

(b) arrangements required by section 18(1) or 19(2) to be implemented, or the appropriate rules, are not being implemented,

sections 3 and 10 apply to the company.

(3) No such arrangements or rules as are required by section 16(1) or 17(2), or any corresponding provisions in force in Northern Ireland, to be made or implemented shall be treated as effecting an alteration to the scheme in question for the purposes of section 591B of the Taxes Act 1988.

(4) Regulations may make provision for determining the time by which—

(a) such arrangements (or further arrangements) as are referred to in section 16(1), 17(2), 18(1) or 19(2) are required to be made, and

(b) trustees or directors are required to be selected in pursuance of the appropriate rules.

(5) Regulations may make provision for determining when any approval under the statutory consultation procedure—

(a) of the appropriate rules, or

(b) of arrangements for selecting the trustees of a scheme, or the directors of a company, given on a proposal by the employer,

is to cease to have effect.

(6) The Secretary of State may by regulations modify sections 16 to 20 and this section in their application to prescribed cases.

(7) In sections 16 to 20 and this section, 'the statutory consultation procedure' means the prescribed procedure for obtaining the views of members of schemes.

(8) For the purposes of this and those sections—

(a) approval of the appropriate rules, or of arrangements, under the statutory consultation procedure must be given by—

(i) the active and pensioner members of the scheme, and

(ii) if the trustees so determine, such deferred members of the scheme as the trustees may determine,

taken as a whole, and

(b) references to the approval of the appropriate rules, or of arrangements under section 17 or 19, by any persons under the statutory consultation procedure are to prescribed conditions in respect of those rules or, as the case may be, arrangements being satisfied in the case of those persons in pursuance of the procedure, and those conditions may relate to the extent to which those persons have either endorsed, or not objected to, the rules or, as the case may be, arrangements.

Independent trustees

22. Circumstances in which following provisions apply

(1)   This section applies in relation to a trust scheme—

(a)   if a person (referred to in this section and sections 23 to 26 as 'the practitioner') begins to act as an insolvency practitioner in relation to a company which, or an individual who, is the employer in relation to the scheme, or

(b)   if the official receiver becomes—

(i)   the liquidator or provisional liquidator of a company which is the employer in relation to the scheme, or

(ii)   the receiver and the manager, or the trustee, of the estate of a bankrupt who is the employer in relation to the scheme.

(2)   Where this section applies in relation to a scheme, it ceases to do so—

(a)   if some person other than the employer mentioned in subsection (1) becomes the employer, or

(b)   if at any time neither the practitioner nor the official receiver is acting in relation to the employer;

but this subsection does not affect the application of this section in relation to the scheme on any subsequent occasion when the conditions specified in subsection (1)(a) or (b) are satisfied in relation to it.

(3)   In this section and sections 23 to 26—

'acting as an insolvency practitioner' and 'official receiver' shall be construed in accordance with sections 388 and 399 of the Insolvency Act 1986,

'bankrupt' has the meaning given by section 381 of the Insolvency Act 1986,

'company' means a company within the meaning given by section 735(1) of the Companies Act 1985 or a company which may be wound up under Part V of the Insolvency Act 1986 (unregistered companies), and

'interim trustee' and 'permanent trustee' have the same meanings as they have in the Bankruptcy (Scotland) Act 1985.

23. Requirement for independent trustee

(1)   While section 22 applies in relation to a scheme, the practitioner or official receiver must—

(a)   satisfy himself that at all times at least one of the trustees of the scheme is an independent person, and

(b)   if at any time he is not so satisfied, appoint under this paragraph, or secure the appointment of, an independent person as a trustee of the scheme.

(2)   The duty under subsection (1)(b) must be performed as soon as reasonably practicable and, if a period is prescribed for the purposes of that subsection, within that period.

(3)   For the purposes of subsection (1) a person is independent only if—

(a)   he has no interest in the assets of the employer or of the scheme, otherwise than as trustee of the scheme,

(b)   he is neither connected with, nor an associate. of—

(i)   the employer,

(ii)   any person for the time being acting as an insolvency practitioner in relation to the employer, or

(iii)   the official receiver, acting in any of the capacities mentioned in section 22(1)(b) in relation to the employer, and

(c) he satisfies any prescribed requirements;
and any reference in this Part to an independent trustee shall be construed accordingly.

(4) Where, apart from this subsection, the duties imposed by subsection (1) in relation to a scheme would fall to be discharged at the same time by two or more persons acting in different capacities, those duties shall be discharged—

(a) if the employer is a company, by the person or persons acting as the company's liquidator, provisional liquidator or administrator, or

(b) if the employer is an individual, by the person or persons acting as his trustee in bankruptcy or interim receiver of his property or as permanent or interim trustee in the sequestration of his estate.

(5) References in this section to an individual include, except where the context otherwise requires, references to a partnership and to any debtor within the meaning of the Bankruptcy (Scotland) Act 1985.

24. Members' powers to apply to court to enforce duty

(1) If—

(a) section 22 applies in relation to a trust scheme, but

(b) the practitioner or official receiver neglects or refuses to discharge any duty imposed on him by section 23(1) in relation to the scheme,
any member of the scheme may apply to the appropriate court for an order requiring him to discharge his duties under section 23(1).

(2) In subsection (1) 'the appropriate court' means—

(a) if the employer in question is a company—

(i) where a winding-up order has been made or a provisional liquidator appointed, the court which made the order or appointed the liquidator,

(ii) in any other case, any court having jurisdiction to wind up the company, and

(b) in any other case—

(i) in England and Wales, the court (as defined in section 385 of the Insolvency Act 1986), or

(ii) in Scotland, where a sequestration has been awarded or, by virtue of the proviso to section 13(1) of the Bankruptcy (Scotland) Act 1985 (petition presented by creditor or trustee acting under trust deed) an interim trustee has been appointed, the court which made the award or appointment and, if no such award or appointment has been made, any court having jurisdiction under section 9 of that Act.

25. Appointment and powers of independent trustees: further provisions

(1) If, immediately before the appointment of an independent trustee under section 23(1)(b), there is no trustee of the scheme other than the employer, the employer shall cease to be a trustee upon the appointment of the independent trustee.

(2) While section 22 applies in relation to a scheme—

(a) any power vested in the trustees of the scheme and exercisable at their discretion may be exercised only by the independent trustee, and

(b) any power—

(i) which the scheme confers on the employer (otherwise than as trustee of the scheme), and

(ii)   which is exercisable by him at his discretion but only as trustee of the power,

may be exercised only by the independent trustee,

but if, in either case, there is more than one independent trustee, the power may also be exercised with the consent of at least half of those trustees by any person who could exercise it apart from this subsection.

(3)   While section 22 applies in relation to a scheme, no independent trustee of the scheme may be removed from being a trustee by virtue only of any provision of the scheme.

(4)   If a trustee appointed under section 23(1)(b) ceases to be an independent person, then—

(a)   he must immediately give written notice of that fact to the practitioner or official receiver by whom the duties under that provision fall to be discharged, and

(b)   subject to subsection (5), he shall cease to be a trustee of the scheme.

(5)   If, in a case where subsection (4) applies, there is no other trustee of the scheme than the former independent trustee, he shall not cease by virtue of that subsection to be a trustee until such time as another trustee is appointed.

(6)   A trustee appointed under section 23(1)(b) is entitled to be paid out of the scheme's resources his reasonable fees for acting in that capacity and any expenses reasonably incurred by him in doing so, and to be so paid in priority to all other claims falling to be met out of the scheme's resources.

26. Insolvency practitioner or official receiver to give information to trustees

(1)   Notwithstanding anything in section 155 of the Insolvency Act 1986 (court orders for inspection etc.), while section 22 applies in relation to a scheme, the practitioner or official receiver must provide the trustees of the scheme, as soon as practicable after the receipt of a request, with any information which the trustees may reasonably require for the purposes of the scheme.

(2)   Any expenses incurred by the practitioner or official receiver in complying with a request under subsection (1) are recoverable by him as part of the expenses incurred by him in discharge of his duties.

(3)   The practitioner or official receiver is not required under subsection (1) to take any action which involves expenses that cannot be so recovered, unless the trustees of the scheme undertake to meet them.

Trustees: general

27. Trustee not to be auditor or actuary of the scheme

(1)   A trustee of a trust scheme, and any person who is connected with, or an associate of, such a trustee, is ineligible to act as an auditor or actuary of the scheme.

(2)   Subsection (1) does not make a person who is a director, partner or employee of a firm of actuaries ineligible to act as an actuary of a trust scheme merely because another director, partner or employee of the firm is a trustee of the scheme.

(3)   Subsection (1) does not make a person who falls within a prescribed class or description ineligible to act as an auditor or actuary of a trust scheme.

(4)   A person must not act as an auditor or actuary of a trust scheme if he is ineligible under this section to do so.

(5)   In this section and section 28 references to a trustee of a trust scheme do not include—

(a)   a trustee, or

(b)   a trustee of a scheme,

falling within a prescribed class or description.

28.   Section 27: consequences

(1)   Any person who acts as an auditor or actuary or a trust scheme in contravention of section 27(4) is guilty of an offence and liable—

(a)   on summary conviction, to a fine not exceeding the statutory maximum, and

(b)   on conviction on indictment, to imprisonment or a fine, or both.

(2)   An offence under subsection (1) may be charged by reference to any day or longer period of time; and a person may be convicted of a second or subsequent offence under that subsection by reference to any period of time following the preceding conviction of the offence.

(3)   Acts done as an auditor or actuary of a trust scheme by a person who is ineligble under section 27 to do so are not invalid merely because of that fact.

(4)   Where—

(a)   a trustee of a trust scheme acts as auditor or actuary of the scheme, or

(b)   a person acts as auditor or actuary of a trust scheme when he is ineligible under section 27 to do so by reason of being connected with, or an associate of, a trustee of the scheme,

section 3 applies to the trustee.

29.   Persons disqualified for being trustees

(1)   Subject to subsection (5), a person is disqualified for being a trustee of any trust scheme if—

(a)   he has been convicted of any offence involving dishonesty or deception,

(b)   he has been adjudged bankrupt or sequestration of his estate has been awarded and (in either case) he has not been discharged,

(c)   where the person is a company, if any director of the company is disqualified under this section,

(d)   where the person is a Scottish partnership, if any partner is disqualified under this section,

(e)   he has made a composition contract or an arrangement with, or granted a trust deed for the behoof of, his creditors and has not been discharged in respect of it, or

(f)   he is subject to a disqualification order under the Company Directors Disqualification Act 1986 or to an order made under section 429(2)(b) of the Insolvency Act 1986 (failure to pay under county court administration order).

(2)   In subsection (1)—

(a)   paragraph (a) applies whether the conviction occurred before or after the coming into force of that subsection, but does not apply in relation to any conviction which is a spent conviction for the purposes of the Rehabilitation of Offenders Act 1974,

(b)   paragraph (b) applies whether the adjudication of bankruptcy or the sequestration occurred before or after the coming into force of that subsection,

(c)   paragraph (e) applies whether the composition contract or arrangement was made, or the trust deed was granted, before or after the coming into force of that subsection, and

(d)   paragraph (f) applies in relation to orders made before or after the coming into force of that subsection.

(3)   Where a person—

(a)   is prohibited from being a trustee of a trust scheme by an order under section 3, or

(b)   has been removed as a trustee of a trust scheme by an order made (whether before or after the coming into force of this subsection) by the High Court or the Court of Session on the grounds of misconduct or mismanagement in the administration of the scheme for which he was responsible or to which he was privy, or which he by his conduct contributed to or facilitated,

the Authority may, if in their opinion it is not desirable for him to be a trustee of any trust scheme, by order disqualify him for being a trustee of any trust scheme.

(4)   The Authority may by order disqualify a person for being a trustee of any trust scheme where—

(a)   in their opinion he is incapable of acting as such a trustee by reason of mental disorder (within the meaning of the Mental Health Act 1983 or, as respects Scotland, the Mental Health (Scotland) Act 1984), or

(b)   the person is a company which has gone into liquidation (within the meaning of section 247(2) of the Insolvency Act 1986).

(5)   The Authority may, on the application of any person disqualified under this section—

(a)   give notice in writing to him waiving his disqualification,

(b)   in the case of a person disqualified under subsection (3) or (4), by order revoke the order disqualifying him,

either generally or in relation to a particular scheme or particular class of schemes.

(6)   A notice given or revocation made at any time by virtue of subsection (5) cannot affect anything done before that time.

30.   Persons disqualified: consequences

(1)   A trustee of a trust scheme who becomes disqualified under section 29 shall, while he is so disqualified, cease to be a trustee.

(2)   Where—

(a)   a trustee of a trust scheme becomes disqualified under section 29, or

(b)   in the case of a trustee of a trust scheme who has become so disqualified, his disqualification is waived or the order disqualifying him is revoked or he otherwise ceases to be disqualified,

the Authority may exercise the same jurisdiction and powers as are exercisable by the High Court or, in relation to a trust scheme subject to the law of Scotland, the Court of Session for vesting any property in, or transferring any property to, the trustees.

(3)   A person who purports to act as a trustee of a trust scheme while he is disqualified under section 29 is guilty of an offence and liable—

(a)   on summary conviction to a fine not exceeding the statutory maximum, and

(b)   on conviction on indictment, to a fine or imprisonment or both.

(4)   An offence under subsection (3) may be charged by reference to any day or longer period of time; and a person may be convicted of a second or subsequent offence under that subsection by reference to any period of time following the preceding conviction of the offence.

(5)   Things done by a person disqualified under section 29 while purporting to act as trustee of a trust scheme are not invalid merely because of that disqualification.

(6)   Nothing in section 29 or this section affects the liability of any person for things done, or omitted to be done, by him while purporting to act as trustee of a trust scheme.

(7)   The Authority must keep, in such manner as they think fit, a register of all persons who are disqualified under section 29(3) or (4); and the Authority must, if requested to do so, disclose whether the name of a person specified in the request is included in the register in respect of a scheme so specified.

31.   Trustees not to be indemnified for fines or civil penalties

(1)   No amount may be paid out of the assets of a trust scheme for the purpose of reimbursing, or providing for the reimbursement of, any trustee of the scheme in respect of—

(a)   a fine imposed by way of penalty for an offence of which he is convicted, or

(b)   a penalty which he is required to pay under section 10 or under section 168(4) of the Pension Schemes Act 1993.

(2)   For the purposes of subsection (1), providing for the reimbursement of a trustee in respect of a fine or penalty includes (among other things) providing for the payment of premiums in respect of a policy of insurance where the risk is or includes the imposition of such a fine or the requirement to pay such a penalty.

(3)   Where any amount is paid out of the assets of a trust scheme in contravention of this section, sections 3 and 10 apply to any trustee who fails to take all such steps as are reasonable to secure compliance.

(4)   Where a trustee of a trust scheme—

(a)   is reimbursed, out of the assets of the scheme or in consequence of provision for his reimbursement made out of those assets, in respect of any of the matters referred to in subsection (1)(a) or (b), and

(b)   knows, or has reasonable grounds to believe, that he has been reimbursed as mentioned in paragraph (a),

then, unless he has taken all such steps as are reasonable to secure that he is not so reimbursed, he is guilty of an offence.

(5)   A person guilty of an offence under subsection (4) is liable—

(a)   on summary conviction, to a fine not exceeding the statutory maximum, and

(b)   on conviction on indictment, to imprisonment, or a fine, or both.

Functions of trustees

32.   Decisions by majority

(1)   Decisions of the trustees of a trust scheme may, unless the scheme provides otherwise, be taken by agreement of a majority of the trustees.

(2)   Where decisions of the trustees of a trust scheme may be taken by agreement of a majority of the trustees—

(a) the trustees may, unless the scheme provides otherwise, by a determination under this subsection require not less than the number of trustees specified in the determination to be present when any decision is so taken, and

(b) notice of any occasions at which decisions may be so taken must, unless the occasion falls within a prescribed class or description, be given to each trustee to whom it is reasonably practicable to give such notice.

(3) Notice under subsection (2)(b) must be given in a prescribed manner and not later than the beginning of a prescribed period.

(4) This section is subject to sections 8(4)(b), 16(3)(b) and 25(2).

(5) If subsection (2)(b) is not complied with, sections 3 and 10 apply to any trustee who has failed to take all such steps as are reasonable to secure compliance.

33. Investment powers: duty of care

(1) Liability for breach of an obligation under any rule of law to take care or exercise skill in the performance of any investment functions, where the function is exercisable—

(a) by a trustee of a trust scheme, or

(b) by a person to whom the function has been delegated under section 34, cannot be excluded or restricted by any instrument or agreement.

(2) In this section, references to excluding or restricting liability include—

(a) making the liability or its enforcement subject to restrictive or onerous conditions,

(b) excluding or restricting any right or remedy in respect of the liability, or subjecting a person to any prejudice in consequence of his pursuing any such right or remedy, or

(c) excluding or restricting rules of evidence or procedure.

(3) This section does not apply—

(a) to a scheme falling within any prescribed class or description, or

(b) to any prescribed description of exclusion or restriction.

34. Power of investment and delegation

(1) The trustees of a trust scheme have, subject to any restriction imposed by the scheme, the same power to make an investment of any kind as if they were absolutely entitled to the assets of the scheme.

(2) Any discretion of the trustees of a trust scheme to make any decision about investments—

(a) may be delegated by or on behalf of the trustees to a fund manager to whom subsection (3) applies to be exercised in accordance with section 36, but

(b) may not otherwise be delegated except under section 25 of the Trustee Act 1925 (delegation of trusts during absence abroad) or subsection (5) below.

(3) This subsection applies to a fund manager who, in relation to the decisions in question, falls, or is treated as falling, within any of paragraphs (a) to (c) of section 191(2) of the Financial Services Act 1986 (occupational pension schemes: exemptions where decisions taken by authorised and other persons).

(4) The trustees are not responsible for the act or default of any fund manager in the exercise of any discretion delegated to him under subsection (2)(a) if they have taken all such steps as are reasonable to satisfy themselves or the person who made the delegation on their behalf has taken all such steps as are reasonable to satisfy himself—

(a)   that the fund manager has the appropriate knowledge and experience for managing the investments of the scheme, and

(b)   that he is carrying out his work competently and complying with section 36.

(5)   Subject to any restriction imposed by a trust scheme—

(a)   the trustees may authorise two or more of their number to exercise on their behalf any discretion to make any decision about investments, and

(b)   any such discretion may, where giving effect to the decision would not constitute carrying on investment business in the United Kingdom (within the meaning of the Financial Services Act 1986), be delegated by or on behalf of the trustees to a fund manager to whom subsection (3) does not apply to be exercised in accordance with section 36;

but in either case the trustees are liable for any acts or defaults in the exercise of the discretion if they would be so liable if they were the acts or defaults of the trustees as a whole.

(6)   Section 33 does not prevent the exclusion or restriction of any liability of the trustees of a trust scheme for the acts or defaults of a fund manager in the exercise of a discretion delegated to him under subsection (5)(b) where the trustees have taken all such steps as are reasonable to satisfy themselves, or the person who made the delegation on their behalf has taken all such steps as are reasonable to satisfy himself—

(a)   that the fund manager has the appropriate knowledge and experience for managing the investments of the scheme, and

(b)   that he is carrying out his work competently and complying with section 36;

and subsection (2) of section 33 applies for the purposes of this subsection as it applies for the purposes of that section.

(7)   The provisions of this section override any restriction inconsistent with the provisions imposed by any rule of law or by or under any enactment, other than an enactment contained in, or made under, this Part or the Pension Schemes Act 1993.

35.   Investment principles

(1)   The trustees of a trust scheme must secure that there is prepared, maintained and from time to time revised a written statement of the principles governing decisions about investments for the purposes of the scheme.

(2)   The statement must cover, among other things—

(a)   the trustees' policy for securing compliance with sections 36 and 56, and

(b)   their policy about the following matters.

(3)   Those matters are—

(a)   the kinds of investments to be held,

(b)   the balance between different kinds of investments,

(c)   risk,

(d)   the expected return on investments,

(e)   the realisation of investments, and

(f)   such other matters as may be prescribed.

(4)   Neither the trust scheme nor the statement may impose restrictions (however expressed) on any power to make investments by reference to the consent of the employer.

(5) The trustees of a trust scheme must, before a statement under this section is prepared or revised—

(a) obtain and consider the written advice of a person who is reasonably believed by the trustees to be qualified by his ability in and practical experience of financial matters and to have the appropriate knowledge and experience of the management of the investments of such schemes, and

(b) consult the employer.

(6) If in the case of any trust scheme—

(a) a statement under this section has not been prepared or is not being maintained, or

(b) the trustees have not obtained and considered advice in accordance with subsection (5),

sections 3 and 10 apply to any trustee who has failed to take all such steps as are reasonable to secure compliance.

(7) This section does not apply to any scheme which falls within a prescribed class or description.

36. Choosing investments

(1) The trustees of a trust scheme must exercise their powers of investment in accordance with subsections (2) to (4) and any fund manager to whom any discretion has been delegated under section 34 must exercise the discretion in accordance with subsection (2).

(2) The trustees or fund manager must have regard—

(a) to the need for diversification of investments, in so far as appropriate to the circumstances of the scheme, and

(b) to the suitability to the scheme of investments of the description of investment proposed and of the investment proposed as an investment of that description.

(3) Before investing in any manner (other than in a manner mentioned in Part I of Schedule 1 to the Trustee Investments Act 1961) the trustees must obtain and consider proper advice on the question whether the investment is satisfactory having regard to the matters mentioned in subsection (2) and the principles contained in the statement under section 35.

(4) Trustees retaining any investment must—

(a) determine at what intervals the circumstances, and in particular the nature of the investment, make it desirable to obtain such advice as is mentioned in subsection (3), and

(b) obtain and consider such advice accordingly.

(5) The trustees, or the fund manager to whom any discretion has been delegated under section 34, must exercise their powers of investment with a view to giving effect to the principles contained in the statement under section 35, so far as reasonably practicable.

(6) For the purposes of this section 'proper advice' means—

(a) where giving the advice constitutes carrying on investment business in the United Kingdom (within the meaning of the Financial Services Act 1986), advice—

(i) given by a person authorised under Chapter III of Part I of that Act,

(ii) given by a person exempted under Chapter IV of that Part who, in giving the advice, is acting in the course of the business in respect of which he is exempt,

(iii)   given by a person where, by virtue of paragraph 27 of Schedule 1 to that Act, paragraph 15 of that Schedule does not apply to giving the advice, or

(iv)   given by a person who, by virtue of regulation 5 of the Banking Coordination (Second Council Directive) Regulations 1992, may give the advice though not authorised as mentioned in sub-paragraph (i) above.

(b)   in any other case, the advice of a person who is reasonably believed by the trustees to be qualified by his ability in and practical experience of financial matters and to have the appropriate knowledge and experience of the management of the investments of trust schemes.

(7)   Trustees shall not be treated as having complied with subsection (3) or (4) unless the advice was given or has subsequently been confirmed in writing.

(8)   If the trustees of a trust scheme do not obtain and consider advice in accordance with this section, sections 3 and 10 apply to any trustee who has failed to take all such steps as are reasonable to secure compliance.

37.   Payment of surplus to employer

(1)   This section applies to a trust scheme if—

(a)   apart from this section, power is conferred on any person (including the employer) to make payments to the employer out of funds which are held for the purposes of the scheme,

(b)   the scheme is one to which Schedule 22 to the Taxes Act 1988 (reduction of pension fund surpluses in certain exempt approved schemes) applies, and

(c)   the scheme is not being wound up.

(2)   Where the power referred to in subsection (1)(a) is conferred by the scheme on a person other than the trustees, it cannot be exercised by that person but may be exercised instead by the trustees; and any restriction imposed by the scheme on the exercise of the power shall, so far as capable of doing so, apply to its exercise by the trustees.

(3)   The power referred to in subsection (1)(a) cannot be exercised unless the requirements of subsection (4) and (in prescribed circumstances) (5), and any prescribed requirements, are satisfied.

(4)   The requirements of this subsection are that—

(a)   the power is exercised in pursuance of proposals approved under paragraph 6(1) of Schedule 22 to the Taxes Act 1988,

(b)   the trustees are satisfied that it is in the interests of the members that the power be exercised in the manner so proposed,

(c)   where the power is conferred by the scheme on the employer, the employer has asked for the power to be exercised, or consented to it being exercised, in the manner so proposed,

(d)   the annual rates of the pensions under the scheme which commence or have commenced are increased by the appropriate percentage, and

(e)   notice has been given in accordance with prescribed requirements to the members of the scheme of the proposal to exercise the power.

(5)   The requirements of this subsection are that the Authority are of the opinion that—

(a)   any requirements prescribed by virtue of subsection (3) are satisfied, and

(b)   the requirements of subsection (4) are satisfied.

(6)   In subsection (4)—

(a) 'annual rate' and 'appropriate percentage' have the same meaning as in section 54, and

(b) 'pension' does not include—

(i) any guaranteed minimum pension (as defined in section 8(2) of the Pension Schemes Act 1993) or any increase in such a pension under section 109 of that Act, or

(ii) any money purchase benefit (as defined in section 181(1) of that Act).

(7) This section does not apply to any payment to which, by virtue of section 601(3) of the Taxes Act 1988, section 601(2) of that Act does not apply.

(8) If, where this section applies to any trust scheme, the trustees purport to exercise the power referred to in subsection (1)(a) by making a payment to which this section applies without complying with the requirements of this section, sections 3 and 10 apply to any trustee who has failed to take all such steps as are reasonable to secure compliance.

(9) If, where this section applies to any trust scheme, any person, other than the trustees, purports to exercise the power referred to in subsection (1)(a) by making a payment to which this section applies, section 10 applies to him.

(10) Regulations may provide that, in prescribed circumstances, this section does not apply to schemes falling within a prescribed class or description, or applies to them with prescribed modifications.

38. Power to defer winding up

(1) If, apart from this section, the rules of a trust scheme would require the scheme to be wound up, the trustees may determine that the scheme is not for the time being to be wound up but that no new members are to be admitted to the scheme.

(2) Where the trustees make a determination under subsection (1), they may also determine—

(a) that no further contributions are to be paid towards the scheme, or

(b) that no new benefits are to accrue to, or in respect of, members of the scheme;

but this subsection does not authorise the trustees to determine, where there are accrued rights to any benefit, that the benefit is not to be increased.

(3) This section does not apply to—

(a) a money purchase scheme, or

(b) a scheme falling within a prescribed class or description.

39. Exercise of powers by member trustees

No rule of law that a trustee may not exercise the powers vested in him so as to give rise to a conflict between his personal interest and his duties to the beneficiaries shall apply to a trustee of a trust scheme, who is also a member of the scheme, exercising the powers vested in him in any manner, merely because their exercise in that manner benefits, or may benefit, him as a member of the scheme.

Functions of trustees or managers

40. Restriction on employer-related investments

(1) The trustees or managers of an occupational pension scheme must secure that the scheme complies with any prescribed restrictions with respect to the

proportion of its resources that may at any time be invested in, or in any description of, employer-related investments.

(2) In this section—

'employer-related investments' means—

(a) shares or other securities issued by the employer or by any person who is connected with, or an associate of, the employer,

(b) land which is occupied or used by, or subject to a lease in favour of, the employer or any such person,

(c) property (other than land) which is used for the purposes of any business carried on by the employer or any such person,

(d) loans to the employer or any such person, and

(e) other prescribed investments,

'securities' means any asset, right or interest falling within paragraph 1, 2, 4 or 5 of Schedule 1 to the Financial Services Act 1986.

(3) To the extent (if any) that sums due and payable by a person to the trustees or managers of an occupational pension scheme remain unpaid—

(a) they shall be regarded for the purposes of this section as loans made to that person by the trustees or managers, and

(b) resources of the scheme shall be regarded as invested accordingly.

(4) If in the case of a trust scheme subsection (1) is not complied with, sections 3 and 10 apply to any trustee who fails to take all such steps as are reasonable to secure compliance.

(5) If any resources of an occupational pension scheme are invested in contravention of subsection (1), any trustee or manager who agreed in the determination to make the investment is guilty of an offence and liable—

(a) on summary conviction, to a fine not exceeding the statutory maximum, and

(b) on conviction on indictment, to a fine or imprisonment, or both.

41. Provision of documents for members

(1) Regulations may require the trustees or managers of an occupational pension scheme—

(a) to obtain at prescribed times the documents mentioned in subsection (2), and

(b) to make copies of them, and of the documents mentioned in subsection (3), available to the persons mentioned in subsection (4).

(2) The documents referred to in subsection (1)(a) are—

(a) the accounts audited by the auditor of the scheme,

(b) the auditor's statement about contributions under the scheme,

(c) a valuation by the actuary of the assets and liabilities of the scheme, and a statement by the actuary concerning such aspects of the valuation as may be prescribed,

(3) The documents referred to in subsection (1)(b) are—

(a) any valuation, or certificate, prepared under section 57 or 58 by the actuary of the scheme,

(b) any report prepared by the trustees or managers under section 59(3).

(4) The persons referred to in subsection (1)(b) are—

(a) members and prospective members of the scheme,

(b)   spouses of members and of prospective members,

(c)   persons within the application of the scheme and qualifying or prospectively qualifying for its benefits,

(d)   independent trade unions recognised to any extent for the purposes of collective bargaining in relation to members and prospective members of the scheme.

(5)   Regulations may in the case of occupational pension schemes to which section 47 does not apply—

(a)   prescribe the persons who may act as auditors or actuaries for the purposes of subsection (2), or

(b)   provide that the persons who may so act shall be—

(i)   persons with prescribed professional qualifications or experience, or

(ii)   persons approved by the Secretary of State.

(6)   Regulations shall make provision for referring to an industrial tribunal any question on whether an organisation is such a trade union as is mentioned in subsection (4)(d) and may make provision as to the form and content of any such document as is referred to in subsection (2).

Employee trustees

42.   Time off for performance of duties and for training

(1)   The employer in relation to a trust scheme must permit any employee of his who is a trustee of the scheme to take time off during his working hours for the purpose of—

(a)   performing any of his duties as such a trustee, or

(b)   undergoing training relevant to the performance of those duties.

(2)   The amount of time off which an employee is to be permitted to take under this section and the purposes for which, the occasions on which and any conditions subject to which time off may be so taken are particular to—

(a)   how much time off is required for the performance of the duties of a trustee of the scheme and the undergoing of relevant training, and how much time off is required for performing the particular duty or, as the case may be, for undergoing the particular training, and

(b)   the circumstances of the employer's business and the effect of the employee's absence on the running of that business.

(3)   An employee may present a complaint to an industrial tribunal that his employer has failed to permit him to take time off as required by this section.

(4)   For the purposes of this section, the working hours of an employee are any time when in accordance with his contract of employment he is required to be at work.

43.   Payment for time off

(1)   An employer who permits an employee to take time off under section 42 must pay him for the time taken off pursuant to the permission.

(2)   Where the employee's remuneration for the work he would ordinarily have been doing during that time does not vary with the amount of work done, he must be paid as if he had worked at that work for the whole of that time.

(3)   Where the employee's remuneration for the work he would ordinarily have been doing during time varies with the amount of work done, he must be paid an amount calculated by reference to the average hourly earnings for that work.

(4)   The average hourly earnings mentioned in subsection (3) are those of the employee concerned or, if no fair estimate can be made of those earnings, the average hourly earnings for work of that description of persons in comparable employment with the same employer or, if there are no such persons, a figure of average hourly earnings which is reasonable in the circumstances.

(5)   A right to be paid an amount under this section does not affect any right of an employee in relation to remuneration under his contract of employment, but—

(a)   any contractual remuneration paid to an employee in respect of a period of time off to which this section applies shall go towards discharging any liability of the employer under this section in respect of that period, and

(b)   any payment under this section in respect of a period shall go towards discharging any liability of the employer to pay contractual remuneration in respect of that period.

(6)   An employee may present a complaint to an industrial tribunal that his employer has failed to pay him in accordance with this section.

44.   Time limit for proceedings

An industrial tribunal must not consider a complaint under section 42 or 43 unless it is presented to the tribunal—

(a)   within three months of the date when the failure occurred, or

(b)   where the tribunal is satisfied that it was not reasonably practicable for the complaint to be presented within that period, within such further period as the tribunal considers reasonable.

45.   Remedies

(1)   Where the tribunal finds a complaint under section 42 is well-founded, it must make a declaration to that effect and may make an award of compensation to be paid by the employer to the employee.

(2)   The amount of the compensation shall be such as the tribunal considers just and equitable in all the circumstances having regard to the employer's default in failing to permit time off to be taken by the employee and to any loss sustained by the employee which is attributable to the matters complained of.

(3)   Where on a complaint under section 43 the tribunal finds that the employer has failed to pay the employee in accordance with that section, it must order him to pay the amount which it finds to be due.

(4)   The remedy of an employee for infringement of the rights conferred on him by section 42 or 43 is by way of complaint to an industrial tribunal in accordance with this Part, and not otherwise.

46.   Right not to suffer detriment in employment or be unfairly dismissed

(1)   Subject to subsection (2), an employee has the right not to be subjected to any detriment by any act, or any deliberate failure to act, by his employer done on the ground that, being a trustee of a trust scheme which relates to his employment, the employee performed (or proposed to perform) any functions as such a trustee.

(2)   Subsection (1) does not apply where the detriment in question amounts to dismissal, except where an employee is dismissed in circumstances in which, by virtue of section 142 of the Employment Protection (Consolidation) Act 1978 ('the 1978 Act'), section 54 of that Act does not apply to the dismissal.

(3) Sections 22B and 22C of the 1978 Act (which relate to proceedings brought by an employee on the grounds that he has been subjected to a detriment in contravention of section 22A of that Act) shall have effect as if the reference in section 22B(1) to section 22A included a reference to subsection (1).

(4) In the following provisions of the 1978 Act—

    (a)   section 129 (remedy for infringement of certain rights),

    (b)   section 141(2) (employee ordinarily working outside Great Britain), and

    (c)   section 150 and Schedule 12 (death of employee or employer),

any reference to Part II of that Act includes a reference to subsection (1).

(5) The dismissal of an employee by an employer shall be regarded for the purposes of Part V of the 1978 Act as unfair if the reason (or, if more than one, the principal reason) for it is that, being a trustee of a trust scheme which relates to his employment, the employee performed (or proposed to perform) any functions; as such a trustee.

(6) Where the reason or the principal reason for which an employee was selected for dismissal was that he was redundant, but it is shown—

    (a)   that the circumstances constituting the redundancy applied equally to one or more other employees in the same undertaking who held positions similar to that held by him and who have not been dismissed by the employer, and

    (b)   that the reason (or, if more than one, the principal reason) for which he was selected for dismissal was that specified in subsection (5),

then, for the purposes of Part V of the 1978 Act, the dismissal shall be regarded as unfair.

(7) Section 54 of the 1978 Act (right of employee not to be unfairly dismissed) applies to a dismissal regarded as unfair by virtue of subsection (5) or (6) regardless of the period for which the employee has been employed and of his age; and accordingly section 64(1) of that Act (which provides a qualifying period and an upper age limit) does not apply to such a dismissal.

(8) Any provision in an agreement (whether a contract of employment or not) shall be void in so far as it purports—

    (a)   to exclude or limit the operation of any provision of this section, or

    (b)   to preclude any person from presenting a complaint to an industrial tribunal by virtue of any provision of this section.

(9) Subsection (8) does not apply to an agreement to refrain from presenting or continuing with a complaint where—

    (a)   a conciliation officer has taken action under section 133(2) or (3) of the 1978 Act (general provisions as to conciliation) or under section 134(1), (2) or (3) (conciliation in case of unfair dismissal) of that Act, or

    (b)   the conditions regulating compromise agreements under the 1978 Act (as set out in section 140(3) of that Act) are satisfied in relation to the agreement.

(10) In this section, 'dismissal' has the same meaning as in Part V of the 1978 Act.

(11) Section 153 of the 1978 Act (general interpretation) has effect for the purposes of this section as it has effect for the purposes of that Act.

Advisers

47. Professional advisers

(1) For every occupational pension scheme there shall be—

(a) an individual, or a firm, appointed by the trustees or managers as auditor (referred to in this Part, in relation to the scheme, as 'the auditor'), and

(b) an individual appointed by the trustees or managers as actuary (referred to in this Part, in relation to the scheme, as 'the actuary').

(2) For every occupational pension scheme the assets of which consist of or include investments (within the meaning of the Financial Services Act 1986) there shall be an individual or a firm appointed by or on behalf of the trustees or managers as fund manager.

(3) If in the case of an occupational pension scheme any person—

(a) is appointed otherwise than by the trustees or managers as legal adviser or to exercise any prescribed functions in relation to the scheme, or

(b) is appointed otherwise than by or on behalf of the trustees or managers as a fund manager,

sections 3 and 10 apply to any trustee, and section 10 applies to any manager, who in exercising any of his functions places reliance on the skill or judgement of that person.

(4) In this Part, in relation to an occupational pension scheme—

(a) the auditor, actuary and legal adviser appointed by the trustees or managers,

(b) any fund manager appointed by or on behalf of the trustees or managers, and

(c) any person appointed by the trustees or managers to exercise any of the functions referred to in subsection (3)(a),

are referred to as 'professional advisers'.

(5) This section does not apply to an occupational pension scheme falling within a prescribed class or description and regulations may—

(a) make exceptions to subsections (1) to (3),

(b) specify the qualifications and experience, or approval, required for appointment as a professional adviser.

(6) Regulations may make provision as to—

(a) the manner in which professional advisers may be appointed and removed,

(b) the terms on which professional advisers may be appointed (including the manner in which the professional advisers may resign).

(7) Subject to regulations made by virtue of subsection (6), professional advisers shall be appointed on such terms as the trustees or managers may determine.

(8) If in the case of an occupational pension scheme an auditor, actuary or fund manager is required under this section to be appointed but the appointment has not been made, or not been made in accordance with any requirements imposed under this section, sections 3 and 10 apply to any trustee, and section 10 applies to any manager, who has failed to take all such steps as are reasonable to secure compliance.

(9) Regulations may in the case of occupational pension schemes—

(a) impose duties on any person who is or has been the employer, and on any person who acts as auditor or actuary to such a person, to disclose information to the trustees or managers and to the scheme's professional advisers,

(b) impose duties on the trustees or managers to disclose information to, and make documents available to, the scheme's professional advisers.

(10)   If in the case of an occupational pension scheme a person fails to comply with any duty imposed under subsection (9)(a), section 10 applies to him.

(11)   If in the case of an occupational pension scheme any duty imposed under subsection (9)(b) is not complied with, sections 3 and 10 apply to any trustee, and section 10 applies to any manager, who has failed to take all such steps as are reasonable to secure compliance.

48.   'Blowing the whistle'

(1)   If the auditor or actuary of any occupational pension scheme has reasonable cause to believe that—

(a)   any duty relevant to the administration of the scheme imposed by any enactment or rule of law on the trustees or managers, the employer, any professional adviser or any prescribed person acting in connection with the scheme has not been or is not being complied with, and

(b)   the failure to comply is likely to be of material significance in the exercise by the Authority of any of their functions,
he must immediately give a written report of the matter to the Authority.

(2)   The auditor or actuary of any occupational pension scheme must, in any prescribed circumstances, immediately give a written report of any prescribed matter to the Authority.

(3)   No duty to which the auditor or actuary of any occupational pension scheme is subject shall be regarded as contravened merely because of any information or opinion contained in a written report under this section.

(4)   If in the case of any occupational pension scheme any professional adviser (other than the auditor or actuary), any trustee or manager or any person involved in the administration of the scheme has reasonable cause to believe as mentioned in paragraphs (a) and (b) of subsection (1), he may give a report of the matter to the Authority.

(5)   In the case of any such scheme, no duty to which any such adviser, trustee or manager or other person is subject shall be regarded as contravened merely because of any information or opinion contained in a report under this section; but this subsection does not apply to any information disclosed in such a report by the legal adviser of an occupational pension scheme if he would be entitled to refuse to produce a document containing the information in any proceedings in any court on the grounds that it was the subject of legal professional privilege or, in Scotland, that it contained a confidential communication made by or to an advocate or solicitor in that capacity.

(6)   Subsections (1) to (5) apply to any occupational pension scheme to which section 47 applies.

(7)   Section 10 applies to any auditor or actuary who fails to comply with subsection (1) or (2).

(8)   If it appears to the Authority that an auditor or actuary has failed to comply with subsection (1) or (2), the Authority may by order disqualify him for being the auditor or, as the case may be, actuary of any occupational pension scheme specified in the order.

(9)   An order under subsection (8) may specify the scheme to which the failure relates, all schemes falling within any class or description of occupational pension scheme or all occupational pension schemes.

(10) The Authority may, on the application of any person disqualified under this section who satisfies the Authority that he will in future comply with those subsections, by order revoke the order disqualifying him; but a revocation made at any time cannot affect anything done before that time.

(11) An auditor or actuary of an occupational pension scheme who becomes disqualified under this section shall, while he is so disqualified, cease to be auditor or, as the case may be, actuary of any scheme specified in the order disqualifying him.

(12) A person who, while he is disqualified under this section, purports to act as auditor or actuary of an occupational pension scheme specified in the order disqualifying him is guilty of an offence and liable—

    (a) on summary conviction, to a fine not exceeding the statutory maximum, and

    (b) on conviction on indictment, to a fine or imprisonment, or both.

(13) An offence under subsection (12) may be charged by reference to any day or longer period of time; and a person may be convicted of a second or subsequent offence under that subsection by reference to any period of time following the preceding conviction of the offence.

Receipts, payments and records

49. Other responsibilities of trustees, employers, etc.

(1) The trustees of any trust scheme must, except in any prescribed circumstances, keep any money received by them in a separate account kept by them at an institution authorised under the Banking Act 1987.

(2) Regulations may require the trustees of any trust scheme to keep—

    (a) records of their meetings (including meetings of any of their number), and

    (b) books and records relating to any prescribed transaction.

(3) Regulations may, in the case of any trust scheme, require the employer, and any prescribed person acting in connection with the scheme, to keep books and records relating to any prescribed transaction.

(4) Regulations may require books or records kept under subsection (2) or (3) to be kept in a prescribed form and manner and for a prescribed period.

(5) Regulations must, in cases where payments of benefit to members of trust schemes are made by the employer, require the employer to make into a separate account kept by him at an institution authorised under the Banking Act 1987 any payments of benefit which have not been made to the members within any prescribed period.

(6) If in the case of any trust scheme any requirements imposed by or under subsection (1) or (2) are not complied with, sections 3 and 10 apply to any trustee who has failed to take all such steps as are reasonable to secure compliance.

(7) If in the case of any trust scheme any person falls to comply with any requirement imposed under subsection (3) or (5), section 10 applies to him.

(8) Where—

    (a) on making a payment of any earnings in respect of any employment there is deducted any amount corresponding to any contribution payable on behalf of an active member of an occupational pension scheme, and

    (b) the amount deducted is not, within a prescribed period, paid to the trustees or managers of the scheme and there is no reasonable excuse for the failure to do so, the employer is guilty of an offence and liable, on summary conviction, to a fine not exceeding the statutory maximum and, on conviction on indictment, to imprisonment, or a fine, or both.

Resolution of disputes

50. Resolution of disputes

(1) The trustees or managers of an occupational pension scheme must secure that such arrangements as are required by or under this section for the resolution of disagreements between prescribed persons about matters in relation to the scheme are made and implemented.

(2) The arrangements must—

(a) provide for a person, on the application of a complainant of a prescribed description, to give a decision on such a disagreement, and

(b) require the trustees or managers, on the application of such a complainant following a decision given in accordance with paragraph (a), to reconsider the matter in question and confirm the decision or give a new decision in its place.

(3) Regulations may make provision about—

(a) applications for decisions under such arrangements, and

(b) the procedure for reaching and giving such decisions,

including the times by which applications are to be made and decisions given.

(4) Applications and decisions under subsection (2) must be in writing.

(5) Arrangements under subsection (1) must, in the case of existing schemes, have effect as from the commencement of this section.

(6) If, in the case of any occupational pension scheme, such arrangements as are required by this section to be made have not been made, or are not being implemented, section 10 applies to any of the trustees or managers who have failed to take all such steps as are reasonable to secure that such arrangements are made or implemented.

(7) This section does not apply to a scheme of a prescribed description and subsection (1) does not apply to prescribed matters in relation to the scheme.

Indexation

51. Annual increase in rate of pensions

(1) Subject to subsection (6) this section applies to a pension under an occupational pension scheme if—

(a) the scheme—

(i) is an approved scheme, within the meaning of Chapter I of Part XIV of the Taxes Act 1988 (retirement benefit schemes approved by the Commissioners of Inland Revenue) or is a scheme for which such approval has been applied for under that Chapter and not refused, and

(ii) is not a public service pension scheme, and

(b) apart from this section, the annual rate of the pension would not be increased each year by at least the appropriate percentage of that rate.

(2) Subject to section 52, where a pension to which this section applies, or any part of it, is attributable to pensionable service on or after the appointed day or, in the case of money purchase benefits, to payments in respect of employment carried on on or after the appointed day—

(a) the annual rate of the pension, or

(b)   if only part of the pension is attributable to pensionable service or, as the case may be, to payments in respect of employment carried on on or after the appointed day, so much of the annual rate as is attributable to that part,
must be increased annually by at least the appropriate percentage.

(3)   Subsection (2) does not apply to a pension under an occupational pension scheme if the rules of the scheme require—

(a)   the annual rate of the pension, or

(b)   if only part of the pension is attributable to pensionable service or, as the case may be, to payments in respect of employment carried on on or after the appointed day, so much of the annual rate as is attributable to that part,
to be increased at intervals of not more than twelve months by at least the relevant percentage and the scheme complies with any prescribed requirements.

(4)   For the purposes of subsection (3) the relevant percentage is—

(a)   the percentage increase in the retail prices index for the reference period, being a period determined, in relation to each periodic increase, under the rules, or

(b)   the percentage for that period which corresponds to 5 per cent per annum,
whichever is the lesser.

(5)   Regulations may provide that the provisions of subsections (2) and (3) apply in relation to a pension as if so much of it as would not otherwise be attributable to pensionable service or to payments in respect of employment were attributable to pensionable service or, as the case may be, payments in respect of employment—

(a)   before the appointed day,

(b)   on or after that day, or

(c)   partly before and partly on or after that day.

(6)   This section does not apply to any pension or part of a pension which, in the opinion of the trustees or managers, is derived from the payment by any member of the scheme of voluntary contributions.

52.   Restriction on increase where member is under 55

(1)   Subject to subsection (2), no increase under section 51 is required to be paid to or for a member of a scheme whose pension is in payment but who has not attained the age of 55 at the time when the increase takes effect.

(2)   Subsection (1) does not apply if the member—

(a)   is permanently incapacitated by mental or physical infirmity from engaging in regular full-time employment, or

(b)   has retired on account of mental or physical infirmity from the employment in respect of which, or on retirement from which, the pension is payable.

(3)   The rules of a scheme may provide that if, in a case where a pension has been paid to or for a member under the age of 55 at an increased rate in consequence of subsection (2), the member—

(a)   ceases to suffer from the infirmity in question before he attains the age of 55, but

(b)   continues to be entitled to the pension,
any increases subsequently taking effect under section 51 in the annual rate of the pension shall not be paid or shall not be paid in full.

(4)   In any case where—

(a)   by virtue only of subsection (1) or (3), increases are not paid to or for a member or are not paid in full, but

(b)   the member attains the age of 55 or, in a case falling within subsection (3), again satisfies the condition set out in subsection (2)(a) or (b),

his pension shall then become payable at the annual rate at which it would have been payable apart from subsection (1) or (3).

53.   Effect of increases above the statutory requirement

(1)   Where in any tax year the trustees or managers of an occupational pension scheme make an increase in a person's pension, not being an increase required by section 109 of the Pension Schemes Act 1993 or section 51 of this Act, they may deduct the amount of the increase from any increase which, but for this subsection, they would be required to make under either of those sections in the next tax year.

(2)   Where in any tax year the trustees or managers of such a scheme make an increase in a person's pension and part of the increase is not required by section 109 of the Pension Schemes Act 1993 or section 51 of this Act, they may deduct that part of the increase from any increase which, but for this subsection, they would be required to make under either of those sections in the next tax year.

(3)   Where by virtue of subsection (1) or (2) any pensions are not required to be increased in pursuance of section 109 of the Pension Schemes Act 1993 or section 51 of this Act, or not by the full amount that they otherwise would be, their amount shall be calculated for any purpose as if they had been increased in pursuance of the section in question or, as the case may be, by that full amount.

(4)   In section 110 of the Pension Schemes Act 1993 (resources for annual increase of guaranteed minimum pension)—

(a)   subsections (2) to (4) are omitted, and

(b)   in subsection (1), for 'subsection (2) or (3)' there is substituted 'section 53 of the Pensions Act 1995'.

54.   Sections 51 to 53: supplementary

(1)   The first increase required by section 51 in the rate of a pension must take effect not later than the first anniversary of the date on which the pension is first paid; and subsequent increases must take effect at intervals of not more than twelve months.

(2)   Where the first such increase is to take effect on a date when the pension has been in payment for a period of less than twelve months, the increase must be of an amount at least equal to one twelfth of the amount of the increase so required (apart from this subsection) for each complete month in that period.

(3)   In sections 51 to 53 and this section—

'annual rate', in relation to a pension, means the annual rate of the pension, as previously increased under the rules of the scheme or under section 51,

'the appointed day' means the day appointed under section 180 for the commencement of section 51,

'appropriate percentage', in relation to an increase in the whole or part of the annual rate of a pension, means the revaluation percentage for the revaluation period the reference period for which ends with the last preceding 30th September before the increase is made (expressions used in this definition having the same meaning as in paragraph 2 of Schedule 3 to the Pension Schemes Act 1993 (methods of revaluing accrued pension benefits)), 'pension', in relation to a scheme, means any pension in payment under the scheme and includes an annuity.

55. Section 51: end of annual increase in GMP

In section 109 of the Pension Schemes Act 1993 (annual increase of guaranteed minimum pensions)—

(a) in subsection (2) (increase in rate of that part of guaranteed minimum pension attributable to earnings factors for tax year 1988-89 and subsequent tax years) for 'the tax year 1988-89 and subsequent tax years' there is substituted 'the tax years in the relevant period', and

(b) after subsection (3) there is inserted—

'(3A) The relevant period is the period—

(a) beginning with the tax year 1988-89, and

(b) ending with the last tax year that begins before the principal appointed day for the purposes of Part III of the Pensions Act 1995'.

Minimum funding requirement

56. Minimum funding requirement

(1) Every occupational pension scheme to which this section applies is subject to a requirement (referred to in this Part as 'the minimum funding requirement') that the value of the assets of the scheme is not less than the amount of the liabilities of the scheme.

(2) This section applies to an occupational pension scheme other than—

(a) a money purchase scheme, or

(b) a scheme falling within a prescribed class or description.

(3) For the purposes of this section and sections 57 to 61, the liabilities and assets to be taken into account, and their amount or value, shall be determined, calculated and verified by a prescribed person and in the prescribed manner.

(4) In calculating the value of any liabilities for those purposes, a provision of the scheme which limits the amount of its liabilities by reference to the amount of its assets is to be disregarded.

(5) In sections 57 to 61, in relation to any occupational pension scheme to which this section applies—

(a) the amount of the liabilities referred to in subsection (1) is referred to as 'the amount of the scheme liabilities',

(b) the value of the assets referred to in that subsection is referred to as 'the value of the scheme assets',

(c) an 'actuarial valuation' means a written valuation prepared and signed by the actuary of the scheme of the assets and liabilities referred to in subsection (1), and

(d) the 'effective 'date' of an actuarial valuation is the date by reference to which the assets and liabilities are valued.

57. Valuation and certification of assets and liabilities

(1) The trustees or managers of an occupational pension scheme to which section 56 applies must—

(a) obtain, within a prescribed period, an actuarial valuation and afterwards obtain such a valuation before the end of prescribed intervals, and

(b) on prescribed occasions or within prescribed periods, obtain a certificate prepared by the actuary of the scheme—

(i)   stating whether or not in his opinion the contributions payable towards the scheme are adequate for the purpose of securing that the minimum funding requirement will continue to be met throughout the prescribed period or, if it appears to him that it is not met, will be met by the end of that period, and

(ii)   indicating any relevant changes that have occurred since the last actuarial valuation was prepared.

(2)   Subject to subsection (3), the trustees or managers must—

(a)   if the actuary states in such a certificate that in his opinion the contributions payable towards the scheme are not adequate for the purpose of securing that the minimum funding requirement will continue to be met throughout the prescribed period or, if it appears to him that it is not met, will be met by the end of that period, or

(b)   in prescribed circumstances,

obtain an actuarial valuation within the period required by subsection (4).

(3)   In a case within subsection (2)(a), the trustees or managers are not required to obtain an actuarial valuation if—

(a)   in the opinion of the actuary of the scheme, the value of the scheme assets is not less than 90 per cent, of the amount of the scheme liabilities, and

(b)   since the date on which the actuary signed the certificate referred to in that subsection, the schedule of contributions for the scheme has been revised under section 58(3)(b).

(4)   If the trustees or managers obtain a valuation under subsection (2) they must do so—

(a)   in the case of a valuation required by paragraph (a), within the period of six months beginning with the date on which the certificate was signed, and

(b)   in any other case, within a prescribed period.

(5)   A valuation or certificate obtained under subsection (1) or (2) must be prepared in such manner, give such information and contain such statements as may be prescribed.

(6)   The trustees or managers must secure that any valuation or certificate obtained under this section's made available to the employer within seven days of their receiving it.

(7)   Where, in the case of an occupational pension scheme to which section 56 applies, subsection (1), (2) or (6) is not complied with—

(a)   section 3 applies to any trustee who has failed to take all such steps as are reasonable to secure compliance, and

(b)   section 10 applies to any trustee or manager who has failed to take all such steps.

58. Schedules of contributions

(1)   The trustees or managers of an occupational pension scheme to which section 56 applies must secure that there is prepared, maintained and from time to time revised a schedule (referred to in sections 57 to 59 as a 'schedule of contributions') showing—

(a)   the rates of contributions payable towards the scheme by or on behalf of the employer and the active members of the scheme, and

(b)   the dates on or before which such contributions are to be paid.

(2)   The schedule of contributions for a scheme must satisfy prescribed requirements.

(3) The schedule of contributions for a scheme—

(a) must be prepared before the end of a prescribed period beginning with the signing of the first actuarial valuation for the scheme,

(b) may be revised from time to time where the revisions are previously agreed by the trustees or managers and the employer and any revision in the rates of contributions is certified by the actuary of the scheme, and

(c) must be revised before the end of a prescribed period beginning with the signing of each subsequent actuarial valuation.

(4) The matters shown in the schedule of contributions for a scheme—

(a) must be matters previously agreed by the trustees or managers and the employer, or

(b) if no such agreement has been made as to all the matters shown in the schedule, must be—

(i) rates of contributions determined by the trustees or managers, being such rates as in their opinion are adequate for the purpose of securing that the minimum funding requirement will continue to be met throughout the prescribed period or, if it appears to them that it is not met, will be met by the end of that period, and

(ii) other matters determined by the trustees or managers;

and the rates of contributions shown in the schedule must be certified by the actuary of the scheme.

(5) An agreement for the purposes of subsection (4)(a) is one which is made by the trustees or managers and the employer during the prescribed period beginning with the signing of the last preceding actuarial valuation for the scheme.

(6) The actuary may not certify the rates of contributions shown in the schedule of contributions—

(a) in a case where on the date he signs the certificate it appears to him that the minimum funding requirement is met, unless he is of the opinion that the rates are adequate for the purpose of securing that the requirement will continue to be met throughout the prescribed period, and

(b) in any other case, unless he is of the opinion that the rates are adequate for the purpose of securing that the requirement will be met by the end of that period.

(7) The Authority may in prescribed circumstances extend (or further extend) the period referred to in subsection (6).

(8) Where, in the case of any occupational pension scheme to which section 56 applies, this section is not complied with—

(a) section 3 applies to any trustee who has failed to take all such steps as are reasonable to secure compliance, and

(b) section 10 applies to any trustee or manager who has failed to take all such steps.

59. Determinations of contributions: supplementary

(1) Except in prescribed circumstances, the trustees or managers of an occupational pension scheme to which section 56 applies must, where any amounts payable by or on behalf of the employer or the active members of the scheme in accordance with the schedule of contributions have not been paid on or before the due date, give notice of that fact, within the prescribed period, to the Authority and to the members of the scheme.

(2)   Any such amounts which for the time being remain unpaid after that date (whether payable by the employer or not) shall, if not a debt due from the employer to the trustees or managers apart from this subsection, be treated as such a debt.

(3)   If, in the case of an occupational pension scheme to which section 56 applies, it appears to the trustees or managers, at the end of any prescribed period that the minimum funding requirement is not met, they must prepare a report giving the prescribed information about the failure to meet that requirement.

(4)   If in the case of any such scheme, subsection (1) or (3) is not complied with—

(a)   section 3 applies to any trustee who has failed to take all such steps as are reasonable to secure compliance, and

(b)   section 10 applies to any trustee or manager who has failed to take all such steps.

60.   Serious underprovision

(1)   Subsection (2) applies where, in the case of an occupational pension scheme to which section 56 applies, an actuarial valuation shows that, on the effective date of the valuation, the value of the scheme assets is less than 90 per cent of the amount of the scheme liabilities (the difference shown in the valuation being referred to in this section as 'the shortfall').

(2)   The employer must—

(a)   by making an appropriate payment to the trustees or managers, or

(b)   by a prescribed method,

secure an increase in the value of the scheme assets which, taken with any contributions paid, is not less than the shortfall.

(3)   The required increase in that value must be secured—

(a)   before the end of a prescribed period beginning with the signing of the valuation, or

(b)   if the actuarial valuation was obtained by reason of such a statement in a certificate as is referred to in section 57(2), before the end of a prescribed period beginning with the signing of the certificate.

(4)   Except in prescribed circumstances, if the employer fails to secure the required increase in value before the end of the period applicable under subsection (3), the trustees or managers must, within the period of fourteen days (or such longer period as is prescribed) beginning with the end of that period, give written notice of that fact to the Authority and to the members of the scheme.

(5)   If the employer fails to secure the required increase in value before the end of the period applicable under subsection (3), then so much of the shortfall as, at any subsequent time, has not been met by an increase in value under subsection (2) made—

(a)   by making an appropriate payment to the trustees or managers,

(b)   by a prescribed method, or

(c)   by contributions made before the end of that period,

shall, if not a debt due from the employer to the trustees or managers apart from this subsection, be treated at that time as such a debt.

(6)   Where an increase in value is secured by a prescribed method, the increase is to be treated for the purposes of this section as being of an amount determined in accordance with regulations.

(7)   The Authority may in prescribed circumstances extend (or further extend) the period applicable under subsection (3).

(8)   If subsection (4) is not complied with—

(a)   section 3 applies to any trustee who has failed to take all such steps as are reasonable to secure compliance, and

(b)   section 10 applies to any trustee or manager who has failed to take all such steps.

61. Sections 56 to 60: supplementary

Regulations may modify sections 56 to 60 as they apply in prescribed circumstances.

Equal treatment

62. The equal treatment rule

(1)   An occupational pension scheme which does not contain an equal treatment rule shall be treated as including one.

(2)   An equal treatment rule is a rule which relates to the terms on which—

(a)   persons become members of the scheme, and

(b)   members of the scheme are treated.

(3)   Subject to subsection (6), an equal treatment rule has the effect that where—

(a)   a woman is employed on like work with a man in the same employment,

(b)   a woman is employed on work rated as equivalent with that of a man in the same employment, or

(c)   a woman is employed on work which, not being work in relation to which paragraph (a) or (b) applies, is, in terms of the demands made on her (for instance under such headings as effort, skill and decision) of equal value to that of a man in the same employment,

but (apart from the rule) any of the terms referred to in subsection (2) is or becomes less favourable to the woman than it is to the man, the term shall be treated as so modified as not to be less favourable.

(4)   An equal treatment rule does not operate in relation to any difference as between a woman and a man in the operation of any of the terms referred to in subsection (2) if the trustees or managers of the scheme prove that the difference is genuinely due to a material factor which—

(a)   is not the difference of sex, but

(b)   is a material difference between the woman's case and the man's case.

(5)   References in subsection (4) and sections 63 to 65 to the terms referred to in subsection (2), or the effect of any of those terms, include—

(a)   a term which confers on the trustees or managers of an occupational pension scheme, or any other person, a discretion which, in a case within any of paragraphs (a) to (c) of subsection (3)—

(i)   may be exercised so as to affect the way in which persons become members of the scheme, or members of the scheme are treated, and

(ii)   may (apart from the equal treatment rule) be so exercised in a way less favourable to the woman than to the man, and

(b) the effect of any exercise of such a discretion;

and references to the terms on which members of the scheme are treated are to be read accordingly.

(6)   In the case of a term within subsection (5)(a) the effect of an equal treatment rule is that the term shall be treated as so modified as not to permit the discretion to be exercised in a way less favourable to the woman than to the man.

63.   Equal treatment rule: supplementary

(1)   The reference in section 62(2) to the terms on which members of a scheme are treated includes those terms as they have effect for the benefit of dependants of members, and the reference in section 62(5) to the way in which members of a scheme are treated includes the way they are treated as it has effect for the benefit of dependants of members.

(2)   Where the effect of any of the terms referred to in section 62(2) on persons of the same sex differs according to their family or marital status, the effect of the term is to be compared for the purposes of section 62 with its effect on persons of the other sex who have the same status.

(3)   An equal treatment rule has effect subject to paragraphs 5 and 6 of Schedule 5 to the Social Security Act 1989 (employment-related benefit schemes: maternity and family leave provisions).

(4)   Section 62 shall be construed as one with section 1 of the Equal Pay Act 1970 (requirement of equal treatment for men and women in the same employment); and sections 2 and 2A of that Act (disputes and enforcement) shall have effect for the purposes of section 62 as if—

(a)   references to an equality clause were to an equal treatment rule,

(b)   references to employers and employees were to the trustees or managers of the scheme (on the one hand) and the members, or prospective members, of the scheme (on the other),

(c)   for section 2(4) there were substituted—

'(4) No claim in respect of the operation of an equal treatment rule in respect of an occupational pension scheme shall be referred to an industrial tribunal otherwise than by virtue of subsection (3) above unless the woman concerned has been employed in a description or category of employment to which the scheme relates within the six months preceding the date of the reference', and

(d)   references to section 1(2)(c) of the Equal Pay Act 1970 were to section 62(3)(c) of this Act.

(5)   Regulations may make provision for the Equal Pay Act 1970 to have effect, in relation to an equal treatment rule, with prescribed modifications; and subsection (4) shall have effect subject to any regulations made by virtue of this subsection.

(6)   Section 62, so far as it relates to the terms on which members of a scheme are treated, is to be treated as having had effect in relation to any pensionable service on or after 17th May 1990.

64.   Equal treatment rule: exceptions

(1)   An equal treatment rule does not operate in relation to any variation as between a woman and a man in the effect of any of the terms referred to in section 62(2) if the variation is permitted by or under any of the provisions of this section.

(2)   Where a man and a woman are eligible, in prescribed circumstances, to receive different amounts by way of pension, the variation is permitted by this subsection if, in prescribed circumstances, the differences are attributable only to differences between men and women in the benefits under sections 43 to 55 of the

Social Security Contributions and Benefits Act 1992 (State retirement pensions) to which, in prescribed circumstances, they are or would be entitled.

(3) A variation is permitted by this subsection if—

(a) the variation consists of the application of actuarial factors which differ for men and women to the calculation of contributions to a scheme by employers, being factors which fall within a prescribed class or description, or

(b) the variation consists of the application of actuarial factors which differ for men and women to the determination of benefits falling within a prescribed class or description;

and in this subsection 'benefits' include any payment or other benefit made to or in respect of a person as a member of the scheme.

(4) Regulations may—

(a) permit further variations, or

(b) amend or repeal subsection (2) or (3);

and regulations made by virtue of this subsection may have effect in relation to pensionable service on or after 17th May 1990 and before the date on which the regulations are made.

65. Equal treatment rule: consequential alteration of schemes

(1) The trustees or managers of an occupational pension scheme may, if—

(a) they do not (apart from this section) have power to make such alterations to the scheme as may be required to secure conformity with an equal treatment rule, or

(b) they have such power but the procedure for doing so—

(i) is liable to be unduly complex or protracted, or

(ii) involves the obtaining of consents which cannot be obtained, or can only be obtained with undue delay or difficulty,

by resolution make such alterations to the scheme.

(2) The alterations may have effect in relation to a period before the alterations are made.

66. Equal treatment rule: effect on terms of employment, etc.

(1) In section 6 of the Equal Pay Act 1970 (exclusions), for subsections (1A) and (2) (exclusion for terms related to death or retirement) there is substituted—

'(1B) An equality clause shall not operate in relation to terms relating to a person's membership of, or rights under, an occupational pension scheme, being terms in relation to which, by reason only of any provision made by or under sections 62 to 64 of the Pensions Act 1995 (equal treatment), an equal treatment rule would not operate if the terms were included in the scheme.

(1C) In subsection (1B), 'occupational pension scheme' has the same meaning as in the Pension Schemes Act 1993 and 'equal treatment rule' has the meaning given by section 62 of the Pensions Act 1995'.

(2) In section 4(1) of the Sex Discrimination Act 1975 (victimisation of complainants etc.)—

(a) in paragraphs (a), (b) and (c), after 'Equal Pay Act 1970' there is inserted 'or sections 62 to 65 of the Pensions Act 1995', and

(b) at the end of paragraph (d) there is added 'or under sections 62 to 65 of the Pensions Act 1995'.

(3) In section 6 of the Sex Discrimination Act 1975 (discrimination against applicants and employees), for subsection (4) there is substituted—

'(4)   Subsections (1)(b) and (2) do not render it unlawful for a person to discriminate against a woman in relation to her membership of, or rights under, an occupational pension scheme in such a way that, were any term of the scheme to provide for discrimination in that way, then, by reason only of any provision made by or under sections 62 to 64 of the Pensions Act 1995 (equal treatment), an equal treatment rule would not operate in relation to that term.

(4A)   In subsection (4), 'occupational pension scheme' has the same meaning as in the Pension Schemes Act 1993 and 'equal treatment rule' has the meaning given by section 62 of the Pensions Act 1995'.

(4)   Regulations may make provision—

(a)   for the Equal Pay Act 1970 to have effect, in relation to terms of employment relating to membership of, or rights under, an occupational pension scheme with prescribed modifications, and

(b)   for imposing requirements on employers as to the payment of contributions and otherwise in case of their failing or having failed to comply with any such terms.

(5)   References in subsection (4) to terms of employment include (where the context permits)—

(a)   any collective agreement or pay structure, and

(b)   an agricultural wages order within section 5 of the Equal Pay Act 1970.

Modification of schemes

67.   Restriction on powers to alter schemes

(1)   This section applies to any power conferred on any person by an occupational pension scheme (other than a public service pension scheme) to modify the scheme.

(2)   The power cannot be exercised on any occasion in a manner which would or might affect any entitlement, or accrued right, of any member of the scheme acquired before the power is exercised unless the requirements under subsection (3) are satisfied.

(3)   Those requirements are that, in respect of the exercise of the power in that manner on that occasion—

(a)   the trustees have satisfied themselves that—

(i)   the certification requirements, or

(ii)   the requirements for consent,

are met in respect of that member, and

(b)   where the power is exercised by a person other than the trustees, the trustees have approved the exercise of the power in that manner on that occasion.

(4)   In subsection (3)—

(a)   'the certification requirements' means prescribed requirements for the purpose of securing that no power to which this section applies is exercised in any manner which, in the opinion of an actuary, would adversely affect any member of the scheme (without his consent) in respect of his entitlement, or accrued rights, acquired before the power is exercised, and

(b)   'the consent requirements' means prescribed requirements for the purpose of obtaining the consent of members of a scheme to the exercise of a power to which this section applies.

(5)   Subsection (2) does not apply to the exercise of a power in a prescribed manner.

(6)   Where a power to which this section applies may not (apart from this section) be exercised without the consent of any person, regulations may make provision for treating such consent as given in prescribed circumstances.

68.   Power of trustees to modify schemes by resolution

(1)   The trustees of a trust scheme may by resolution modify the scheme with a view to achieving any of the purposes specified in subsection (2).

(2)   The purposes referred to in subsection (1) are—

(a)   to extend the class of persons who may receive benefits under the scheme in respect of the death of a member of the scheme,

(b)   to enable the scheme to conform with such arrangements as are required by section 16(1) or 17(2),

(c)   to enable the scheme to comply with such terms and conditions as may be imposed by the Compensation Board in relation to any payment made by them under section 83 or 84,

(d)   to enable the scheme to conform with section 37(2), 76(2), 91 or 92, and

(e)   prescribed purposes.

(3) No modification may be made by virtue of subsection (2)(a) without the consent of the employer.

(4)   Modifications made by virtue of subsection (2)(b) may include in particular—

(a)   modification of any limit on the number of, or of any category of, trustees, or

(b)   provision for the transfer or vesting of property.

(5)   Nothing done by virtue of subsection (2)(d), or any corresponding provisions in force in Northern Ireland, shall be treated as effecting an alteration to the scheme in question for the purposes of section 591B (cessation of approval) of the Taxes Act 1988.

(6)   Regulations may provide that this section does not apply to trust schemes falling within a prescribed class or description.

69.   Grounds for applying for modifications

(1)   The Authority may, on an application made to them by persons competent to do so, make an order in respect of an occupational pension scheme (other than a public service pension scheme)—

(a)   authorising the modification of the scheme with a view to achieving any of the purposes mentioned in subsection (3), or

(b)   modifying the scheme with a view to achieving any such purpose.

(2)   Regulations may make provision about the manner of dealing with applications under this section.

(3)   The purposes referred to in subsection (1) are—

(a)   in the case of a scheme to which Schedule 22 to the Taxes Act 1988 (reduction of pension fund surpluses in certain exempt approved schemes) applies, to reduce or eliminate on any particular occasion any excess in accordance with any proposal submitted under paragraph 3(1) of that Schedule, where any requirements mentioned in section 37(4), and any other prescribed requirements, will be satisfied in relation to the reduction or elimination,

(b)   in the case of an exempt approved scheme (within the meaning given by section 592(1) of the Taxes Act 1988) which is being wound up, to enable assets remaining after the liabilities of the scheme have been fully discharged to be distributed to the employer, where prescribed requirements in relation to the distribution are satisfied, or

(c)   to enable the scheme to be so treated during a prescribed period that an employment to which the scheme applies may be contracted-out employment by reference to it.

(4)   The persons competent to make an application under this section are—

(a)   in the case of the purposes referred to in paragraph (a) or (b) of subsection (3), the trustees of the scheme, and

(b)   in the case of the purposes referred to in paragraph (c) of that subsection—

(i)   the trustees or managers of the scheme,

(ii)   the employer, or

(iii)   any person other than the trustees or managers who has power to alter the rules of the scheme.

(5)   An order under subsection (1)(a) must be framed—

(a)   if made with a view to achieving either of the purposes referred to in subsection (3)(a) or (b), so as to confer the power of modification on the trustees, and

(b)   if made with a view to achieving the purposes referred to in subsection (3)(c), so as to confer the power of modification on such persons (who may include persons who were not parties to the application made to the Authority) as the Authority think appropriate.

(6)   Regulations may provide that in prescribed circumstances this section does not apply to occupational pension schemes falling within a prescribed class or description or applies to them with prescribed modifications.

70.   Section 69: supplementary

(1)   The Authority may not make an order under section 69 unless they are satisfied that the purposes for which the application for the order was made—

(a)   cannot be achieved otherwise than by means of such an order, or

(b)   can only be achieved in accordance with a procedure which—

(i)   is liable to be unduly complex or protracted, or

(ii)   involves the obtaining of consents which cannot be obtained, or can only be obtained with undue delay or difficulty.

(2)   The extent of the Authority's powers to make such an order is not limited, in relation to any purposes for which they are exercisable, to the minimum necessary to achieve those purposes.

(3)   The Authority may not make an order under section 69 with a view to achieving the purpose referred to in subsection (3)(c) of that section unless they are satisfied that it is reasonable in all the circumstances to make it.

71.   Effect of orders under section 69

(1)   An order under paragraph (a) of subsection (1) of section 69 may enable those exercising any power conferred by the order to exercise it retrospectively (whether or not the power could otherwise be so exercised) and an order under paragraph (b) of that subsection may modify a scheme retrospectively.

(2) Any modification of a scheme made in pursuance of an order of the Authority under section 69 is as effective in law as if it had been made under powers conferred by or under the scheme.

(3) An order under section 69 may be made and complied with in relation to a scheme—

(a) in spite of any enactment or rule of law, or any rule of the scheme, which would otherwise operate to prevent the modification being made, or

(b) without regard to any such enactment, rule of law or rule of the scheme as would otherwise require, or might otherwise be taken to require, the implementation of any procedure or the obtaining of any consent, with a view to the making of the modification.

(4) In this section, 'retrospectively' means with effect from a date before that on which the power is exercised or, as the case may be, the order is made.

72. Modification of public service pension schemes

(1) The appropriate authority may make such provision for the modification of a public service pension scheme as could be made in respect of a scheme other than a public service pension scheme by an order of the Authority under section 69(1)(b).

(2) In this section 'the appropriate authority', in relation to a scheme, means such Minister of the Crown or government department as may be designated by the Treasury as having responsibility for the particular scheme.

(3) The powers of the appropriate authority under this section are exercisable by means of an order—

(a) directly modifying the scheme (without regard, in the case of a scheme contained in or made under powers conferred by an enactment, to the terms of the enactment or any of its restrictions), or

(b) modifying an enactment under which the scheme was made or by virtue of which it has effect.

(4) Any such order may adapt, amend or repeal any such enactment as is referred to in paragraph (a) or (b) of subsection (3) as that authority thinks appropriate.

Winding up

73. Preferential liabilities on winding up

(1) This section applies, where a salary related occupational pension scheme to which section 56 applies is being wound up, to determine the order in which the assets of the scheme are to be applied towards satisfying the liabilities in respect of pensions and other benefits (including increases in pensions).

(2) The assets of the scheme must be applied first towards satisfying the amounts of the liabilities mentioned in subsection (3) and, if the assets are insufficient to satisfy those amounts in full, then—

(a) the assets must be applied first towards satisfying the amounts of the liabilities mentioned in earlier paragraphs of subsection (3) before the amounts of the liabilities mentioned in later paragraphs, and

(b) where the amounts of the liabilities mentioned in one of those paragraphs cannot be satisfied in full, those amounts must be satisfied in the same proportions.

(3) The liabilities referred to in subsection (2) are—

(a)   any liability for pensions or other benefits which, in the opinion of the trustees, are derived from the payment by any member of the scheme of voluntary contributions,

(b)   where a person's entitlement to payment of pension or other benefit has arisen, liability for that pension or benefit and for any pension or other benefit which will be payable to dependants of that person on his death (but excluding increases to pensions),

(c)   any liability for—

(i)   pensions or other benefits which have accrued to or in respect of any · members of the scheme (but excluding increases to pensions), or

(ii)   (in respect of members with less than two years pensionable service) the return of contributions,

(d)   any liability for increases to pensions referred to in paragraphs (b) and (c);

and, for the purposes of subsection (2), the amounts of the liabilities mentioned in paragraphs (b) to (d) are to be taken to be the amounts calculated and verified in the prescribed manner.

(4)   To the extent that any liabilities, as calculated in accordance with the rules of the scheme, have not been satisfied under subsection (2), any remaining assets of the scheme must then be applied towards satisfying those liabilities (as so calculated) in the order provided for in the rules of the scheme.

(5)   If the scheme confers power on any person other than the trustees or managers to apply the assets of the scheme in respect of pensions or other benefits (including increases in pensions), it cannot be exercised by that person but may be exercised instead by the trustees or managers.

(6)   If this section is not complied with—

(a)   section 3 applies to any trustee who has failed to take all such steps as are reasonable to secure compliance, and

(b)   section 10 applies to any trustee or manager who has failed to take all such steps.

(7)   Regulations may modify subsection (3).

(8)   This section does not apply to an occupational pension scheme falling within a prescribed class or description.

(9)   This section shall have effect with prescribed modifications in cases where part of a salary related occupational pension scheme to which section 56 applies is being wound up.

74.   Discharge of liabilities by insurance, etc

(1)   This section applies where a salary related occupational pension scheme to which section 56 applies, other than a scheme falling within a prescribed class or description, is being wound up.

(2)   A liability to or in respect of a member of the scheme in respect of pensions or other benefits (including increases in pensions) is to be treated as discharged (to the extent that it would not be so treated apart from this section) if the trustees or managers of the scheme have, in accordance with prescribed arrangements, provided for the discharge of the liability in one or more of the ways mentioned in subsection (3).

(3)   The ways referred to in subsection (2) are—

(a)   by acquiring transfer credits allowed under the rules of another occupational pension scheme which satisfies prescribed requirements and the trustees or managers of which are able and willing to accept payment in respect of the member,

(b)   by acquiring rights allowed under the rules of a personal pension scheme which satisfies prescribed requirements and the trustees or managers of which are able and willing to accept payment in respect of the member's accrued rights,

(c)   by purchasing one or more annuities which satisfy prescribed requirements from one or more insurance companies, being companies willing to accept payment in respect of the member from the trustees or managers,

(d)   by subscribing to other pension arrangements which satisfy prescribed requirements.

(4)   If   the assets of the scheme are insufficient to satisfy in full the liabilities, as calculated in accordance with the rules of the scheme, in respect of pensions and other benefits (including increases in pensions), the reference in subsection (2) to providing for the discharge of any liability in one or more of the ways mentioned in subsection (3) is to applying any amount available, in accordance with section 73, in one or more of those ways.

(5)   Regulations may provide for this section—

(a)   to have effect in relation to so much of any liability as may be determined in accordance with the regulations, or

(b)   to have effect with prescribed modifications in relation to schemes falling within a prescribed class or description.

75.   Deficiencies in the assets

(1)   If, in the case of an occupational pension scheme which is not a money purchase scheme, the value at the applicable time of the assets of the scheme is less than the amount at that time of the liabilities of the scheme, an amount equal to the difference shall be treated as a debt due from the employer to the trustees or managers of the scheme.

(2)   If in the case of an occupational pension scheme which is not a money purchase scheme—

(a)   a relevant insolvency event occurs in relation to the employer, and

(b)   a debt due from the employer under subsection (1) has not been discharged at the time that event occurs,

the debt in question shall be taken, for the purposes of the law relating to winding up, bankruptcy or sequestration as it applies in relation to the employer, to arise immediately before that time.

(3)   In this section 'the applicable time' means —

(a)   if the scheme is being wound up before a relevant insolvency event occurs in relation to the employer, any time when it is being wound up before such an event occurs, and

(b)   otherwise, immediately before the relevant insolvency event occurs.

(4)   For the purposes of this section a relevant insolvency event occurs in relation to the employer—

(a)   in England and Wales—

(i)   where the employer is a company, when it goes into liquidation, within the meaning of section 247(2) of the Insolvency Act 1986, or

(ii)   where the employer is an individual, at the commencement of his bankruptcy, within the meaning of section 278 of that Act, or

(b)   in Scotland—

(i)   where the employer is a company, at the commencement of its winding up, within the meaning of section 129 of that Act, or

(ii)   where the employer is a debtor within the meaning of the Bankruptcy (Scotland) Act 1985, on the date of sequestration as defined in section 12(4) of that Act.

(5)   For the purposes of subsection (1), the liabilities and assets to be taken into account, and their amount or value, must be determined, calculated and verified by a prescribed person and in the prescribed manner.

(6)   In calculating the value of any liabilities for those purposes, a provision of the scheme which limits the amount of its liabilities by reference to the amount of its assets is to be disregarded.

(7)   This section does not prejudice any other right or remedy which the trustees or managers may have in respect of a deficiency in the scheme's assets.

(8)   A debt due by virtue only of this section shall not be regarded—

(a)   as a preferential debt for the purposes of the Insolvency Act 1986, or

(b)   as a preferred debt for the purposes of the Bankruptcy (Scotland) Act 1985.

(9)   This section does not apply to an occupational pension scheme falling within a prescribed class or description.

(10)   Regulations may modify this section as it applies in prescribed circumstances.

76.   Excess assets on winding up

(1)   This section applies to a trust scheme in any circumstances if—

(a)   it is an exempt approved scheme, within the meaning given by section 592(1) of the Taxes Act 1988,

(b)   the scheme is being wound up, and

(c)   in those circumstances power is conferred on the employer or the trustees to distribute assets to the employer on a winding up.

(2)   The power referred to in subsection (1)(c) cannot be exercised unless the requirements of subsections (3) and (in prescribed circumstances) (4), and any prescribed requirements, are satisfied.

(3)   The requirements of this subsection are that—

(a)   the liabilities of the scheme have been fully discharged,

(b)   where there is any power under the scheme, after the discharge of those liabilities, to distribute assets to any person other than the employer, the power has been exercised or a decision has been made not to exercise it,

(c)   the annual rates of the pensions under the scheme which commence or have commenced are increased by the appropriate percentage, and

(d)   notice has been given in accordance with prescribed requirements to the members of the scheme of the proposal to exercise the power.

(4)   The requirements of this subsection are that the Authority are of the opinion that—

(a)   any requirements prescribed by virtue of subsection (2) are satisfied, and

(b)   the requirements of subsection (3) are satisfied.

(5)   In subsection (3)—

(a)   'annual rate' and 'appropriate percentage' have the same meaning as in section 54, and

(b)   'pension' does not include—

(i)   any guaranteed minimum pension (as defined in section 8(2) of the Pension Schemes Act 1993) or any increase in such a pension under section 109 of that Act, or

(ii)   any money purchase benefit (as defined in section 181(1) of that Act).

(6)   If, where this section applies to any trust scheme, the trustees purport to exercise the power referred to in subsection (1)(c) without complying with the requirements of this section, sections 3 and 10 apply to any of them who have failed to take all such steps as are reasonable to secure compliance.

(7)   If, where this section applies to any trust scheme, any person other than the trustees purports to exercise the power referred to in subsection (1)(c) without complying with the requirements of this section, section 10 applies to him.

(8)   Regulations may provide that, in prescribed circumstances, this section does not apply to schemes falling within a prescribed class or description, or applies to them with prescribed modifications.

77.   Excess assets remaining after winding up: power to distribute

(1)   This section applies to a trust scheme in any circumstances if—

(a)   it is an exempt approved scheme, within the meaning given by section 592(1) of the Taxes Act 1988,

(b)   the scheme is being wound up,

(c)   the liabilities of the scheme have been fully discharged,

(d)   where there is any power under the scheme, after the discharge of those liabilities, to distribute assets to any person other than the employer, the power has been exercised or a decision has been made not to exercise it,

(e)   any assets remain undistributed, and

(f)   the scheme prohibits the distribution of assets to the employer in those circumstances.

(2)   The annual rates of the pensions under the scheme which commence or have commenced must be increased by the appropriate percentage, so far as the value of the undistributed assets allows.

(3)   In subsection (2)—

(a)   'annual rate' and 'appropriate percentage' have the same meaning as in section 54, and

(b)   'pension' does not include—

(i)   any guaranteed minimum pension (as defined in section 8(2) of the Pension Schemes Act 1993) or any increase in such a pension under section 109 of that Act, or

(ii)   any money purchase benefit (as defined in section 181(1) of that Act).

(4)   Where any assets remain undistributed after the discharge of the trustees' duty under subsection (2)—

(a)   the trustees must use those assets for the purpose of providing additional benefits or increasing the value of any benefits, but subject to prescribed limits, and

(b)   the trustees may then distribute those assets (so far as undistributed) to the employer.

(5) If, where this section applies to a trust scheme, the requirements of this section are not complied with, section 3 applies to any trustee who has failed to take all such steps as are reasonable to secure compliance.

(6) Regulations may modify this section as it applies in prescribed circumstances.

The Pensions Compensation Board

78. The Compensation Board

(1) There shall be a body corporate called the Pensions Compensation Board (referred to in this Part as 'the Compensation Board').

(2) The Compensation Board shall consist of not less than three members appointed by the Secretary of State, one of whom shall be so appointed as chairman.

(3) In addition to the chairman, the Board shall comprise—
    (a) a member appointed after the Secretary of State has consulted—
        (i) organisations appearing to him to be representative of employers, and
        (ii) the chairman,
    (b) a member appointed after the Secretary of State has consulted—
        (i) organisations appearing to him to be representative of employees, and
        (ii) the chairman,
and such other member or members as the Secretary of State may appoint after consultation with the chairman.

(4) Payments made by the Compensation Board may be made on such terms (including terms requiring repayment in whole or in part) and on such conditions as the Board think appropriate.

(5) The Compensation Board may borrow from an institution authorised under the Banking Act 1987 such sums as they may from time to time require for exercising any of their functions.

(6) The aggregate amount outstanding in respect of the principal of any money borrowed by the Compensation Board under subsection (5) must not exceed the prescribed amount.

(7) Neither the Compensation Board nor any person who is a member or employee of the Compensation Board shall be liable in damages for anything done or omitted in the discharge or purported discharge of the functions of the Compensation Board under this Part, or any corresponding provisions in force in Northern Ireland, unless it is shown that the act or omission was in bad faith.

(8) Schedule 2 (constitution, procedure, etc. of the Compensation Board) shall have effect.

79. Reports to Secretary of State

(1) The Compensation Board must prepare a report for the first twelve months of their existence, and a report for each succeeding period of twelve months, and must send each report to the Secretary of State as soon as practicable after the end of the period for which it is prepared.

(2) A report prepared under this section for any period must deal with the activities of the Compensation Board in the period.

(3) The Secretary of State must lay before each House of Parliament a copy of every report received by him under this section.

80. Review of decisions

(1) Subject to the following provisions of this section, any determination by the Compensation Board of a question which it is within their functions to determine shall be final.

(2) The Compensation Board may on the application of a person appearing to them to be interested—

(a) at any time review any such determination of theirs as is mentioned in subsection (1) (including a determination given by them on a previous review), if they are satisfied that there has been a relevant change of circumstances since the determination was made, or that the determination was made in ignorance of a material fact or based on a mistake as to a material fact or was erroneous in point of law, and

(b) at any time within a period of three months from the date of the determination, or within such longer period as they may allow in any particular case, review such a determination on any ground.

(3) The Compensation Board's powers on a review under this section include power—

(a) to vary or revoke any determination previously made,

(b) to substitute a different determination, and

(c) generally to deal with the matters arising on the review as if they had arisen on the original determination;

and also include power to make savings and transitional provisions.

(4) Subject to subsection (5), regulations may make provision with respect to the procedure to be adopted on any application for a review under this section, or under any corresponding provision in force in Northern Ireland, and generally with respect to such applications and reviews.

(5) Nothing in subsection (4) shall be taken to prevent such a review being entered upon by the Compensation Board without an application being made.

The compensation provisions

81. Cases where compensation provisions apply

(1) Subject to subsection (2), this section applies to an application for compensation under section 82 in respect of an occupational pension scheme if all the following conditions are met—

(a) the scheme is a trust scheme,

(b) the employer is insolvent,

(c) the value of the assets of the scheme has been reduced, and there are reasonable grounds for believing that the reduction was attributable to an act or omission constituting a prescribed offence,

(d) in the case of a salary related trust scheme, immediately before the date of the application the value of the assets of the scheme is less than 90 per cent of the amount of the liabilities of the scheme, and

(e) it is reasonable in all the circumstances that the members of the scheme should be assisted by the Compensation Board paying to the trustees of the scheme, out of funds for the time being held by them, an amount determined in accordance with the compensation provisions.

(2) Subsection (1) does not apply in respect of a trust scheme falling within a prescribed class or description; and paragraph (c) applies only to reductions in value since the appointed day.

(3) In this Part the 'compensation provisions' means the provisions of this section and sections 82 to 85; and below in the compensation provisions as they relate to a trust scheme—

(a) 'the application date' means the date of the application for compensation under section 82,

(b) 'the appointed day' means the day appointed under section 180 for the commencement of this section,

(c) 'the insolvency date' means the date on which the employer became insolvent,

(d) 'the settlement date' means the date determined by the Compensation Board, after consulting the trustees, to be the date after which further recoveries of value are unlikely to be obtained without disproportionate cost or within a reasonable time,

(e) 'the shortfall at the application date' means the amount of the reduction falling within subsection (1)(c) or (if there was more than one such reduction) the aggregate of the reductions, being the amount or aggregate immediately before the application date,

(f) 'recovery of value' means any increase in the value of the assets of the scheme, being an increase attributable to any payment received (otherwise than from the Compensation Board) by the trustees of the scheme in respect of any act or omission—

(i) which there are reasonable grounds for believing constituted a prescribed offence, and

(ii) to which any reduction in value failing within subsection (1)(c) was attributable.

(4) It is for the Compensation Board to determine whether anything received by the trustees of the scheme is to be treated as a payment received for any such act or omission as is referred to in subsection (3)(f); and in this section 'payment' includes any money or money's worth.

(5) Where this section applies to an application for compensation under section 82, the trustees must obtain any recoveries of value, to the extent that they may do so without disproportionate cost and within a reasonable time.

(6) If subsection (5) is not complied with, section 3 applies to any trustee who has failed to take all such steps as are reasonable to secure compliance.

(7) Section 56(3) and (4) applies for the purposes of the compensation provisions as it applies for the purposes of sections 56 to 61.

(8) Section 123 of the Pension Schemes Act 1993 (meaning of insolvency) applies for the purposes of the compensation provisions as it applies for the purposes of Chapter II of Part VII of that Act (unpaid scheme contributions).

82. Applications for payments

(1) Compensation may be paid under section 83 only on an application to which section 81 applies made within the qualifying period by a prescribed person.

(2) An application under this section must be made in the manner, and give the information, required by the Compensation Board.

(3) For the purposes of this section the 'qualifying period', subject to subsection (5), is the period expiring with the period of twelve months mentioned in subsection (4).

(4) The period of twelve months referred to in subsection (3) is that beginning with the later of the following times—

(a) the insolvency date,

(b) when the auditor or actuary of the scheme, or the trustees, knew or ought reasonably to have known that a reduction of value falling within section 81(1)(c) had occurred,

being, in each case, a time after the appointed day.

(5) The Compensation Board may extend, or further extend, the qualifying period.

83. Amount of compensation

(1) Where in the opinion of the Compensation Board section 81 applies to an application for compensation under section 82 in respect of a trust scheme, and the Board have determined the settlement date, the Board may make a payment or payments to the trustees of the scheme in accordance with this section.

(2) The amount of any payment must be determined in accordance with regulations and must take account of any payment already made under section 84, and the Compensation Board must give written notice of their determination to the person who made the application under section 82 and (if different) to the trustees.

(3) The amount of the payment or (if there is more than one) the aggregate—

(a) must not exceed 90 per cent of the shortfall at the application date, together with interest at the prescribed rate for the prescribed period on the shortfall or (if the shortfall comprises more than one reduction in value) on each of the reductions, and also,

(b) in the case of a salary related scheme, must not exceed the amount which, on the settlement date, is required to be paid to the trustees of the scheme in order to secure that the value on that date of the assets of the scheme is equal to 90 per cent of the amount on that date of the liabilities of the scheme.

84. Payments made in anticipation

(1) The Compensation Board may, on an application for compensation under section 82, make a payment or payments to the trustees of a trust scheme where in their opinion—

(a) section 81 applies, or may apply, to the application, and

(b) the trustees would not otherwise be able to meet liabilities falling within a prescribed class,

but the Board have not determined the settlement date.

(2) Amounts payable under this section must be determined in accordance with regulations.

(3) Where any payment is made under this section, the Compensation Board may, except in prescribed circumstances—

scheme, or

(a) if they subsequently form the opinion that section 81 does not apply to the application for compensation in respect of the scheme, or

(b) if they subsequently form the opinion that the amount of the payment was excessive,

recover so much of the payment as they consider appropriate.

85. Surplus funds

(1)   If the Secretary of State, after consultation with the Compensation Board, considers that the funds for the time being held by the Board exceed what is reasonably required for the purpose of exercising their functions under this Part, he may by order require them to distribute any of those funds appearing to him to be surplus to their requirements among occupational pension schemes.

(2)   A distribution under subsection (1) must be made in the prescribed manner and subject to the prescribed conditions.

(3)   The Compensation Board may invest any funds for the time being held by them which appear to them to be surplus to their requirements—

(a)   in any investment for the time being falling within Part I, Part II or Part III of Schedule 1 to the Trustee Investments Act 1961, or

(b)   in any prescribed investment.

86. Modification of compensation provisions

Regulations may modify the compensation provisions in their application to trust schemes falling within a prescribed class or description.

Money purchase schemes

87. Schedules of payments to money purchase schemes

(1)   This section applies to an occupational pension scheme which is a money purchase scheme, other than one falling within a prescribed class or description.

(2)   The trustees or managers of every occupational pension scheme to which this section applies must secure that there is prepared, maintained and from time to time revised a schedule (referred to in this section and section 88 as a 'payment schedule') showing—

(a)   the rates of contributions payable towards the scheme by or on behalf of the employer and the active members of the scheme,

(b)   such other amounts payable towards the scheme as may be prescribed, and

(c)   the dates on or before which payments of such contributions or other amounts are to be made (referred to in those sections as 'due dates').

(3)   The payment schedule for a scheme must satisfy prescribed requirements.

(4)   The matters shown in the payment schedule for a scheme—

(a)   to the extent that the scheme makes provision for their determination, must be so determined, and

(b)   otherwise,

(i)   must be matters previously agreed between the employer and the trustees or managers of the scheme, or

(ii)   if no such agreement has been made as to all matters shown in the schedule (other than those for whose determination the scheme makes provision), must be matters determined by the trustees or managers of the scheme.

(5)   Where in the case of a scheme this section is not complied with—

(a)   section 3 applies to any trustee who has failed to take all such steps as are reasonable to secure compliance, and

(b)   section 10 applies to any trustee or manager who has failed to take all such steps.

88. Schedules of payments to money puchase schemes: supplementary

(1) Except in prescribed circumstances, the trustees or managers of an occupational pension scheme to which section 87 applies must, where any amounts payable in accordance with the payment schedule have not been paid on or before the due date, give notice of that fact, within the prescribed period, to the Authority and to the members of the scheme.

(2) Any such amounts which for the time being remain unpaid after that date (whether payable by the employer or not) shall, if not a debt due from the employer to the trustees or managers apart from this subsection, be treated as such a debt.

(3) Where any amounts payable in accordance with the payment schedule by or on behalf of the employer have not been paid on or before the due date, section 10 applies to the employer.

(4) If, in the case of an occupational pension scheme to which section 87 applies, subsection (1) is not complied with—

(a) section 3 applies to any trustee who has failed to take all such steps as are reasonable to secure compliance, and

(b) section 10 applies to any trustee or manager who has failed to take all such steps.

89. Application of further provisions to money puchase schemes

(1) In the case of money purchase schemes falling within a prescribed class or description, regulations may—

(a) provide for any of the provisions of sections 56 to 60 to apply, or apply with prescribed modifications (in spite of anything in those sections), and

(b) provide for any of the provisions of sections 87 and 88 to apply with prescribed modifications or not to apply,

to such extent as may be prescribed.

(2) Regulations may provide for any of the provisions of section 75 to apply, or apply with prescribed modifications, to money purchase schemes to such extent as may be prescribed (in spite of anything in that section), and the power conferred by this subsection includes power to apply section 75 in circumstances other than those in which the scheme is being wound up or a relevant insolvency event occurs (within the meaning of that section).

90. Unpaid contributions in cases of insolvency

In section 124 of the Pension Schemes Act 1993 (duty of Secretary of State to pay unpaid contributions to schemes), after subsection (3) there is inserted—

'(3A) Where the scheme in question is a money purchase scheme, the sum payable under this section by virtue of subsection (3) shall be the lesser of the amounts mentioned in paragraphs (a) and (c) of that subsection',

and, accordingly, at the beginning of subsection (3) there is inserted 'Subject to subsection (3A)'.

Assignment, forfeiture, bankruptcy etc.

91. Inalienability of occupational pension

(1) Subject to subsection (5), where a person is entitled, or has an accrued right, to a pension under an occupational pension scheme—

(a) the entitlement or right cannot be assigned, commuted or surrendered,

(b)   the entitlement or right cannot be charged or a lien exercised in respect of it, and

(c)   no set-off can be exercised in respect of it,

and an agreement to effect any of those things is unenforceable.

(2)   Where by virtue of this section a person's entitlement, or accrued right, to a pension under an occupational pension scheme cannot, apart from subsection (5), be assigned, no order can be made by any court the effect of which would be that he would be restrained from receiving that pension.

(3)   Where a bankruptcy order is made against a person, any entitlement or right of his which by virtue of this section cannot, apart from subsection (5), be assigned is excluded from his estate for the purposes of Parts VIII to XI of the Insolvency Act 1986 or the Bankruptcy (Scotland) Act 1985.

(4)   Subsection (2) does not prevent the making of—

(a)   an attachment of earnings order under the Attachment of Earnings Act 1971, or

(b)   an income payments order under the Insolvency Act 1986.

(5)   In the case of a person ('the person in question') who is entitled, or has an accrued right, to a pension under an occupational pension scheme, subsection (1) does not apply to any of the following, or any agreement to effect any of the following—

(a)   an assignment in favour of the person in question's widow, widower or dependant,

(b)   a surrender, at the option of the person in question, for the purpose of—

(i)   providing benefits for that person's widow, widower or dependant,or

(ii)   acquiring for the person in question entitlement to further benefits under the scheme,

(c)   a commutation—

(i)   of the person in question's benefit on or after retirement or in exceptional circumstances of serious ill health,

(ii)   in prescribed circumstances, of any benefit for that person's widow, widower or dependant, or

(iii)   in other prescribed circumstances,

(d)   subject to subsection (6), a charge or lien on, or set-off against, the person in question's entitlement, or accrued right, to pension (except to the extent that it includes transfer credits other than prescribed transfer credits) for the purpose of enabling the employer to obtain the discharge by him of some monetary obligation due to the employer and arising out of a criminal, negligent or fraudulent act or omission by him,

(e)   subject to subsection (6), except in prescribed circumstances a charge or lien on, or set-off against, the person in question's entitlement, or accrued right, to pension, for the purpose of discharging some monetary obligation due from the person in question to the scheme and—

(i)   arising out of a criminal, negligent or fraudulent act or omission by him, or

(ii)   in the case of a trust scheme of which the person in question is a trustee, arising out of a breach of trust by him.

(6)   Where a charge, lien or set-off is exercisable by virtue of subsection (5)(d) or (e)—

(a) its amount must not exceed the amount of the monetary obligation in question, or (if less) the value (determined in the prescribed manner) of the person in question's entitlement or accrued right, and

(b) the person in question must be given a certificate showing the amount of the charge, lien or set-off and its effect on his benefits under the scheme,
and where there is a dispute as to its amount, the charge, lien or set-off must not be exercised unless the obligation in question has become enforceable under an order of a competent court or in consequence of an award of an arbitrator or, in Scotland, an arbiter to be appointed (failing agreement between the parties) by the sheriff.

(7) This section is subject to section 159 of the Pension Schemes Act 1993 (inalienability of guaranteed minimum pension and protected rights payments).

92. Forfeiture, etc.

(1) Subject to the provisions of this section and section 93, an entitlement, or accrued right, to a pension under an occupational pension scheme cannot be forfeited.

(2) Subsection (1) does not prevent forfeiture by reference to—

(a) a transaction or purported transaction which under section 91 is of no effect, or

(b) the bankruptcy of the person entitled to the pension or whose right to it has accrued,
whether or not that event occurred before or after the pension became payable.

(3) Where such forfeiture as is mentioned in subsection (2) occurs, any pension which was, or would but for the forfeiture have become, payable may, if the trustees or managers of the scheme so determine, be paid to all or any of the following—

(a) the member of the scheme to or in respect of whom the pension was, or would have become, payable,

(b) the spouse, widow or widower of the member,

(c) any dependant of the member, and

(d) any other person falling within a prescribed class.

(4) Subsection (1) does not prevent forfeiture by reference to the person entitled to the pension, or whose right to it has accrued, having been convicted of one or more offences—

(a) which are committed before the pension becomes payable, and

(b) which are—

(i) offences of treason,

(ii) offences under the Official Secrets Acts 1911 to 1989 for which the person has been sentenced on the same occasion to a term of imprisonment of, or to two or more consecutive terms amounting in the aggregate to, at least 10 years, or

(iii) prescribed offences.

(5) Subsection (1) does not prevent forfeiture by reference to a failure by any person to make a claim for pension—

(a) where the forfeiture is in reliance on any enactment relating to the limitation of actions, or

(b) where the claim is not made within six years of the date on which the pension becomes due.

(6)   Subsection (1) does not prevent forfeiture in prescribed circumstances.

(7)   In this section and section 93, references to forfeiture include any manner of deprivation or suspension.

93.   Forfeiture by reference to obligation to employer

(1)   Subject to subsection (2), section 92(1) does not prevent forfeiture of a person's entitlement, or accrued right, to a pension under an occupational pension scheme by reference to the person having incurred some monetary obligation due to the employer and arising out of a criminal, negligent or fraudulent act or omission by the person.

(2)   A person's entitlement or accrued right to a pension may be forfeited by reason of subsection (1) to the extent only that it does not exceed the amount of the monetary obligation in question, or (if less) the value (determined in the prescribed manner) of the person's entitlement or accrued right to a pension under the scheme.

(3)   Such forfeiture as is mentioned in subsection (1) must not take effect where there is a dispute as to the amount of the monetary obligation in question, unless the obligation has become enforceable under an order of a competent court or in consequence of an award of an arbitrator or, in Scotland, an arbiter to be appointed (failing agreement between the parties) by the sheriff.

(4)   Where a person's entitlement or accrued right to a pension is forfeited by reason of subsection (1), the person must be given a certificate showing the amount forfeited and the effect of the forfeiture on his benefits under the scheme.

(5)   Where such forfeiture as is mentioned in subsection (1) occurs, an amount not exceeding the amount forfeited may, if the trustees or managers of the scheme so determine, be paid to the employer.

94.   Sections 91 to 93: supplementary

(1)   Regulations may—

(a)   modify sections 91 to 93 in their application to public service pension schemes or to other schemes falling within a prescribed class or description, or

(b)   provide that those sections do not apply in relation to schemes falling within a prescribed class or description.

(2)   In those sections, 'pension' in relation to an occupational pension scheme, includes any benefit under the scheme and any part of a pension and any payment by way of pension.

(3)   In the application of sections 91 and 92 to Scotland—

(a)   references to a charge are to be read as references to a right in security or a diligence and 'charged' is to be interpreted accordingly,

(b)   references to assignment are to be read as references to assignation and 'assign' is to be interpreted accordingly,

(c)   the reference to a person's bankruptcy is to be read as a reference to the sequestration of his estate or the appointment on his estate of a judicial factor under section 41 of the Solicitors (Scotland) Act 1980,

(d)   the reference to an income payments order under the Insolvency Act 1986 is to be read as a reference to an order under section 32(2) of the Bankruptcy (Scotland) Act 1985, and

(e)   the reference to the making of a bankruptcy order is to be read as a reference to the award of sequestration or the making of the appointment of such a judicial factor.

95. Pension rights of individuals adjudged bankrupt etc.

(1)   After section 342 of the Insolvency Act 1986 (adjustment of certain transactions entered into by individuals subsequently adjudged bankrupt), there is inserted—

342A.   Recovery of excessive pension contributions

(1)   Where an individual is adjudged bankrupt and—

(a)   he has during the relevant period made contributions as a member of an occupational pension scheme, or

(b)   contributions have during the relevant period been made to such a scheme on his behalf,

the trustee of the bankrupt's estate may apply to the court for an order under this section.

(2)   If on an application for an order under this section, the court is satisfied that the making of any of the contributions ('the excessive contributions') has unfairly prejudiced the individual's creditors, the court may make such order as it thinks fit for restoring the position to what it would have been if the excessive contributions had not been made.

(3)   The court shall, in determining whether it is satisfied under subsection (2), consider in particular—

(a)   whether any of the contributions were made by or on behalf of the individual for the purpose of putting assets beyond the reach of his creditors or any of them,

(b)   whether the total amount of contributions made by or on behalf of the individual (including contributions made to any other occupational pension scheme) during the relevant period was excessive in view of the individual's circumstances at the time when they were made, and

(c)   whether the level of benefits under the scheme,

together with benefits under any other occupational pension scheme, to which the individual is entitled, or is likely to become entitled, is excessive in all the circumstances of the case.

342B.   Orders under sections 342A

(1)   Without prejudice to the generality of section 342A(2), an order under that section may include provision—

(a)   requiring the trustees or managers of the scheme to pay an amount to the individual's trustee in bankruptcy,

(b)   reducing the amount of any benefit to which the individual (or his spouse, widow, widower or dependant) is entitled, or to which he has an accrued right, under the scheme,

(c)   reducing the amount of any benefit to which, by virtue of any assignment, commutation or surrender of the individual's entitlement (or that of his spouse, widow, widower or dependant) or accrued right under the scheme, another person is entitled or has an accrued right,

(d)   otherwise adjusting the liabilities of the scheme in respect of any such person as is mentioned in paragraph (b) or (c).

(2)   The maximum amount by which an order under section 342A may require the assets of an occupational pension scheme to be reduced is the lesser of—

(a)   the amount of the excessive contributions, and

(b)   the value (determined in the prescribed manner) of the assets of the scheme which represent contributions made by or on behalf of the individual.

(3)   Subject to subsections (4) and (5), an order under section 342A must reduce the amount of the liabilities of the scheme by an amount equal to the amount of the reduction made in the value of the assets of the scheme.

(4)   Subsection (3) does not apply where the individual's entitlement or accrued right to benefits under the scheme which he acquired by virtue of the excessive contributions (his 'excessive entitlement') has been forfeited.

(5)   Where part of the individual's excessive entitlement has been forfeited, the amount of the reduction in the liabilities of the scheme required by subsection (3) is the value of the remaining part of his excessive entitlement.

(6)   An order under section 342A in respect of an occupational pension scheme shall be binding on the trustees or managers of the scheme.

342C.   Orders under section 342A: supplementary

(1)   Nothing in—

(a)   any provision of section 159 of the Pension Schemes Act 1993 or section 91 of the Pensions Act 1995 (which prevent assignment, or orders being made restraining a person from receiving anything which he is prevented from assigning, and make provision in relation to a person's pension on bankruptcy),

(b)   any provision of any enactment (whether passed or made before or after the passing of the Pensions Act 1995) corresponding to any of the provisions mentioned in paragraph (a), or

(c)   any provision of the scheme in question corresponding to any of those provisions,

applies to a court exercising its powers under section 342A.

(2)   Where any sum is required by an order under section 342A to be paid to the trustee in bankruptcy, that sum shall be comprised in the bankrupt's estate.

(3)   Where contributions have been made during the relevant period to any occupational pension scheme and the entitlement or accrued right to benefits acquired thereby has been transferred to a second or subsequent occupational pension scheme ('the transferee scheme'), sections 342A and 342B and this section shall apply as though the contributions had been made to the transferee scheme.

(4)   For the purposes of this section and sections 342A and 342B—

(a)   contributions are made during the relevant period if—

(i)   they are made by or on behalf of the individual at any time during the period of 5 years ending with the day of presentation of the bankruptcy petition on which the individual is adjudged bankrupt, or

(ii)   they are made on behalf of the individual at any time during the period between the presentation of the petition and the commencement of the bankruptcy,

and

(b)   the accrued rights of an individual under an occupational pension scheme at any time are the rights which have accrued to or in respect of him at that time to future benefits under the scheme.

(5)   In this section and sections 342A and 342B—
'occupational pension scheme' has the meaning given by section 1 of the Pension Schemes Act 1993, and
'trustees or managers', in relation to an occupational pension scheme, means—
(a)   in the case of a scheme established under a trust, the trustees of the scheme, and
(b)   in any other case, the managers of the scheme.'

(2)   After section 36 of the Bankruptcy (Scotland) Act 1985 there is inserted —

36A.   Recovery of excessive pension contributions

(1)   Where a debtor's estate has been sequestrated and—
(a)   he has during the relevant period made contributions as a member of an occupational pension scheme; or
(b)   contributions have during the relevant period been made to such a scheme on his behalf;
the permanent trustee may apply to the court for an order under this section.

(2)   If on an application for an order under this section, the court is satisfied that the making of any of the contributions ('the excessive contributions') has unfairly prejudiced the debtor's creditors, the court may make such order as it thinks fit for restoring the position to what it would have been if the excessive contributions had not been made.

(3)   The court shall, in determining whether it is satisfied under subsection (2) above, consider in particular—
(a)   whether any of the contributions were made by or on behalf of the debtor for the purpose of putting assets beyond the reach of his creditors or any of them;
(b)   whether the total amount of contributions made by or on behalf of the debtor (including contributions made to any other occupational pension scheme) during the relevant period was excessive in view of the debtor's circumstances at the time when they were made; and
(c)   whether the level of benefits under the scheme, together with benefits under any other occupational pension scheme, to which the debtor is entitled, or is likely to become entitled, is excessive in all the circumstances of the case.

36B.   Orders under section 36A

(1)   Without prejudice to the generality of subsection (2) of section 36A of this Act, an order under that section may include provision—
(a)   requiring the trustees or managers of the scheme to pay an amount to the permanent trustee;
(b)   reducing the amount of any benefit to which the debtor (or his spouse, widow, widower or dependant) is entitled, or to which he has an accrued right, under the scheme;
(c)   reducing the amount of any benefit to which, by virtue of any assignation, commutation or surrender of the debtor's entitlement (or that of his spouse, widow, widower or dependant) or accrued right under the scheme, another person is entitled or has an accrued right;
(d)   otherwise adjusting the liabilities of the scheme in respect of any such person as is mentioned in paragraph (b) or (c) above.

(2)   The maximum amount by which an order under section 36A of this Act may require the assets of an occupational pension scheme to be reduced is the lesser of —

(a)   the amount of the excessive contributions; and

(b)   the value (determined in the prescribed manner) of the assets of the scheme which represent contributions made by or on behalf of the debtor.

(3)   Subject to subsections (4) and (5) below, an order under section 36A of this Act must reduce the amount of the liabilities of the scheme by an amount equal to the amount of the reduction made in the value of the assets of the scheme.

(4)   Subsection (3) above does not apply where the debtor's entitlement or accrued right to benefits under the scheme which he acquired by virtue of the excessive contributions (his 'excessive entitlement') has been forfeited.

(5)   Where part of the debtor's excessive entitlement has been forfeited, the amount of the reduction in the liabilities of the scheme required by subsection (3) above is the value of the remaining part of his excessive entitlement.

(6)   An order under section 36A of this Act in respect of an occupational pension scheme shall be binding on the trustees or managers of the scheme.

(7)   The court may, on the application of any person having an interest, review, rescind or vary an order under section 36A of this Act.

36C.   Orders under section 36A: supplementary

(1)   Nothing in—

(a)   any provision of section 159 of the Pension Schemes Act 1993 or 91 of the Pensions Act 1995 (which prevent assignation, or orders being made restraining a person from receiving anything which he is prevented from assigning, and make provision in relation to a person's pension on sequestration);

(b)   any provision of any enactment (whether passed or made before or after the passing of the Pensions Act 1995) corresponding to any of the provisions mentioned in paragraph (a) above; or

(c)   any provision of the scheme in question corresponding to any of those provisions,

applies to a court exercising its powers under section 36A of this Act.

(2)   Where any sum is required by an order under section 36A of this Act to be paid to the permanent trustee, that sum shall be comprised in the debtor's estate.

(3)   Where contributions have been made during the relevant period to any occupational pension scheme and the entitlement or accrued right to benefits acquired thereby has been transferred to a second or subsequent occupational pension scheme ('the transferee scheme'), sections 36A and 36B of this Act and this section shall apply as though the contributions had been made to the transferee scheme.

(4)   For the purposes of this section and sections 36A and 36B of this Act—

(a)   contributions are made during the relevant period if they are made at any time during the period of 5 years ending with the date of sequestration; and

(b)   the accrued rights of a debtor under an occupational pension scheme at any time are the rights which have accrued to or in respect of him at that time to future benefits under the scheme.

(5)   In this section and sections 36A and 36B of this Act—
'occupational pension scheme' has the meaning given by section 1 of the Pension Schemes Act 1993; and
'trustees or managers', in relation to an occupational pension scheme, means—

(a)   in the case of a scheme established under a trust, the trustees of the scheme; and

(b)   in any other case, the managers of the scheme.'

Questioning the decisions of the Authority

96.   Review of decisions

(1)   Subject to the following provisions of this section and to section 97, any determination by the Authority of a question which it is within their functions to determine shall be final.

(2)   The Authority must, on the application of any person ('the applicant') at any time within the prescribed period, review any determination of theirs—

(a)   to make an order against the applicant under section 3,

(b)   to require the applicant to pay a penalty under section 10 of this Act or section 168(4) of the Pension Schemes Act 1993, or

(c)   to disqualify the applicant from being a trustee of any trust scheme under section 29(3) or (4).

(3)   The Authority may on the application of a person appearing to them to be interested—

(a)   at any time review any other such determination of theirs as is mentioned in subsection (1) (including a determination given by them on a previous review), if they are satisfied that there has been a relevant change of circumstances since the determination was made, or that the determination was made in ignorance of a material fact or based on a mistake as to a material fact or was erroneous in point of law,

(b)   at any time within a period of six months from the date of the determination, or within such longer period as they may allow in any particular case, review such a determination on any ground.

(4)   The Authority's powers on a review under subsection (2) or (3) include power—

(a)   to vary or revoke any determination or order previously made,

(b)   to substitute a different determination or order, and

(c)   generally to deal with the matters arising on the review as if they had arisen on the original determination;
and also include power to make savings and transitional provisions.

(5)   Subject to subsection (6), regulations may make provision with respect to the procedure to be adopted on any application for a review under subsection (2) or (3) or under any corresponding provision in force in Northern Ireland and generally with respect to such applications and reviews.

(6)   Nothing in subsection (5) shall be taken to prevent such a review being entered upon by the Authority without an application being made.

97.   References and appeals from the Authority

(1)   Any question of law arising in connection with—

(a)   any matter arising under this Part for determination, or

(b)   any matter arising on an application to the Authority for a review of a determination, or on a review by them entered upon without an application,
may, if the Authority think fit, be referred for decision to the court.

(2)   If the Authority determine in accordance with subsection (1) to refer any question of law to the court, they must give notice in writing of their intention to do so—

(a)   in a case where the question arises on an application made to the Authority, to the applicant, and

(b)   in any case to such persons as appear to them to be concerned with the question.

(3)   Any person who is aggrieved—

(a)   by a determination of the Authority given on a review under section 96, or

(b)   by the refusal of the Authority to review a determination,
where the determination involves a question of law and that question is not referred by the Authority to the court under subsection (1), may on that question appeal from the determination to the court.

(4)   The Authority is entitled to appear and be heard on any reference or appeal under this section.

(5)   The rules of court must include provision for regulating references and appeals to the court under this section and for limiting the time within which such appeals may be brought.

(6)   The decision of the court on a reference or appeal under this section is final, and this subsection overrides any other enactment.

(7)   On any such reference or appeal the court may order the Authority to pay the costs or, in Scotland, the expenses of any other person, whether or not the decision is in that other person's favour and whether or not the Authority appear on the reference or appeal.

(8)   In this section 'the court' means the High Court or the Court of Session.

Gathering information: the Authority

98.   Provision of information

(1)   In the case of any occupational pension scheme—

(a)   a trustee, manager, professional adviser or employer, and

(b)   any other person appearing to the Authority to be a person who holds, or is likely to hold, information relevant to the discharge of the Authority's functions,
must, if required to do so by them by notice in writing, produce any document relevant to the discharge of those functions.

(2)   To comply with subsection (1) the document must be produced in such a manner, at such a place and within such a period as may be specified in the notice.

(3)   In this section and sections 99 to 101, 'document' includes information recorded in any form, and any reference to production of a document, in relation to information recorded otherwise than in legible form, is to producing a copy of the information in legible form.

99.   Inspection of premises

(1)   An inspector may, for the purposes of investigating whether, in the case of any occupational pension scheme, the regulatory provisions are being, or have

been, complied with, at any reasonable time enter premises liable to inspection and, while there—

    (a)   may make such examination and inquiry as may be necessary for such purposes,

    (b)   may require any person on the premises to produce, or secure the production of, any document relevant to compliance with those provisions for his inspection, and

    (c)   may, as to any matter relevant to compliance with those provisions, examine, or require to be examined, either alone or in the presence of another person, any person on the premises whom he has reasonable cause to believe to be able to give information relevant to that matter.

    (2)   In subsection (1), 'the regulatory provisions' means provisions made by or under—

    (a)   the provisions of this Part, other than the following provisions: sections 51 to 54, 62 to 65 and 110 to 112,

    (b)   the following provisions of the Pension Schemes Act 1993: section 6 (registration), Chapter IV of Part IV (transfer values), section 113 (information) or section 175 (levy), or

    (c)   any corresponding provisions in force in Northern Ireland.

    (3)   Premises are liable to inspection for the purposes of this section if the inspector has reasonable grounds to believe that—

    (a)   members of the scheme are employed there,

    (b)   documents relevant to the administration of the scheme are being kept there, or

    (c)   the administration of the scheme, or work connected with the administration of the scheme, is being carried out there,

unless the premises are a private dwelling-house not used by, or by permission of, the occupier for the purposes of a trade or business.

    (4)   An inspector applying for admission to any premises for the purposes of this section must, if so required, produce his certificate of appointment.

    (5)   In this Part 'inspector' means a person appointed by the Authority as an inspector.

100. Warrants

    (1)   A justice of the peace may issue a warrant under this section if satisfied on information on oath given by or on behalf of the Authority that there are reasonable grounds for believing—

    (a)   that there are on any premises documents whose production has been required under section 98(1) or 99(1)(b), or any corresponding provisions in force in Northern Ireland, and which have not been produced in compliance with the requirement,

    (b)   that there are on any premises documents whose production could be so required and that if their production were so required the documents would not be produced but would be removed from the premises, hidden, tampered with or destroyed, or

    (c)   that—

        (i)   an offence has been committed under this Act or the Pension Schemes Act 1993, or any enactment in force in Northern Ireland corresponding to either of them,

(ii)   a person will do any act which constitutes a misuse or misappropriation of the assets of an occupational pension scheme,

(iii)   a person is liable to pay a penalty under section 10 of this Act or section 168(4) of the Pension Schemes Act 1993, or any enactment in force in Northern Ireland corresponding to either of them, or

(iv)   a person is liable to be prohibited from being a trustee of a trust scheme under section 3,

and that there are on any premises documents which relate to whether the offence has been committed, whether the act will be done, or whether the person is so liable, and whose production could be required under section 98(1) or 99(1)(b) or any corresponding provisions in force in Northern Ireland.

(2)   A warrant under this section shall authorise an inspector—

(a)   to enter the premises specified in the information, using such force as is reasonably necessary for the purpose,

(b)   to search the premises and take possession of any documents appearing to be such documents as are mentioned in subsection (1) or to take in relation to such documents any other steps which appear necessary for preserving them or preventing interference with them,

(c)   to take copies of any such documents, or

(d)   to require any person named in the warrant to provide an explanation of them or to state where they may be found.

(3)   A warrant under this section shall continue in force until the end of the period of one month beginning with the day on which it is issued.

(4)   Any documents of which possession is taken by virtue of a warrant under this section may be retained—

(a)   for a period of six months, or

(b)   if within that period proceedings to which the documents are relevant are commenced against any person for any offence under this Act or the Pension Schemes Act 1993, or any enactment in force in Northern Ireland corresponding to either of them, until the conclusion of those proceedings.

(5)   In the application of this section in Scotland—

(a)   the reference to a justice of the peace is to be read as a reference to a justice within the meaning of the Criminal Procedure (Scotland) Act 1975, and

(b)   the references to information are to be read as references to evidence.

101.   Information and inspection: penalties

(1)   A person who, without reasonable excuse, neglects or refuses to produce a document when required to do so under section 98 is guilty of an offence.

(2)   A person who without reasonable excuse—

(a)   intentionally delays or obstructs an inspector exercising any power under section 99,

(b)   neglects or refuses to produce, or secure the production of, any document when required to do so under that section, or

(c)   neglects or refuses to answer a question or to provide information when so required,

is guilty of an offence.

(3)   A person guilty of an offence under subsection (1) or (2) is liable on summary conviction to a fine not exceeding level 5 on the standard scale.

(4) An offence under subsection (1) or (2)(b) or (c) may be charged by reference to any day or longer period of time; and a person may be convicted of a second or subsequent offence by reference to any period of time following the preceding conviction of the offence.

(5) Any person who knowingly or recklessly provides the Authority with information which is false or misleading in a material particular is guilty of an offence if the information—

(a) is provided in purported compliance with a requirement under section 99, or

(b) is provided otherwise than as mentioned in paragraph (a) above but in circumstances in which the person providing the information intends, or could reasonably be expected to know, that it would be used by the Authority for the purpose of discharging their functions under this Act.

(6) Any person who intentionally and without reasonable excuse alters, suppresses, conceals or destroys any document which he is or is liable to be required under section 98 or 99 to produce to the Authority is guilty of an offence.

(7) Any person guilty of an offence under subsection (5) or (6) is liable—

(a) on summary conviction, to a fine not exceeding the statutory maximum,

(b) on conviction on indictment, to imprisonment or a fine, or both.

102. Savings for certain privileges etc

(1) Nothing in sections 98 to 101 requires a person to answer any question or give any information if to do so would incriminate that person or that person's spouse.

(2) Nothing in those sections requires any person to produce any document to the Authority, or to any person acting on their behalf, if he would be entitled to refuse to produce the document in any proceedings in any court on the grounds that it was the subject of legal professional privilege or, in Scotland, that it contained a confidential communication made by or to an advocate or solicitor in that capacity.

(3) Where a person claims a lien on a document, its production under section 98 or 99 shall be without prejudice to the lien.

103. Publishing reports

(1) The Authority may, if they consider it appropriate to do so in any particular case, publish in such form and manner as they think fit a report of any investigation under this Part and of the result of that investigation.

(2) For the purposes of the law of defamation, the publication of any matter by the Authority shall be absolutely privileged.

Disclosure of information: the Authority

104. Restricted information

(1) Except as provided by sections 106 to 108, restricted information must not be disclosed by the Authority or by any person who receives the information directly or indirectly from them, except with the consent of the person to whom it relates and (if different) the person from whom the Authority obtained it.

(2) For the purposes of this section and sections 105 to 108, 'restricted information' means any information obtained by the Authority in the exercise of

their functions which relates to the business or other affairs of any person, except for information—

    (a)   which at the time of the disclosure is or has already been made available to the public from other sources, or

    (b)   which is in the form of a summary or collection of information so framed as not to enable information relating to any particular person to be ascertained from it.

(3) Any person who discloses information in contravention of this section is guilty of an offence and liable—

    (a)   on summary conviction, to a fine not exceeding the statutory maximum, and

    (b)   on conviction on indictment, to a fine or imprisonment, or both.

105. Information supplied to the Authority by corresponding overeseas authorities

(1)   Subject to subsection (2), for the purposes of section 104, 'restricted information' includes information which has been supplied to the Authority for the purposes of their functions by an authority which exercises functions corresponding to the functions of the Authority in a country or territory outside the United Kingdom.

(2)   Sections 106 to 108 do not apply to such information as is mentioned in subsection (1), and such information must not be disclosed except—

    (a)   as provided in section 104,

    (b)   for the purpose of enabling or assisting the Authority to discharge their functions, or

    (c)   with a view to the institution of, or otherwise for the purposes of, criminal proceedings, whether under this Act or otherwise.

106. Disclosure for facilitating discharge of functions by the Authority

(1)   Section 104 does not preclude the disclosure of restricted information in any case in which disclosure is for the purpose of enabling or assisting the Authority to discharge their functions.

(2)   If, in order to enable or assist the Authority properly to discharge any of their functions, the Authority consider it necessary to seek advice from any qualified person on any matter of law, accountancy, valuation or other matter requiring the exercise of professional skill, section 104 does not preclude the disclosure by the Authority to that person of such information as appears to the Authority to be necessary to ensure that he is properly informed with respect to the matters on which his advice is sought.

107. Disclosure for facilitating discharge of functions by other supervisory authorities

(1)   Section 104 does not preclude the disclosure by the Authority of restricted information to any person specified in the first column of the following Table if the Authority consider that the disclosure would enable or assist that person to discharge the functions specified in relation to him in the second column of that Table.

TABLE

Persons	*Functions*
The Secretary of State.	Functions under the Insurance Companies Act 1982, Part XIV of the Companies Act 1985, the Insolvency Act 1986, the Financial Services Act 1986, Part III of the Companies Act 1989 or Part III of the Pension Schemes Act 1993.
The Treasury.	Functions under the Financial Services Act 1986.
The Bank of England.	Functions under the Banking Act 1987 or any other functions.
The Charity Commissioners.	Functions under the Charities Act 1993.
The Lord Advocate.	Functions under Part I of the Law Reform (Miscellaneous Provisions) (Scotland) Act 1990.
The Pensions Ombudsman and the Registrar of Occupational and Personal Pension Schemes.	Functions under the Pension Schemes Act 1993 or the Pension Schemes (Northern Ireland) Act 1993.
The Compensation Board.	Functions under this Act or any corresponding enactment in force in Northern Ireland.
The Policyholders Protection Board.	Functions under the Policyholders Protection Act 1975.
The Deposit Protection Board.	Functions under the Banking Act 1987.
The Investor Protection Board.	Functions under the Building Societies Act 1986.
The Friendly Societies Commission.	Functions under the enactments relating to friendly societies.
The Building Societies Commission.	Functions under the Building Societies Act 1986.
The Commissioners of Inland Revenue or their officers.	Functions under the Taxes Act 1988 or the Taxation of Chargeable Gains Act 1992.
The Official Receiver, or, in Northern Ireland, the Official Receiver for Northern Ireland.	Functions under the enactments relating to insolvency.
An inspector appointed by the Secretary of State.	Functions under Part XIV of the Companies Act 1985 or section 94 or 177 of the Financial Services Act 1986.

Persons	*Functions*
A person authorised to exercise powers under section 43A or 44 of the Insurance Companies Act 1982, section 447 of the Companies Act 1985, section 106 of the Financial Services Act 1986, Article 440 of the Companies (Northern Ireland) Order 1986, or section 84 of the Companies Act 1989.	Functions under those sections or that Article.
A designated agency or transferee body or the competent authority (within the meaning of the Financial Services Act 1986).	Functions under the Financial Services Act 1986.
A recognised self-regulating organisation, recognised professional body, recognised investment exchange or recognised clearing house (within the meaning of the Financial Services Act 1986).	Functions in its capacity as an organisation, body, exchange or clearing house recognised under the Financial Services Act 1986.
A person administering a scheme for compensating investors under section 54 of the Financial Services Act 1986.	Functions under that section.
A recognised professional body (within the meaning of section 391 of the Insolvency Act 1986).	Functions in its capacity as such a body under that Act.
The Department of Economic Development in Northern Ireland.	Functions under Part XV of the Companies (Northern Ireland) Order 1986, the Insolvency (Northern Ireland) Order 1989 or Part II of the Companies (No. 2) (Northern Ireland) Order 1990.
The Department of Health and Social Services for Northern Ireland.	Functions under Part III of the Pension Schemes (Northern Ireland) Act 1993.
An inspector appointed by the Department of Economic Development in Northern Ireland.	Functions under Part XV of the Companies (Northern Ireland) Order 1986.
A recognised professional body within the meaning of Article 350 of the Insolvency (Northern Ireland) Order 1989.	Functions in its capacity as such a body under that Order.

(2)   The Secretary of State may after consultation with the Authority—

(a)   by order amend the Table in subsection (1) by—

(i)   adding any person exercising regulatory functions and specifying functions in relation to that person,

(ii)   removing any person for the time being specified in the Table, or

(iii)   altering the functions for the time being specified in the Table in relation to any person, or

(b)   by order restrict the circumstances in which, or impose conditions subject to which, disclosure may be made to any person for the time being specified in the Table.

108.   Other permitted disclosures

(1)   Section 104 does not preclude the disclosure by the Authority of restricted information to—

(a)   the Secretary of State, or

(b)   the Department of Health and Social Services for Northern Ireland,

if the disclosure appears to the Authority to be desirable or expedient in the interests of members of occupational pension schemes or in the public interest.

(2)   Section 104 does not preclude the disclosure of restricted information—

(a)   with a view to the institution of, or otherwise for the purposes of, criminal proceedings, whether under this Act or otherwise,

(b)   in connection with any other proceedings arising out of—

(i)   this Act, or

(ii)   the Pension Schemes Act 1993,

or any corresponding enactment in force in Northern Ireland or any proceedings for breach of trust in relation to an occupational pension scheme,

(c)   with a view to the institution of, or otherwise for the purposes of, proceedings under section 7 or 8 of the Company Directors Disqualification Act 1986 or Article 10 or 11 of the Companies (Northern Ireland) Order 1989,

(d)   in connection with any proceedings under the Insolvency Act 1986 or the Insolvency (Northern Ireland) Order 1989 which the Authority have instituted or in which they have a right to be heard,

(e)   with a view to the institution of, or otherwise for the purposes of, any disciplinary proceedings relating to the exercise of his professional duties by a solicitor, an actuary or an accountant,

(f)   with a view to the institution of, or otherwise for the purposes of, any disciplinary proceedings relating to the discharge by a public servant of his duties,

(g)   for the purpose of enabling or assisting an authority in a country outside the United Kingdom to exercise functions corresponding to those of the Authority under this Act, or

(h)   in pursuance of a Community obligation.

(3)   Section 104 does not preclude the disclosure by the Authority of information to the Director of Public Prosecutions, the Director of Public Prosecutions for Northern Ireland, the Lord Advocate, a procurator fiscal or a constable.

(4)   Section 104 does not preclude the disclosure by any person mentioned in subsection (1) or (3) of information obtained by the person by virtue of that subsection, if the disclosure is made with the consent of the Authority.

(5)   Section 104 does not preclude the disclosure by any person specified in the first column of the Table in section 107 of information obtained by the person by virtue of that subsection, if the disclosure is made—

(a)   with the consent of the Authority, and

(b)   for the purpose of enabling or assisting the person to discharge any functions specified in relation to him in the second column of the Table.

(6)   The Authority must, before deciding whether to give their consent to such a disclosure as is mentioned in subsection (4) or (5), take account of any representations made to them by the person seeking to make the disclosure as to the desirability of the disclosure or the necessity for it.

(7)   In subsection (2), 'public servant' means an officer or servant of the Crown or of any prescribed authority.

109.   Disclosure of information by the Inland Revenue

(1)   This section applies to information held by any person in the exercise of tax functions about any matter relevant, for the purposes of those functions, to tax or duty in the case of an identifiable person (in this section referred to as 'tax information').

(2)   No obligation as to secrecy imposed by section 182 of the Finance Act 1989 or otherwise shall prevent the disclosure of tax information to the Authority for the purpose of enabling or assisting the Authority to discharge their functions.

(3)   Where tax information is disclosed to the Authority by virtue of subsection (2), it shall, subject to subsection (4), be treated for the purposes of section 104 as restricted information.

(4)   Sections 106 to 108 do not apply to tax information and such information must not be disclosed except—

(a)   to, or in accordance with authority duly given by, the Commissioners of Inland Revenue or the Commissioners of Customs and Excise, or

(b)   with a view to the institution of, or otherwise for the purposes of, criminal proceedings under this Act or the Pension Schemes Act 1993, or any enactment in force in Northern Ireland corresponding to either of them.

(5)   In this section 'tax functions' has the same meaning as in section 182 of the Finance Act 1989.

Gathering information: the Compensation Board

110.   Provision of information

(1)   In the case of any trust scheme—

(a)   a trustee, professional adviser or employer, and

(b)   any other person appearing to the Compensation Board to be a person who holds, or is likely to hold, information relevant to the discharge of the Board's functions,

must, if required to do so by the Board by notice in writing, produce any document relevant to the discharge of those functions.

(2)   To comply with subsection (1) the document must be produced in such a manner, at such a place and within such a period as may be specified in the notice.

(3)   In this section and section 111, 'document' includes information recorded in any form, and any reference to production of a document, in relation to information recorded otherwise than in legible form, is to producing a copy of the information in legible form.

111.   Information: penalties

(1)   A person who without reasonable excuse neglects or refuses to produce a document when required to do so under section 110 is guilty of an offence.

(2)   A person guilty of an offence under subsection (1) is liable on summary conviction to a fine not exceeding level 5 on the standard scale.

(3) An offence under subsection (1) may be charged by reference to any day or longer period of time; and a person may be convicted of a second or subsequent offence by reference to any period of time following the preceding conviction of the offence.

(4) Any person who knowingly or recklessly provides the Compensation Board with information which is false or misleading in a material particular is guilty of an offence if the information is provided in circumstances in which the person providing the information intends, or could reasonably be expected to know, that it would be used by the Board for the purpose of discharging their functions under this Act or any corresponding enactment in force in Northern Ireland.

(5) Any person who intentionally and without reasonable excuse alters, suppresses, conceals or destroys any document which he is or is liable to be required under section 110 to produce to the Compensation Board is guilty of an offence.

(6) Any person guilty of an offence under subsection (4) or (5) is liable—

    (a)   on summary conviction, to a fine not exceeding the statutory maximum,

    (b)   on conviction on indictment, to imprisonment or a fine, or both.

112. Savings for certain privileges

Nothing in section 110 or 111 requires a person—

    (a)   to answer any question or give any information if to do so would incriminate that person or that person's spouse, or

    (b)   to produce any document if he would be entitled to refuse to produce the document in any proceedings in any court on the grounds that it was the subject of legal professional privilege or, in Scotland, that it contained a confidential communication made by or to an advocate or solicitor in that capacity.

113. Publishing reports

(1) The Compensation Board may, if they consider it appropriate to do so in any particular case, publish in such form and manner as they think fit a report of any investigation under this Part and of the result of that investigation.

(2) For the purposes of the law of defamation, the publication of any matter by the Compensation Board shall be absolutely privileged.

114. Disclosure of information

(1) A person to whom this section applies may disclose to the Compensation Board any information received by him or for the purposes of any enactment if the disclosure is made by him for the purpose of enabling or assisting the Board to discharge any of their functions.

(2) In the case of information which a person holds or has held in the exercise of functions—

    (a)   of the Commissioners of Inland Revenue or their officers, and

    (b)   relating to any tax within the general responsibility of the Commissioners,

subsection (1) does not authorise any disclosure unless made in accordance with an authorisation given by the Commissioners.

(3) Subject to subsection (4), the Compensation Board may disclose to a person to whom this section applies any information received by them under or for the purposes of any enactment, where the disclosure is made by the Board—

(a)   for any purpose connected with the discharge of their functions, or

(b)   for the purpose of enabling or assisting that person to discharge any of his functions.

(4)   Where any information disclosed to the Compensation Board under this section is so disclosed subject to any express restriction on the disclosure of the information by the Board, the Board's power of disclosure under subsection (3) is, in relation to the information, exercisable by them subject to any such restriction.

(5)   In the case of any such information as is mentioned in subsection (2), subsection (3) does not authorise any disclosure of that information by the Compensation Board unless made—

(a)   to, or in accordance with authority duly given by, the Commissioners of Inland Revenue or the Commissioners of Customs and Excise, or

(b)   with a view to the institution of, or otherwise for the purposes of, criminal proceedings under this Act or the Pension Schemes Act 1993, or any enactment in force in Northern Ireland corresponding to either of them.

(6)   Nothing in this section shall be construed as affecting any power of disclosure exercisable apart from this section.

(7)   This section applies to the following (and, accordingly, in this section 'person' shall be construed as including any of them)—

(a)   any department of the Government (including the government of Northern Ireland),

(b)   the Director of Public Prosecutions,

(c)   the Director of Public Prosecutions for Northern Ireland,

(d)   the Lord Advocate,

(e)   any constable,

(f)   any designated agency or recognised self-regulating organisation (within the meaning of the Financial Services Act 1986),

(g)   a recognised professional body (within the meaning of section 391 of the Insolvency Act 1986),

(h)   the Pensions Ombudsman,

(j)   the Policyholders Protection Board,

(k)   the Authority,

(l)   the Registrar of Occupational and Personal Pension Schemes,

(m)   the Official Receiver, or, in Northern Ireland, the Official Receiver for Northern Ireland, and

(n)   such other persons as may be prescribed.

General

115.   Offences by bodies corporate and partnerships

(1)   Where an offence under this Part committed by a body corporate is proved to have been committed with the consent or connivance of, or to be attributable to any neglect on the part of, a director, manager, secretary or other similar officer of the body, or a person purporting to act in any such capacity, he as well as the body corporate is guilty of the offence and liable to be proceeded against and punished accordingly.

(2)   Where the affairs of a body corporate are managed by its members, subsection (1) applies in relation to the acts and defaults of a member in connection with his functions of management as to a director of a body corporate.

(3)   Where an offence under this Part committed by a Scottish partnership is proved to have been committed with the consent or connivance of, or to be attributable to any neglect on the part of, a partner, he as well as the partnership is guilty of the offence and liable to be proceeded against and punished accordingly.

116.   Breach of regulations

(1)   Regulations made by virtue of any provision of this Part may provide for the contravention of any provision contained in any such regulations to be an offence under this Part and for the recovery on summary conviction for any such offence of a fine not exceeding level 5 on the standard scale.

(2)   An offence under any provision of the regulations may be charged by reference to any day or longer period of time; and a person may be convicted of a second or subsequent offence under such a provision by reference to any period of time following the preceding conviction of the offence.

(3)   Where by reason of the contravention of any provision contained in regulations made by virtue of this Part—

(a)   a person is convicted of an offence under this Part, or

(b)   a person pays a penalty under section 10,

then, in respect of that contravention, he shall not, in a case within paragraph (a), be liable to pay such a penalty or, in a case within paragraph (b), be convicted of such an offence.

117.   Overriding requirements

(1)   Where any provision mentioned in subsection (2) conflicts with the provisions of an occupational pension scheme—

(a)   the provision mentioned in subsection (2), to the extent that it conflicts, overrides the provisions of the scheme, and

(b)   the scheme has effect with such modifications as may be required in consequence of paragraph (a).

(2)   The provisions referred to in subsection (1) are those of—

(a)   this Part,

(b)   any subordinate legislation made or having effect as if made under this Part, or

(c)   any arrangements under section 16(1) or 17(2).

118.   Powers to modify this Part

(1)   Regulations may modify any provisions of this Part, in their application—

(a)   to a trust scheme which applies to earners in employments under different employers,

(b)   to a trust scheme of which there are no members who are in pensionable service under the scheme, or

(c)   to any case where a partnership is the employer, or one of the employers, in relation to a trust scheme.

(2)   Regulations may provide for sections 22 to 26, and section 117 (so far as it applies to those sections), not to apply in relation to a trust scheme falling within a prescribed class or description.

119. Calculations etc. under regulations: sub-delegation

Regulations made by virtue of section 56(3), 73(3) or 75 may provide for the values of the assets and the amounts of the liabilities there mentioned to be calculated and verified in accordance with guidance—

(a) prepared and from time to time revised by a prescribed body, and

(b) approved by the Secretary of State.

120. Consultations about regulations

(1) Before the Secretary of State makes any regulations by virtue of this Part, he must consult such persons as he considers appropriate.

(2) Subsection (1) does not apply—

(a) to regulations made for the purpose only of consolidating other regulations revoked by them,

(b) to regulations in the case of which the Secretary of State considers consultation inexpedient because of urgency,

(c) to regulations made before the end of the period of six months beginning with the coming into force of the provision of this Part by virtue of which the regulations are made, or

(d) to regulations which—

(i) state that they are consequential upon a specified enactment, and

(ii) are made before the end of the period of six months beginning with the coming into force of that enactment.

121. Crown application

(1) This Part applies to an occupational pension scheme managed by or on behalf of the Crown as it applies to other occupational pension schemes; and, accordingly, references in this Part to a person in his capacity as a trustee or manager of an occupational pension scheme include the Crown, or a person acting on behalf of the Crown, in that capacity.

(2) References in this Part to a person in his capacity as employer in relation to an occupational pension scheme include the Crown, or a person acting on behalf of the Crown, in that capacity.

(3) This section does not apply to any provision made by or under this Part under which a person may be prosecuted for an offence; but such a provision applies to persons in the public service of the Crown as it applies to other persons.

(4) This section does not apply to sections 42 to 46.

(5) Nothing in this Part applies to Her Majesty in Her private capacity (within the meaning of the Crown Proceedings Act 1947).

122. Consequential amendments

Schedule 3 (amendments consequential on this Part) shall have effect.

123. 'Connected' and 'associated' persons

(1) Sections 249 and 435 of the Insolvency Act 1986 (connected and associated persons) shall apply for the purposes of the provisions of this Act listed in subsection (3) as they apply for the purposes of that Act.

(2) Section 74 of the Bankruptcy (Scotland) Act 1985 (associated persons) shall apply for the purposes of the provisions so listed as it applies for the purposes of that Act.

(3) The provisions referred to in subsections (1) and (2) are—

(a) section 23(3)(b),

(b) sections 27 and 28,

(c) section 40,

but in the case of section 40 the provisions mentioned in subsections (1) and (2) shall apply for those purposes with any prescribed modifications.

124. Interpretation of Part I

(1) In this Part—

'active member', in relation to an occupational pension scheme, means a person who is in pensionable service under the scheme,

'the actuary' and 'the auditor', in relation to an occupational pension scheme, have the meanings given by section 47,

'the Authority' has the meaning given by section 1(1),

'the Compensation Board' has the meaning given by section 78(1),

'the compensation provisions' has the meaning given by section 81(3),

'contravention' includes failure to comply,

'deferred member', in relation to an occupational pension scheme, means a person (other than an active or pensioner member) who has accrued rights under the scheme,

'employer', in relation to an occupational pension scheme, means the employer of persons in the description or category of employment to which the scheme in question relates (but see section 125(3)),

'equal treatment rule' has the meaning given by section 62,

'firm' means a body corporate or a partnership,

'fund manager', in relation to an occupational pension scheme, means a person who manages the investments held for the purposes of the scheme,

'independent trustee' has the meaning given by section 23(3),

'managers', in relation to an occupational pension scheme other than a trust scheme, means the persons responsible for the management of the scheme,

'member', in relation to an occupational pension scheme, means any active, deferred or pensioner member (but see section 125(4)),

'member-nominated director' has the meaning given by section 18(2),

'member-nominated trustee' has the meaning given by section 16(2),

'the minimum funding requirement' has the meaning given by section 56,

'normal pension age' has the meaning given by section 180 of the Pension Schemes Act 1993,

'payment schedule' has the meaning given by section 87(2),

'pensionable service', in relation to a member of an occupational pension scheme, means service in any description or category of employment to which the scheme relates which qualifies the member (on the assumption that it continues for the appropriate period) for pension or other benefits under the scheme,

'pensioner member', in relation to an occupational pension scheme, means a person who in respect of his pensionable service under the scheme or by reason of transfer credits, is entitled to the present payment of pension or other benefits,

'prescribed' means prescribed by regulations,

'professional adviser', in relation to a scheme, has the meaning given by section 47, 'public service pension scheme' has the meaning given by section 1 of the Pension Schemes Act 1993,

'regulations' means regulations made by the Secretary of State,

'resources', in relation to an occupational pension scheme, means the funds out of which the benefits provided by the scheme are payable from time to time, including the proceeds of any policy of insurance taken out, or annuity contract entered into, for the purposes of the scheme,

'Scottish partnership' means a partnership constituted under the law of Scotland,

'the Taxes Act 1988' means the Income and Corporation Taxes Act 1988,

'transfer credits' means rights allowed to a member under the rules of an occupational pension scheme by reference to a transfer to that scheme of his accrued rights from another scheme (including any transfer credits allowed by that scheme),

'trustees or managers', in relation to an occupational pension scheme, means—

    (a)   in the case of a trust scheme, the trustees of the scheme, and

    (b)   in any other case, the managers of the scheme,

'trust scheme' means an occupational pension scheme established under a trust.

(2)   For the purposes of this Part—

    (a)   the accrued rights of a member of an occupational pension scheme at any time are the rights which have accrued to or in respect of him at that time to future benefits under the scheme, and

    (b)   at any time when the pensionable service of a member of an occupational pension scheme is continuing, his accrued rights are to be determined as if he had opted, immediately before that time, to terminate that service;

and references to accrued pension or accrued benefits are to be interpreted accordingly.

(3)   In determining what is 'pensionable service' for the purposes of this Part—

    (a)   service notionally attributable for any purpose of the scheme is to be disregarded, and

    (b)   no account is to be taken of any rules of the scheme by which a period of service can be treated for any purpose as being longer or shorter than it actually is.

(4)   In the application of this Part to Scotland, in relation to conviction on indictment, references to imprisonment are to be read as references to imprisonment for a term not exceeding two years.

(5)   Subject to the provisions of this Act, expressions used in this Act and in the Pension Schemes Act 1993 have the same meaning in this Act as in that.

125. Section 124: supplementary

(1)   For the purposes of this Part, an occupational pension scheme is salary related if—

    (a)   the scheme is not a money purchase scheme, and

    (b)   the scheme does not fall within a prescribed class or description,

and 'salary related trust scheme' is to be read accordingly.

(2)   Regulations may apply this Part with prescribed modifications to occupational pension schemes—

(a) which are not money purchase schemes, but

(b) where some of the benefits that may be provided are money purchase benefits.

(3) Regulations may, in relation to occupational pension schemes, extend for the purposes of this Part the meaning of 'employer' to include persons who have been the employer in relation to the scheme.

(4) For any of the purposes of this Part, regulations may in relation to occupational pension schemes—

(a) extend or restrict the meaning of 'member',

(b) determine who is to be treated as a prospective member, and

(c) determine the times at which a person is to be treated as becoming, or as ceasing to be, a member or prospective member.

PART II
STATE PENSIONS

126. Equalisation of pensionable age and of entitlement to certain benefits
Schedule 4 to this Act, of which—

(a) Part I has effect to equalise pensionable age for men and women progressively over a period of ten years beginning with 6th April 2010,

(b) Part II makes provision for bringing equality for men and women to certain pension and other benefits, and

(c) Part III makes consequential amendments of enactments, shall have effect.

127. Enhancement of additional pension, etc. where family credit or disability working allowance paid

(1) After section 45 of the Social Security Contributions and Benefits Act 1992 (additional pension in a Category A retirement pension) there is inserted—

'**45A. Effect of family credit and disability working allowance on earnings factor**

(1) For the purpose of calculating additional pension under sections 44 and 45 above where, in the case of any relevant year, family credit is paid in respect of any employed earner, or disability working allowance is paid to any employed earner, section 44(6)(a)(i) above shall have effect as if—

(a) where that person had earnings of not less than the qualifying earnings factor for that year, being earnings upon which primary Class 1 contributions were paid or treated as paid ('qualifying earnings') in respect of that year, the amount of those qualifying earnings were increased by the aggregate amount (call it 'AG') of family credit or, as the case may be, disability working allowance paid in respect of that year, and

(b) in any other case, that person had qualifying earnings in respect of that year and the amount of those qualifying earnings were equal to AG plus the qualifying earnings factor for that year.

(2) The reference in subsection (1) above to the person in respect of whom family credit is paid—

(a) where it is paid to one of a married or unmarried couple, is a reference to the prescribed member of the couple, and

(b) in any other case, is a reference to the person to whom it is paid.

(3)   A person's qualifying earnings in respect of any year cannot be treated by virtue of subsection (1) above as exceeding the upper earnings limit for that year multiplied by fifty-three.

(4)   Subsection (1) above does not apply to any woman who has made, or is treated as having made, an election under regulations under section 19(4) above, which has not been revoked, that her liability in respect of primary Class 1 contributions shall be at a reduced rate.

(5)   In this section—

'married couple' and 'unmarried couple' (defined in section 137 below) have the same meaning as in Part VII, and

'relevant year' has the same meaning as in section 44 above.'

(2)   Accordingly, in the following provisions of the Social Security Contributions and Benefits Act 1992, for 'sections 44 and 45' there is substituted 'sections 44 to 45A': sections 39(1) to (3), 50(3) to (5) and 51(2) and (3).

(3)   Subject to subsections (4) and (5) below, this section applies to a person ('the pensioner') who attains pensionable age after 5th April 1999 and, in relation to such persons, has effect for 1995-96 and subsequent tax years.

(4)   Where the pensioner is a woman, this section has effect in the case of additional pension falling to be calculated under sections 44 and 45 of the Social Security Contributions and Benefits Act 1992 by virtue of section 39 of that Act (widowed mother's allowance and widow's pension), including Category B retirement pension payable under section 48B(4), if her husband—

(a)   dies after 5th April 1999, and

(b)   has not attained pensionable age on or before that date.

(5)   This section has effect where additional pension falls to be calculated under sections 44 and 45 of the Social Security Contributions and Benefits Act 1992 as applied by sections 48A or 48B(2) of that Act (other Category B retirement pension) if—

(a)   the pensioner attains pensionable age after 5th April 1999, and

(b)   the pensioner's spouse has not attained pensionable age on or before that date.

128.   Additional pension: calculation of surpluses

(1)   In section 44 of the Social Security Contributions and Benefits Act 1992 (Category A retirement pension), for subsection (5) (surplus on which additional pension is calculated) there is substituted—

'(5A) For the purposes of this section and section 45 below—

(a)   there is a surplus in the pensioner's earnings factor for a relevant year if that factor exceeds the qualifying earnings factor for that year, and

(b)   the amount of the surplus is the amount of that excess, as increased by the last order under section 148 of the Administration Act to come into force before the end of the final relevant year'.

(2)   In subsection (6) of that section (calculation of earnings factors), for paragraphs (a)(ii) and (b) there is substituted—

'(ii)   his earnings factors derived from Class 2 and Class 3 contributions actually paid in respect of that year, or, if less, the qualifying earnings factor for that year; and

(b)   where the relevant year is an earlier tax year, to the aggregate of—
    (i)   his earnings factors derived from Class 1 contributions actually paid by him in respect of that year, and
    (ii)   his earnings factors derived from Class 2 and Class 3 contributions actually paid by him in respect of that year, or, if less, the qualifying earnings factor for that year.'

(3)   Section 148 of the Social Security Administration Act 1992 (revaluation of earnings factors) shall have effect in relation to surpluses in a person's earnings factors under section 44(5A) of the Social Security Contributions and Benefits Act 1992 as it has effect in relation to earnings factors.

(4)   Subject to subsections (5) and (6) below, this section has effect in relation to a person ('the pensioner') who attains pensionable age after 5th April 2000.

(5)   Where the pensioner is a woman, this section has effect in the case of additional pension falling to be calculated under sections 44 and 45 of the Social Security Contributions and Benefits Act 1992 by virtue of section 39 of that Act (widowed mother's allowance and widow's pension), including Category B retirement pension payable under section 48B(4), if her husband—
(a)   dies after 5th April 2000, and
(b)   has not attained pensionable age on or before that date.

(6)   This section has effect where additional pension falls to be calculated under sections 44 and 45 of the Social Security Contributions and Benefits Act 1992 as applied by section 48A or 48B(2) of that Act (other Category B retirement pension) if—
(a)   the pensioner attains pensionable age after 5th April 2000, and
(b)   the pensioner's spouse has not attained pensionable age on or before that date.

129.   Contribution conditions

In Schedule 3 to the Social Security Contributions and Benefits Act 1992 (contribution conditions), in paragraph 5(3)(a) (conditions for widowed mother's allowance, widow's pension and Category A and Category B retirement pension), after 'class' there is inserted 'or been credited (in the case of 1987-88 or any subsequent year) with earnings'.

130.   Up-rating of pensions increased under section 52 of the Social Security Contributions and Benefits Act

(1)   For section 156 of the Social Security Administration Act 1992 there is substituted—

'156.   Up-rating under section 150 above of pensions increased under section 52(3) of the Contributions and Benefits Act

(1)   This section applies in any case where a person is entitled to a Category A retirement pension with an increase, under section 52(3) of the Contributions and Benefits Act, in the additional pension on account of the contributions of a spouse who has died.

(2)   Where in the case of any up-rating order under section 150 above—
(a)   the spouse's final relevant year is the tax year preceding the tax year in which the up-rating order comes into force, but
(b)   the person's final relevant year was an earlier tax year,

then the up-rating order shall not have effect in relation to that part of the additional pension which is attributable to the spouse's contributions.

(3) Where in the case of any up-rating order under section 150 above—

(a) the person's final relevant year is the tax year preceding the tax year in which the up-rating order comes into force, but

(b) the spouse's final relevant year was an earlier tax year,

then the up-rating order shall not have effect in relation to that part of the additional pension which is attributable to the person's contributions.'

(2) In section 151(1) of that Act (effect of up-rating orders on additional pensions), after 'and shall apply' there is inserted 'subject to section 156 and'.

131. Graduated retirement benefit

(1) In section 62(1) of the Social Security Contributions and Benefits Act 1992 (graduated retirement benefit), after paragraph (a) there is inserted—

'(aa) for amending section 36(7) of that Act (persons to be treated as receiving nominal retirement pension) so that where a person has claimed a Category A or Category B retirement pension but—

(i) because of an election under section 54(1) above, or

(ii) because he has withdrawn his claim for the pension,

he is not entitled to such a pension, he is not to be treated for the purposes of the preceding provisions of that section as receiving such a pension at a nominal weekly rate;'.

(2) In section 150(11) of the Social Security Administration Act 1992 (application of up-rating provisions to graduated retirement benefit) for the words following 'provisions of this section' there is substituted—

'(a) to the amount of graduated retirement benefit payable for each unit of graduated contributions,

(b) to increases of such benefit under any provisions made by virtue of section 24(1)(b) of the Social Security Pensions Act 1975 or section 62(1)(a) of the Contributions and Benefits Act, and

(c) to any addition under section 37(1) of the National Insurance Act 1965 (addition to weekly rate of retirement pension for widows and widowers) to the amount of such benefit.'

(3) In section 155(7) of that Act (effect of alteration of rates of graduated retirement benefit) for the words following 'provisions of this section' there is substituted—

'(a) to the amount of graduated retirement benefit payable for each unit of graduated contributions,

(b) to increases of such benefit under any provisions made by virtue of section 24(1)(b) of the Social Security Pensions Act 1975 or section 62(1)(a) of the Contributions and Benefits Act, and

(c) to any addition under section 37(1) of the National Insurance Act 1965 (addition to weekly rate of retirement pension for widows and widowers) to the amount of such benefit'.

132. Extension of Christmas bonus for pensioners

(1) Section 150 of the Social Security Contributions and Benefits Act 1992 (Christmas bonus: interpretation) is amended as follows.

(2) In subsection (1), after paragraph (k) there is inserted—

'(l)   a mobility supplement'.

(3)   In subsection (2)—

(a)   after the definition of 'attendance allowance' there is inserted—

'mobility supplement' means a supplement awarded in respect of disablement which affects a person's ability to walk and for which the person is in receipt of war disablement pension;',

(b)   in the definition of 'retirement pension', 'if paid periodically' is omitted,

(c)   in paragraph (b) of the definition of 'unemployability supplement or allowance', after sub-paragraph (iv) there is inserted 'or

(v)   under the Pensions (Navy, Army, Air Force and Mercantile Marine) Act 1939.'

and accordingly, the 'or' immediately following sub paragraph (iii) is omitted.

133.   Contributions paid in error

After section 61 of the Social Security Contributions and Benefits
Act 1992 there is inserted—

'61A.   Contributions paid in error

(1)   This section applies in the case of any individual if—

(a)   the individual has paid amounts by way of primary Class 1 contributions which, because the individual was not an employed earner, were paid in error, and

(b)   prescribed conditions are satisfied.

(2)   Regulations may, where—

(a)   this section applies in the case of any individual, and

(b)   the Secretary of State is of the opinion that it is appropriate for the regulations to apply to the individual,

provide for entitlement to, and the amount of, additional pension to be determined as if the individual had been an employed earner and, accordingly, those contributions had been properly paid.

(3)   The reference in subsection (2) above to additional pension is to additional pension for the individual or the individual's spouse falling to be calculated under section 45 above for the purposes of—

(a)   Category A retirement pension,

(b)   Category B retirement pension for widows or widowers,

(c)   widowed mother's allowance and widow's pension, and

(d)   incapacity benefit (except in transitional cases).

(4)   Regulations may, where—

(a)   this section applies in the case of any individual, and

(b)   the Secretary of State is of the opinion that it is appropriate for regulations made by virtue of section 4(8) of the Social Security (Incapacity for Work) Act 1994 (provision during transition from invalidity benefit to incapacity benefit for incapacity benefit to include the additional pension element of any invalidity pension) to have the following effect in the case of the individual,

provide for the regulations made by virtue of that section to have effect as if, in relation to the provisions in force before the commencement of that section with respect to that additional pension element, the individual had been an employed earner and, accordingly, the contributions had been properly paid.

(5)   Where such provision made by regulations as is mentioned in subsection (2) or (4) above applies in respect of any individual regulations under paragraph 8(1)(m) of Schedule 1 to this Act may not require the amounts paid by way of primary Class 1 contributions to be repaid.

(6)   Regulations may provide, where—

(a)   such provision made by regulations as is mentioned in subsection (2) or (4) above applies in respect of any individual,

(b)   prescribed conditions are satisfied, and

(c)   any amount calculated by reference to the contributions in question has been paid in respect of that individual by way of minimum contributions under section 43 of the Pension Schemes Act 1993 (contributions to personal pension schemes),

for that individual to be treated for the purposes of that Act as if that individual had been an employed earner and, accordingly, the amount had been properly paid'.

134.   Minor amendments

(1)   In section 23(1) of the Social Security Contributions and Benefits Act 1992 (contribution conditions: supplemental), for '22(1)(a)' there is substituted '22(1)'.

(2)   Section 54(4) of that Act (effect on advance claims for retirement pension of deferral of entitlement) is omitted.

(3)   For section 55 of that Act (deferred entitlement) there is substituted—

'55.   Increase of retirement pension where entitlement is deferred

(1)   Where a person's entitlement to a Category A or Category B retirement pension is deferred, Schedule 5 to this Act shall have effect for increasing the rate of pension.

(2)   For the purposes of this Act a person's entitlement to a Category A or Category B retirement pension is deferred if and so long as that person—

(a)   does not become entitled to that pension by reason only—

(i)   of not satisfying the conditions of section 1 of the Administration Act (entitlement to benefit dependent on claim), or

(ii)   in the case of a Category B retirement pension payable by virtue of a spouse's contributions, of the spouse not satisfying those conditions with respect to his Category A retirement pension; or

(b)   in consequence of an election under section 54(1) above, falls to be treated as not having become entitled to that pension;

and, in relation to any such pension, 'period of deferment' shall be construed accordingly'.

(4)   In section 122(1) of that Act (interpretation of Parts I to VI), after the definition of 'week' there is inserted—

'working life' has the meaning given by paragraph 5(8) of Schedule 3 to this Act'.

(5)   In paragraph 5(8) of Schedule 3 to that Act (contribution conditions: meaning of 'working life') for 'this paragraph' there is substituted 'Parts I to VI of this Act'.

PART III
CERTIFICATION OF PENSION SCHEMES AND EFFECTS ON MEMBERS' STATE SCHEME RIGHTS AND DUTIES

Introductory

135. The 'principal appointed day' for Part III

An order under section 180 of this Act appointing a day for the coming into force of any provisions of this Part, being 6th April in any year, may designate that day as the principal appointed day for the purposes of this Part.

New certification requirements applying as from the principal appointed day

136. New requirements for contracted-out schemes

(1) In section 7 of the Pension Schemes Act 1993 (issue of contracting-out etc. certificates), after subsection (2) there is inserted—

'(2A) The regulations may provide, in the case of contracting out certificates issued before the principal appointed day, for their cancellation by virtue of the regulations—

(a) at the end of a prescribed period beginning with that day, or

(b) if prescribed conditions are not satisfied at any time in that period,

but for them to continue to have effect until so cancelled; and the regulations may provide that a certificate having effect on and after that day by virtue of this subsection is to have effect, in relation to any earner's service on or after that day, as if issued on or after that day.

(2B) In this Part, 'the principal appointed day' means the day designated by an order under section 180 of the Pensions Act 1995 as the principal appointed day for the purposes of Part III of that Act'.

(2) In section 8 of that Act (definition of terms), for subsection (1)(a)(i) there is substituted—

'(i) his service in the employment is for the time being service which qualifies him for a pension provided by an occupational pension scheme contracted out by virtue of satisfying section 9(2) (in this Act referred to as 'a salary related contracted-out scheme')'.

(3) In section 9 of that Act (requirements for certification of schemes: general), for subsection (2) (requirement for guaranteed minimum pension) there is substituted—

'(2) An occupational pension scheme satisfies this subsection only if—

(a) in relation to any earner's service before the principal appointed day, it satisfies the conditions of subsection (2A), and

(b) in relation to any earner's service on or after that day, it satisfies the conditions of subsection (2B).

(2A) The conditions of this subsection are that—

(a) the scheme complies in all respects with sections 13 to 23 or, in such cases or classes of case as may be prescribed, with those sections as modified by regulations, and

(b) the rules of the scheme applying to guaranteed minimum pensions are framed so as to comply with the relevant requirements.

(2B) The conditions of this subsection are that the Secretary of State is satisfied that—

(a)   the scheme complies with section 12A,

(b)   restrictions imposed under section 40 of the Pensions Act 1995 (restriction on employer-related investments) apply to the scheme and the scheme complies with those restrictions,

(c)   the scheme satisfies such other requirements as may be prescribed (which—

(i)   must include requirements as to the amount of the resources of the scheme and,

(ii)   may include a requirement that, if the only members of the scheme were those falling within any prescribed class or description, the scheme would comply with section 12A); and

(d)   the scheme does not fall within a prescribed class or description,

and is satisfied that the rules of the scheme are framed so as to comply with the relevant requirements.

(2C)   Regulations may modify subsection (2B)(a) and (b) in their application to occupational pension schemes falling within a prescribed class or description.'

(4)   In subsection (3) of that section (requirement for protected rights, etc.) after 'case' in paragraph (a) there is inserted—

'(aa)   the Secretary of State is satisfied that the scheme does not fall within a prescribed class or description'.

(5)   After section 12 of that Act there is inserted—

Requirements for certification of occupational pension schemes applying from the principal appointed day of the Pensions Act 1995

12A.   The statutory standard

(1)   Subject to the provisions of this Part, the scheme must, in relation to the provision of pensions for earners in employed earner's employment, and for their widows or widowers, satisfy the statutory standard.

(2)   Subject to regulations made by virtue of section 9(2B)(c)(ii), in applying this section regard must only be had to—

(a)   earners in employed earner's employment, or

(b)   their widows or widowers,

collectively, and the pensions to be provided for persons falling within paragraph (a) or (b) must be considered as a whole.

(3)   For the purposes of this section, a scheme satisfies the statutory standard if the pensions to be provided for such persons are broadly equivalent to, or better than, the pensions which would be provided for such persons under a reference scheme.

(4)   Regulations may provide for the manner of, and criteria for, determining whether the pensions to be provided for such persons under a scheme are broadly equivalent to, or better than, the pensions which would be provided for such persons under a reference scheme.

(5)   Regulations made by virtue of subsection (4) may provide for the determination to be made in accordance with guidance prepared from time to time by a prescribed body and approved by the Secretary of State.

(6)   The pensions to be provided for such persons under a scheme are to be treated as broadly equivalent to or better than the pensions which would

be provided for such persons under a reference scheme if and only if an actuary (who, except in prescribed circumstances, must be the actuary appointed for the scheme in pursuance of section 47 of the Pensions Act 1995) so certifies.

12B. Reference scheme

(1) This section applies for the purposes of section 12A.

(2) A reference scheme is an occupational pension scheme which—

    (a) complies with each of subsections (3) and (4), and

    (b) complies with any prescribed requirements.

(3) In relation to earners employed in employed earner's employment, a reference scheme is one which provides—

    (a) for them to be entitled to a pension under the scheme commencing at a normal pension age of 65 and continuing for life, and

    (b) for the annual rate of the pension at that age to be—

        (i) 1/80th of average qualifying earnings in the last three tax years preceding the end of service,

multiplied by

        (ii) the number of years service, not exceeding such number as would produce an annual rate equal to half the earnings on which it is calculated.

(4) In relation to widows or widowers, a reference scheme is one which provides—

    (a) for the widows or widowers of earners employed in employed earner's employment (whether the earners die before or after attaining the age of 65) to be entitled, except in prescribed circumstances, to pensions under the scheme, and

    (b) except in prescribed circumstances, for the annual rate of the pensions, at the time when the widows or widowers first become entitled to them, to be—

        (i) in the case of widows or widowers of persons whose age when they died was, or was greater than, normal pension age, 50 per cent. of the annual rate which a reference scheme is required to provide for persons of that age, and

        (ii) in the case of widows or widowers of other persons, 50 per cent. of the annual rate which a reference scheme would have been required to provide in respect of the persons' actual periods of service if those persons had attained that age.

(5) For the purposes of this section, an earner's qualifying earnings in any tax year are 90 per cent. of the amount by which the earner's earnings—

    (a) exceed the qualifying earnings factor for that year, and

    (b) do not exceed the upper earnings limit for that year multiplied by fifty-three.

(6) Regulations may modify subsections (2) to (5).

(7) In this section—

    'normal pension age', in relation to a scheme, means the age specified in the scheme as the earliest age at which pension becomes payable under the scheme (apart from any special provision as to early retirement on grounds of ill-health or otherwise), 'qualifying earnings factor', in relation to a tax year, has the meaning given by section 122(1) of the Social Security Contributions and Benefits Act 1992, and

'upper earnings limit', in relation to a tax year, means the amount specified for that year by regulations made by virtue of section 5(3) of that Act as the upper earnings limit for Class 1 contributions.

12C. Transfer commutation, etc.

(1) Regulations may prohibit or restrict—

    (a) the transfer of any liability—

        (i) for the payment of pensions under a relevant scheme, or

        (ii) in respect of accrued rights to such pensions,

    (b) the discharge of any liability to provide pensions under a relevant scheme, or

    (c) the payment of a lump sum instead of a pension payable under a relevant scheme,

except in prescribed circumstances or on prescribed conditions.

(2) In this section 'relevant scheme' means a scheme contracted out by virtue of section 9(2B) of this Act and references to pensions and accrued rights under the scheme are to such pensions and rights so far as attributable to an earner's service on or after the principal appointed day.

(3) Regulations under subsection (1) may provide that any provision of this Part shall have effect subject to such modifications as may be specified in the regulations.

12D. Entitlement to benefit

In the case of a scheme contracted out by virtue of section 9(2B) of this Act, regulations may make provision as to the ages by reference to which benefits under the scheme are to be paid'.

Reduction in State scheme contributions, payment of rebates and reduction in State scheme benefits

137. State scheme contributions and rebates

(1) In section 40 of the Pension Schemes Act 1993 (scope of Chapter II of Part III), in paragraph (b), after 'members of' there is inserted 'money purchase contracted-out schemes and members of'.

(2) For section 41 (1) of that Act (reduced rates of Class 1 contributions for earners in contracted-out employment), including the sidenote and the preceding heading, there is substituted—

'Reduced rates of contributions for members of salary related contracted-out schemes

41. Reduced rates of Class 1 contributions

(1) Where—

    (a) the earnings paid to or for the benefit of an earner in any tax week are in respect of an employment which is contracted-out employment at the time of the payment, and

    (b) the earner's service in the employment is service which qualifies him for a pension provided by a salary related contracted-out scheme,

the amount of a Class 1 contribution in respect of so much of the earnings
paid in that week as exceeds the current lower earnings limit but not the
current upper earnings limit for that week (or the prescribed equivalents if he
is paid otherwise than weekly) shall be reduced by the following amount.

(1A)   The amount is—

(a)   in the case of a primary Class 1 contribution, an amount equal to
1.8 per cent. of that part of those earnings, and

(b)   in the case of a secondary Class 1 contribution, an amount equal to
3 per cent. of that part of those earnings'.

(3)   In section 42 of that Act (review and alteration of rates of contributions
applicable under section 41), for subsection (1)(a) there is substituted—

'(a)   a report by the Government Actuary or the Deputy Government Actuary
on—

(i)   the percentages for the time being applying under section
41(1A)(a) and (b), and

(ii)   any changes since the preparation of the last report under this
paragraph in the factors in his opinion affecting the cost of providing benefits of
an actuarial value equivalent to that of the benefits which, under section 48A, are
foregone by or in respect of members of salary related contracted-out schemes'.

(4)   In relation to the first report under section 42(1)(a) of that Act laid after
the passing of this Act, that section shall have effect as if—

(a)   in subsection (1)(a), sub-paragraph (i) and, in sub-paragraph (ii), 'any
changes since the preparation of the last report under this paragraph in' were omitted,

(b)   for subsection (1)(b) there were substituted—

'(b)   a report by the Secretary of State stating what, in view of the report
under paragraph (a), he considers the percentages under section 41(1A)(a)
should be',

(c)   for subsections (3) and (4) there were substituted—

'(3)   The Secretary of State shall prepare and lay before each House of
Parliament with the report the draft of an order specifying the percentages;
and if the draft is approved by resolution of each House the Secretary of State
shall make the order in the form of the draft.

(4)   An order under subsection (3) shall have effect from the beginning of
the tax year which begins with the principal appointed day, not being a tax
year earlier than the second after that in which the order is made',

(d)   in subsection (5), for 'alteration' there were substituted 'determination', and

(e)   in subsection (6), for 'an order making alterations in either or both
of those percentages' there were substituted 'such an order'.

(5)   After that section there is inserted—

*'Reduced rates of contributions, and rebates, for members of money
purchase contracted-out schemes*

42A.   Reduced rates of Class 1 contributions, and rebates

(1)   Subsections (2) and (3) apply where—

(a)   the earnings paid to or for the benefit of an earner in any tax week
are in respect of an employment which is contracted-out employment at the
time of the payment, and

(b)   the earner's service in the employment is service which qualifies him for a pension provided by a money purchase contracted-out scheme.

(2)   The amount of a Class 1 contribution in respect of so much of the earnings paid in that week in respect of that employment as exceeds the current lower earnings limit but not the current upper earnings limit for that week (or the prescribed equivalents if he is paid otherwise than weekly) shall be reduced by an amount equal to the appropriate flat-rate percentage of that part of those earnings.

(3)   The Secretary of State shall except in prescribed circumstances or in respect of prescribed periods pay in respect of that earner and that tax week to the trustees or managers of the scheme or, in prescribed circumstances, to a prescribed person the amount by which—

(a)   the appropriate age-related percentage of that part of those earnings,
exceeds

(b)   the appropriate flat-rate percentage of that part of those earnings.

(4)   Regulations may make provision—

(a)   as to the manner in which and time at which or period within which payments under subsection (3) are to be made,

(b)   for the adjustment of the amount which would otherwise be payable under that subsection so as to avoid the payment of trivial or fractional amounts,

(c)   for earnings to be calculated or estimated in such manner and on such basis as may be prescribed for the purpose of determining whether any, and if so what, payments under subsection (3) are to be made.

(5)   If the Secretary of State pays an amount under subsection (3) which he is not required to pay or is not required to pay to the person to whom, or in respect of whom, he pays it, he may recover it from any person to whom, or in respect of whom, he paid it.

(6)   Where—

(a)   an earner has ceased to be employed in an employment, and

(b)   earnings are paid to him or for his benefit within the period of six weeks, or such other period as may be prescribed, from the day on which he so ceased,
that employment shall be treated for the purposes of this section as contracted-out employment at the time when the earnings are paid if it was contracted-out employment in relation to the earner when he was last employed in it.

(7)   Subsection (3) of section 41 applies for the purposes of this section as it applies for the purposes of that.

42B.   Determination and alteration of rates of contributions, and rebates, applicable under section 42A.

(1)   The Secretary of State shall at intervals of not more than five years lay before each House of Parliament—

(a)   a report by the Government Actuary or the Deputy Government Actuary on the percentages which, in his opinion, are required to be specified in an order under this section so as to reflect the cost of providing benefits of an actuarial value equivalent to that of the benefits which, under section 48A, are foregone by or in respect of members of money purchase contracted-out schemes,

(b) a report by the Secretary of State stating what, in view of the report under paragraph (a), he considers those percentages should be, and

(c) a draft of an order under subsection (2).

(2) An order under this subsection shall have effect in relation to a period of tax years (not exceeding five) and may—

(a) specify different percentages for primary and secondary Class 1 contributions, and

(b) for each of the tax years for which it has effect—

(i) specify a percentage in respect of all earners which is 'the appropriate flat-rate percentage' for the purposes of section 42A, and

(ii) specify different percentages (not being less than the percentage specified by virtue of sub-paragraph (i)) in respect of earners by reference to their ages on the last day of the preceding year (the percentage for each group of earners being 'the appropriate age-related percentage' in respect of earners in that group for the purposes of section 42A).

(3) If the draft of an order under subsection (2) is approved by resolution of each House of Parliament, the Secretary of State shall make the order in the form of the draft.

(4) An order under subsection (2) shall have effect from the beginning of such tax year as may be specified in the order, not being a tax year earlier than the second after that in which the order is made.

(5) Subsection (2) is without prejudice to the generality of section 182'.

(6) In Schedule 4 to that Act (priority in bankruptcy, etc.), in paragraph 2(3)—

(a) in paragraph (a), for '4.8 per cent.' there is substituted 'the percentage for non-contributing earners',

(b) in paragraph (b), for '3 per cent.' there is substituted 'the percentage for contributing earners'.

(7) In paragraph 2(5) of that Schedule—

(a) before the definition of 'employer' there is inserted—

'appropriate flat-rate percentage' has the same meaning as in section 42A', and

(b) after the definition there is inserted—

'the percentage for contributing earners' means—

(a) in relation to a salary related contracted-out scheme, 3 per cent, and

(b) in relation to a money purchase contracted-out scheme, the percentage which is the appropriate flat-rate percentage for secondary Class 1 contributions,

'the percentage for non-contributing earners' means—

(a) in relation to a salary related contracted-out scheme, 4.8 per cent, and

(b) in relation to a money purchase contracted-out scheme, a percentage equal to the sum of the appropriate flat-rate percentages for primary and secondary Class 1 contributions'.

138. Minimum contributions towards appropriate personal pension schemes
   (1)   Section 45 of the Pension Schemes Act 1993 (minimum contributions to personal pension schemes) is amended as follows.
   (2)   For subsection (1) there is substituted—
   '(1)   In relation to any tax week falling within a period for which the Secretary of State is required to pay minimum contributions in respect of an earner, the amount of those contributions shall be an amount equal to the appropriate age-related percentage of so much of the earnings paid in that week (other than earnings in respect of contracted-out employment) as exceeds the current lower earnings limit but not the current upper earnings limit for that week (or the prescribed equivalents if he is paid otherwise than weekly)'.
   (3)   Subsection (2) is omitted.
   (4)   In subsection (3)(e), the words following 'prescribed period' are omitted.
   (5)   After that section there is inserted—

45A. Determination and alteration of rates of minimum contributions under section 45
   (1)   The Secretary of State shall at intervals of not more than five years lay before each House of Parliament—
   (a)   a report by the Government Actuary or the Deputy Government Actuary on the percentages which, in his opinion, are required to be specified in an order under this section so as to reflect the cost of providing benefits of an actuarial value equivalent to that of the benefits which, under section 48A, are foregone by or in respect of members of appropriate personal pension schemes,
   (b)   a report by the Secretary of State stating what, in view of the report under paragraph (a), he considers those percentages should be, and
   (c)   a draft of an order under subsection (2).
   (2)   An order under this subsection—
   (a)   shall have effect in relation to a period of tax years (not exceeding five), and
   (b)   may, for each of the tax years for which it has effect, specify different percentages in respect of earners by reference to their ages on the last day of the preceding year (the percentage for each group of earners being 'the appropriate age related percentage' in respect of earners in that group for the purposes of section 45).
   (3)   If the draft of an order under subsection (2) is approved by resolution of each House of Parliament, the Secretary of State shall make the order in the form of the draft.
   (4)   An order under subsection (2) shall have effect from the beginning of such tax year as may be specified in the order, not being a tax year earlier than the second after that in which the order is made.
   (5)   Subsection (2) is without prejudice to the generality of section 182'.

139. Money purchase and personal pension schemes: verification of ages
After section 45A of the Pension Schemes Act 1993 (inserted by section 138) there is inserted—

45B. 'Money purchase and personal pension schemes: verification of ages.

(1)   Regulations may make provision for the manner in which an earner's age is to be verified in determining the appropriate age-related percentages for the purposes of sections 42A and 45(1).

(2)   Information held by the Secretary of State as to the age of any individual may, whether or not it was obtained in pursuance of regulations under subsection (1), be disclosed by the Secretary of State—

(a)   to the trustees or managers of a money purchase contracted-out scheme or an appropriate personal pension scheme, and

(b)   to such other persons as may be prescribed,

in connection with the making of payments under section 42A(3) or the payment of minimum contributions.'

140.   Reduction in benefits for members of certified schemes

(1)   After section 48 of the Pension Schemes Act 1993 there is inserted—

'Effect of reduced contributions and rebates on social security benefits

48A.   Additional pension and other benefits

(1)   In relation to any tax week where—

(a)   the amount of a Class 1 contribution in respect of the earnings paid to or for the benefit of an earner in that week is reduced under section 41 or 42A, or

(b)   an amount is paid under section 45(1) in respect of the earnings paid to or for the benefit of an earner,

section 44(6) of the Social Security Contributions and Benefits Act 1992 (earnings factors for additional pension) shall have effect, except in prescribed circumstances, as if no primary Class 1 contributions had been paid or treated as paid upon those earnings for that week and section 45A of that Act did not apply (where it would, apart from this subsection, apply).

(2)   Where the whole or part of a contributions equivalent premium has been paid or treated as paid in respect of the earner, the Secretary of State may make a determination reducing or eliminating the application of subsection (1).

(3)   Subsection (1) is subject to regulations under paragraph 5(3A) to (3E) of Schedule 2.

(4)   Regulations may, so far as is required for the purpose of providing entitlement to additional pension (such as is mentioned in section 44(3)(b) of the Social Security Contributions and Benefits Act 1992) but to the extent only that the amount of additional pension is attributable to provision made by regulations under section 45(5) of that Act, disapply subsection (1).

(5)   In relation to earners where, by virtue of subsection (1), section 44(6) of the Social Security Contributions and Benefits Act 1992 has effect, in any tax year, as mentioned in that subsection in relation to some but not all of their earnings, regulations may modify the application of section 44(5) of that Act.'

(2)   In section 48 of the Pension Schemes Act 1993 (effect of membership of money purchase contracted-out scheme or appropriate scheme on payment of

social security benefits) in subsection (2), paragraph (b) is omitted and, in paragraph (c), 'if the earner dies before reaching pensionable age' is omitted.

(3)   Section 48 of that Act shall cease to have effect in relation to minimum payments made, or minimum contributions paid, on or after the principal appointed day.

Premiums and return to State scheme

141.   State scheme etc. premiums and buyback into State scheme

(1)   In section 55 of the Pension Schemes Act 1993 (payment of state scheme premiums on termination of certified status), for subsection (2)   there is sub-stituted—

'(2)   Where—

(a)   an earner is serving in employment which is contracted-out employ-ment by reference to an occupational pension scheme (other than a money purchase contracted-out scheme),

(b)   paragraph (a) ceases to apply, by reason of any of the following circumstances, before the earner attains the scheme's normal pension age or (if earlier) the end of the tax year preceding that in which the earner attains pensionable age, and

(c)   the earner has served for less than two years in the employment, the prescribed person may elect to pay a premium under this subsection (referred to in this Act as a 'contributions equivalent premium').

(2A)   The circumstances referred to in subsection (2) are that—

(a)   the earner's service in the employment ceases otherwise than on the earner's death,

(b)   the earner ceases to be a member of the scheme otherwise than on the earner's death,

(c)   the earner's service in the employment ceases on the earner's death and the earner dies leaving a widow or widower,

(d)   the scheme is wound up,

(e)   the scheme ceases to be a contracted-out occupational pension scheme;

but paragraph (a), (b), (d) or (e) does not apply if the earner has an accrued right to short service benefit'.

(2)   In Schedule 2 to that Act, in paragraph 5 (state scheme premiums)—

(a)   in sub-paragraph (3)—

(i)   'in relation to state scheme premiums' is omitted,

(ii)   paragraph (b) is omitted, and

(iii)   at the end there is added—

'and in this sub-paragraph and the following provisions of this paragraph 'premium' means a contributions equivalent premium',

(b)   after sub-paragraph (3) there is inserted—

'(3A)   Sub-paragraph (3B) applies in relation to a member of a contracted-out occupational pension scheme which is being wound up if, in the opinion of the Secretary of State—

(a)   the resources of the scheme are insufficient to meet the whole of the liability for the cash equivalent of the member's rights under the scheme, and

(b)   if the resources of the scheme are sufficient to meet a part of that liability, that part is less than the amount required for restoring his State scheme rights.

(3B)   Where this sub-paragraph applies—

(a)   regulations may provide for treating the member as if sections 46 to 48 or, as the case may be, section 48A(1) did not apply, or applied only to such extent as is determined in accordance with the regulations, and

(b)   the amount required for restoring the member's State scheme rights, or a prescribed part of that amount, shall be a debt due from the trustees or managers of the scheme to the Secretary of State.

(3C)   Regulations may make provision—

(a)   for determining the cash equivalent of a member's rights under a scheme and the extent (if any) to which the resources of the scheme are insufficient to meet the liability for that cash equivalent,

(b)   for the recovery of any debt due under sub-paragraph (3B)(b), and

(c)   for determining the amount required for restoring a member's State scheme rights including provision requiring the Secretary of State to apply whichever prescribed actuarial table in force at the appropriate time is applicable.

(3D)   Section 155 shall apply as if sub-paragraphs (3A) and (3B)(a), and regulations made by virtue of this sub-paragraph and sub-paragraph (3B)(b), were included among the provisions there referred to.

(3E)   In sub-paragraphs (3A) and (3B), 'State scheme rights', in relation to a member of a scheme, are the rights for which, if the scheme had not been a contracted-out scheme, the member would have been eligible by virtue of section 44(6) of the Social Security Contributions and Benefits Act 1992 (earnings factors for additional pension).', and

(c)   sub-paragraph (5) is omitted.

Protected rights

142.   Interim arrangements for giving effect to protected rights

(1)   Section 28 of the Pension Schemes Act 1993 (ways of giving effect to protected rights) is amended as follows.

(2)   In subsection (1), after paragraph (a) there is inserted—

'(aa)   in any case where subsection (1A) so requires, by the making of such payments as are mentioned in that subsection,'.

(3)   After that subsection there is inserted—

'(1A)   In the case of a personal pension scheme, where the member so elects, effect shall be given to his protected rights—

(a)   during the interim period, by the making of payments under an interim arrangement which—

(i)   complies with section 28A,

(ii)   satisfies such conditions as may be prescribed,

and

(b)   at the end of the interim period, in such of the ways permitted by the following subsections as the rules of the scheme may specify.'

(4)   In subsection (3)—

(a)   in paragraph (b), after 'the member' there is inserted 'or, where section 28A(2) applies, the member's widow or widower', and

(b)   in the words following that paragraph, after 'subsection' there is inserted '(1A)(a) or'.

(5)   In subsection (4)(a), for the words from '65' to the end there is substituted—

'65 or such later date as has been agreed by him, or

(ii)   in the case of a personal pension scheme, where the member has elected to receive payments under an interim arrangement, the date by reference to which the member elects to terminate that arrangement, and otherwise such date as has been agreed by him and is not earlier than his 60th birthday nor later than his 75th birthday.'

(6)   In subsection (5), after 'subsection' there is inserted '(1A)'.

(7)   After subsection (7) there is added—

'(8)   In this section and sections 28A, 28B and 29—

'the interim period' means the period beginning with the starting date in relation to the member in question and ending with the termination date;

'the starting date' means the date, which must not be earlier than the member's 60th birthday, by reference to which the member elects to begin to receive payments under the interim arrangement;

'the termination date means the date by reference to which the member (or, where section 28A(2) applies, the member's widow or widower) elects to terminate the interim arrangement, and that date must be not later than—

(i)   the member's 75th birthday, or

(ii)   where section 28A(2) applies, the earlier of the member's widow or widower's 75th birthday and the 75th anniversary of the member's birth.'

143.   Requirements for interim arrangements

After section 28 of the Pension Schemes Act 1993 there is inserted—

28A.   'Requirements for interim arrangements

(1)   An interim arrangement must provide for payments to be made to the member, and, where subsection (2) applies, to the member's widow or widower, throughout the interim period, at intervals not exceeding twelve months.

(2)   This subsection applies where the member dies during the interim period and is survived by a widow or widower who at the date of the member's death has not yet attained the age of 75 years.

(3)   The aggregate amount of payments made to a person under an interim arrangement in each successive period of twelve months must not be—

(a)   greater than the annual amount of the annuity which would have been purchasable by him on the relevant reference date, or

(b)   less than the prescribed percentage of that amount.

(4)   The percentage prescribed under subsection (3)(b) may be zero.

(5)   For the purposes of this section—

(a)   the annual amount of the annuity which would have been purchasable by a person on any date shall be calculated in the prescribed manner by reference to—

(i)   the value on that date, determined by or on behalf of the trustees or managers of the scheme, of the person's protected rights, and

(ii)   the current published tables of rates of annuities prepared in the prescribed manner by the Government Actuary for the purposes of this section, and

(b)   the relevant reference date is—

(i)   in relation to payments made to the member during the three years beginning with the member's starting date, that date, and in relation to such payments made during each succeeding period of three years, the first day of the period of three years in question, or

(ii)   where subsection (2) applies, in relation to payments made to the member's widow or widower during the three years beginning with the date of the member's death, that date, and in relation to such payments made during each succeeding period of three years, the first day of the period of three years in question.

28B.   Information about interim arrangements

(1)   The trustees or managers of a personal pension scheme must, if required to do so by the Secretary of State, produce any document relevant to—

(a)   the level of payments made under any interim arrangement, or

(b)   the value of protected rights to which such an arrangement gives effect,

or otherwise connected with the making of payments under such an arrangement.

(2)   In this section, 'document' includes information recorded in any form, and the reference to the production of a document, in relation to information recorded otherwise than in legible form, is a reference to producing a copy of the information in legible form.'

144.   Interim arrangements: supplementary

(1)   Section 29 of the Pension Schemes Act 1993 (the pension and annuity requirements) is amended as follows.

(2)   In subsection (1) for paragraph (a) there is substituted—

'(a)   in the case of an occupational pension scheme it commences on a date—

(i)   not earlier than the member's 60th birthday, and

(ii)   not later than his 65th birthday,

or on such later date as has been agreed by him, and continues until the date of his death, or

(aa)   in the case of a personal pension scheme—

(i)   where the member has elected under section 28(1A) to receive payments under an interim arrangement, it commences on the termination date, and continues until the date of the member's death or, where section 28A(2) applies, until the death of the member's widow or widower, or

(ii)   otherwise, it commences on such a date as has been agreed by the member and is not earlier than his 60th birthday nor later than his 75th birthday, and continues until the date of his death;'.

(3)   In subsection (3)(b)(iii), after 'member' there is inserted 'or, where section 28A(2) applies, the member's widow or widower'.

(4)   In subsection (4), after 'member' there is inserted '(or a member's widow or widower)'.

145. Extension of interim arrangements to occupational pension schemes

Regulations made by the Secretary of State may provide that sections 141 to 143 shall have effect, subject to prescribed modifications, in relation to protected rights under an occupational pension scheme as they have effect in relation to protected rights under a personal pension scheme.

146. Discharge of protected rights on winding up: insurance policies

(1) After section 32 of the Pension Schemes Act 1993 there is inserted—

> **32A. 'Discharge of protected rights on winding up: insurance policies**
>
> (1) Where an occupational pension scheme is being wound up and such conditions as may be prescribed are satisfied, effect may be given to the protected rights of a member of the scheme (in spite of section 28) by—
>
> (a) taking out an appropriate policy of insurance, or a number of such policies, under which the member is the beneficiary, or
>
> (b) assuring the benefits of a policy of insurance, or a number of such policies, to the member, where the policy assured is an appropriate policy.
>
> (2) A policy of insurance is appropriate for the purposes of this section if—
>
> (a) the insurance company with which it is or was taken out or entered into—
>
> (i) is, or was at the time when the policy was taken out or (as the case may be) the benefit of it was assured, carrying on ordinary long-term insurance business (within the meaning of the Insurance Companies Act 1982) in the United Kingdom or any other Member State, and
>
> (ii) satisfies, or at that time satisfied, prescribed requirements, and
>
> (b) it may not be assigned or surrendered except on conditions which satisfy such requirements as may be prescribed, and
>
> (c) it contains or is endorsed with terms whose effect is that the amount secured by it may not be commuted except on conditions which satisfy such requirements as may be prescribed, and
>
> (d) it satisfies such other requirements as may be prescribed'.

(2) At the end of section 28 of that Act, as amended by this Act, (ways of giving effect to protected rights) there is inserted—

'(9) This section is subject to section 32A'.

Miscellaneous

147. Monitoring personal pension schemes

After section 33 of the Pension Schemes Act 1993 there is inserted—

> **33A. 'Appropriate schemes: 'Blowing the whistle'**
>
> (1) If any person acting as an auditor or actuary of an appropriate scheme has reasonable cause to believe that—
>
> (a) any requirement which, in the case of the scheme, is required by section 9(5)(a) to be satisfied is not satisfied, and
>
> (b) the failure to satisfy the requirement is likely to be of material significance in the exercise by the Secretary of State of any of his functions relating to appropriate schemes,
>
> that person must immediately give a written report of the matter to the Secretary of State.

(2)   No duty to which a person acting as auditor or actuary of an appropriate scheme is subject shall be regarded as contravened merely because of any information or opinion contained in a written report under this section.'

148.   Earner employed in more than one employment.

(1)   Paragraph 1 of Schedule 1 to the Social Security Contributions and Benefits Act 1992 (Class 1 contributions where earner in more than one employment) is amended as follows.

(2)   For sub-paragraph (3) there is substituted—

'(3)   The amount of the primary Class 1 contribution shall be the aggregate of the amounts determined under the following paragraphs (applying earlier paragraphs before later ones)—

(a)   if the aggregated earnings are paid to or for the benefit of an earner in respect of whom minimum contributions are payable under section 43(1) of the Pension Schemes Act 1993 (contributions to personal pension schemes), the amount obtained by applying the rate of primary Class 1 contributions that would apply if all the aggregated earnings were attributable to employments which are not contracted-out to such part of the aggregated earnings so attributable as does not exceed the current upper earnings limit (referred to in this paragraph as 'the APPS earnings'),

(b)   if some of the aggregated earnings are attributable to COMPS service, the amount obtained by applying the rate of primary Class 1 contributions that would apply if all the aggregated earnings were attributable to COMPS service—

(i)   to such part of the aggregated earnings attributable to COMPS service as does not exceed the current upper earnings limit, or

(ii)   if paragraph (a) applies, to such part of the earnings attributable to COMPS service as, when added to the APPS earnings, does not exceed the current upper earnings limit,

(c)   if some of the aggregated earnings are attributable to COSRS service, the amount obtained by applying the rate of primary Class 1 contributions that would apply if all the aggregated earnings were attributable to COSRS service—

(i)   to such part of the aggregated earnings attributable to COSRS service as does not exceed the current upper earnings limit, or

(ii)   if paragraph (a) or (b) applies, to such part of the earnings attributable to COSRS service as, when added to the APPS earnings or the part attributable to COMPS service (or both), does not exceed the current upper earnings limit,

(d)   the amount obtained by applying the rate of primary Class 1 contributions that would apply if all the aggregated earnings were attributable to employments which are not contracted-out to such part of the aggregated earnings as, when added to the part or parts attributable to COMPS or COSRS service, does not exceed the current upper earnings limit'.

(3)   For sub-paragraph (6) there is substituted—

'(6)   The amount of the secondary Class 1 contribution shall be the aggregate of the amounts determined under the following paragraphs (applying earlier paragraphs before later ones)—

(a) if the aggregated earnings are paid to or for the benefit of an earner in respect of whom minimum contributions are payable under section 43(1) of the Pension Schemes Act 1993, the amount obtained by applying the rate of secondary Class 1 contributions that would apply if all the aggregated earnings were attributable to employments which are not contracted-out to the APPS earnings,

(b) if some of the aggregated earnings are attributable to COMPS service, the amount obtained by applying the rate of secondary Class 1 contributions that would apply if all the aggregated earnings were attributable to COMPS service to the part of the aggregated earnings attributable to such service,

(c) if some of the aggregated earnings are attributable to COSRS service, the amount obtained by applying the rate of secondary Class 1 contributions that would apply if all the aggregated earnings were attributable to COSRS service to the part of the aggregated earnings attributable to such service,

(d) the amount obtained by applying the rate of secondary Class 1 contributions that would apply if all the aggregated earnings were attributable to employments which are not contracted-out to the remainder of the aggregated earnings'.

(4) At the end of that paragraph there is added—

'(9) In this paragraph—

'COMPS service' means service in employment in respect of which minimum payments are made to a money purchase contracted-out scheme,

'COSRS service' means service in employment which qualifies the earner for a pension provided by a salary related contracted-out scheme'.

(5) Until the principal appointed day, that paragraph, as amended by this section, shall have effect as if—

(a) for sub-paragraph (3)(b) there were substituted—

'(b) if some of the aggregated earnings are attributable to service in contracted-out employment, the amount obtained by applying the rate of primary Class 1 contributions that would apply if all the aggregated earnings were attributable to such service—

(i) to such part of the aggregated earnings attributable to such service as does not exceed the current upper earnings limit, or

(ii) if paragraph (a) applies, to such part of the earnings attributable to such service as, when added to the APPS earnings, does not exceed the current upper earnings limit',

(b) sub-paragraph (3)(c) were omitted,

(c) in sub-paragraph (3)(d), for 'COMPS or COSRS service' there

(d) were substituted 'service in contracted-out employment', for sub-paragraph (6)(b) there were substituted—

'(b) if some of the aggregated earnings are attributable to service in contracted-out employment, the amount obtained by applying the rate of secondary Class 1 contributions that would apply if all the aggregated earnings were attributable to such service to the part of the aggregated earnings attributable to such service',

(e) sub-paragraph (6)(c) were omitted, and

(f) in sub-paragraph (9) the definitions of 'COMPS service' and 'COSRS service' were omitted.

149. Hybrid occupational pension schemes

(1) In spite of anything in sections 9 and 12 of the Pension Schemes Act 1993 (requirements for certification and determination of basis on which scheme is contracted-out), the Secretary of State may by regulations provide, where the pensions provided by an occupational pension scheme include both—

(a) such pensions that, if the scheme provided only those pensions, it would satisfy section 9(2) of that Act. and

(b) such other pensions that, if the scheme provided only those other pensions, it would satisfy section 9(3) of that Act,

for Part III of that Act to have effect as if the scheme were two separate schemes providing, respectively, the pensions referred to in paragraphs (a) and (b).

(2) Regulations made by the Secretary of State may, in connection with any provision made by virtue of subsection (1), make such modifications of the following Acts, and the instruments made or having effect as if made under them, as appear to the Secretary of State desirable: the Social Security Contributions and Benefits Act 1992, the Pension Schemes Act 1993 and Part I of this Act.

150. Dissolution of Occupational Pensions Board

(1) The Occupational Pensions Board (referred to in this section as 'the Board') is hereby dissolved.

(2) An order under section 180 appointing the day on which subsection (1) is to come into force may provide—

(a) for all property, rights and liabilities to which the Board is entitled or subject immediately before that day to become property, rights and liabilities of the Authority or the Secretary of State, and

(b) for any function of the Board falling to be exercised on or after that day, or which fell to be exercised before that day but has not been exercised, to be exercised by the Authority, the Secretary of State or the Department of Health and Social Services for Northern Ireland.

Minor and consequential amendments

151. Minor and consequential amendments related to sections 136 to 150

Schedule 5 (which makes amendments related to sections 136 to 150) shall have effect.

PART IV
MISCELLANEOUS AND GENERAL

Transfer values

152. Extension of scope of right to cash equivalent

(1) Section 93 of the Pension Schemes Act 1993 (scope of provisions relating to transfer values) is amended as follows.

(2) For subsection (1)(a) there is substituted—

'(a) to any member of an occupational pension scheme—

(i) whose pensionable service has terminated at least one year before normal pension age, and

(ii)   who on the date on which his pensionable service terminated had accrued rights to benefit under the scheme,

except a member of a salary related occupational pension scheme whose pensionable service terminated before 1st January 1986 and in respect of whom prescribed requirements are satisfied'.

(3)   After subsection (1) there is inserted—

'(1A)   For the purposes of this section and the following provisions of this Chapter, an occupational pension scheme is salary related if—

(a)   the scheme is not a money purchase scheme, and

(b)   the scheme does not fall within a prescribed class.

(1B)   Regulations may—

(a)   provide for this Chapter not to apply in relation to a person of a prescribed description, or

(b)   apply this Chapter with prescribed modifications to occupational pension schemes—

(i)   which are not money purchase schemes, but

(ii)   where some of the benefits that may be provided are money purchase benefits.'

153.   Right to guaranteed cash equivalent

After section 93 of the Pension Schemes Act 1993 there is inserted—

93A.   'Salary related schemes: right to statement of entitlement

(1)   The trustees or managers of a salary related occupational pension scheme must, on the application of any member, provide the member with a written statement (in this Chapter referred to as a 'statement of entitlement') of the amount of the cash equivalent at the guarantee date of any benefits which have accrued to or in respect of him under the applicable rules.

(2)   In this section—

'the applicable rules' has the same meaning as in section 94;

'the guarantee date' means the date by reference to which the value of the cash equivalent is calculated, and must be—

(a)   within the prescribed period beginning with the date of the application, and

(b)   within the prescribed period ending with the date on which the statement of entitlement is provided to the member.

(3)   Regulations may make provision in relation to applications for a statement of entitlement, including, in particular, provision as to the period which must elapse after the making of such an application before a member may make a further such application.

(4)   If, in the case of any scheme, a statement of entitlement has not been provided under this section, section 10 of the Pensions Act 1995 (power of the Regulatory Authority to impose civil penalties) applies to any trustee or manager who has failed to take all such steps as are reasonable to secure compliance with this section.'

154.   Right to guaranteed cash equivalent: supplementary

(1)   In paragraph (a) of section 94(1) of the Pension Schemes Act 1993—

(a) after 'occupational pension scheme' there is inserted 'other than a salary related scheme', and

(b) after 'terminates' there is inserted '(whether before or after 1st January 1986)'.

(2) After that paragraph there is inserted—

'(aa) a member of a salary related occupational pension scheme who has received a statement of entitlement and has made a relevant application within three months beginning with the guarantee date in respect of that statement acquires a right to his guaranteed cash equivalent'.

(3) After that subsection there is inserted—

'(1A) For the purposes of subsection (1)(aa), a person's 'guaranteed cash equivalent' is the amount stated in the statement of entitlement mentioned in that subsection.'

(4) In subsection (2) of that section, after the definition of 'the applicable rules' there is inserted—

'"the guarantee date' has the same meaning as in section 93A(2)'.

(5) After that subsection there is inserted—

'(3) Regulations may provide that, in prescribed circumstances, subsection (1)(aa) does not apply to members of salary related occupational pension schemes or applies to them with prescribed modifications.'

Penalties

155. Breach of regulations under the Pension Schemes Act 1993

(1) For section 168 of the Pension Schemes Act 1993 (penalties for breach of regulations) there is substituted—

'168. Breach of regulations

(1) Regulations under any provision of this Act (other than Chapter II of Part VII) may make such provision as is referred to in subsection (2) or (4) for the contravention of any provision contained in regulations made or having effect as if made under any provision of this Act.

(2) The regulations may provide for the contravention to be an offence under this Act and for the recovery on summary conviction of a fine not exceeding level 5 on the standard scale.

(3) An offence under any provision of the regulations may be charged by reference to any day or longer period of time; and a person may be convicted of a second or subsequent offence under such a provision by reference to any period of time following the preceding conviction of the offence.

(4) The regulations may provide for a person who has contravened the provision to pay to the Regulatory Authority, within a prescribed period, a penalty not exceeding an amount specified in the regulations; and the regulations must specify different amounts in the case of individuals from those specified in other cases and any amount so specified may not exceed the amount for the time being specified in the case of individuals or, as the case may be, others in section 10(2)(a) of the Pensions Act 1995.

(5) Regulations made by virtue of subsection (4) do not affect the amount of any penalty recoverable under that subsection by reason of an act or omission occurring before the regulations are made.

(6)   Where—

(a)   apart from this subsection, a penalty under subsection (4) is recoverable from a body corporate or Scottish partnership by reason of any act or omission of the body or partnership as a trustee of a trust scheme, and

(b)   the act or omission was done with the consent or connivance of, or is attributable to any neglect on the part of, any persons mentioned in subsection (7),

such a penalty is recoverable from each of those persons who consented to or connived in the act or omission or to whose neglect the act or omission was attributable.

(7)   The persons referred to in subsection (6)(b)—

(a)   in relation to a body corporate, are—

(i)   any director, manager, secretary, or other similar officer of the body, or a person purporting to act in any such capacity, and

(ii)   where the affairs of a body corporate are managed by its members, any member in connection with his functions of management, and

(b)   in relation to a Scottish partnership, are the partners.

(8)   Where the Regulatory Authority requires any person to pay a penalty by virtue of subsection (6), they may not also require the body corporate, or Scottish partnership, in question to pay a penalty in respect of the same act or omission.

(9)   A penalty under subsection (4) is recoverable by the Authority and any such penalty recovered by the Authority must be paid to the Secretary of State.

(10)   Where by reason of the contravention of any provision contained in regulations made, or having effect as if made, under this Act—

(a)   a person is convicted of an offence under this Act, or

(b)   a person pays a penalty under subsection (4),

then, in respect of that contravention, he shall not, in a case within paragraph (a), be liable to pay such a penalty or, in a case within paragraph (b), be convicted of such an offence.

(11)   In this section 'contravention' includes failure to comply, and 'Scottish partnership' means a partnership constituted under the law of Scotland.

168A.   Offence in connection with the Registrar

(1)   Any person who knowingly or recklessly provides the Registrar with information which is false or misleading in a material particular is guilty of an offence if the information—

(a)   is provided in purported compliance with a requirement under section 6, or

(b)   is provided otherwise than as mentioned in paragraph (a) above but in circumstances in which the person providing the information intends, or could reasonably be expected to know, that it would be used by the Registrar for the purpose of discharging his functions under this Act.

(2)   Any person guilty of an offence under subsection (1) is liable—

(a)   on summary conviction, to a fine not exceeding the statutory maximum,

(b)   on conviction on indictment, to imprisonment or a fine, or both'.

(2)   In section 186 of that Act (Parliamentary control of orders and regulations), in subsection (3), after paragraph (c) there is inserted 'or

(d)   regulations made by virtue of section 168(2)'.

Pensions Ombudsman

156.   Employment of staff by the Pensions Ombudsman

For section 145(4) of the Pension Schemes Act 1993 (staff of the Pensions Ombudsman), there is substituted—

'(4A)   The Pensions Ombudsman may (with the approval of the Secretary of State as to numbers) appoint such persons to be employees of his as he thinks fit, on such terms and conditions as to remuneration and other matters as the Pensions Ombudsman may with the approval of the Secretary of State determine.

(4B)   The Secretary of State may, on such terms as to payment by the Pensions Ombudsman as the Secretary of State thinks fit, make available to the Pensions Ombudsman such additional staff and such other facilities as he thinks fit.

(4C)   Any function of the Pensions Ombudsman, other than the determination of complaints made and disputes referred under this Part, may be performed by any—

(a)   employee appointed by the Pensions Ombudsman under subsection (4A), or

(b)   member of staff made available to him by the Secretary of State under subsection (4B),

who is authorised for that purpose by the Pensions Ombudsman.'

157.   Jurisdiction of Pensions Ombudsman

(1)   Sections 146 to 151 of the Pension Schemes Act 1993 are amended as shown in subsections (2) to (11).

(2)   In section 146 (investigations concerning the trustees or managers of schemes), for subsections (1) to (4) there is substituted—

'(1)   The Pensions Ombudsman may investigate and determine the following complaints and disputes—

(a)   a complaint made to him by or on behalf of an actual or potential beneficiary of an occupational or personal pension scheme who alleges that he has sustained injustice in consequence of maladministration in connection with any act or omission of a person responsible for the management of the scheme,

(b)   a complaint made to him—

(i)   by or on behalf of a person responsible for the management of an occupational pension scheme who in connection with any act or omission of another person responsible for the management of the scheme, alleges maladministration of the scheme, or

(ii)   by or on behalf of the trustees or managers of an occupational pension scheme who in connection with any act or omission of any trustee or manager of another such scheme, allege maladministration of the other scheme, and in any case falling within sub-paragraph (ii) references in this Part to the scheme to which the complaint relates is to the other scheme referred to in that paragraph,

(c)   any dispute of fact or law which arises in relation to an occupational or personal pension scheme between—

(i)   a person responsible for the management of the scheme, and

(ii)   an actual or potential beneficiary,

and which is referred to him by or on behalf of the actual or potential beneficiary, and

(d)   any dispute of fact or law which arises between the trustees or managers of an occupational pension scheme and—

(i)   another person responsible for the management of the scheme, or

(ii)   any trustee or manager of another such scheme,

and which is referred to him by or on behalf of the person referred to in sub-paragraph (i) or (ii); and in any case falling within sub-paragraph (ii) references in this Part to the scheme to which the reference relates is to the scheme first mentioned in that paragraph.

(2)   Complaints and references made to the Pensions Ombudsman must be made to him in writing.

(3)   For the purposes of this Part, the following persons (subject to subsection (4)) are responsible for the management of an occupational pension scheme—

(a)   the trustees or managers, and

(b)   the employer;

but, in relation to a person falling within one of those paragraphs, references in this Part to another person responsible for the management of the same scheme are to a person falling within the other paragraph.

(3A)   For the purposes of this Part, a person is responsible for the management of a personal pension scheme if he is a trustee or manager of the scheme.

(4)   Regulations may provide that, subject to any prescribed modifications or exceptions, this Part shall apply in the case of an occupational or personal pension scheme in relation to any prescribed person or body of persons where the person or body—

(a)   is not a trustee or manager or employer, but

(b)   is concerned with the financing or administration of, or the provision of benefits under, the scheme,

as if for the purposes of this Part he were a person responsible for the management of the scheme'.

(3)   In subsection (7) of that section, for 'authorised complainants' there is substituted 'actual or potential beneficiaries'.

(4)   In section 147 (death, insolvency etc.), in subsections (1) and (2), for 'authorised complainant' there is substituted 'actual or potential beneficiary' and for 'the authorised complainant's' there is substituted 'his'.

(5)   In subsection (3) of that section, for 'an authorised complainant' there is substituted 'a person by whom, or on whose behalf, a complaint or reference has been made under this Part'.

(6) In section 148 (staying court proceedings), in subsection (5), for paragraphs (a) and (b) there is substituted—

'(a) the person by whom, or on whose behalf, the complaint or reference has been made,

(b) any person responsible for the management of the scheme to which the complaint or reference relates'.

(7) In section 149 (procedure on investigation), in subsection (1)(a), for 'the trustees and managers of the scheme concerned' there is substituted 'any person (other than the person by whom, or on whose behalf, the complaint or reference was made) responsible for the management of the scheme to which the complaint or reference relates.'

(8) In section 150 (investigations: futher provisions), in subsection (1)(a), for any 'trustee or manager of the scheme concerned' there is substituted 'any person responsible for the management of the scheme to which the complaint or reference relates.'

(9) In section 151 (determinations of Pensions Ombudsman), for subsection (1)(a) and (b) there is substituted—

'(a) to the person by whom, or on whose behalf, the complaint or reference was made, and

(b) to any person (if different) responsible for the management of the scheme to which the complaint or reference relates'.

(10) In subsection (2) of that section, for 'the trustees or managers of the scheme concerned' there is substituted 'any person responsible for the management of the scheme to which the complaint or reference relates'.

(11) In subsection (3) of that section, for paragraphs (a) to (c) there is substituted—

'(a) the person by whom, or on whose behalf, the complaint or reference was made,

(b) any person (if different) responsible for the management of the scheme to which the complaint or reference relates, and

(c) any person claiming under a person falling within paragraph (a) or (b)'.

(12) In Part I of Schedule 1 to the Tribunals and Inquiries Act 1992 (tribunals under the direct supervision of the Council on Tribunals), in paragraph 35(e), for 'section 146(2)' there is substituted 'section 146(1)(c) and (d)'.

158. Costs and expenses

In section 149 of the Pension Schemes Act 1993—

(a) after subsection (3)(b) there is inserted 'and

(c) for the payment by the Ombudsman of such travelling and other allowances (including compensation for loss of remunerative time) as the Secretary of State may determine, to—

(i) actual or potential beneficiaries of a scheme to which a complaint or reference relates, or

(ii) persons appearing and being heard on behalf of such actual or potential beneficiaries,

who attend at the request of the Ombudsman any oral hearing held in connection with an investigation into the complaint or dispute.', and

(b)   at the end of subsection (3)(a), 'and' is omitted.

159.   Disclosing information

(1)   In section 149 of the Pension Schemes Act 1993, after subsection (4) there is added—

'(5)   The Pensions Ombudsman may disclose any information which he obtains for the purposes of an investigation under this Part to any person to whom subsection (6) applies, if the Ombudsman considers that the disclosure would enable or assist that person to discharge any of his functions.

(6)   This subsection applies to the following—

(a)   the Regulatory Authority,

(b)   the Pensions Compensation Board,

(c)   the Registrar,

(d)   any department of the Government (including the government of Northern Ireland),

(e)   the Bank of England,

(f)   the Friendly Societies Commission,

(g)   the Building Societies Commission,

(h)   an inspector appointed by the Secretary of State under Part XIV of the Companies Act 1985 or section 94 or 177 of the Financial Services Act 1986,

(j)   an inspector appointed by the Department of Economic Development in Northern Ireland under Part XV of the Companies (Northern Ireland) Order 1986,

(k)   a person authorised under section 106 of the Financial Services Act 1986 to exercise powers conferred by section 105 of that Act,

(l)   a designated agency or transferee body or the competent authority within the meaning of that Act, and

(m)   a recognised self-regulating organisation, recognised professional body, recognised investment exchange or recognised clearing house, within the meaning of that Act.

(7)   The Secretary of State may by order—

(a)   amend subsection (6) by adding any person or removing any person for the time being specified in that subsection, or

(b)   restrict the circumstances in which, or impose conditions subject to which, disclosure may be made to any person for the time being specified in that subsection.'

(2)   In section 151 of that Act, in subsection (7)(a), after 'this section' there is inserted—

'(aa) in disclosing any information under section 149(5)'.

160.   Interest on late payment of benefit

After section 151 of the Pension Schemes Act 1993 there is inserted—

'151A.   Interest on late payment of benefit

Where under this Part the Pensions Ombudsman directs a person responsible for the management of an occupational or personal pension scheme to make any payment in respect of benefit under the scheme which, in his opinion, ought to have been paid earlier, his direction may also require the payment of interest at the prescribed rate'.

Modification and winding up of schemes

161. Repeal of sections 136 to 143 of the Pension Schemes Act 1993

Sections 136 to 141 (modification) and 142 and 143 (winding up) of the Pension Schemes Act 1993 are repealed.

Personal pensions

162. Annual increase in rate of personal pension

(1)   This section applies to any pension provided to give effect to protected rights of a member of a personal pension scheme if—

(a)   there is in force, or was in force at any time after the appointed day, an appropriate scheme certificate issued in accordance with Chapter I of Part III (certification) of the Pension Schemes Act 1993, and

(b)   apart from this section, the annual rate of the pension would not be increased each year by at least the appropriate percentage of that rate.

(2)   Where a pension to which this section applies, or any part of it, is attributable to contributions in respect of employment carried on on or after the appointed day—

(a)   the annual rate of the pension, or

(b)   if only part of the pension is attributable to contributions in respect of employment carried on on or after the appointed day, so much of the annual rate as is attributable to that part,

must be increased annually by at least the appropriate percentage.

163. Section 162: supplementary

(1)   The first increase required by section 162 in the rate of a pension must take effect not later than the first anniversary of the date on which the pension is first paid; and subsequent increases must take effect at intervals of not more than twelve months.

(2)   Where the first such increase is to take effect on a date when the pension has been in payment for a period of less than 12 months, the increase must be of an amount at least equal to one twelfth of the amount of the increase so required (apart from this subsection) for each complete month in that period.

(3)   In section 162 and this section—

'annual rate', in relation to a pension, means the annual rate of the pension, as previously increased under the rules of the scheme or under section 162,

'the appointed day' means the day appointed under section 180 for the commencement of section 162,

'appropriate percentage', in relation to an increase in the whole or part of the annual rate of a pension, means the revaluation percentage for the revaluation period the reference period for which ends with the last preceding 30th September before the increase is made (expressions used in this definition having the same meaning as in paragraph 2 of Schedule 3 to the Pension Schemes Act 1993 (methods of revaluing accrued pension benefits)),

'pension', in relation to a scheme, means any pension in payment under the scheme and includes an annuity,

'protected rights' has the meaning given by section 10 of the Pension Schemes Act 1993 (money purchase benefits).

164. Power to reject notice choosing appropriate personal pension scheme

In section 44 of the Pension Schemes Act 1993 (earner's chosen scheme)—

    (a) in subsection (1), after paragraph (b) there is inserted—

'then, unless the Secretary of State rejects the notice on either or both of the grounds mentioned in subsection (1A)', and

    (b) after that subsection there is inserted—

'(1A) The grounds referred to in subsection (1) are that the Secretary of State is of the opinion—

    (a) that section 31(5) is not being complied with in respect of any members of the scheme,

    (b) that, having regard to any other provisions of sections 26 to 32 and 43 to 45, it is inexpedient to allow the scheme to be the chosen scheme of any further earners'.

Levy

165. Levy

For section 175 of the Pension Schemes Act 1993 (levies towards meeting certain costs and grants) there is substituted—

'175. Levies towards certain expenditure

    (1) For the purpose of meeting expenditure—

    (a) under section 6,

    (b) under Part X and section 174, or

    (c) of the Regulatory Authority (including the establishment of the authority and, if the authority are appointed as Registrar under section 6 of this Act, their expenditure as Registrar),

regulations may make provision for imposing levies in respect of prescribed occupational or prescribed personal pension schemes.

    (2) Any levy imposed under subsection (1) is payable to the Secretary of State by or on behalf of—

    (a) the administrators of any prescribed public service pension scheme,

    (b) the trustees or managers of any other prescribed occupational or prescribed personal pension scheme, or

    (c) any other prescribed person,

at prescribed rates and at prescribed times.

    (3) Regulations made by virtue of subsection (1)—

    (a) in determining the amount of any levy in respect of the Regulatory Authority, must take account (among other things) of any amounts paid to the Secretary of State under section 168(4) of this Act or section 10 of the Pensions Act 1995, and

    (b) in determining the amount of expenditure in respect of which any levy is to be imposed, may take one year with another and, accordingly, may have regard to expenditure estimated to be incurred in current or future periods and to actual expenditure incurred in previous periods (including periods ending before the coming into force of this subsection).

    (4) Regulations may make provision for imposing a levy in respect of prescribed occupational pension schemes for the purpose of meeting expenditure of the Pensions Compensation Board (including the establishment of the Board).

(5) Any levy imposed under subsection (4) is payable to the Board by or on behalf of—

(a) the trustees of any prescribed occupational pension scheme, or

(b) any other prescribed person,

at prescribed times and at a rate, not exceeding the prescribed rate, determined by the Board.

(6) In determining the amount of expenditure in respect of which any levy under subsection (4) is to be imposed, the Board, and regulations made by virtue of subsection (5), may take one year with another and, accordingly, may have regard to expenditure estimated to be incurred in current or future periods and to actual expenditure incurred in previous periods (including periods ending before the coming into force of this subsection).

(7) Notice of the rates determined by the Board under subsection (5) must be given to prescribed persons in the prescribed manner.

(8) An amount payable by a person on account of a levy imposed under this section shall be a debt due from him to the appropriate person, that is—

(a) if the levy is imposed under subsection (1), the Secretary of State, and

(b) if the levy is imposed under subsection (4), the Board,

and an amount so payable shall be recoverable by the appropriate person accordingly or, if the appropriate person so determines, be recoverable by the Registrar on behalf of the appropriate person.

(9) Without prejudice to the generality of subsections (1) and (4), regulations under this section may include provision relating to—

(a) the collection and recovery of amounts payable by way of levy under this section, or

(b) the circumstances in which any such amount may be waived.'

Pensions on divorce, etc.

166. Pensions on divorce etc.

(1) In the Matrimonial Causes Act 1973, after section 25A there is inserted——

'25B. Pensions

(1) The matters to which the court is to have regard under section 25(2) above include—

(a) in the case of paragraph (a), any benefits under a pension scheme which a party to the marriage has or is likely to have, and

(b) in the case of paragraph (h), any benefits under a pension scheme which, by reason of the dissolution or annulment of the marriage, a party to the marriage will lose the chance of acquiring,

and, accordingly, in relation to benefits under a pension scheme, section 25(2)(a) above shall have effect as if 'in the foreseeable future' were omitted.

(2) In any proceedings for a financial provision order under section 23 above in a case where a party to the marriage has, or is likely to have, any benefit under a pension scheme, the court shall, in addition to considering any other matter which it is required to consider apart from this subsection, consider—

(a) whether, having regard to any matter to which it is required to have regard in the proceedings by virtue of subsection (1) above, such an order (whether deferred or not) should be made, and

(b)   where the court determines to make such an order, how the terms of the order should be affected, having regard to any such matter.

(3)   The following provisions apply where, having regard to any benefits under a pension scheme, the court determines to make an order under section 23 above.

(4)   To the extent to which the order is made having regard to any benefits under a pension scheme, the order may require the trustees or managers of the pension scheme in question, if at any time any payment in respect of any benefits under the scheme becomes due to the party with pension rights, to make a payment for the benefit of the other party.

(5)   The amount of any payment which, by virtue of subsection (4) above, the trustees or managers are required to make under the order at any time shall not exceed the amount of the payment which is due at that time to the party with pension rights.

(6)   Any such payment by the trustees or managers—

(a)   shall discharge so much of the trustees or managers liability to the party with pension rights as corresponds to the amount of the payment, and

(b)   shall be treated for all purposes as a payment made by the party with pension rights in or towards the discharge of his liability under the order.

(7)   Where the party with pension rights may require any benefits which he has or is likely to have under the scheme to be commuted, the order may require him to commute the whole or part of those benefits; and this section applies to the payment of any amount commuted in pursuance of the order as it applies to other payments in respect of benefits under the scheme.

25C.   Pensions: lump sums

(1)   The power of the court under section 23 above to order a party to a marriage to pay a lump sum to the other party includes, where the benefits which the party with pension rights has or is likely to have under a pension scheme include any lump sum payable in respect of his death, power to make any of the following provision by the order.

(2)   The court may—

(a)   if the trustees or managers of the pension scheme in question have power to determine the person to whom the sum, or any part of it, is to be paid, require them to pay the whole or part of that sum, when it becomes due, to the other party,

(b)   if the party with pension rights has power to nominate the person to whom the sum, or any part of it, is to be paid, require the party with pension rights to nominate the other party in respect of the whole or part of that sum,

(c)   in any other case, require the trustees or managers of the pension scheme in question to pay the whole or part of that sum, when it becomes due, for the benefit of the other party instead of to the person to whom, apart from the order, it would be paid.

(3)   Any payment by the trustees or managers under an order made under section 23 above by virtue of this section shall discharge so much of the trustees, or managers, liability in respect of the party with pension rights as corresponds to the amount of the payment.

25D. Pensions: supplementary

(1) Where—

(a) an order made under section 23 above by virtue of section 25B or 25C above imposes any requirement on the trustees or managers of a pension scheme ('the first scheme') and the party with pension rights acquires transfer credits under another pension scheme ('the new scheme') which are derived (directly or indirectly) from a transfer from the first scheme of all his accrued rights under that scheme (including transfer credits allowed by that scheme), and

(b) the trustees or managers of the new scheme have been given notice in accordance with regulations,

the order shall have effect as if it has been made instead in respect of the trustees or managers of the new scheme; and in this subsection 'transfer credits' has the same meaning as in the Pension Schemes Act 1993.

(2) Regulations may—

(a) in relation to any provision of sections 25B or 25C above which authorises the court making an order under section 23 above to require the trustees or managers of a pension scheme to make a payment for the benefit of the other party, make provision as to the person to whom, and the terms on which, the payment is to be made,

(b) require notices to be given in respect of changes of circumstances relevant to such orders which include provision made by virtue of sections 25B and 25C above,

(c) make provision for the trustees or managers of any pension scheme to provide, for the purposes of orders under section 23 above, information as to the value of any benefits under the scheme,

(d) make provision for the recovery of the administrative expenses of—

(i) complying with such orders, so far as they include provision made by virtue of sections 25B and 25C above, and

(ii) providing such information,

from the party with pension rights or the other party,

(e) make provision for the value of any benefits under a pension scheme to be calculated and verified, for the purposes of orders under section 23 above, in a prescribed manner,

and regulations made by virtue of paragraph (e) above may provide for that value to be calculated and verified in accordance with guidance which is prepared and from time to time revised by a prescribed person and approved by the Secretary of State.

(3) In this section and sections 25B and 25C above—

(a) references to a pension scheme include—

(i) a retirement annuity contract, or

(ii) an annuity, or insurance policy, purchased or transferred for the purpose of giving effect to rights under a pension scheme,

(b) in relation to such a contract or annuity, references to the trustees or managers shall be read as references to the provider of the annuity,

(c) in relation to such a policy, references to the trustees or managers shall be read as references to the insurer,

and in section 25B(1) and (2) above, references to benefits under a pension scheme include any benefits by way of pension, whether under a pension scheme or not.

(4)   In this section and sections 25B and 25C above—
    'the party with pension rights' means the party to the marriage who has or is likely to have benefits under a pension scheme and 'the other party' means the other party to the marriage,
    'pension scheme' means an occupational pension scheme or a personal pension scheme (applying the definitions in section 1 of the Pension Schemes Act 1993, but as if the reference to employed earners in the definition of 'personal pension scheme' were to any earners),
    'prescribed' means prescribed by regulations, and
    'regulations' means regulations made by the Lord Chancellor;
    and the power to make regulations under this section shall be exercisable by statutory instrument, which shall be subject to annulment in pursuance of a resolution of either House of Parliament.'

(2)   In section 25(2)(h) of that Act (loss of chance to acquire benefits), '(for example, a pension)' is omitted.

(3)   In section 31 of that Act (variation, discharge, etc. of orders)—
    (a)   in subsection (2), after paragraph (d) there is inserted—
        '(dd)   any deferred order made by virtue of section 23(1)(c) (lump sums) which includes provision made by virtue of—
            (i)   section 25B(4), or
            (ii)   section 25C,
    (provision in respect of pension rights)', and
    (b)   after subsection (2A) there is inserted—
        '(2B)   Where the court has made an order referred to in subsection (2)(dd)(ii) above, this section shall cease to apply to the order on the death of either of the parties to the marriage'.

(4)   Nothing in the provisions mentioned in subsection (5) applies to a court exercising its powers under section 23 of the Matrimonial Causes Act 1973 (financial provision in connection with divorce proceedings, etc.) in respect of any benefits under a pension scheme (within the meaning of section 25B(1) of the Matrimonial Causes Act 1973) which a party to the marriage has or is likely to have.

(5)   The provisions referred to in subsection (4) are—
    (a)   section 203(1) and (2) of the Army Act 1955, 203(1) and (2) of the Air Force Act 1955, 128G(1) and (2) of the Naval Discipline Act 1957 or 159(4) and (4A) of the Pension Schemes Act 1993 (which prevent assignment, or orders being made restraining a person from receiving anything which he is prevented from assigning),
    (b)   section 91 of this Act,
    (c)   any provision of any enactment (whether passed or made before or after this Act is passed) corresponding to any of the enactments mentioned in paragraphs (a) and (b), and
    (d)   any provision of the scheme in question corresponding to any of those enactments.

(6)   Subsections (3) to (7) of section 25B, and section 25C of the Matrimonial Causes Act 1973, as inserted by this section, do not affect the powers of the court under section 31 of that Act (variation, discharge, etc.) in relation to any order made before the commencement of this section.

167. Pensions on divorce, etc.: Scotland

(1) In section 8(1) (orders for financial provision) of the Family Law (Scotland) Act 1985 ('the 1985 Act'), after paragraph (b) there is inserted—

'(ba)   an order under section 12A(2) or (3) of this Act;'.

(2) In section 10 of the 1985 Act (sharing of value of matrimonial property)—

(a) in subsection (5)—

(i)   after 'party' there is inserted '(a)'; and

(ii)   for 'or occupational pension scheme or similar arrangement' there is substituted—

'or similar arrangement; and

(b) in any benefits under a pension scheme which either party has or may have (including such benefits payable in respect of the death of either party),

which is'; and

(b) after subsection (7) there is inserted—

'(8)   The Secretary of State may by regulations make provision—

(a) for the value of any benefits under a pension scheme to be calculated and verified, for the purposes of this Act, in a prescribed manner;

(b) for the trustees or managers of any pension scheme to provide, for the purposes of this Act, information as to that value, and for the recovery of the administrative expenses of providing such information from either party,

and regulations made by virtue of paragraph (a) above may provide for that value to be calculated and verified in accordance with guidance which is prepared and from time to time revised by a prescribed body and approved by the Secretary of State.

(9)   Regulations under subsection (8) above shall be made by statutory instrument which shall be subject to annulment in pursuance of a resolution of either House of Parliament.

(10)   In this section—

'benefits under a pension scheme' includes any benefits by way of pension, whether under a pension scheme or not;

'pension scheme' means—

(a) an occupational pension scheme or a personal pension scheme (applying the definitions in section 1 of the Pension Schemes Act 1993, but as if the reference to employed earners in the definition of 'personal pension scheme' were to any earners);

(b) a retirement annuity contract; or

(c) an annuity, or insurance policy, purchased or transferred for the purpose of giving effect to rights under a pension scheme falling within paragraph (a) above; and

'prescribed' means prescribed by regulations.

(11)   In this section, references to the trustees or managers of a pension scheme—

(a) in relation to a contract or annuity referred to in paragraph (b) or (c) of the definition of 'pension scheme' in subsection (10) above, shall be read as references to the provider of the annuity;

(b) in relation to an insurance policy referred to in paragraph (c) of that definition, shall be read as a reference to the insurer.'.

(3) After section 12 of the 1985 Act there is inserted—

'12A. Orders for payment of capital sum: pensions lump sums

(1) This section applies where the court makes an order under section 8(2) of this Act for payment of a capital sum (a 'capital sum order') by a party to the marriage ('the liable party') in circumstances where—

(a) the matrimonial property within the meaning of section 10 of this Act includes any rights or interests in benefits under a pension scheme which the liable party has or may have (whether such benefits are payable to him or in respect of his death); and

(b) those benefits include a lump sum payable to him or in respect of his death.

(2) Where the benefits referred to in subsection (1) above include a lump sum payable to the liable party, the court, on making the capital sum order, may make an order requiring the trustees or managers of the pension scheme in question to pay the whole or part of that sum, when it becomes due, to the other party to the marriage ('the other party').

(3) Where the benefits referred to in subsection (1) above include a lump sum payable in respect of the death of the liable party, the court, on making the capital sum order, may make an order—

(a) if the trustees or managers of the pension scheme in question have power to determine the person to whom the sum, or any part of it, is to be paid, requiring them to pay the whole or part of that sum, when it becomes due, to the other party;

(b) if the liable party has power to nominate the person to whom the sum, or any part of it, is to be paid, requiring the liable party to nominate the other party in respect of the whole or part of that sum;

(c) in any other case, requiring the trustees or managers of the pension scheme in question to pay the whole or part of that sum, when it becomes due, to the other party instead of to the person to whom, apart from the order, it would be paid.

(4) Any payment by the trustees or managers under an order under subsection (2) or (3) above—

(a) shall discharge so much of the trustees' or managers' liability to or in respect of the liable party as corresponds to the amount of the payment; and

(b) shall be treated for all purposes as a payment made by the liable party in or towards the discharge of his liability under the capital sum order.

(5) Where the liability of the liable party under the capital sum order has been discharged in whole or in part, other than by a payment by the trustees or managers under an order under subsection (2) or (3) above, the court may, on an application by any person having an interest, recall any order under either of those subsections or vary the amount specified in such an order, as appears to the court appropriate in the circumstances.

(6) Where—

(a) an order under subsection (2) or (3) above imposes any requirement on the trustees or managers of a pension scheme ('the first scheme') and the liable party acquires transfer credits under another scheme ('the new scheme') which are derived (directly or indirectly) from a transfer from the first scheme of all his accrued rights under that scheme; and

    (b) the trustees or managers of the new scheme have been given notice in accordance with regulations under subsection (8) below,
the order shall have effect as if it had been made instead in respect of the trustees or managers of the new scheme; and in this subsection 'transfer credits' has the same meaning as in the Pension Schemes Act 1993.

    (7) Without prejudice to subsection (6) above, the court may, on an application by any person having an interest, vary an order under subsection (2) or (3) above by substituting for the trustees or managers specified in the order the trustees or managers of any other pension scheme under which any lump sum referred to in subsection (1) above is payable to the liable party or in respect of his death.

    (8) The Secretary of State may by regulations—

    (a) require notices to be given in respect of changes of circumstances relevant to orders under subsection (2) or (3) above;

    (b) make provision for the recovery of the administrative expenses of complying with such orders from the liable party or the other party.

    (9) Regulations under subsection (8) above shall be made by statutory instrument which shall be subject to annulment in pursuance of a resolution of either House of Parliament.

    (10) Subsection (10) (other than the definition of 'benefits under a pension scheme') and subsection (11) of section 10 of this Act shall apply for the purposes of this section as those subsections apply for the purposes of that section.'

  (4) Nothing in the provisions mentioned in section 166(5) above applies to a court exercising its powers under section 8 (orders for financial provision on divorce, etc.) or 12A (orders for payment of capital sum: pensions lump sums) of the 1985 Act in respect of any benefits under a pension scheme which fall within subsection (5)(b) of section 10 of that Act ('pension scheme' having the meaning given in subsection (10) of that section).

168. War pensions for widows: effect of remarriage

  (1) In determining whether a pension is payable to a person as a widow under any of the enactments mentioned in subsection (3) in respect of any period beginning on or after the commencement of this section, no account may be taken of the fact that the widow has married another if, before the beginning of that period, the marriage has been terminated or the parties have been judicially separated.

  (2) For the purposes of this section—

    (a) the reference to the termination of a marriage is to the termination of the marriage by death, dissolution or annulment, and

    (b) the reference to judicial separation includes any legal separation obtained in a country or territory outside the British Islands and recognised in the United Kingdom;
and for those purposes a divorce, annulment or legal separation obtained in a country or territory outside the British Islands must, if the Secretary of State so determines, be treated as recognised in the United Kingdom even though no declaration as to its validity has been made by any court in the United Kingdom.

(3)   The enactments referred to in subsection (1) are—

(a)   The Naval, Military and Air Forces Etc. (Disablement and Death) Service Pensions Order 1983, and any order re-enacting the provisions of that order,

(b)   The Personal Injuries (Civilians) Scheme 1983, and any subsequent scheme made under the Personal Injuries (Emergency Provisions) Act 1939,

(c)   any scheme made under the Pensions (Navy, Army, Air Force and Mercantile Marine) Act 1939 or the Polish Resettlement Act 1947 applying the provisions of any such order as is referred to in paragraph (a),

(d)   the order made under section 1(5) of the Ulster Defence Regiment Act 1969 concerning pensions and other grants in respect of disablement or death due to service in the Ulster Defence Regiment.

169.   Extensions of Pensions Appeal Tribunals Act 1943

(1)   The Pensions Appeal Tribunals Act 1943 is amended as follows.

(2)   In section 1 (appeals against rejection of war pension claims made in respect of members of armed forces)—

(a)   in subsection (1), after 'administered by the Minister' there is inserted 'or under a scheme made under section 1 of the Polish Resettlement Act 1947', and

(b)   in subsections (3) and (3A), for 'or Order of His Majesty' there is substituted ', Order of Her Majesty or scheme'.

(3)   In section 7 (application of Act to past decisions and assessments)—

(a)   in subsection (2), at the beginning there is inserted 'Subject to subsection (2A) of this section,', and

(b)   after that subsection, there is inserted—

'(2A)   Subsection (2) of this section shall not apply in relation to any decision given by the Minister before the passing of this Act which corresponds, apart from any difference of the kind referred to in that subsection, with such a decision as is referred to in section 1 of this Act in respect of claims made under the scheme referred to in that section.'

(4)   In section 10 (power to modify sections 1 to 4 by Order in Council), in subsections (1) and (2), for 'or Order of His Majesty' there is substituted ', Order of Her Majesty or scheme'.

(5)   In section 12 (interpretation), in the definition of 'relevant service'—

(a)   for 'or Order of His Majesty' there is substituted ', Order of Her Majesty or scheme', and

(b)   for 'or Order' there is substituted ', Order or scheme'.

(6)   In the Schedule (constitution, jurisdiction and procedure of Pensions Appeal Tribunals), in paragraph 3(2), after paragraph (b) there is inserted—

'(ba)   if the claim was made under the scheme referred to in section 1 of this Act in respect of a person who is treated under the scheme as an officer, shall be a retired or demobilised officer of Her Majesty's naval, military or air forces;

(bb)   if the claim was made under the aforesaid scheme in respect of a person who is treated under the scheme as a soldier, shall be a discharged or demobilised member of any of the said forces who was not at the time of his discharge or demobilisation an officer;'.

Official and public service pensions

170. Pensions for dependants of the Prime Minister etc.

(1) Section 27 of the Parliamentary and Other Pensions Act 1972 (application of certain provisions with modifications in relation to the Prime Minister and the Speaker) is amended as follows.

(2) For subsection (1)(b) (amount by reference to which dependant's pension calculated) there is substituted—

'(b) for the purposes of that scheme, that person's basic or prospective pension were of an amount equal to his section 26 entitlement'.

(3) After subsection (1) there is inserted—

'(1A) For the purposes of subsection (1)(b), the amount of a person's section 26 entitlement—

(a) where at the time of his death he was entitled to receive a pension under section 26 of this Act (whether or not, by virtue of subsection (2) of that section, the pension was payable), is the annual amount of the pension to which he was entitled under that section at the time when he ceased to hold that office or (if later) on 28th February 1991, and

(b) where at the time of his death he held office as Prime Minister and First Lord of the Treasury or as Speaker of the House of Commons, is the annual amount of the pension to which he would have been entitled under that section if he had ceased to hold office immediately before his death,

but in either case, any provision which deems such a pension to have begun on a day earlier than the day referred to in section 8(2) of the Pensions (Increase) Act 1971 shall be disregarded.'

(4) For the purposes of the Pensions (Increase) Act 1971, a pension payable under section 27 of the Parliamentary and Other Pensions Act 1972 in respect of a person who ceased to hold the office of Prime Minister and First Lord of the Treasury or Speaker of the House of Commons before 28th February 1991 shall be deemed to have begun on that date.

(5) Where a person—

(a) is entitled to receive a pension under that section by reason of the death of a person who, at any time before the commencement of this section, held the office of Prime Minister and First Lord of the Treasury or Speaker of the House of Commons, and

(b) the amount of that pension determined in accordance with subsection (6) is greater than the amount of the pension determined in accordance with subsections (1) to (4),

it shall be determined in accordance with subsection (6).

(6) The annual amount of the pension shall be determined as if—

(a) subsections (1) to (3) had not been enacted, and

(b) for the purposes of the Pensions (Increase) Act 1971, the pension had begun on the day following the date of the death.

(7) This section has effect, and shall be treated as having had effect, in relation to any person who becomes entitled to a pension payable under section 27 of the Parliamentary and Other Pensions Act 1972 on or after 15th December 1994.

171. Equal treatment in relation to official pensions

(1)   Section 3 of the Pensions (Increase) Act 1971 (qualifying conditions for pensions increase) is amended as follows.

(2)   In subsection (2)(c), 'is a woman who' is omitted.

(3)   In subsection (10)—

(a)   for 'woman is in receipt of a pension' there is substituted 'person is in receipt of a pension the whole or any part of', and

(b)   for 'woman and that pension' there is substituted 'person and that pension or part'.

(4)   In subsection (11)—

(a)   for 'woman's' there is substituted 'person's', and

(b)   for 'woman' there is substituted 'person',

and accordingly for 'she' there is substituted 'he'.

(5)   This section shall have effect, and shall be deemed to have had effect, in relation to pensions commencing after 17th May 1990, and in relation to so much of any such pension as is referable to service on or after that date.

172. Information about public service schemes

(1)   In prescribed circumstances, the Secretary of State may provide information to any prescribed person in connection with the following questions—

(a)   whether an individual who during any period—

(i)   has been eligible to be an active member of an occupational pension scheme under the Superannuation Act 1972, but

(ii)   has instead made contributions to a personal pension scheme,

has suffered loss as a result of a contravention which is actionable under section 62 of the Financial Services Act 1986 (actions for damages in respect of contravention of rules etc. made under the Act), and

(b)   if so, what payment would need to be made to the occupational scheme in respect of the individual to restore the position to what it would have been if the individual had been an active member of the occupational scheme throughout the period in question,

and may impose on that person reasonable fees in respect of administrative expenses incurred in providing that information.

(2)   Where—

(a)   such an individual as is mentioned in subsection (1) is admitted or readmitted as an active member of an occupational pension scheme under the Superannuation Act 1972, or

(b)   a payment is made to the Secretary of State in respect of such an individual for the purpose mentioned in paragraph (b) of that subsection,

the Secretary of State may impose on any prescribed person reasonable fees in respect of administrative expenses incurred in connection with the admission, readmission or payment.

(3)   In the case of an occupational pension scheme under section 1 of the Superannuation Act 1972 (superannuation of civil servants), the references in subsections (1) and (2) to the Secretary of State shall be read as references to the Minister for the Civil Service, or such person as may be prescribed.

(4)   In the case of an occupational pension scheme under section 7 of the Superannuation Act 1972 (superannuation of persons employed in local

government etc.), the references in subsections (1) and (2) to the Secretary of State shall be read as references to a prescribed person.

(5) In this section—

'prescribed' means—

(i) in the case of a scheme made under section 1 of the Superannuation Act 1972, prescribed by a scheme made by the Minister for the Civil Service, or

(ii) in any other case, prescribed by regulations made by the Secretary of State, and

'active member', in relation to an occupational pension scheme, has the same meaning as in Part I.

General minor and consequential amendments

173. General minor and consequential amendments

Schedule 6, which makes general minor and consequential amendments, shall have effect.

Subordinate legislation etc.

174. Orders and regulations (general provisions)

(1) Any power under this Act to make regulations or orders (except a power of the court or the Authority to make orders) shall be exercisable by statutory instrument.

(2) Except in so far as this Act provides otherwise, any power conferred by it to make regulations or an order may be exercised—

(a) either in relation to all cases to which the power extends, or in relation to those cases subject to specified exceptions, or in relation to any specified cases or classes of case,

(b) so as to make, as respects the cases in relation to which it is exercised—

(i) the full provision to which the power extends or any less provision (whether by way of exception or otherwise),

(ii) the same provision for all cases in relation to which the power is exercised, or different provision for different cases or different classes of case or different provision as respects same case or class of case for different purposes of this Act, or

(iii) any such provision either unconditionally or subject to any specified condition,

and where such a power is expressed to be exercisable for alternative purposes it may be exercised in relation to the same case for any or all of those purposes; and any power to make regulations or an order for the purposes of any one provision of this Act shall be without prejudice to any power to make regulations or an order for the purposes of any other provision.

(3) Any power conferred by this Act to make regulations or an order includes power to make such incidental, supplementary, consequential or transitional provision as appears to the authority making the regulations or order to be expedient for the purposes of the regulations or order.

(4) Regulations made by the Secretary of State may, for the purposes of or in connection with the coming into force of any provisions of this Act, make any such

provision as could be made, by virtue of subsection (4)(a) of section 180, by an order bringing those provisions into force.

175. Parliamentary control of orders and regulations

(1) Subject to subsections (2) and (3), a statutory instrument which contains any regulations or order made under this Act shall be subject to annulment in pursuance of a resolution of either House of Parliament.

(2) A statutory instrument which contains any regulations made by virtue of—

    (a) section 64(4),

    (b) section 78(6),

    (c) section 116(1), or

    (d) section 149

or order under section 10(2) must not be made unless a draft of the instrument has been laid before and approved by a resolution of each House of Parliament.

(3) Subsection (1) does not apply to an order under section 180.

General

176. Interpretation

In this Act—

    'enactment' includes an enactment comprised in subordinate legislation (within the meaning of the Interpretation Act 1978),

    'occupational pension scheme' and 'personal pension scheme' have the meaning given by section 1 of the Pension Schemes Act 1993,

and the definition of 'enactment' shall apply for the purposes of section 114 as if 'Act' in section 21(1) of the Interpretation Act 1978 included any enactment.

177. Repeals

The enactments shown in Schedule 7 are repealed to the extent specified in the third column.

178. Extent

(1) Subject to the following provisions, this Act does not extend to Northern Ireland.

(2) Sections 1, 2, 21(3), 68(5), 78, 79, 80(4), 150, 168, 170(4) to (7), 172 and 179 extend to Northern Ireland.

(3) The amendment by this Act of an enactment which extends to Northern Ireland extends also to Northern Ireland.

179. Northern Ireland

An Order in Council under paragraph 1(1)(b) of Schedule 1 to the Northern Ireland Act 1974 (legislation for Northern Ireland in the interim period) which states that it is made only for purposes corresponding to those of this Act—

    (a) shall not be subject to paragraph 1(4) and (5) of that Schedule (affirmative resolution of both Houses of Parliament), but

    (b) shall be subject to annulment in pursuance of a resolution of either House.

180. Commencement

(1) Subject to the following provisions, this Act shall come into force on such day as the Secretary of State may by order made by statutory instrument appoint and different days may be appointed for different purposes.

(2) The following provisions shall come into force on the day this Act is passed—

    (a) subject to the provisions of Schedule 4, Part 11,

    (b) section 168,

    (c) sections 170 and 171,

    (d) section 179,

and any repeal in Schedule 7 for which there is a note shall come into force in accordance with that note.

(3) Section 166 shall come into force on such day as the Lord Chancellor may by order made by statutory instrument appoint and different days may be appointed for different purposes.

(4) Without prejudice to section 174(3), the power to make an order under this section includes power—

    (a) to make transitional adaptations or modifications—

        (i) of the provisions brought into force by the order, or

        (ii) in connection with those provisions, of any provisions of this Act, or the Pension Schemes Act 1993, then in force, or

    (b) to save the effect of any of the repealed provisions of that Act, or those provisions as adapted or modified by the order,

as it appears to the Secretary of State expedient, including different adaptations or modifications for different periods.

181. Short title

This Act may be cited as the Pensions Act 1995.

SCHEDULES

Section 1

SCHEDULE 1
OCCUPATIONAL PENSIONS REGULATORY AUTHORITY

General

1. The Authority shall not be regarded as the servant or agent of the Crown, or as enjoying any status, privilege or immunity of the Crown; and its property shall not be regarded as property of, or property held on behalf of, the Crown.

2. The Authority may do anything (except borrow money) which is calculated to facilitate the discharge of their functions, or is incidental or conducive to their discharge.

Tenure of members

3. Subject to the following provisions, a person shall hold and vacate office as chairman or other member of the Authority in accordance with the terms of the instrument appointing him.

4. If a member of the Authority becomes or ceases to be chairman, the Secretary of State may vary the terms of the instrument appointing him to be a member so as to alter the date on which he is to vacate office.

5. A person may at any time resign office as chairman or other member of the Authority by giving written notice of his resignation signed by him to the Secretary of State.

6.—(1) The chairman of the Authority may at any time be removed from office by notice in writing given to him by the Secretary of State.

(2) If a person ceases to be chairman by virtue of sub-paragraph (1), he shall cease to be a member of the Authority.

7.—(1) If the Secretary of State is satisfied that a member of the Authority other than the chairman—

(a) has been absent from meetings of the Authority for a period longer than three consecutive months without the Authority's permission,

(b) has become bankrupt or made an arrangement with his creditors, or

(c) is unable or unfit to discharge the functions of a member,

the Secretary of State may remove that member by notice in writing.

(2) In the application of sub-paragraph (1) to Scotland—

(a) the reference to a member's having become bankrupt shall be read as a reference to sequestration of the member's estate having been awarded, and

(b) the reference to a member having made an arrangement with his creditors shall be read as a reference to his having made a trust deed for the behoof of his creditors or a composition contract.

Expenses, remuneration, etc.

8.—(1) The Secretary of State may pay the Authority such sums as he thinks fit towards their expenses.

(2) The Authority may pay, or make provision for paying, to or in respect of the chairman or any other member such salaries or other remuneration, and such pensions, allowances, fees, expenses or gratuities, as the Secretary of State may determine.

(3) Where a person ceases to be a member of the Authority otherwise than on the expiration of his term of office and it appears to the Secretary of State that there are circumstances which make it right for that person to receive compensation, the Authority may make to that person a payment of such amount as the Secretary of State may determine.

Parliamentary disqualification

9. In Part II of Schedule 1 to the House of Commons Disqualification Act 1975, and in Part II of Schedule 1 to the Northern Ireland Assembly Disqualification Act 1975 (bodies all members of which are disqualified), there is inserted at the appropriate place—

'The Occupational Pensions Regulatory Authority'.

The Ombudsman

10. In the Parliamentary Commissioner Act 1967, in Schedule 2 (departments and authorities subject to investigation), there is inserted at the appropriate place—

'The Occupational Pensions Regulatory Authority'.

Staff

11.—(1) There shall be a chief executive and, with the approval of the Secretary of State as to numbers, other employees of the Authority.

(2) The first chief executive shall be appointed by the Secretary of State on such terms and conditions as to remuneration and other matters as the Secretary of State may determine.

(3)   Any reappointment of the first chief executive, and the appointment of the second and any subsequent chief executive, shall be made by the Authority, with the approval of the Secretary of State, on such terms and conditions as to remuneration and other matters as the Authority may, with the approval of the Secretary of State, determine.

(4)   The other employees shall be appointed by the Authority on such terms and conditions as to remuneration and other matters as the Authority may, with the approval of the Secretary of State, determine.

(5)   The Secretary of State may, on such terms as to payment by the Authority as he thinks fit, make available to the Authority such additional staff and such other facilities as he thinks fit.

The Superannuation Act 1972 (c. 11)

12.—(1)   Employment with the Authority shall be included among the kinds of employment to which a scheme under section 1 of the Superannuation Act 1972 can apply, and accordingly in Schedule 1 to that Act (in which those kinds of employment are listed), at the end of the list of Other Bodies there is inserted—

'The Occupational Pensions Regulatory Authority'

(2)   The Authority must pay to the Treasury, at such times as the Treasury may direct, such sums as the Treasury may determine in respect of the increase attributable to this paragraph in the sums payable out of money provided by Parliament under the Superannuation Act 1972.

Proceedings

13.—(1)   The Secretary of State may make regulations generally as to the procedure to be followed by the Authority in the exercise of their functions and the manner in which their functions are to be exercised.

(2)   Such regulations may in particular make provision—

(a)   as to the hearing of parties, the taking of evidence and the circumstances (if any) in which a document of any prescribed description is to be treated, for the purposes of any proceedings before the Authority, as evidence, or conclusive evidence, of any prescribed matter,

(b)   as to the time to be allowed for making any application or renewed application to the Authority (whether for an order or determination of the Authority or for the review of a determination, or otherwise),

(c)   as to the manner in which parties to any proceedings before the Authority may or are to be represented for the purposes of the proceedings.

(3)   Regulations under sub-paragraph (1) may provide for enabling the Authority to summon persons—

(a)   to attend before them and give evidence (including evidence on oath) for any purposes of proceedings in connection with an occupational pension scheme,

(b)   to produce any documents required by the Authority for those purposes, or

(c)   to furnish any information which the Authority may require relating to any such scheme which is the subject matter of proceedings pending before them.

14.—(1)   The Authority may establish a committee for any purpose.

(2)   The quorum of the Authority shall be such as they may determine, and the Authority may regulate their own procedure and that of any of their committees.

(3) The Authority may authorise the chairman or any other member, the chief executive or any committee established by the Authority to exercise such of the Authority's functions as they may determine.

(4) This paragraph is subject to regulations made by virtue of paragraph 13 and to section 96(5).

Validity

15. The validity of any proceedings of the Authority, or of any of their committees, shall not be affected by any vacancy among the members or by any defect in the appointment of any member.

Accounts

16.—(1) It shall be the duty of the Authority—

(a) to keep proper accounts and proper records in relation to the accounts,

(b) to prepare in respect of each financial year of the Authority a statement of accounts, and

(c) to send copies of the statement to the Secretary of State and to the Comptroller and Auditor General before the end of the month of August next following the financial year to which the statement relates.

(2) The statement of accounts shall comply with any directions given by the Secretary of State with the approval of the Treasury as to—

(a) the information to be contained in it,

(b) the manner in which the information contained in it is to be presented, or

(c) the methods and principles according to which the statement is to be prepared,

and shall contain such additional information as the Secretary of State may with the approval of the Treasury require to be provided for the information of Parliament.

(3) The Comptroller and Auditor General shall examine, certify and report on each statement received by him in pursuance of this paragraph and shall lay copies of each statement and of his report before each House of Parliament.

(4) In this paragraph, 'financial year' means the period beginning with the date on which the Authority is established and ending with the next following 31st March, and each successive period of twelve months.

Other expenses

17. The Authority may—

(a) pay to persons attending meetings of the Authority at the request of the Authority such travelling and other allowances (including compensation for loss of remunerative time) as the Secretary of State may determine, and

(b) pay to persons from whom the Authority may decide to seek advice, as being persons considered by the Authority to be specially qualified to advise them on particular matters, such fees as the Secretary of State may determine.

Fees

18. Regulations made by the Secretary of State may authorise the Authority to charge fees for their services in respect of the modification of an occupational

pension scheme on an application made under section 69, or under any corresponding provision in force in Northern Ireland, including services in connection with
the drawing up of any order of the Authority made on application.

Application of seal and proof of instruments

19.—(1)   The fixing of the common seal of the Authority shall be authenticated
by the signature of the secretary of the Authority or some other person authorised
by them to act for that purpose.

(2)   Sub-paragraph (1) does not apply in relation to any document which is or
is to be signed in accordance with the law of Scotland.

20.   A document purporting to be duly executed under the seal of the Authority
shall be received in evidence and shall, unless the contrary is proved, be deemed
to be so executed.

Section 78   SCHEDULE 2
                          PENSIONS COMPENSATION BOARD

General

1.   The Compensation Board shall not be regarded as the servant or agent of
the Crown, or as enjoying any status, privilege or immunity of the Crown; and their
property shall not be regarded as property of, or property held on behalf of, the
Crown.

2.   The Compensation Board may do anything which is calculated to facilitate
the discharge of their functions, or is incidental or conducive to their discharge,
including in particular—

(a)   giving guarantees or indemnities in favour of any person, or

(b)   making any other agreement or arrangement with or for the benefit of
any person.

Tenure of members

3.   Subject to the following provisions, a person shall hold and vacate office as
chairman or other member of the Compensation Board in accordance with the
terms of the instrument appointing him.

4.   If a member of the Compensation Board becomes or ceases to be chairman,
the Secretary of State may vary the terms of the instrument appointing him to be
a member so as to alter the date on which he is to vacate office.

5.   A person may at any time resign office as chairman or other member of the
Compensation Board by giving written notice of his resignation signed by him to
the Secretary of State.

6.   The chairman or any other member of the Compensation Board may at any
time be removed from office by notice in writing given to him by the Secretary of
State.

Expenses, remuneration, etc.

7.—(1)   The Compensation Board may pay, or make provision for paying, to
or in respect of the chairman or any other member such salaries or other
remuneration, and such pensions, allowances, fees, expenses or gratuities, as the
Secretary of State may determine.

(2) Where a person ceases to be a member of the Compensation Board otherwise than on the expiration of his term of office and it appears to the Secretary of State that there are circumstances which make it right for that person to receive compensation, the Compensation Board may make to that person a payment of such amount as the Secretary of State may determine.

Parliamentary disqualification

8. In Part II of Schedule 1 to the House of Commons Disqualification Act 1975, and in Part II of Schedule 1 to the Northern Ireland Assembly Disqualification Act 1975 (bodies all members of which are disqualified), there is inserted at the appropriate place—
'The Pensions Compensation Board'.

The Ombudsman

9. In the Parliamentary Commissioner Act 1967, in Schedule 2 (departments and authorities subject to investigation), there is inserted at the appropriate place—
'The Pensions Compensation Board'.

Staff

10.—(1) The Compensation Board may (with the approval of the Secretary of State as to numbers) appoint such persons to be employees of theirs as the Board think fit, on such terms and conditions as to remuneration and other matters as the Board may with the approval of the Secretary of State determine.

(2) The Secretary of State may, on such terms as to payment by the Compensation Board as he thinks fit, make available to the Compensation Board such additional staff and such other facilities as he thinks fit.

(3) The Pensions Ombudsman may, on such terms as to payment by the Compensation Board as he thinks fit, make available to the Compensation Board such of his employees as he thinks fit.

The Superannuation Act 1972 (c. 11)

11.—(1) Employment with the Compensation Board shall be included among the kinds of employment to which a scheme under section 1 of the Superannuation Act 1972 can apply, and accordingly in Schedule 1 to that Act (in which those kinds of employment are listed), at the end of the list of Other Bodies there is inserted—
'The Pensions Compensation Board'.

(2) The Compensation Board must pay to the Treasury, at such times as the Treasury may direct, such sums as the Treasury may determine in respect of the increase attributable to this paragraph in the sums payable out of money provided by Parliament under the Superannuation Act 1972.

Proceedings

12. The Secretary of State may make regulations generally as to the procedure to be followed by the Compensation Board in the exercise of their functions and the manner in which their functions are to be exercised.

13. The Compensation Board must meet at least once in the first twelve months of their existence, and at least once in each succeeding period of twelve months.

14.—(1) The Compensation Board may (subject to sub-paragraph (2)) authorise any of their members to exercise such of the Compensation Board's functions as the Board may determine.

(2) The Compensation Board may not authorise any of their members to—

(a) determine whether section 81 applies to an application for compensation under section 82 in respect of any occupational pension scheme,

(b) determine the amount of any payment under section 83,

(c) determine whether any payment should be made under section 84 or the amount of any such payment, or

(d) exercise such functions of the Compensation Board as may be prescribed.

(3) The quorum of the Compensation Board shall be such as they may determine, and the Board may regulate their own procedure.

(4) The decisions of the Compensation Board must be taken by agreement of a majority of the members of the Compensation Board who are present at the meeting where the decision is taken.

(5) This paragraph is subject to regulations made by virtue of paragraph 12.

15.—(1) Where the Compensation Board notify any person of a decision on any matter dealt with by them by means of a formal hearing, or on review, they shall furnish a written statement of the reasons for the decision.

(2) Any statement by the Compensation Board of their reasons for a decision, whether the statement is given by them in pursuance of this paragraph or otherwise, shall be taken to form part of the decision, and accordingly to be incorporated in the record.

Validity

16. The validity of any proceedings of the Compensation Board shall not be affected by any vacancy among the members or by any defect in the appointment of any member.

Accounts

17.—(1) The Compensation Board must—

(a) keep proper accounts and proper records in relation to the accounts,

(b) prepare in respect of each financial year of the Compensation Board a statement of accounts, and

(c) send copies of the statement to the Secretary of State and to the Comptroller and Auditor General before the end of the month of August next following the financial year to which the statement relates.

(2) The statement of accounts must comply with any directions given by the Secretary of State with the approval of the Treasury as to—

(a) the information to be contained in it,

(b) the manner in which the information contained in it is to be presented, or

(c) the methods and principles according to which the statement is to be prepared,

and must contain such additional information as the Secretary of State may with the approval of the Treasury require to be provided for the information of Parliament.

(3)   The Comptroller and Auditor General must examine, certify and report on each statement received by him in pursuance of this paragraph and must lay copies of each statement and of his report before each House of Parliament.

(4)   In this paragraph, 'financial year' means the period beginning with the date on which the Board is established and ending with the next following 5th April, and each successive period of twelve months.

Other expenses

18.—(1)   The Compensation Board may—

(a)   pay to persons attending meetings of the Compensation Board at the request of the Board such travelling and other allowances (including compensation for loss of remunerative time) as the Board may determine, and

(b)   pay to persons from whom the Compensation Board may decide to seek advice, as being persons considered by the Board to be specially qualified to advise them on particular matters, such fees as the Board may determine.

(2)   A determination under sub-paragraph (1) requires the approval of the Secretary of State.

Application of seal and proof of instruments

19.—(1)   The fixing of the common seal of the Compensation Board shall be authenticated by the signature of the chairman of the Compensation Board or some other person authorised by them to act for that purpose.

(2)   Sub-paragraph (1) above does not apply in relation to any document which is or is to be signed in accordance with the law of Scotland.

20.   A document purporting to be duly executed under the seal of the Compensation Board shall be received in evidence and shall, unless the contrary is proved, be deemed to be so executed.

Section 122   SCHEDULE 3
                    AMENDMENTS CONSEQUENTIAL ON PART I

The Employment Protection (Consolidation) Act 1978 (c. 44)

1.   The Employment Protection (Consolidation) Act 1978 is amended as follows.

2.   In section 60A(4) (dismissal on grounds of assertion of statutory right), after paragraph (c) there is added—

'(d)   the rights conferred by sections 42, 43 and 46 of the Pensions Act 1995.'

3.   In section 71(2B) (compensation award for failure to comply with section 69 not to be made), at the end there is added 'of this Act or section 46 of the Pensions Act 1995.'

4.   In section 72(2) (special award), at the end there is added 'of this Act or section 46 of the Pensions Act 1995.'

5.   In section 73(6B) (calculation of basic award), at the end there is added 'of this Act or section 46 of the Pensions Act 1995.'

6.   In section 77(1) (interim relief), after '57A(1)(a) and (b)' there is inserted 'of this Act or section 46 of the Pensions Act 1995'.

7.   In section 77A(1) (procedure on application for interim relief), after '57A (1)(a) and (b)' there is inserted 'of this Act or section 46 of the Pensions Act 1995'.

8.   In section 133(1) (conciliation officers), after paragraph (e) there is added—
'or
(ea)   arising out of a contravention, or alleged contravention, of section 42, 43 or 46 of the Pensions Act 1995.'
9.   In section 136(1) (appeals to Employment Appeal Tribunal), after paragraph (f) there is added—
'(g)   the Pensions Act 1995;'
10.   In section 138 (application of Act to Crown employment), in subsection (1), after 'and section 53' there is inserted 'of this Act and sections 42 to 46 of the Pensions Act 1995;'

The Insurance Companies Act 1982 (c. 50)

11.—(1)   In the Table in sub-paragraph (1) of paragraph 3 of Schedule 2B to the Insurance Companies Act 1982, after the entry relating to the Building Societies Commission there is inserted—

'The Occupational Pensions Regulatory Authority.	Functions under the Pension Schemes Act 1993 or the Pensions Act 1995, or any enactment in force in Northern Ireland corresponding to either of them.'

(2)   In sub-paragraph (9) of that paragraph, after paragraph (b) there is added—
'or
(c)   persons involved in the operation of occupational pension schemes (within the meaning of the Pension Schemes Act 1993 or, in Northern Ireland, the Pension Schemes (Northern Ireland) Act 1993)',
and accordingly the 'or' after paragraph (a) is omitted.

The Companies Act 1985 (c. 6)

12.   In section 449(1) of the Companies Act 1985, after paragraph (df) there is inserted—
'(dg)   for the purpose of enabling or assisting the Occupational Pensions Regulatory Authority to discharge their functions under the Pension Schemes Act 1993 or the Pensions Act 1995 or any enactment in force in Northern Ireland corresponding to either of them,'.

The Bankruptcy (Scotland) Act 1985 (c. 66)

13.   In section 31(1) of the Bankruptcy (Scotland) Act 1985 (vesting in permanent trustee of debtor's estate on sequestration), after 'Act' there is inserted 'and section 91(3) of the Pensions Act 1995'.
14.   In section 32 of that Act (vesting of estate, and dealings of debtor, after sequestration), after subsection (2) there is inserted—
'(2A)   The amount allowed for the purposes specified in paragraphs (a) and (b) of subsection (2) above shall not be less than the total amount of any income received by the debtor—
(a)   by way of guaranteed minimum pension; and

(b) in respect of his protected rights as a member of a pension scheme, 'guaranteed minimum pension' and 'protected rights' having the same meanings as in the Pension Schemes Act 1993.'.

The Insolvency Act 1986 (c. 45)

15. In section 310 of the Insolvency Act 1986 (income payments orders)—

(a) in subsection (2), after 'income of the bankrupt' there is inserted 'when taken together with any payments to which subsection (8) applies', and

(b) at the end of subsection (7), there is added—

'and any payment under a pension scheme but excluding any payment to which subsection (8) applies.

(8) This subsection applies to—

(a) payments by way of guaranteed minimum pension; and

(b) payments giving effect to the bankrupt's protected rights as a member of a pension scheme.

(9) In this section, 'guaranteed minimum pension' and 'protected rights' have the same meaning as in the Pension Schemes Act 1993.'

The Building Societies Act 1986 (c. 53)

16. In section 53(15) of the Building Societies Act 1986, after paragraph (b) there is added—

'or

(c) persons involved in the operation of occupational pension schemes (within the meaning of the Pension Schemes Act 1993 or, in Northern Ireland, the Pension Schemes (Northern Ireland) Act 1993)',

and accordingly the 'or' after paragraph (a) is omitted.

The Financial Services Act 1986 (c. 60)

17. In section 180(1) of the Financial Services Act 1986, after paragraph (m) there is inserted—

'(mm) for the purpose of enabling or assisting the Occupational Pensions Regulatory Authority or the Pensions Compensation Board to discharge their functions under the Pension Schemes Act 1993 or the Pensions Act 1995 or any enactment in force in Northern Ireland corresponding to either of them;'

The Banking Act 1987 (c. 22)

18.—(1) In the Table in subsection (1) of section 84 of the Banking Act 1987, at the end there is added—

'20. The Occupational Pensions Regulatory Authority.	Functions under the Pension Schemes Act 1993 or the Pensions Act 1995, or any enactment in force in Northern Ireland corresponding to either of them.'

(2) In subsection (10) of that section, after paragraph (b) there is added—

'or

(c) persons involved in the operation of occupational pension schemes (within the meaning of the Pension Schemes Act 1993 or, in Northern Ireland, the Pension Schemes (Northern Ireland) Act 1993)', and accordingly the 'or' after paragraph (a) is omitted.

The Companies Act 1989 (c. 40)

19.   In the Table in section 87(4) of the Companies Act 1989, after the entry relating to the Building Societies Commission there is inserted—

'The Occupational Pensions Regulatory Authority.	Functions under the Pension Schemes Act 1993 or the Pensions Act 1995, or any enactment in force in Northern Ireland corresponding to either of them.'

The Friendly Societies Act 1992 (c. 40)

20.   In the Table in section 64(5) of the Friendly Societies Act 1992, after the entry relating to the Building Societies Commission there is inserted—

'The Occupational Pensions Regulatory Authority.	Functions under the Pension Schemes Act 1993 or the Pensions Act 1995, or any enactment in force in Northern Ireland corresponding to either of them.'

The Tribunals and Inquiries Act 1992 (c. 53)

21.   The Tribunals and Inquiries Act 1992 is amended as follows—
      (a)   in section 7(2) (concurrence required for removal of tribunal members), after '(e)' there is inserted '(g) or (h)',
      (b)   in section 10 (reasons to be given on request), at the end of subsection (5) there is added—
         '(ba)   to decisions of the Pensions Compensation Board referred to in paragraph 35(h) of Schedule 1',
      (c)   in section 14 (restricted application of the Act in relation to certain tribunals), after subsection (1) there is inserted—
         '(1A)   In this Act—
            (a)   references to the working of the Occupational Pensions Regulatory Authority referred to in paragraph 35(g) of Schedule 1 are references to their working so far as relating to matters dealt with by them by means of a formal hearing or on review, and
            (b)   references to procedural rules for the Authority are references to regulations under—
               (i)   section 96(5) of the Pensions Act 1995 (procedure to be adopted with respect to reviews), or
               (ii)   paragraph 13 of Schedule 1 to that Act (procedure of the Authority), so far as the regulations relate to procedure on any formal hearing by the Authority.', and
      (d)   in paragraph 35 of Schedule 1 (tribunals under the direct supervision of the Council on Tribunals: pensions), after paragraph (f) there is inserted—
         '(g)   the Occupational Pensions Regulatory Authority established by section 1 of the Pensions Act 1995;

(h)   the Pensions Compensation Board established by section 78 of that Act'.

The Pension Schemes Act 1993 (c. 48)

22.   The Pension Schemes Act 1993 is amended as follows.

23.   In section 6 (registration)—

(a)   after subsection (5) there is inserted—

'(5A)   The regulations may make provision for information obtained by or furnished to the Registrar under or for the purposes of this Act to be disclosed to the Regulatory Authority or the Pensions Compensation Board', and

(b)   in subsection (7), for '(5)' there is substituted '(5A)'.

24.   Sections 77 to 80 (assignment, forfeiture etc. of short service benefit) are repealed.

25.   Sections 102 to 108 (annual increase in pensions in payment) are repealed.

26.   Section 112 (restriction on investment in employer-related assets) is repealed.

27.   Section 114 (documents for members etc.) is repealed.

28.   Section 116 (regulations as to auditors) is repealed.

29.   Section 118 (equal access) is repealed.

30.   Sections 119 to 122 (independent trustees) are repealed.

31.   In section 129 (overriding requirements)—

(a)   in subsection (1), 'Chapter I of Part V', 'sections 119 to 122', 'under Chapter I of Part V or' and 'or sections 119 to 122' are omitted,

(b)   in subsection (2), for the words from 'Chapter III' to 'section 108)' there is substituted 'and Chapter III of that Part', and

(c)   subsection (3)(a) is omitted.

32.   In section 132 (conformity of schemes with requirements), 'the equal access requirements' is omitted.

33.   In section 133(1) (advice of the Board), 'the equal access requirements' is omitted.

34.   In section 134 (determination of questions)—

(a)   in subsection (3), 'the equal access requirements', and

(b)   in subsection (4), 'or the equal access requirements' and 'or, as the case may be, section 118(1)',

are omitted.

35.   In section 136(2)(e)(iv) (applications to modify schemes), 'or the equal access requirements' is omitted.

36.   In section 139(2) (functions of the Board), 'the equal access requirements' is omitted.

37.   In section 140(4) (effect of orders), paragraph (c) and the 'and' immediately preceding it are omitted.

38.   Section 144 (deficiencies in assets on winding up) is repealed.

39.   In section 153 (power to modify Act)—

(a)   in subsection (1), the words from 'and Chapter 1' to 'section 108)' are omitted,

(b)   subsections (3) and (4) are omitted,

    (c)   in subsection (5), 'Chapter I of Part VII' is omitted, at the end of paragraph (b) there is inserted 'or', and paragraph (d) and the preceding 'or' are omitted, and

    (d)   subsections (6) and (7) are omitted.

    40.   In section 154(1) (application of provisions to personal pension schemes), after 'provision of this Act' there is inserted 'or of sections 22 to 26 and 40 of the Pensions Act 1995'.

    41.   In section 159 (inalienability of certain pensions), after subsection (4) there is inserted—

    '(4A)   Where a person—

    (a)   is entitled or prospectively entitled as is mentioned in subsection (1), or

    (b)   is entitled to such rights or to such a payment as is mentioned in subsection (4),

no order shall be made by any court the effect of which would be that he would be restrained from receiving anything the assignment of which is or would be made void by either of those subsections.

    (4B)   Subsection (4A) does not prevent the making of an attachment of earnings order under the Attachment of Earnings Act 1971.'

    42.   In section 170 (determination of questions by Secretary of State), subsections (5) and (6) are omitted.

    43.   In section 178 (meaning of 'trustee' and 'manager') in paragraph (a), after 'Administration Act 1992' there is inserted 'or of sections 22 to 26 of the Pensions Act 1995', and the 'or' after 'Social Security Acts 1975 to 1991' is omitted.

    44.   In section 181 (general interpretation)—

    (a)   in subsection (1)—

    (i)   the definition of 'equal access requirements' is omitted, and

    (ii)   after the definition of 'regulations' there is inserted—

''the Regulatory Authority' means the Occupational Pensions Regulatory Authority;', and

    (b)   in subsection (2), for the words from '160' to 'requirements' there is substituted 'and 160'.

    45.   In section 183 (sub-delegation), in subsection (3)—

    (a)   for '97(1), 104(8) and 144(5)' there is substituted 'and 97(1)',

    (b)   the words from 'or, in the case of' to 'determined' are omitted, and

    (c)   the words following paragraph (b) are omitted.

    46.   In section 185(1) (consultation about regulations), 'I or' is omitted.

    47.   In Schedule 7 (re-enactment or amendment of certain provisions not in force), paragraphs 1 and 3 are omitted.

Section 125   SCHEDULE 4

EQUALISATION

PART I

PENSIONABLE AGES FOR MEN AND WOMEN

Rules for determining pensionable age

    1.   The following rules apply for the purposes of the enactments relating to social security, that is, the following Acts and the instruments made, or having

effect as if made, under them: the Social Security Contributions and Benefits Act 1992, the Social Security Administration Act 1992 and the Pension Schemes Act 1993.

Rules

(1)   A man attains pensionable age when he attains the age of 65 years.

(2)   A woman born before 6th April 1950 attains pensionable age when she attains the age of 60.

(3)   A woman born on any day in a period mentioned in column 1 of the following table attains pensionable age at the commencement of the day shown against that period in column 2.

(4)   A woman born after 5th April 1955 attains pensionable age when she attains the age of 65.

TABLE

(1) *Period within which woman's birthday falls*	*(2)* *Day pensionable age attained*
6th April 1950 to 5th May 1950	6th May 2010
6th May 1950 to 5th June 1950	6th July 2010
6th June 1950 to 5th July 1950	6th September 2010
6th July 1950 to 5th August 1950	6th November 2010
6th August 1950 to 5th September 1950	6th January 2011
6th September 1950 to 5th October 1950	6th March 2011
6th October 1950 to 5th November 1950	6th May 2011
6th November 1950 to 5th December 1950	6th July 2011
6th December 1950 to 5th January 1951	6th September 2011
6th January 1951 to 5th February 1951	6th November 2011
6th February 1951 to 5th March 1951	6th January 2012
6th March 1951 to 5th April 1951	6th March 2012
6th April 1951 to 5th May 1951	6th May 2012
6th May 1951 to 5th June 1951	6th July 2012
6th June 1951 to 5th July 1951	6th September 2012
6th July 1951 to 5th August 1951	6th November 2012
6th August 1951 to 5th September 1951	6th January 2013
6th September 1951 to 5th October 1951	6th March 2013
6th October 1951 to 5th November 1951	6th May 2013
6th November 1951 to 5th December 1951	6th July 2013
6th December 1951 to 5th January 1952	6th September 2013
6th January 1952 to 5th February 1952	6th November 2013
6th February 1952 to 5th March 1952	6th January 2014
6th March 1952 to 5th April 1952	6th March 2014
6th April 1952 to 5th May 1952	6th May 2014
6th May 1952 to 5th June 1952	6th July 2014
6th June 1952 to 5th July 1952	6th September 2014
6th July 1952 to 5th August 1952	6th November 2014
6th August 1952 to 5th September 1952	6th January 2015

(1) Period within which woman's birthday falls	(2) Day pensionable age attained
6th September 1952 to 5th October 1952	6th March 2015
6th October 1952 to 5th November 1952	6th May 2015
6th November 1952 to 5th December 1952	6th July 2015
6th December 1952 to 5th January 1953	6th September 2015
6th January 1953 to 5th February 1953	6th November 2015
6th February 1953 to 5th March 1953	6th January 2016
6th March 1953 to 5th April 1953	6th March 2016
6th April 1953 to 5th May 1953	6th May 2016
6th May 1953 to 5th June 1953	6th July 2016
6th June 1953 to 5th July 1953	6th September 2016
6th July 1953 to 5th August 1953	6th November 2016
6th August 1953 to 5th September 1953	6th January 2017
6th September 1953 to 5th October 1953	6th March 2017
6th October 1953 to 5th November 1953	6th May 2017
6th November 1953 to 5th December 1953	6th July 2017
6th December 1953 to 5th January 1954	6th September 2017
6th January 1954 to 5th February 1954	6th November 2017
6th February 1954 to 5th March 1954	6th January 2018
6th March 1954 to 5th April 1954	6th March 2018
6th April 1954 to 5th May 1954	6th May 2018
6th May 1954 to 5th June 1954	6th July 2018
6th June 1954 to 5th July 1954	6th September 2018
6th July 1954 to 5th August 1954	6th November 2018
6th August 1954 to 5th September 1954	6th January 2019
6th September 1954 to 5th October 1954	6th March 2019
6th October 1954 to 5th November 1954	6th May 2019
6th November 1954 to 5th December 1954	6th July 2019
6th December 1954 to 5th January 1955	6th September 2019
6th January 1955 to 5th February 1955	6th November 2019
6th February 1955 to 5th March 1955	6th January 2020
6th March 1955 to 5th April 1955	6th March 2020

PART II
ENTITLEMENT TO CERTAIN PENSION AND OTHER BENEFITS

Pension increases for dependent spouses

2.—(1) For sections 83 and 84 of the Social Security Contributions and Benefits Act 1992 (pension increases for dependent wife or husband) there is substituted—

'83A. Pension increase for spouse

(1) Subject to subsection (3) below, the weekly rate of a Category A or Category C retirement pension payable to a married pensioner shall, for any period mentioned in subsection (2) below, be increased by the amount specified in relation to the pension in Schedule 4, Part IV, column (3).

(2)   The periods referred to in subsection (1) above are—

(a)   any period during which the pensioner is residing with the spouse, and

(b)   any period during which the pensioner is contributing to the maintenance of the spouse at a weekly rate not less than the amount so specified, and the spouse does not have weekly earnings which exceed that amount.

(3)   Regulations may provide that for any period during which the pensioner is residing with the spouse and the spouse has earnings there shall be no increase of pension under this section'.

(2)   This paragraph shall have effect on or after 6th April 2010.

Category B retirement pensions

3.—(1)   For sections 49 and 50 of the Social Security Contributions and Benefits Act 1992 (Category B retirement pensions for women) there is substituted—

'48A.   Category B retirement pension for married person

(1)   A person who—

(a)   has attained pensionable age, and

(b)   on attaining that age was a married person or marries after attaining that age,

shall be entitled to a Category B retirement pension by virtue of the contributions of the other party to the marriage ('the spouse') if the following requirement is met.

(2)   The requirement is that the spouse—

(a)   has attained pensionable age and become entitled to a Category A retirement pension, and

(b)   satisfies the conditions specified in Schedule 3, Part I, paragraph 5.

(3)   During any period when the spouse is alive, a Category B retirement pension payable by virtue of this section shall be payable at the weekly rate specified in Schedule 4, Part I, paragraph 5.

(4)   During any period after the spouse is dead, a Category B retirement pension payable by virtue of this section shall be payable at a weekly rate corresponding to—

(a)   the weekly rate of the basic pension, plus

(b)   half of the weekly rate of the additional pension,

determined in accordance with the provisions of sections 44 to 45A above as they apply in relation to a Category A retirement pension, but subject to section 46(2) above and the modification in section 48C(4) below.

(5)   A person's Category B retirement pension payable by virtue of this section shall not be payable for any period falling before the day on which the spouse's entitlement is to be regarded as beginning for that purpose by virtue of section 5(1)(k) of the Administration Act.

48B.   Category B retirement pension for widows and widowers

(1)   A person ('the pensioner') whose spouse died—

(a)   while they were married, and

(b)   after the pensioner attained pensionable age,

shall be entitied to a Category B retirement pension by virtue of the contributions of the spouse if the spouse satisfied the conditions specified in Schedule 3, Part I, paragraph 5.

(2) A Category B retirement pension payable by virtue of subsection (1) above shall be payable at a weekly rate corresponding to—

(a) the weekly rate of the basic pension, plus

(b) half of the weekly rate of the additional pension,

determined in accordance with the provisions of sections 44 to 45A above as they apply in relation to a Category A retirement pension, but subject to section 46(2) above and the modifications in subsection (3) below and section 48C(4) below.

(3) Where the spouse died under pensionable age, references in the provisions of sections 44 to 45A above as applied by subsection (2) above to the tax year in which the pensioner attained pensionable age shall be taken as references to the tax year in which the spouse died.

(4) A person who has attained pensionable age ('the pensioner') whose spouse died before the pensioner attained that age shall be entitled to a Category B retirement pension by virtue of the contributions of the spouse if—

(a) where the pensioner is a woman, the following condition is satisfied, and

(b) where the pensioner is a man, the following condition would have been satisfied on the assumption mentioned in subsection (7) below.

(5) The condition is that the pensioner—

(a) is entitled (or is treated by regulations as entitled) to a widow's pension by virtue of section 38 above, and

(b) became entitled to that pension in consequence of the spouse's death.

(6) A Category B retirement pension payable by virtue of subsection (4) above shall be payable—

(a) where the pensioner is a woman, at the same weekly rate as her widow's pension, and

(b) where the pensioner is a man, at the same weekly rate as that of the pension to which he would have been entitled by virtue of section 38 above on the assumption mentioned in subsection (7) below.

(7) The assumption referred to in subsections (4) and (6) above is that a man is entitled to a pension by virtue of section 38 above on the same terms and conditions, and at the same rate, as a woman.

48C. Category B retirement pension: general

(1) Subject to the provisions of this Act, a person's entitlement to a Category B retirement pension shall begin on the day on which the conditions of entitlement become satisfied and shall continue for life.

(2) In any case where—

(a) a person would, apart from section 43(1) above, be entitled both to a Category A and to a Category B retirement pension, and

(b) section 47(1) above would apply for the increase of the Category A retirement pension, section 47(1) above shall be taken as applying also for the increase of the Category B retirement pension, subject to reduction or extinguishment of the increase by the application of section 47(2) above or section 46(5) of the Pensions Act.

(3) In the case of a pensioner whose spouse died on or before 5th April 2000, sections 48A(4)(b) and 48B(2)(b) above shall have effect with the omission of the words 'half of'.

(4) In the application of the provisions of sections 44 to 45A above by virtue of sections 48A(4) or 48B(2) above, references in those provisions to the pensioner shall be taken as references to the spouse'.

(2) Section 48A of that Act (as inserted by this paragraph) does not confer a right to a Category B retirement pension on a man by reason of his marriage to a woman who was born before 6th April 1950.

(3) Section 48B of that Act (as inserted by this paragraph) does not confer a right to a Category B retirement pension on a man who attains pensionable age before 6th April 2010; and section 51 of that Act does not confer a right to a Category B retirement pension on a man who attains pensionable age on or after that date.

Home responsibilities protection

4.—(1) In paragraph 5 of Schedule 3 to the Social Security Contributions and Benefits Act 1992 (contribution conditions for entitlement to retirement pension), in sub-paragraph (7)(a) (condition that contributor must have paid or been credited with contributions of the relevant class for not less than the requisite number of years modified in the case of those precluded from regular employment by responsibilities at home), '(or at least 20 of them, if that is less than half)' is omitted.

(2) This paragraph shall have effect in relation to any person attaining pensionable age on or after 6th April 2010.

Additional pension

5. In section 46(2) of the Social Security Contributions and Benefits Act 1992 (benefits calculated by reference to Category A retirement pension), for the words following '45(4)(b) above-' there is substituted—

"N" =

(a) the number of tax years which begin after 5th April 1978 and end before the date when the entitlement to the additional pension commences, or

(b) the number of tax years in the period—

(i) beginning with the tax year in which the deceased spouse ('S') attained the age of 16 or if later 1978-79, and

(ii) ending immediately before the tax year in which S would have attained pensionable age if S had not died earlier,

whichever is the smaller number'.

Increments

6.—(1) In section 54(1) of the Social Security Contributions and Benefits Act 1992 (election to defer right to pension), in paragraph (a), the words from 'but' to '70' are omitted.

(2)   In Schedule 5 to that Act—

(a)   in paragraph 2(2), the definition of 'period of enhancement' (and the preceding 'and') are omitted, and

(b)   for 'period of enhancement' (in every other place in paragraphs 2 and 3 where it appears) there is substituted 'period of deferment'.

(3)   In paragraph 2(3) of that Schedule, for '1/7th per cent.' there is substituted '1/5th per cent.'

(4)   In paragraph 8 of that Schedule, sub-paragraphs (1) and (2) are omitted.

(5)   Sub-paragraph (1) above shall come into force on 6th April 2010; and sub-paragraphs (2) to (4) above shall have effect in relation to incremental periods beginning on or after that date.

Graduated retirement benefit

7.   In section 62(1) of the Social Security Contributions and Benefits Act 1992 (graduated retirement benefit continued in force by regulations)—

(a)   in paragraph (a), for 'replacing section 36(4) of the National Insurance Act 1965' there is substituted 'amending section 36(2) of the National Insurance Act 1965 (value of unit of graduated contributions) so that the value is the same for women as it is for men and for replacing section 36(4) of that Act', and

(b)   at the end of paragraph (b) there is added 'and for that section (except subsection (5)) so to apply as it applies to women and their late husbands'.

Christmas bonus for pensioners

8.   In section 149(4) of that Act (Christmas bonus: supplementary), for '70 in the case of a man or 65 in the case of a woman' there is substituted '65'.

PART III
CONSEQUENTIAL AMENDMENTS

Pensionable age

9.   In section 50 of the London Regional Transport Act 1984 (travel concessions), for subsection (7)(a) there is substituted—

'(a)   persons who have attained pensionable age (within the meaning given by the rules in paragraph 1 of Schedule 4 to the Pensions Act 1995)'.

10.   In section 93 of the Transport Act 1985 (travel concessions), for subsection (7)(a) there is substituted—

'(a)   persons who have attained pensionable age (within the meaning given by the rules in paragraph 1 of Schedule 4 to the Pensions Act 1995)'.

11.   In section 73B(2)(b)(ii) of the Housing (Scotland) Act 1987 (rent loan scheme), for 'of the Social Security Act 1975' there is substituted 'given by the rules in paragraph 1 of Schedule 4 to the Pensions Act 1995)'.

12.   In the Income and Corporation Taxes Act 1988—

(a)   in section 187(2) (interpretation), the definition of 'pensionable age' is omitted,

(b)   in the words following paragraph (d) of paragraph 2 of Schedule 10 (retention of shares in connection with profit sharing schemes), for 'to pensionable age' there is substituted 'in the case of a man, to the age of 65, and in the case of a woman, to the age of 60'.

(c)   in sub-paragraph (2) of paragraph 3A of that Schedule, for 'pensionable age' there is substituted—

'(a)   in the case of a man, 65, and

(b)   in the case of a woman, 60.', and

(d)   in sub-paragraph (4) of that paragraph, for 'pensionable age' there is substituted 'in the case of a man, 65, and in the case of a woman, 60.'

13.   In the Social Security Contributions and Benefits Act 1992—

(a)   in section 122(1) (interpretation of Parts I to VI), for the definition of 'pensionable age' there is substituted—

''pensionable age' has the meaning given by the rules in paragraph 1 of Schedule 4 to the Pensions Act 1995', and

(b)   in section 150(2) (interpretation of Part X), for the definition of 'pensionable age' there is substituted—

''pensionable age' has the meaning given by the rules in paragraph 1 of Schedule 4 to the Pensions Act 1995'.

14.   In section 191 of the Social Security Administration Act 1992 (interpretation), for the definition of 'pensionable age' there is substituted—

''pensionable age' has the meaning given by the rules in paragraph 1 of Schedule 4 to the Pensions Act 1995'.

15.   In section 58 of the Trade Union and Labour Relations (Consolidation) Act 1992 (exemption from requirement for election), in subsection (3)(b), for the words following 'pensionable age' there is substituted '(within the meaning given by the rules in paragraph 1 of Schedule 4 to the Pensions Act 1995)'.

16.   For section 49 of the Pension Schemes Act 1993 (married women and widows), including the cross heading preceding it, there is substituted—

'Women, married women and widows

49.   Women, married women and widows

The Secretary of State may make regulations modifying, in such manner as he thinks proper—

(a)   this Chapter in its application to women born on or after 6th April 1950, and

(b)   sections 41, 42, 46(1), 47(2) and (5) and 48, in their application to women who are or have been married'.

17.   In section 181(1) of that Act (interpretation), for the definition of 'pensionable age' there is substituted—

''pensionable age'—

(a)   so far as any provisions (other than sections 46 to 48) relate to guaranteed minimum pensions, means the age of 65 in the case of a man and the age of 60 in the case of a woman, and

(b)   in any other case, has the meaning given by the rules in paragraph 1 of Schedule 4 to the Pensions Act 1995'.

Pension increases for dependent spouses

18.   In the Social Security Contributions and Benefits Act 1992—

(a)   in section 25(6)(c) (unemployment benefit), for '83' there is substituted '83A',

(b) in section 30B(3) (incapacity benefit: rate, inserted by the Social Security (Incapacity for Work) Act 1994), for '83' there is substituted '83A',

(c) in section 78(4)(d) (benefits for the aged), for '83' there is substituted '83A',

(d) in section 85(4) (pension increase: care of children), for '83(3)' there is substituted '83A(3)',

(e) in section 88 (pension increase: supplementary), for '83' there is substituted '83A',

(f) in section 114(4) (persons maintaining dependants, etc.), for '84' there is substituted '83A', and

(g) in section 149(3)(b) (Christmas bonus), for '83(2) or (3)' there is substituted '83A(2) or (3)'.

19. In the Social Security (Incapacity for Work) Act 1994, in Schedule 1, paragraphs 20 and 21 are omitted.

20. Paragraphs 18 and 19 shall have effect on or after 6th April 2010.

Category B retirement pensions

21.—(1) In section 20(1)(f) of the Social Security Contributions and Benefits Act 1992 (general description of benefits), for sub-paragraph (ii) there is substituted—

'(ii) Category B, payable to a person by virtue of the contributions of a spouse (with increase for child dependants)'.

(2) In section 25(6) of that Act, in paragraph (b), for '(for married women) under section 53(2)' there is substituted '(for married people) under section 51A(2)'.

(3) In section 30B of that Act (incapacity benefit), in paragraph (a) of the proviso to subsection (3), for '(for married women) under section 53(2)' there is substituted '(for married people) under section 51A(2)'.

(4) In section 41(5)(a) of that Act (long-term incapacity benefit for widowers), for 'section 51 below' there is substituted 'the contributions of his wife'.

(5) In section 46(2) of that Act (calculation of additional pension in certain benefits), for '50(3)' there is substituted '48A(4) or 48B(2)'.

(6) After section 51 of that Act there is inserted—

'51A. Special provision for married people

(1) This section has effect where, apart from section 43(1) above, a married person would be entitled both—

(a) to a Category A retirement pension, and

(b) to a Category B retirement pension by virtue of the contributions of the other party to the marriage.

(2) If by reason of a deficiency of contributions the basic pension in the Category A retirement pension falls short of the weekly rate specified in Schedule 4, Part I, paragraph 5, that basic pension shall be increased by the lesser of—

(a) the amount of the shortfall, or

(b) the amount of the weekly rate of the Category B retirement pension.

(3) This section does not apply in any case where both parties to the marriage attained pensionable age before 6th April 1979',

and section 53 of that Act (special provision for married women) is omitted.

(7)   In section 52 of that Act (special provision for surviving spouses), for subsection (1)(b) there is substituted—

'(b)   to a Category B retirement pension by virtue of the contributions of a spouse who has died'.

(8) In section 54 of that Act (supplemental provisions), for subsection (3) there is substituted—

'(3)   Where both parties to a marriage (call them 'P' and 'S') have become entitled to retirement pensions and—

(a)   P's pension is Category A, and

(b)   S's pension is—

(i)   Category B by virtue of P's contributions, or

(ii)   Category A with an increase under section 51A(2) above by virtue of P's contributions,

P shall not be entitled to make an election in accordance with regulations made under subsection (1) above without S's consent, unless that consent is unreasonably withheld'.

(9)   In section 60 of that Act (complete or partial failure to satisfy contribution conditions)—

(a)   in subsection (2), for 'him' (in paragraph (b)) there is substituted 'the employed earner' and for 'his widow's entitlement' there is substituted 'the entitlement of the employed earner's widow or widower', and

(b)   for subsection (3)(d) there is substituted—

'(d)   a Category B retirement pension payable by virtue of section 48B above'.

(10)   In section 85 of that Act (pension increase for person with care of children), in subsection (3), for 'man whose wife' there is substituted 'person whose spouse'.

(11)   In Schedule 4 to that Act (rates of benefit, etc.), in paragraph 5 of Part I, for 'section 50(1)(a)(i)' there is substituted 'section 48A(3)'.

(12)   In Schedule 5 to that Act (increased pension where entitlement deferred), in paragraph 2(5)(a), for '5 or 6' there is substituted '5, 5A or 6'.

(13)   In paragraph 4 of that Schedule, for sub-paragraphs (1) and (2) there is substituted—

'(1)   Subject to sub-paragraph (3) below, where—

(a)   a widow or widower (call that person 'W') is entitled to a Category A or Category B retirement pension and was married to the other party to the marriage (call that person 'S') when S died, and

(b)   S either—

(i)   was entitled to a Category A or Category B retirement pension with an increase under this Schedule, or

(ii)   would have been so entitled if S's period of deferment had ended on the day before S's death,

the rate of W's pension shall be increased by an amount equal to the increase to which S was or would have been entitled under this Schedule apart from paragraphs 5 to 6'.

(14)   Paragraph 4(1) of that Schedule. (as inserted by sub-paragraph (13) above) shall have effect where W is a man who attains pensionable age before 6th

April 2010 as if paragraph (a) also required him to have been over pensionable age when S died.

(15)   For paragraphs 5 and 6 of that Schedule there is substituted—

'5.—(1)   Where—

(a)   a widow or widower (call that person 'W') is entitled to a Category A or Category B retirement pension and was married to the other party to the marriage (call that person 'S') when S died, and

(b)   S either—

(i)   was entitled to a guaranteed minimum pension with an increase under section 15(1) of the Pensions Act, or

(ii)   would have been so entitled if S had retired on the date of S's death,

the rate of W's pension shall be increased by the following amount.

(2)   The amount is—

(a)   where W is a widow, an amount equal to the sum of the amounts set out in paragraph 5A(2) or (3) below (as the case may be), and

(b)   where W is a widower, an amount equal to the sum of the amounts set out in paragraph 6(2), (3) or (4) below (as the case may be).

5A.—(1)   This paragraph applies where W (referred to in paragraph 5 above) is a widow.

(2)   Where the husband dies before 6th April 2000, the amounts referred to in paragraph 5(2)(a) above are the following—

(a)   an amount equal to one-half of the increase mentioned in paragraph 5(1)(b) above,

(b)   the appropriate amount, and

(c)   an amount equal to any increase to which the husband had been entitled under paragraph 5 above.

(3)   Where the husband dies after 5th April 2000, the amounts referred to in paragraph 5(2)(a) above are the following—

(a)   one-half of the appropriate amount after it has been reduced by the amount of any increases under section 109 of the Pensions Act, and

(b)   one-half of any increase to which the husband had been entitled under paragraph 5 above.

6.—(1)   This paragraph applies where W (referred to in paragraph 5 above) is a widower.

(2)   Where the wife dies before 6th April 1989, the amounts referred to in paragraph 5(2)(b) above are the following—

(a)   an amount equal to the increase mentioned in paragraph 5(1)(b) above,

(b)   the appropriate amount, and

(c)   an amount equal to any increase to which the wife had been entitled under paragraph 5 above.

(3)   Where the wife dies after 5th April 1989 but before 6th April 2000, the amounts referred to in paragraph 5(2)(b) above are the following—

(a)   the increase mentioned in paragraph 5(1)(b) above, so far as attributable to employment before 6th April 1988,

(b)   one-half of that increase, so far as attributable to employment after 5th April 1988,

(c)   the appropriate amount reduced by the amount of any increases under section 109 of the Pensions Act, and

(d)   any increase to which the wife had been entitled under paragraph 5 above.

(4)   Where the wife dies after 5th April 2000, the amounts referred to in paragraph 5(2)(b) above are the following—

(a)   one-half of the increase mentioned in paragraph 5(1)(b) above, so far as attributable to employment before 6th April 1988,

(b)   one-half of the appropriate amount after it has been reduced by the amount of any increases under section 109 of the Pensions Act, and

(c)   one-half of any increase to which the wife had been entitled under paragraph 5 above'.

(16)   Paragraph 5(1) of that Schedule (inserted by sub-paragraph (15) above) shall have effect, where W is a man who attained pensionable age before 6th April 2010, as if paragraph (a) also required him to have been over pensionable age when S died.

(17)   In paragraph 7 of that Schedule—

(a)   in sub-paragraph (1), for 'paragraphs 5 and 6' there is substituted 'paragraphs 5 to 6', and

(b)   in sub-paragraph (2), for 'paragraph 5 or 6' there is substituted 'paragraph 5, 5A or 6'.

(18)   In paragraph 8 of that Schedule, for sub-paragraphs (3) and (4) there is substituted—

'(3)   In the case of the following pensions (where 'P' is a married person and 'S' is the other party to the marriage), that is—

(a)   a Category B retirement pension to which P is entitled by virtue of the contributions of S, or

(b)   P's Category A retirement pension with an increase under section 51A(2) above attributable to the contributions of S,

the reference in paragraph 2(3) above to the pension to which a person would have been entitled if that person's entitlement had not been deferred shall be construed as a reference to the pension to which P would have been entitled if neither P's nor S's entitlement to a retirement pension had been deferred.

(4)   Paragraph 4(1)(b) above shall not apply to a Category B retirement pension to which S was or would have been entitled by virtue of W's contributions ('W' and 'S' having the same meaning as in paragraph 4(1)); and where the Category A retirement pension to which S was or would have been entitled includes an increase under section 51A(2) above attributable to W's contributions, the increase to which W is entitled under that paragraph shall be calculated as if there had been no increase under that section'.

22.   In section 46 of the Pension Schemes Act 1993 (effect of entitlement to guaranteed minimum pension on payment of benefits), in subsection (6)(b)(iii), for 'section 49' there is substituted 'section 48A or 48B'.

SCHEDULE 5
AMENDMENTS RELATING TO PART III
The Public Records Act 1958 (c. 51)

1.   In Schedule 1 to the Public Records Act 1958 (definition of 'Public Record'), in the Table—

(a) in Part 1, the entry relating to the Occupational Pensions Board is omitted, and

(b) in Part II—

(i)   after the entry relating to the Nature Conservancy Council for England, there is inserted—

'Occupational Pensions Regulatory Authority.', and

(ii)   after the entry relating to the Office of the Director General of Fair Trading, there is inserted—

'Pensions Compensation Board.'

The Administration of Justice Act 1970 (c. 31)

2.   In Schedule 4 to the Administration of Justice Act 1970 (taxes, social insurance contributions, etc. subject to special enforcement provisions), in paragraph 3, for 'State scheme premiums' there is substituted 'Contributions equivalent premiums'.

The Attachment of Earnings Act 1971 (c. 31)

3.   In Schedule 2 to the Attachment of Earnings Act 1971 (taxes, social security contributions, etc. relevant for purposes of section 3(6)), in paragraph 3, for 'State scheme premiums' there is substituted 'Contributions equivalent premiums'.

The House of Commons Disqualification Act 1975 (c. 24)

4.   In Part II of Schedule 1 to the House of Commons Disqualification Act 1975 (bodies of which all members are disqualified), the entry relating to the Occupational Pensions Board is omitted.

The Northern Ireland Assembly Disqualification Act 1975 (c. 25)

5.   In Part II of Schedule 1 to the Northern Ireland Assembly Disqualification Act 1975 (bodies of which all members are disqualified), the entry relating to the Occupational Pensions Board is omitted.

The Social Security Pensions Act 1975 (c. 60)

6.—(1)   In section 61 of the Social Security Pensions Act 1975 (consultation about regulations) for the words from 'refer the proposals' in subsection (2) to the end of subsection (3) there is substituted 'consult such persons as he may consider appropriate'.

(2)   In section 61B(1) of that Act (orders and regulations: general provisions), 'except any power of the Occupational Pensions Board to make orders' is omitted.

(3)   In section 64(3) of that Act (expenses and receipts), for 'state scheme premium' there is substituted 'contributions equivalent premium'.

The European Parliament (Pay and Pensions) Act 1979 (c. 50)

7.   In section 6(4) of the European Parliament (Pay and Pensions) Act 1979 (provision for payment of block transfer value into another pension scheme), 'and the Occupational Pensions Board' is omitted.

The Justices of the Peace Act 1979 (c. 55)

8.   In section 55(6)(b)(ii) of the Justices of the Peace Act 1979 (duties of local authorities), for 'state scheme premiums' there is substituted 'contributions equivalent premiums'.

The Judicial Pensions Act 1981 (c. 20)

9.   In section 14A(2) of the Judicial Pensions Act 1981 (modifications of that Act in relation to personal pensions), in the definition of 'personal pension scheme', for the words from 'by' to the end there is substituted 'in accordance with section 7 of the Pension Schemes Act 1993;'.

The Insurance Companies Act 1982 (c. 50)

10.   In the Table in paragraph 3(1) of Schedule 2B to the Insurance Companies Act 1982 (restriction on disclosure of information), the entry relating to the Occupational Pensions Board is omitted.

The Companies Act 1985 (c. 6)

11.   In Schedule 2 to the Companies Act 1985 (interpretation of references to 'beneficial interest'), in paragraphs 3(2)(b) and 7(2)(b), for 'state scheme premium' there is substituted 'contributions equivalent premium'.

The Income and Corporation Taxes Act 1988 (c.1)

12.—(1)   In section 649 of the Income and Corporation Taxes Act 1988 (minimum contributions towards approved personal pension schemes), in subsection (2), for the definition of 'the employee's share' there is substituted—

 ''the employee's share' of minimum contributions is the amount that would be the minimum contributions if, for the reference in section 45(1) of the Pension Schemes Act 1993 to the appropriate age-related percentage, there were substituted a reference to the percentage mentioned in section 41(1A)(a) of that Act'.

(2)   This paragraph does not extend to Northern Ireland.

The Social Security Act 1989 (c. 24)

13.—(1)   Section 29(7) of the Social Security Act 1989 (regulations and orders) is omitted.

(2)   In Schedule 5 to that Act (equal treatment in employment related schemes for pensions etc.), paragraph 4 is omitted.

The Social Security Contributions and Benefits Act 1992 (c.4)

14.   In Schedule 1 to the Social Security Contributions and Benefits Act 1992 (supplementary provisions), in paragraph 8(1)(g), for 'state scheme premium' there is substituted 'contributions equivalent premium'.

The Social Security Administration Act 1992 (c.5)

15.—(1)   The Social Security Administration Act 1992 is amended as follows.

(2)   In section 110 (appointment and powers of inspectors)—

 (a)   in subsections (2)(c)(ii) and (6)(a)(ii), for 'state scheme premium' there is substituted 'contributions equivalent premium', and

(b)   in subsection (7)(e)(i), for 'state scheme premiums' there is substituted 'contributions equivalent premiums'.

(3)   In section 120 (proof of previous offences), in subsections (3) and (4), for 'state scheme premiums' there is substituted 'contributions equivalent premiums'.

(4)   In Schedule 4 (persons employed in social security administration etc.), the entries in Part I relating to the Occupational Pensions Board are omitted.

The Tribunals and Inquiries Act 1992 (c. 53)

16.—(1)   The Tribunals and Inquiries Act 1992 is amended as follows.

(2)   In section 7(2) (concurrence needed for removal of members of certain tribunals), '(d) or' is omitted.

(3)   In section 10(5) (reasons to be given for decisions of tribunals and Ministers), paragraph (c) is omitted.

(4)   In section 13(5)(a) (power to amend), 'and (d)' is omitted.

(5)   In section 14 (restricted application of Act in relation to certain tribunals), subsection (2) is omitted.

(6)   In Schedule 1 (Tribunals under the direct supervision of the Council on Tribunals), paragraph 35(d) is omitted.

The Judicial Pensions and Retirement Act 1993 (c. 8)

17.   In section 13(9) of the Judicial Pensions and Retirement Act 1993 (election for personal pension), in the definition of 'personal pension scheme', 'by the Occupational Pensions Board' is omitted.

The Pension Schemes Act 1993 (c. 48)

18.   The Pension Schemes Act 1993 is amended as follows.

19.   Sections 2 to 5 (constitution, membership etc. of the Board) are repealed.

20.   For section 6(8) (Board may be appointed as Registrar), there is substituted—

'(8) Nothing in this Act or the Pensions Act 1995 shall be taken to imply that the Regulatory Authority may not be appointed as the Registrar.'

21.   In the provisions listed in the first column of the table—

(a)   in each place where the word appears, for 'Board' there is substituted 'Secretary of State', and

(b)   the additional amendments listed in the second column of the table in relation to those provisions shall have effect.

TABLE

Provision	Additional amendments
Section 8 (meaning of terms).	—
Section 9 (requirements for certification).	In subsection (4), for 'they think' there is substituted 'he thinks'.
Section 11 (employer's right to elect as to contracting-out).	In subsection (4), for 'consider' and 'they' there is substituted, respectively, 'considers' and 'he'. In subsection (5)(d), for 'they are' there is substituted 'he is'.
Section 30 (protected rights).	—
Section 34 (cancellation etc. of certificates).	In subsection (2)(a), for 'they have' there is substituted 'he has'. In subsections (4) and (5), for 'they consider' (in both places) and 'they' (in both places) there is substituted, respectively, 'he considers' and 'he'.
Section 50 (schemes ceasing to be certified).	In subsection (2), for 'have' (in both places) and 'their' there is substituted, respectively, 'has' and 'his'. In subsection (3), for 'they subsequently approve' there is substituted 'he subsequently approves'. In subsection (4), for the first 'have' there is substituted 'has'.
Section 57 (contribution equivalent premiums).	In subsection (4) for 'consider' and 'they' there is substituted, respectively, 'considers' and 'he'.
Section 163 (rule against perpetuities).	In subsection, (6), for 'consider' there is substituted 'considers'.

22. In section 7—

(a) in subsections (1) and (6), for 'Board' there is substituted 'Secretary of State', and

(b) in subsection (4), 'by the Board' is omitted.

23. In section 8 (definition of terms)—

(a) in subsection (2), for the words following the definition of 'minimum payment' there is substituted—

'and for the purposes of this subsection 'rebate percentage' means the appropriate flat rate percentage for the purposes of section 42A(2)', and

(b) subsection (5) is omitted.

24. In section 9 (requirements for certification), in subsection (3) '22 and' is omitted.

25. In section 10 (protected rights), in subsection (2)(a), after 'minimum payments' there is inserted 'and payments under section 42A(3)'.

26. In section 13 (minimum pensions for earners), in subsection (2)(a), the words from 'and does' to the end are omitted.

27. In section 14 (earner's guaranteed minimum)—

    (a) subsection (3) is omitted,

    (b) in subsection (8) after '1978-79' there is inserted 'or later than the tax year ending immediately before the principal appointed day'.

28. In section 16 (revaluation of earnings factors)—

    (a) in subsection (3), for the words following 'at least' there is substituted 'the prescribed percentage for each relevant year after the last service tax year; and the provisions included by virtue of this subsection may also conform with such additional requirements as may be prescribed', and

    (b) for the definition of 'final relevant year' in subsection (5) there is substituted—

    "final relevant year' means the last tax year in the earner's working life'.

29. In section 17 (minimum pensions for widows and widowers), at the end of subsection (7) there is added 'or widows'.

30. Section 22 (financing of benefits) is repealed.

31. In section 23 (securing of benefits)—

    (a) subsections (1) and (5) are omitted,

    (b) in subsection (4), for '(1) to (3)' there is substituted '(2) and (3)';
and subsections (2) and (3) of that section do not apply where the winding up is begun on or after the principal appointed day.

32. Section 24 (sufficiency of resources) is repealed.

33. In section 25 (conditions as to investments, etc.)—

    (a) subsections (1) and (3) are repealed, and

    (b) for subsection (2) there is substituted—

    '(2) A salary related contracted-out scheme must, in relation to any earner's service before the principal appointed day, comply with any requirements prescribed for the purpose of securing that—

        (a) the Secretary of State is kept informed about any matters affecting the security of the minimum pensions guaranteed under the scheme, and

        (b) the resources of the scheme are brought to and are maintained at a level satisfactory to the Secretary of State'.

34. In section 28 (ways of giving effect to protected rights)—

    (a) in subsection (4)(d), for 'a manner satisfactory to the Board' there is substituted 'the prescribed manner', and

    (b) subsection (7) is omitted.

35. In section 29 (the pension and annuity requirements), in subsection (1)(b)(ii), for 'a manner satisfactory to the Board' there is substituted 'the prescribed manner'.

36. In section 31 (investment and resources of schemes)—

    (a) subsection (1) is omitted,

    (b) in subsection (3)(a), after 'minimum payments' there is inserted 'and payments under section 42A(3)', and

    (c) at the end of that section there is added—

    '(5) Any minimum contributions required by reason of this section to be applied so as to provide money purchase benefits for or in respect of a member of a scheme must be so applied in the prescribed manner and within the prescribed period'.

37. In section 34 (cancellation, etc. of certificates)—
  (a) in subsection (1), for paragraph (a) there is substituted—
       '(a) in the case of a contracting-out certificate—
           (i) on any change of circumstances affecting the treatment of an employment as contracted-out employment, or
           (ii) where the scheme is a salary related contracted-out scheme and the certificate was issued on or after the principal appointed day, if any employer of persons in the description or category of employment to which the scheme in question relates, or the actuary of the scheme, fails to provide the Secretary of State, at prescribed intervals, with such documents as may be prescribed for the purpose of verifying that the conditions of section 9(2B) are satisfied',
  (b) subsection (6) is omitted, and
  (c) for subsection (7) there is substituted—
       '(7) Without prejudice to the previous provisions of this section, failure of a scheme to comply with any requirements prescribed by virtue of section 25(2) shall be a ground on which the Secretary of State may, in respect of any employment to which the scheme relates, cancel a contracting-out certificate'.

38.   Sections 35 (surrender, etc. issue of further certificates) and 36 (surrender etc. cancellation of further certificates) are repealed.

39.   For section 37 (alteration of rules of contracted-out schemes) there is substituted—

'37. Alteration of rules contracted-out schemes

(1) Except in prescribed circumstances, the rules of a contracted-out scheme cannot be altered unless the alteration is of a prescribed description.

(2) Regulations made by virtue of subsection (1) may operate so as to validate with retrospective effect any alteration of the rules which would otherwise be void under this section.

(3) References in this section to a contracted-out scheme include a scheme which has ceased to be contracted-out so long as any person is entitled to receive, or has accrued rights to, any benefits under the scheme attributable to a period when the scheme was contracted-out.

(4) The reference in subsection (3) to a person entitled to receive benefits under a scheme includes a person so entitled by virtue of being the widower of an earner only in such cases as may be prescribed.'

40.   In section 38 (alteration of rules of appropriate schemes)—
  (a) in subsection (1), the words from 'unless' to the end are omitted,
  (b) in subsection (3), the words from 'if' to the end are omitted,
  (c) in subsection (4), for the words from the beginning to 'direct' there is substituted 'Regulations made by virtue of subsection (2) may', and
  (d) subsection (7) is omitted.

41.   In section 42 (review of reduced rates of contributions), in subsection (3), for '41(1)(a)' there is substituted '41(1A)(a)'.

42.   In section 43 (payment of minimum contributions), in subsection (1), after 'circumstances' there is inserted 'or in respect of such periods'.

43.   In section 45 (minimum contributions towards personal pension schemes), subsection (3)(d) is omitted.

44. In section 46(1) (effect of entitlement to guaranteed minimum pensions on payment of social security benefits), for sub-paragraph (i) there is substituted—

'(i) to that part of its additional pension which is attributable to earnings factors for any tax years ending before the principal appointed day'.

45. In section 50 (powers to approve arrangements for scheme ceasing to be certified)—

(a) in subsection (1)(a)—

(i) at the end of sub-paragraph (i) there is inserted 'or accrued rights to pensions under the scheme attributable to their service on or after the principal appointed day', and

(ii) in sub-paragraph (ii), for 'guaranteed minimum pensions under the scheme' there is substituted 'such pensions',

(b) after subsection (1) there is inserted—

'(1A) The power of the Secretary of State to approve arrangements under this section—

(a) includes power to approve arrangements subject to conditions, and

(b) may be exercised either generally or in relation to a particular scheme.

(1B) Arrangements may not be approved under this section unless any prescribed conditions are met', and

(c) subsection (7) is omitted.

46. In section 51 (calculation of GMPs preserved under approved arrangements), in subsection (1)(a), for 'are subject to approved arrangements' there is substituted 'satisfy prescribed conditions'.

47. In section 52 (supervision of schemes which have ceased to be certified)—

(a) in subsection (2), for paragraphs (a) and (b) there is substituted—

'(a) the scheme has ceased to be a contracted-out scheme, and

(b) any persons remain who fall within any of the following categories.

(2A) Those categories are—

(a) any persons entitled to receive, or having accrued rights to—

(i) guaranteed minimum pensions, or

(ii) pensions under the scheme attributable to service on or after the principal appointed day but before the scheme ceased to be contracted-out,

(b) any persons who have protected rights under the scheme or are entitled to any benefit giving effect to protected rights under it',

(b) in subsection (3), for paragraphs (a) and (b) there is substituted—

'(a) the scheme has ceased to be an appropriate scheme, and

(b) any persons remain who have protected rights under the scheme or are entitled to any benefit giving effect to protected rights under it', and

(c) subsections (4) to (6) are omitted.

48. In section 53 (supervision: former contracted-out schemes)—

(a) for subsection (1) there is substituted—

'(1) The Secretary of State may direct the trustees or managers of the scheme, or the employer, to take or refrain from taking such steps as the Secretary of State may specify in writing; and such a direction shall be final and binding on the person directed and any person claiming under him.

(1A)   An appeal on a point of law shall lie to the High Court or, in Scotland, the Court of Session from a direction under subsection (1) at the instance of the trustees or managers or the employer, or any person claiming under them.

(1B)   A direction under subsection (1) shall be enforceable—

(a)   in England and Wales, in a county court as if it were an order of that court, and

(b)   in Scotland, by the sheriff, as if it were an order of the sheriff and whether or not the sheriff could himself have given such an order',

(b)   subsection (2) is omitted,

(c)   for subsection (3) there is substituted—

'(3)   If a certificate has been issued under subsection (2) of section 50 and has not been cancelled under subsection (3) of that section, any liabilities in respect of such entitlement or rights as are referred to in section 52(2A)(a) or (b) must, except in prescribed circumstances, be discharged (subject to any directions under subsection (1)) in a prescribed manner and within a prescribed period or such longer period as the Secretary of State may allow', and

(d)   subsections (4) and (5) are omitted.

49.   In section 54 (supervision: former appropriate personal pension schemes)—

(a)   for subsections (1) and (2) there is substituted—

'(1)   The Secretary of State may direct the trustees or managers of the scheme to take or refrain from taking such steps as the Secretary of State may specify in writing; and such a direction shall be final and binding on the person directed and any person claiming under him.

(1A)   An appeal on a point of law shall lie to the High Court or, in Scotland, the Court of Session from a direction under subsection (1) at the instance of the trustees or managers or the employer, or any person claiming under them.

(1B)   A direction under subsection (1) shall be enforceable—

(a)   in England and Wales, in a county court as if it were an order of that court, and

(b)   in Scotland, by the sheriff, as if it were an order of the sheriff and whether or not the sheriff could himself have given such an order.

(2)   If a certificate has been issued under subsection (2) of section 50 and has not been cancelled under subsection (3) of that section, any liabilities in respect of such entitlement or rights as are referred to in section 52(3)(b) must, except in prescribed circumstances, be discharged (subject to any directions under subsection (1)) in a prescribed manner and within a prescribed period or such longer period as the Secretary of State may allow', and

(b)   subsection (3) is omitted.

50.   In section 55 (state scheme premiums), subsections (1) and (3) to (6) are omitted.

51.   In section 56 (provisions supplementary to section 55)—

(a)   subsection (1), in subsection (2) the words following 'the prescribed period' and subsection (3) are omitted, and

(b) for subsections (5) and (6) there is substituted—

'(5) The references in section 55(2A) to an accrued right to short service benefit include an accrued right to any provision which, under the preservation requirements, is permitted as an alternative to short service benefit (other than provision for return of contributions or for benefit in the form of a lump sum).

(6) Subject to regulations under paragraph 1 of Schedule 2, service in any employment which ceases with the death of the employer shall be treated for the purposes of section 55(2A) as ceasing immediately before the death'.

52. In section 58 (amount of premiums under section 55), subsections (1) to (3), (5) and (6) are omitted.

53. Section 59 (alternative basis for revaluation) is repealed.

54. In section 60 (effect of payment of premiums on rights)—

(a) subsections (1) to (3) are omitted,

(b) in subsection (4)—

(i) for '55(2)(i)' there is substituted '55(2A)(a) and (b), (d) and (e)', and

(ii) at the end there is added 'or (in relation to service on or after the principal appointed day) rights to pensions under the scheme so far as attributable to the amount of the premium', and

(c) in subsection (5), for '55(2)(ii)' there is substituted '55(2A)(c)', and after 'widow' there is added 'or widower', and

(d) subsections (6) to (10) are omitted.

55. In section 61 (deduction of contributions equivalent premium from refund of scheme contributions)—

(a) in subsection (1), for paragraph (a) there is substituted—

'(a) an earner's service in contracted-out employment ceases or his employment ceases to be contracted-out employment, and',

(b) in subsection (8)—

(i) for paragraph (a) there is substituted—

'(a) an earner's service in contracted-out employment ceases or his employment ceases to be contracted-out employment', and

(ii) for 'termination' there is substituted 'cessation', and

(c) in subsection (9), for 'termination' (in both places) there is substituted 'cessation'.

56. In section 62 (no recovery of premiums from earners)—

(a) in subsection (1), for 'state scheme' there is substituted 'contributions equivalent', and

(b) subsection (2) is omitted.

57. In section 63 (further provisions concerning calculations relating to premiums)—

(a) in subsection (1)—

(i) paragraph (a) is omitted,

(ii) in paragraph (b), for 'that section' there is substituted 'section 58', and

(iii) paragraph (c) is omitted,

(b) subsection (2) is omitted,

    (c)   in subsection (3)—

       (i)   paragraph (a) is omitted,

       (ii)   in paragraph (b), for 'subsection (4) of that section' there is substituted 'section 58(4)', and

       (iii)   the words following sub-paragraph (ii) are omitted, and

    (d)   subsection (4) is omitted.

58.   Section 64 (actuarial tables) is repealed.

59.   Section 65 (former and future earners) is repealed.

60.   Section 66 (widowers) is repealed.

61.   In sections 67 and 68 (non-payment of state scheme premiums), for 'state scheme premium' (in each place) there is substituted 'contributions equivalent premium'.

62.   In section 84(5), paragraph (b) and the preceding 'or' are omitted.

63.   In section 96 (right to cash equivalent: exercise of options)—

    (a)   in subsection (2)(a), after 'guaranteed minimum pensions' there is inserted 'his accrued rights so far as attributable to service in contracted-out employment on or after the principal appointed day', and

    (b)   in subsection (3)(a), for 'guaranteed minimum pensions' there is substituted 'pensions, being guaranteed minimum pensions or pensions so far as attributable to service in contracted-out employment on or after the principal appointed day'.

64.   Sections 133 to 135 (advice and determinations as to conformity of schemes with requirements) are repealed.

65.   In section 155 (requirement to give information to the Secretary of State or the Board)—

    (a)   'or the Board' is omitted,

    (b)   for 'or they require' there is substituted 'requires', and

    (c)   for the words from 'sections 7' to 'premiums' there is substituted 'Part III'.

66.   In section 158 (disclosure of information between government departments)—

    (a)   subsections (2) and (3) are omitted,

    (b)   in subsection (6), '(2) or (3)', paragraph (d) and the 'or' immediately preceding it are omitted,

    (c)   in subsection (7)—

       (i)   for 'the Inland Revenue and the Board', there is substituted 'and the Inland Revenue',

       (ii)   after paragraph (a), there is inserted 'or', and

       (iii)   paragraph (c) and the 'or' immediately preceding it are omitted, and

    (d)   subsection (8) is omitted.

67.   In section 164(1)(b)(i) (Crown employment), '2 to 5', '172, 173' and 'and Schedule 1' are omitted.

68.   In section 165 (application of certain provisions to case with foreign element), in subsection (2)(a), for the words from 'sections 7' to 'premiums)' there is substituted 'Part III'.

69.   In section 166(5) (reciprocity with other countries), 'sections 2 to 5', '172, 173' and 'and Schedule 1' are omitted.

70.   In section 170 (determinations by the Secretary of State)—

    (a)   in subsection (1)—

        (i)   in paragraph (b) for 'state scheme premium' (in both places) there is substituted 'contributions equivalent premium',

        (ii)   the 'and' at the end of paragraph (c) is omitted, and

        (iii) for the words following paragraph (d) there is substituted 'and

        (e)   any question whether an employment is, or is to be treated, for the purposes of the Pension Schemes Act 1993 as contracted-out employment or as to the persons in relation to whom, or the period for which, an employment is, or is to be treated, for the purposes of that Act as such employment',

    (b) subsections (3) and (4) are omitted, and

    (c) at the end of that section there is added—

    '(7) Sections 18 and 19 of the Social Security Administration Act 1992 (appeals and reviews) shall have effect as if the questions mentioned in subsection (1) of section 17 of that Act included—

        (a)   any question arising in connection with the issue, cancellation or variation of contracting-out certificates or appropriate scheme certificates, not being a question mentioned in subsection (1)(e) above, and

        (b)   any other question arising under this Act which falls to be determined by the Secretary of State, not being a question mentioned in that subsection.

    (8) Regulations may make provision with respect to the procedure to be adopted on any application for a review made under section 19 of that Act by virtue of subsection (7) above and generally with respect to such applications and reviews, but may not prevent such a review being entered upon without an application being made'.

    71.   In section 171 (questions arising in proceedings), in subsection (1)(b), for 'state scheme premium' there is substituted 'contributions equivalent premium'.

    72.   Sections 172 and 173 (reviews and appeals) are repealed.

    73.   In section 174 (grants), for 'Board' (in both places) there is substituted 'Regulatory Authority'.

    74.   In section 176 (fees), for 'either by the Secretary of State or by the Board on his behalf' there is substituted 'by the Secretary of State'.

    75.   In section 177 (general financial arrangements)—

    (a) in subsection (3)(b)—

        (i)   in sub-paragraph (i), 'sections 2 to 5', '172, 173' and 'and Schedule 1' are omitted, and

        (ii)   in sub-paragraph (ii), the words from 'sections 55' to 'premiums)' are omitted, and

    (b) subsection (7)(b) is omitted.

    76.   In section 178(b) (meaning of 'trustee' and 'manager'), 'sections 2 to 5', 172, 173' and 'and Schedule 1' are omitted.

    77.   In section 181 (general interpretation)—

    (a) in subsection (1)—

        (i)   the definitions of 'accrued rights premium', 'the Board', 'contracted-out protected rights premium', 'limited revaluation premium', 'pensioner's rights premium', 'personal pension protected rights premium', 'state scheme premium' and 'transfer premium' are omitted, and

(ii) in the definition of 'contributions equivalent premium', for ,'section 55(6)(e)' there is substituted 'section 55(2)',

(b) in subsection (3), for 'sections 2 to' there is substituted 'section', and '172, 173' and 'and Schedule 1 ' are omitted, and

(c) in subsection (7), 'and Schedule 1' is omitted.

78. In section 182(1) (orders and regulations), 'the Board or' is omitted.

79. In section 183 (sub-delegation), in subsection (1), 'sections 2 to 5', '172, 173' and 'or Schedule 1', and subsection (2) are omitted.

80. In section 185 (consultation about regulations)—

(a) in subsection (1), for the words from the beginning to 'make' there is substituted 'Subject to subsection (2), before the Secretary of State makes', and for the words from 'refer the proposals' to the end there is substituted 'consult such persons as he may consider appropriate',

(b) in subsection (2), at the end of paragraph (c) there is added—

'(d) regulations in the case of which the Secretary of State considers consultation inexpedient because of urgency, or

(e) regulations which—

(i) state that they are consequential upon a specified enactment, and

(ii) are made before the end of the period of six months beginning with the coming into force of that enactment,'

(c) subsections (3) and (4) are omitted,

(d) in subsection (5), for 'subsections (1) to (4)' there is substituted 'subsection (1)',

(e) subsection (6) is omitted, and

(f) in subsection (8), for '172(4)' there is substituted '170(8)'.

81. In section 186(5) (Parliamentary control of regulations and orders), 'or section 185(4)' is omitted.

82. In section 192(2) (extent), for 'sections 1 to 5' there is substituted 'section 1' and 'section 172(4) and (5)' is omitted.

83. Schedule 1 (the Occupational Pensions Board) is repealed.

84. In Schedule 2 (certification regulations)—

(a) in paragraph 2(1), for 'the Board' there is substituted 'the Secretary of State',

(b) in paragraph 4(3), for the words from 'does not cease' to the end there is substituted 'which, apart from the regulations, would not be contracted-out employment is treated as contracted-out employment where any benefits provided under the scheme are attributable to a period when the scheme was contracted-out',

(c) in paragraph 5(1)—

(i) 'or the Board' and 'or, as the case may be, the Board' are omitted, and

(ii) for '65' there is substituted '63',

(d) in paragraph 5(2), 'to 65' is omitted, and

(e) in paragraph 9, for sub-paragraphs (3) to (5) there is substituted—

'(2A) Sub-paragraphs (3) and (4) shall be omitted'.

85. In Schedule 4 (priority in bankruptcy), in paragraph 3(1), for 'state scheme premium' there is substituted 'contributions equivalent premium'.

86. In Schedule 6 (transitional provisions and savings), paragraph 11 is omitted.

Section 177   SCHEDULE 6
GENERAL MINOR AND CONSEQUENTIAL AMENDMENTS

The Public Records Act 1958 (c. 51)

1. In Schedule 1 to the Public Records Act 1958 (definition of 'Public Record'), in Part II of the Table, there is inserted at the appropriate place—
'Pensions Ombudsman.'

The Pension Schemes Act 1993 (c. 48)

2. The Pension Schemes Act 1993 is amended as follows.

3. In section 95(1) (ways of taking right to cash equivalent), for 'this Chapter' there is substituted 'paragraph (a), (aa) or (b) of section 94(1)'.

4. In section 97 (calculation of cash equivalents)—

(a) in subsection (2)(a) after 'cash equivalents' there is inserted 'except guaranteed cash equivalents',

(b) in subsection (3)(b), for the words from 'the date' to the end there is substituted 'the appropriate date', and

(c) after that subsection there is inserted—

'(3A) For the purposes of subsection (3), the 'appropriate date'—

(a) in the case of a salary related occupational pension scheme, is the guarantee date (within the meaning of section 93A), and

(b) in any other case, is the date on which the trustees receive an application from the member under section 95.'

5. In section 98 (variation and loss of rights to cash equivalents)—

(a) in subsection (1), after 'occupational pension scheme' there is inserted 'other than a salary related scheme',

(b) after that subsection there is inserted—

'(1A) Regulations may provide that a member of a salary related occupational pension scheme who continues in employment to which the scheme applies after his pensionable service in that employment terminates—

(a) acquires a right to only part of his guaranteed cash equivalent, or

(b) acquires no right to his guaranteed cash equivalent.',

(c) in subsection (2), after '(1)' there is inserted 'or (1A)', and

(d) in subsection (3)—

(i) in paragraph (a), after 'occupational pension scheme' there is inserted 'other than a salary related scheme', and

(ii) for paragraph (b) and the 'and' immediately preceding it there is substituted—

'or

(aa) by virtue of regulations under subsection (1A) or (2), a member of a salary related occupational pension scheme does not, on such a termination, acquire a right to the whole or any part of his guaranteed cash equivalent,

and his employment terminates at least one year before normal pension age'.

6. In section 99 (trustee's duties after exercise of an option under section 95)—

(a) in subsection (2), for paragraphs (a) and (b) there is substituted—

'(a)   in the case of a member of a salary related occupational pension scheme, within 6 months of the guarantee date, or (if earlier) by the date on which the member attains normal pension age,

(b)   in the case of a member of any other occupational pension scheme, within 6 months of the date on which they receive the application, or (if earlier) by the date on which the member attains normal pension age, or

(c)   in the case of a member of a personal pension scheme, within 6 months of the date on which they receive the application.',

(b)   after subsection (3) there is inserted—

'(3A)   In this section, 'guarantee date' has the same meaning as in section 93A.',

(c)   for subsections (4) and (5) there is substituted—

'(4)   The Regulatory Authority may, in prescribed circumstances, grant an extension of the period within which the trustees or managers of the scheme are obliged to do what is needed to carry out what a member of the scheme requires.

(4A)   Regulations may make provision in relation to applications for extensions under subsection (4).',

(d)   in subsection (6), for 'Board' there is substituted 'Regulatory Authority', and

(e)   after that subsection there is added—

'(7)   Where the trustees or managers of an occupational pension scheme have not done what is needed to carry out what a member of the scheme requires within six months of the date mentioned in paragraph (a) or (b) of subsection (2)—

(a)   they must, except in prescribed cases, notify the Regulatory Authority of that fact within the prescribed period, and

(b)   section 10 of the Pensions Act 1995 (power of the Regulatory Authority to impose civil penalties) shall apply to any trustee or manager who has failed to take all such steps as are reasonable to ensure that it was so done.

(8)   Regulations may provide that in prescribed circumstances subsection (7) shall not apply in relation to an occupational pension scheme.'

7.   In section 145 (Pensions Ombudsman), in subsection (5) 'with the approval of the Treasury' is omitted.

8.   In section 151(5)(b) (enforcement in Scotland of Pensions Ombudsman's determinations), for the words from 'Scotland,' to the end there is substituted 'in like manner as an extract registered decree arbitral bearing warrant for execution issued by the sheriff court of any sheriffdom in Scotland.'.

9.   After section 158 there is inserted—

'158A.   Other disclosures by the Secretary of State

(1)   The Secretary of State may, in spite of any obligation as to secrecy or confidentiality imposed by statute or otherwise on him or on persons employed in the Department of Social Security, disclose any information received by him in connection with his functions under this Act or the Pensions Act 1995 to any person specified in the first column of the following

Table if he considers that the disclosure would enable or assist the person to discharge the functions specified in relation to the person in the second column of the Table.

TABLE

Persons	*Functions*
The Treasury.	Functions under the Financial Services Act 1986.
The Bank of England.	Functions under the Banking Act 1987 or any other functions.
The Regulatory Authority.	Functions under this Act or the Pensions Act 1995, or any enactment in force in Northern Ireland corresponding to either of them.
The Pensions Compensation Board.	Functions under the Pensions Act 1995 or any corresponding enactment in force in Northern Ireland.
The Friendly Societies Commission.	Functions under the enactments relating to friendly societies.
The Building Societies Commission.	Functions under the Building Societies Act 1986.
An inspector appointed by the Secretary of State.	Functions under section 94 or 177 of the Financial Services Act 1986.
A person authorised to exercise powers under section 106 of the Financial Services Act 1986.	Functions under that section.
A designated agency or transferee body or the competent authority (within the meaning of the Financial Services Act 1986).	Functions under the Financial Services Act 1986.
A recognised self-regulating organisation, recognised professional body, recognised investment exchange or recognised clearing house (within the meaning of the Financial Services Act 1986).	Functions in its capacity as an organisation, body, exchange or clearing house recognised under the Financial Services Act 1986.

(2)   The Secretary of State may by order—

(a)   amend the Table in subsection (1) by—

(i)   adding any person exercising regulatory functions and specifying functions in relation to that person,

(ii)   removing any person for the time being specified in the Table, or

(iii)   altering the functions for the time being specified in the Table in relation to any person, or

(b)   restrict the circumstances in which, or impose conditions subject to which, disclosure may be made to any person for the time being specified in the Table'.

10. In section 164(1)(b)(i)(Crown employment), the words from '136' to '143' are omitted.

11. In section 166(5) (reciprocity with other countries), the words from '136' to '143' are omitted.

12. In section 177 (general financial arrangements), in subsection (3)(b)(i), the words from '136' to '143' are omitted.

13. In section 178 (meaning of 'trustee' and 'manager'), in paragraph (b), the words from '136' to '143' are omitted.

14. In section 181 (general interpretation), in subsection (3), the words from '136' to '143' are omitted.

15. In section 183 (sub-delegation)—

(a) in subsection (1), the words from '136' to '143' are omitted, and

(b) in subsection (3)(b), after 'prepared' there is inserted 'and from time to time revised'.

16.—(1) Schedule 9 (transitory modifications) is amended as follows.

(2) In paragraph 1—

(a) in sub-paragraph (1), sub-paragraphs (ii) to (v) are omitted,

(b) in sub-paragraph (3)(a)(i), for 'provisions mentioned in paragraphs (i) to (v)' there is substituted 'provision mentioned in paragraph (i)', and

(c) sub-paragraph (5) is omitted.

(3) Paragraphs 3 and 4 are omitted.

Section 177

SCHEDULE 7
REPEALS
PART I
OCCUPATIONAL PENSIONS

Chapter	Short title	Extent of repeal
1982 c. 50.	The Insurance Companies Act 1982.	In Schedule 2B, in paragraph 3(9), the 'or' after paragraph (a).
1986 c. 53.	The Building Societies Act 1986.	In Section 53(15), the 'or' after paragraph (a).
1987 c. 22.	The Banking Act 1987.	In section 84(10), the 'or' after paragraph (a).
1989 c. 24.	The Social Security Act 1989.	In Schedule 5, paragraph 14.
1993 c. 48.	The Pension Schemes Act 1993.	Sections 77 to 80. Sections 102 to 108. In section 110, subsections (2) to (4). Section 112. Section 114. Section 116. Section 118. Sections 119 to 122.

Chapter	Short title	Extent of repeal
		In section 129, in subsection (1), 'Chapter I of Part V', 'sections 119 to 122', 'under Chapter I of Part V or' and 'or sections 119 to 122', and subsection (3)(a).
		In section 132, 'the equal access requirements'.
		In section 133(1), 'the equal access requirements'.
		In section 134, in subsection (3), 'the equal access requirements' and, in subsection (4), 'or the equal access requirements' and 'or, as the case may be, section 118(1)'.
		In section 136(2)(e)(iv), 'or the equal access requirements'.
		In section 139(2), 'the equal access requirements'.
		In section 140(4), paragraph (c) and the 'and' immediately preceding it.
		Section 144.
		In section 153, in subsection (1), the words from 'and Chapter I' to 'section 108)', subsections (3) and (4), in subsection (5), 'Chapter I of Part VII', paragraph (d) and the preceding 'or', and subsections (6) and (7).
		In section 170, subsections (5) and (6).
		In section 178, in paragraph (a), the second 'or'.
		In section 181(1), the definition of 'equal access requirements'.
		In section 183, in subsection (3), the words from 'or, in the case of' to 'determined' and the words following paragraph (b).
		In section 185, in subsection (1), 'I or'.
		In Schedule 7, paragraphs 1 and 3.
		In Schedule 8, paragraph 3.

PART II
STATE PENSIONS

Chapter	Short title	Extent of repeal
1988 c. 1.	The Income and Corporation Taxes Act 1988.	In section 187, in subsection (2), the definition of 'pensionable age'.
1992 c. 4.	The Social Security Contributions and Benefits Act 1992.	Section 53. In section 54, in subsection (1)(a), the words from 'but' to '70', and subsection (4). In Schedule 3, in paragraph 5(7)(a), '(or at least 20 of them, if that is less than half'. In Schedule 5, in paragraph 2(2), the definition of 'period of enhancement' and the previous 'and', and in paragraph 8, sub-paragraphs (1) and (2).
1994 c. 18.	The Social Security (Incapacity for Work) Act 1994.	In Schedule 1, paragraphs 20 and 21.

These repeals have effect in accordance with Schedule 4 to this Act.

PART III
CERTIFICATION OF PENSION SCHEMES ETC.

Chapter	Short title	Extent of repeal
1958 c. 51.	The Public Records Act 1958.	In Schedule 1, in the Table, the entry relating to the Occupational Pensions Board.
1975 c. 24	The House of Commons Disqualification Act 1975.	In Part II of Schedule 1, the entry relating to the Occupational Pensions Board.
1975 c. 25.	The Northern Ireland Assembly Disqualification Act 1975.	In Part II of Schedule 1, the entry relating to the Occupational Pensions Board.
1975 c. 60.	The Social Security Pensions Act 1975.	In section 61B(1), 'except any power of the Occupational Pensions Board to make orders'.
1979 c. 50.	The European Parliament (Pay and Pensions) Act 1979.	In section 6(4), 'and the Occupational Pensions Board'.
1982 c. 50.	The Insurance Companies Act 1982.	In Schedule 2B, in paragraph 3(1), in the Table, the entry relating to the Occupational Pensions Board.

Chapter	Short title	Extent of repeal
1989 c. 24.	The Social Security Act 1989.	Section 29(7). In Schedule 5, paragraph 4.
1992 c. 5.	The Social Security Administration Act 1992.	In Schedule 4, the entries in Part I relating to the Occupational Pensions Board.
1992 c. 53.	The Tribunals and Inquiries Act 1992.	In section 7(2), '(d) or'. In section 10(5), paragraph (c). In section 13(5)(a), 'and (d)'. In section 14, subsection (2). In Schedule 1, paragraph 35(d).
1993 c. 8.	The Judicial Pensions and Retirement Act 1993.	In section 13(9), in the definition of 'personal pension scheme', 'by the Occupational Pensions Board'.
1993 c. 48.	The Pension Schemes Act 1993.	Sections 2 to 5. In section 7(4), 'by the Board'. Section 8(5). In section 9(3), '22 and'. In section 13(2)(a), the words from 'and does' to the end. In section 14, subsection (3). Section 22. In section 23, subsections (1) and (5). Section 24. In section 25, subsections (1) and (3). Section 28(7). Section 31(1). Section 34(6). Sections 35 and 36. In section 38, in subsection (1), the words from 'unless' to the end, in subsection (3), the words from 'if' to the end, and subsection (7). In section 45, subsection (2) and, in subsection (3), paragraph (d) and, in paragraph (e), the words following 'prescribed period'. In section 48(2), paragraph (b) and, in paragraph (c), 'if the earner dies before reaching pensionable age'. Section 50(7). In section 52, subsections (4) to (6).

Chapter	Short title	Extent of repeal
		In section 53, subsections (2), (4) and (5). Section 54(3). In section 55, subsection (1) and subsections (3) to (6). In section 56, subsection (1), in subsection (2), the words following 'the prescribed period', and subsection (3). In section 58, subsections (1) to (3), (5) and (6). Section 59. In section 60, subsections (1) to (3) and (6) to (10). In section 62, subsection (2). In section 63, in subsection (1), paragraphs (a) and (c), subsection (2), in subsection (3), paragraph (a) and the words following sub-paragraph (ii), and subsection (4). Sections 64 to 66. In section 84, in subsection (5), paragraph (b) and the preceding 'or'. Sections 133 to 135. In section 155, 'or the Board'. In section 158, subsections (2) and (3), in subsection (6), '(2) or (3)', paragraph (d) (and the 'or' immediately preceding it), in subsection (7), paragraph (c) (and the 'or' immediately preceding it) and subsection (8). In section 164(1)(b)(i), '2 to 5', '172, 173' and 'and Schedule 1'. In section 166(5), 'sections 2 to 5', '172, 173' and 'and Schedule 1'. In section 170, in subsection (1), the 'and' at the end of paragraph (c) and subsections (3) and (4). Sections 172 and 173.

Chapter	Short title	Extent of repeal

In section 177, in subsection 3(b)(i), 'sections 2 to 5', '172, 173' and 'and Schedule 1' in subsection (3)(b)(ii), the words from 'sections 55' to 'premiums)', and in subsection (7), paragraph (b).

In section 178, in paragraph (b), 'sections 2 to 5', '172, 173' and 'and Schedule 1'.

In section 181, in subsection (1), the definitions of 'accrued rights premium', 'the Board', 'contracted-out protected rights premium', 'limited revaluation premium', 'pensioner's rights premium', 'personal pension protected rights premium', 'state scheme premium' and 'transfer premium', in subsection (3) '172, 173' and 'and Schedule 1', and in subsection (7) 'and Schedule 1'.

In section 182(1), 'the Board or'.

In section 183, in subsection (1), 'sections 2 to 5', '172, 173', and 'or Schedule 1' and subsection (2).

In section 185, subsections (3), (4) and (6).

In section 186(5), 'or section 185(4)'.

In section 192(2), 'section 172(4) and (5)'.

Schedule 1.

In Schedule 2, in paragraph 5, in sub-paragraph (1), 'or the Board' and 'or, as the case may be, the Board', in sub-paragraph (2), 'to 65', in sub-paragraph (3), 'in relation to state scheme premiums' and paragraph (b), and sub-paragraph (5).

In Schedule 6, paragraph 11.

In Schedule 8, paragraph 44(a) and (b)(i) and the 'and' immediately following it.

PART IV
MISCELLANEOUS AND GENERAL

Chapter	Short title	Extent of repeal
1971 c. 56.	The Pensions (Increase) Act 1971.	In section 3, in subsection (2)(c), 'is a woman who'.
1993 c. 48	The Pension Schemes Act 1993.	Sections 136 to 143.
		In section 145, 'with the approval of the Treasury'.
		In section 149, in subsection (3), at the end of paragraph (a), 'and'.
		In section 164(1)(b)(i), the words from '136' to '143'.
		In section 166(5), the words from '136' to ' 143'.
		Section 172(1)(b).
		In section 177, in subsection (3)(b)(i), the words from '136' to '143'.
		In section 178, in paragraph (b), the words from '136' to '143'.
		In section 181, in subsection (3), the words from '136' to '143'.
		In section 183, in subsection (1), the words from '136' to '143'.
		In Schedule 9, in paragraph 1, in sub-paragraph (1), sub-paragraphs (ii) to (v), and sub-paragraph (5), and paragraphs 3 and 4.

The repeal in the Pensions (Increase) Act 1971 shall come into force on the day this Act is passed.

Index